DUKE UNIVERSITY PRESS   DURHAM AND LONDON   2021

BOMBAY BROKERS

EDITED BY LISA BJÖRKMAN

Library of Congress Cataloging-in-Publication Data
Names: Björkman, Lisa, [date] editor.
Title: Bombay brokers / edited by Lisa Björkman.
Description: Durham: Duke University Press, 2021. | Includes
index.
Identifiers: LCCN 2020027535 (print) | LCCN 2020027536 (ebook)
ISBN 9781478010531 (hardcover)
ISBN 9781478011491 (paperback)
ISBN 9781478013082 (ebook)
Subjects: LCSH: Urban anthropology—India—Mumbai. |
Ethnology—India—Mumbai.
Classification: LCC GN395. B668 2021 (print) | LCC GN395 (ebook) |
DDC 305.800952—dc23
LC record available at https://lccn.loc.gov/2020027535
LC ebook record available at https://lccn.loc.gov/2020027536

Cover art: Local commuters at Churchgate Railway Station,
Mumbai, 1995. Copyright Raghu Rai/Magnum Photos.

for Bombay

CONTENTS

ACKNOWLEDGMENTS

The ideas that animate this book developed slowly over time—in conjunction with my own deepening ethnographic engagement with Bombay over the past decade or so. The idea to actually rope all my friends and colleagues into this somewhat-unwieldy project, however, came more recently and suddenly, during a particularly fantastic dinner in Bombay with Maura Finklestein, sometime in January 2017. As our dinner conversation turned to stories of the remarkable creativity and skillfulness of people we encountered in our research, I began to think about the generative possibilities of bringing such stories together in an unusual kind of book.

That lively Bombay dinner conversation came on the heels of a research workshop that I co-organized with Nellie Chu at the University of Göttingen—titled "The Entrepreneur and the Broker: Mediating Transnational Flow, Scale, and Belonging." The energetic discussions and engagements during that two-day workshop inspired me to further exploration on these themes; I am grateful to Anderson Blanton, Noelle Brigden, Nellie Chu, Heidi Østbø Haugen, Gerda Heck, Sabine Hess, Deborah James, Ahmed Kanna, Elizabeth Krause, Michael Levien, Johan Lindquist, Saikat Maitra,

Taylor Nelms, Léonie Newhouse, Madeleine Reeves, Srirupa Roy, and Llerena G. Searle for such a fun and fabulous few days together in Göttingen.

Between 2017 and 2019, we convened in various cities around the globe for a series of *Bombay Brokers* authors' workshops, during which we read and reflected on early drafts of the profiles. I wish to thank both authors and noncontributing interlocutors of these workshops, seminars, and conferences. I presented an early version of the project in June 2017 at a two-day conference on "Governing Urbanizing India: Citizenship, Policy, and Politics," organized by Niraja Gopal Jayal, Olle Törnquist, and Kenneth Bo Nielsen in Oslo; the book's conceptualization and organization benefited tremendously from the feedback so generously offered by the Oslo workshop participants. Thank you to Achin Chakraborty, Geir Heierstad, Vinoj Abraham, Praveen Priyadarshi, Heidi Bergsli, Annika Wetlesen, Alf Gunvald Nilsen, Neera Chandhoke, Radhika Chatterjee, Subhanil Chowdhury, Srirupa Roy, Henrik Berglund, Nikita Sud, and especially John Harriss—who not only offered advice and encouragement, but also allowed me more than my fair share of those tiny Norwegian shrimps.

Later that same summer, this project received wonderfully insightful feedback from participants in a workshop on "Building the Dreamworld: Space, Place, and the (Re)Making of 'New India,' 1947–2017," organized by contributing author Lalit Vachani at University of Göttingen. I am grateful to Avijit Mukul Kishore, Rohan Shivkumar, Ajay Gandhi, Sumeet Mhaskar, Srirupa Roy, and Nathaniel Roberts for their incisive comments and interventions. At the fall 2017 Association of American Geographers annual meeting in Boston, Chitra Venkataramani, Ateya Khorakiwala, and Sai Balakrishnan offered invaluable suggestions. In Leiden, I am grateful to David Ehrhardt, Ward Berenschot, Joris Tielemen, Retna Hanani, Prio Sambodho, Flávio Eiro de Oliveira, Sarthak Bagchi, Ajay Gandhi, and Michael Collins for a lively debate about the concept of "brokerage" and for offering their interventions and reflections during a December 2017 meeting. Thank you to Natascha van der Zwan for graciously hosting me in Holland; our conversations pushed the book's conceptualization of value, while your local expertise deepened my love for cheese.

Our largest authors' get-together took place in January 2018 in Bombay, where contributing author Rohan Shivkumar graciously hosted us at the Kamla Raheja Vidyanidhi Institute for Architecture and Environmental Studies. I wish to thank University of Louisville for contributing financial support, and VK Phatak, Rohan Shivkumar, Srimati Basu, Bhushan Korgaonkar, Rachel Sturman, Savitri Medhatul, Lalitha Kamat, Lubaina Rangwala, Aneri

Taskar, Prasad Khanolkar, Namrata Kapoor, Vrushti Mawani, and especially Thomas Blom Hansen for their generous engagements during the workshop. Thomas read an early version of the manuscript in its entirety, and I am deeply grateful for his insights and feedback, from which the book benefited tremendously.

In October 2019, material from the book's second chapter—"Property"— was presented at a full-day symposium titled "From Space into Property: Urban South Asia Symposium," organized by Eric Beverley, Nikhil Rao, and Rachel Sturman in conjunction with the Annual Conference on South Asia in Madison. I wish to thank the participants of that symposium for their enthusiastic engagements with the project more generally, and for pushing the arguments in the chapter on "Property." Thank you to Eric Beverley, Nikhil Rao, Rachel Sturman, Svati Shah, Anant Maringanti, Mircea Rainau, Divya Subramanian, Anish Vanaik, Faiza Moatasim, Curt Gambetta, Sai Balakrishna, Namita Dharia, Michael Sugarman, John Harriss, and Jonathan Spencer. I am especially grateful to Jonathan Spencer for his support and unflagging encouragement throughout the process of bringing this book into being.

The project benefited greatly from the insights offered by participants at a spring 2019 conference on "Emergent Urban Transformations: Explorations of State, Society, and Politics in India," organized by Sanjeev Routray, Gavin Shatkin, Liza Weinstein, and Neil Brenner at Northeastern University. My deep thanks to Asher Ghertner, Jonathan Anjaria, Sai Balakrishnan, Llerena Searle, Swarnabh Ghosh, Sanjeev Routray, Gavin Shatkin, Liza Weinstein, and Neil Brenner for such a sparkling conversation. I am particularly grateful to Llerena and Sai for the delightful walk-and-talk on our way to the restaurant following the meeting, and to Sai for hosting me, and for the long and lovely morning walk over from Cambridge (I also wish to thank the good-humored Uber driver who rescued us from the potential embarrassment of having wildly underestimating how much time that walk would take).

The book's introduction has profited from insights offered by friends and colleagues who both talked with me through various ideas, and generously offered to read and provide feedback. For their generous engagements with the book's introduction, I am especially grateful to Joel Revill, Deborah James, Johan Lindquist, Laura Lieto, Nikhil Rao, Lisa Mitchell, Tarini Bedi, Sudev Sheth, Llerena Searle, William Mazzarella, and especially Rachel Sturman—whose unshakable confidence in this project kept me on track during moments of doubt, and whose formidable intellect is matched only by her generosity of spirit. Rachel's unwavering support and good humor has taught me the meaning of true collegiality and intellectual companionship. Thank you.

At Duke University Press I wish to thank Miriam Angress, whose enthusiasm and confidence in this project has been unwavering. The two reviewers that Miriam recruited to read the manuscript provided wonderfully valuable feedback. Thanks to Susan Albury, our project editor at Duke University Press, who provided guidance through copyediting, design, and production. Thank you to Chitra Venkataramani for the beautiful illustrations in Lubaina Rangwala's chapter, Ranjit Kandalgaonkar for designing the brilliant graphic map in Gautam Pemmaraju's piece, and Anand Prahlad for the lovely drawing in Shailaja Paik's chapter as well as for penning the city maps on which the names of places mentioned throughout the book are indicated. Thanks to Celia Brave for preparing the index and to the Max Planck Institute for Social Anthropology in Halle for their support.

Reading through the final *Bombay Brokers* page proofs in the bleak days of December 2020, I find that, in the face of the dark news filling my inbox each morning, the ethnographic accounts in this book nonetheless fill me with hope: these stories suggest that perhaps too much attention is being paid to conventional and empowered ways of reading and narrating the present. By contrast, the stories that populate these pages shine light through the cracks and contradictions that inhere in those empowered discourses and framings, revealing a world so remarkably full of creativity that it seems anything could happen.

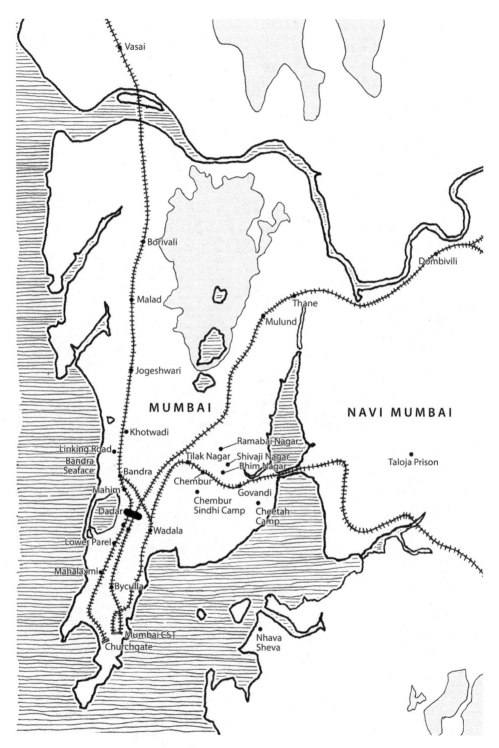

MAP FM.1 Places mentioned in Greater Mumbai. Drawn by Anand Prahlad.

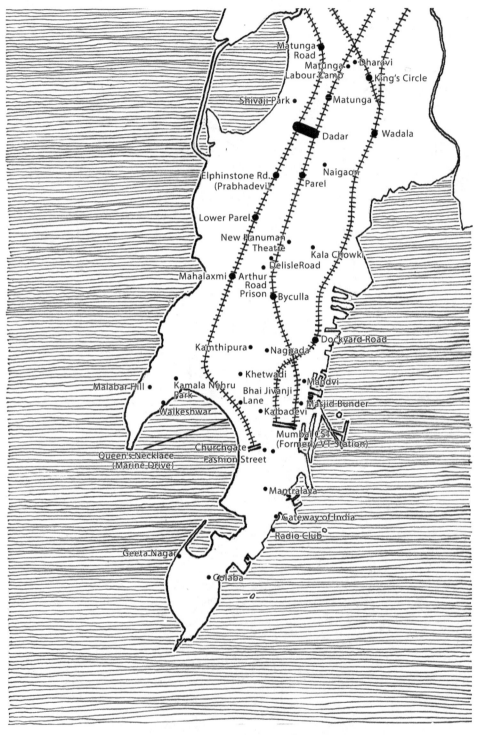

MAP FM.2 Places mentioned in Island City. Drawn by Anand Prahlad.

INTRODUCTION URBAN ETHNOGRAPHY IN THE GLOBAL INTERREGNUM Lisa Björkman

IN APRIL 2014 I moved into one of those lovely crumbling old *chawl**buildings lining L. J. Road in the central Mumbai/Bombay[1] neighborhood of Dadar.[2] The tiny one-room flat had belonged to my friend Kranti's[3] granny, who had recently passed away after living in the flat for more than sixty years. Granny's daughters had long ago moved out of their childhood home in the "Dadar chawl" and into larger and more comfortable residences in Navi Mumbai, in Goa, in Heidelberg. The little room remained shuttered while the building (which had been acquired by one of the city's larger property developers during the giddy turn-of-the-millennium property boom but had been put into cold storage following a protracted market slump) waited for the promised "redevelopment" under one or another of the government's market-driven schemes. In this context, Kranti's idea that "hey, you could stay in Granny's flat!" suggested a fine solution to the perennial problem of where to stay in Mumbai, this time for a six-month visit. Granny's flat it-self was blissfully quiet and peaceful—notwithstanding the chawl's address

---

* The glossary at the end of the book discusses meanings of specialized terms appear-ing in italics. Specialized terms that are more amenable to single-word translations are clarified with parentheticals in the text itself.

along one of the noisiest thoroughfares in a very noisy city—situated as it was on the far side of the internal courtyard, tucked into the back corner of the third-floor corridor farthest from the shared toilet. Getting the place in shape was easy enough: we called in a carpenter to replaster the ceiling and to slap a fresh coat of paint on the walls. The room was already furnished with a bed and a desk, and the kitchen was fully outfitted with pots and pans.

The only catch was the cooking gas.

The problem was that Granny's propane cylinder delivery subscription had been canceled after she passed away. When Kranti called up the propane company to inquire about getting the subscription restarted, she was told that a new subscription would require current residents' proof-of-address documents—documents that, because no one actually lived there anymore, did not exist. Without proof-of-residence documents, it was not possible to get a gas subscription (or "connection" as such subscriptions are so aptly called in Mumbai). And by-the-cylinder direct purchases for domestic purposes were simply not available through any of the city's propane suppliers.

So I called Rasheed.

Rasheed was (among other things) the proprietor of two small-but-bustling roadside tea shops. Neither of Rasheed's tea shops had a commercial license, so I figured Rasheed might be able to "connect" me with other by-the-cylinder retail options. Kranti beseeched me—half-joking—to please keep a low profile and not to scandalize Granny's longtime neighbors with the comings and goings of rough-and-tumble "*dalal*" (broker) types.

Rasheed arrived a few hours later, huffing a propane cylinder up the stairs to Granny's third-floor flat with the help of a young man I'd not met before. I paid Rasheed in cash for the propane: a small deposit for the cylinder plus the price of the gas . . . and not a rupee more. I asked Rasheed, "Didn't you have to pay something . . . extra?" He shook his head, waving his hand dismissively: "Nothing like that." I was puzzled: "But it's not . . . allowed."[4] Rasheed explained, "They don't give these cylinders to just anyone, but they will give to me." He said this with no little pride. I pressed, but without probing the identity of Rasheed's "they": "But how can they be sure that they won't get into trouble?" Rasheed explained, "I'm a businessman. I buy propane from them every day." The men at the warehouse know this, he explained, so they are confident that Rasheed must have "managed" things properly: "Why would I take any risk when my own business depends on it?"

It seemed a good point.

Rasheed's knowledge of where such "risk" might lie, as well as his understanding of how to "manage" those risks, is born of his deep familiarity and vast knowledge of Mumbai: an unquantifiable expertise gained from a life spent navigating and "connecting" the highly complex, constantly changing, and often-contradictory sociopolitical, institutional, and material fabric of the city. To survive and thrive in Mumbai, Rasheed has learned to divine the dangers—financial, social, material, ethical—posed by so many unknowns and contradictions, and to reconcile the risks they pose with the exigencies, possibilities, and pleasures of everyday city life. It was Rasheed's mastery in such matters of divination and reconciliation that inspired me to ring him up that April morning to request his help in resolving my gas cylinder conundrum.

This book is about people like Rasheed—people whose material and practical expertise animate the everyday workings in and of one of the world's more dynamic cities, but whose labors are simultaneously (and paradoxically) subject to much moralizing and hand-wringing. We take this paradox—the ethically fraught yet indispensable character of certain kinds of knowledge and labor—as a methodological and analytical jumping-off point for exploring broader questions about global-level transformations: economic, technological, political, socio-material, ideational. The ethnographic heart of the book comprises thirty-six character profiles, each written by one of the book's authors. Each of us (we are mostly anthropologists but also artists, planners, and activists) has selected some person whom we have come to know through our research in Mumbai: someone who is generally not the protagonist of our research attention in the city (although they might be or become so), but someone whose work and expertise are indispensable to the processes and practices that each of us seeks to understand.[5] As people who are at once central and liminal, their knowledge and know-how, manner and style become portals into urban machinations and meanings.

Taking the city of Bombay as the site for this collective ethnographic undertaking, this book is animated by a four-part set of questions.[6] The first concerns the material-practical work that comes to be characterized in Mumbai in neither-here-nor-there terms such as *brokerage* (*dalali*): What does this work actually entail? What do these labors accomplish (or seek to accomplish) and to what end? What are the stakes of these activities and for whom?

The second part of the questions concerns the knowledge and resources enlisted in these activities: What is required for some crucial work to be done? How and by what means are these varied resources and skills acquired—and by whom? In addition to ethnography, each profile has a biographical component that probes how each profiled person narrates their own history and how they describe the trajectory through which they acquired the technical abilities, embodied expertise, and socio-material resources and relations that enable them to do whatever it is that they do.

The third part concerns the moralizing talk that gathers around these people and their practices. The people profiled in this book emerge in the ethnographies as neither clear heroes nor villains, yet we see that they are rarely spoken of in neutral terms. Rather, they tend to be vilified and/or valorized within their respective domains of activity. We thus ask more questions: in what context—and in whose company—is some person or practice described using such compromising and unflattering terms as *nuisance* or *troublemaker*, *thief* or *khabri*, *dalal* or *agent*? And in what context or company might that same person and their work be characterized using more laudatory terms such as *social worker* or *karyakarta*, *partner* or *sirdar*, *sister* or *friend*? The ethnographies that constitute the chapters of *Bombay Brokers* track the various terms of epithet and praise. The discursive richness and complexity by which people and practices are described beg important questions of such talk: what processes and practices are characterized as ethically fraught—when, where, and by whom? What kinds of normative presumptions underpin opposing characterizations of a singular domain of practice? Attending to the discourse surrounding activities described in either/both complimentary or condemnatory terms reveals how moralizing evaluations are enlisted in the processes thereby set in motion.

Fourth (and finally), bringing these questions together, each ethnographic profile probes the historical and ethnographic specificity of the practices that move in and out of broker-like situations:[7] what renders these particular domains of expertise and activity so salient at this particular historical conjuncture—indeed often valuable enough to command their own price (monetary or otherwise)?[8] *Bombay Brokers* takes the city of Bombay and the paradoxical centrality and liminality of these practices as ethnographic sites and methodological points of entry for probing broader-level transformations characterizing the global present, for thinking about (and disturbing) received concepts and categories, and for raising comparative questions.

Bombay Brokers is about how embodied expertise, enacted at particular moments in particular locations, mediates the material-practical contradictions and "frictions" characterizing the global present.[9] The people profiled demonstrate virtuosity in managing these contradictions, shedding light on the material skills and resources that they enlist in doing so. Using ethnography to probe these frictions—their genealogies, their uneven and contested histories of emergence—is a methodological strategy aiming at generating new insights into our current historical juncture. In this sense, one obvious insight that *Bombay Brokers* yields is methodological, demonstrating the need to attend ethnographically (rather than, say, normatively or conceptually) to the material-practical forms of enacted expertise upon which contemporary life depends. Accounting for the decisive salience in Mumbai of the material dimensions of these liminal-yet-indispensable knowledge practices brings into view profound shifts (institutional, ideational, technological) governing the built form of the city and transforming the lives of its inhabitants: the introduction of market ideas and devices into the city's development planning frameworks, for instance, or the explosion of mobile communication technologies and new media platforms, as well as the new social imaginaries they set in motion.

The comparative question here is not "how and whether similar shifts are or are not happening in other cities" (although this may prove an interesting line of inquiry); our comparative approach seeks neither to read Bombay's particularities alongside empirical work in "comparable" cities (however defined) nor to measure such particularities against ideal-typical arrangements and normative ideals—about, say, the modern state and political mediation, about urban economies and entrepreneurialism, about socio-spatial transformations thought to characterize the global present more generally. Rather, the ethnographic material in this book raises comparative questions concerning how embodied expertise enacted in particular locations mediates the material-practical contradictions to which shifts taking place at different scales (global, national, regional, virtual) are giving rise. It is the contradictions born of these myriad and multi-scalar transformations that the work of these profiled people indexes. The comparative questions that *Bombay Brokers* yields are thus something like these: what new and emerging forms of labor and knowledge are simultaneously indispensable and yet morally suspect in everyday city life? What sorts of socio-material and institutional contradictions or "gaps" come into focus when we shift our empirical and analytical attention to the everyday labor of bridging these gaps? What are "brokers" brokering? What are "fixers" fixing? It is these sorts of comparative questions about the material-practical content of activities glossed as "brokerage" (phenomena that might otherwise be read as idiosyncrasies of particular cities and their histories) from which new understandings and insights about the contemporary historical moment might emerge, insights that push past received concepts and categories in order to glean other meanings and imaginings.

Brokerage

There is a large body of scholarship that labels much of what we are discussing here as "brokerage." Indeed, brokerage is a concept in its own right, with long-standing research traditions clustering largely around questions of political and economic brokerage. Attention to this corpus of scholarship allows us to see how writings on brokers—like emic talk about brokers— speak to the challenges posed to prevailing concepts by historical churnings. Probing this literature on political and economic brokerage allows us to pose questions about the specificity of the current historical juncture that has inspired this book's ethnographic exploration of brokerage.

Scholarship on political brokerage achieved particular prominence during the mid-century "decolonization" moment and the attendant rise of modernization theory in the 1950s. In the South Asian context, mid-century historiographical debates about the nature of anticolonial nationalisms hinged largely on the role of indigenous elites in struggles for independence: whereas Marxian and Dependency School historiography read anticolonialist struggles as an epic battle between colonial oppression and nationalist desires for freedom,[10] historians of the so-called Cambridge School pointed instead to the narrow economic and political self-interest of indigenous political elites, who were held to have been less interested in grand ideals such as freedom than in "jockey[ing] for power and privilege"[11]—whether within a British-controlled or an independent Indian state.[12] Independence-era historiography and sociology characterized the activities of Indian elites in similarly suspect, "agentive" terms, their work now simply consisting of facilitating the political and social incorporation of villages into the political community of the new Indian nation-state. In a classic account—published on the heels of Indian independence—M. N. Srinivas described relations of "patronage" between political parties and individual voters as pyramid-like in structure, with party leadership channeling state resources downward to voters through "intermediary" figures such as higher-caste landowners or moneylenders with whom poorer and lower-caste masses are described to have long-standing ties of social, ritual, and economic obligation.[13]

Modernization theory famously expected that the "critical functions"[14] of these sorts of Independence-era brokers would gradually disappear, that their specialized (even monopoly) expertise and authority would be obviated by "modern" Weberian-style bureaucracies enabling a rationalized and impersonal interface between citizens and states. However, under the influences of both Marxism and poststructuralism since the 1970s (a period that presided over what Jonathan Spencer calls "the death of political anthropology"),[15] Euro-American social theory turned away from brokers and brokerage as interesting sites where trials and transformations of the political present might be explored. On the one hand, structural Marxists—for whom the state was simply the locus and apparatus of capitalist power—theorized the "agentive" broker out of existence; on the other hand, for poststructuralists (especially of the Foucauldian variety), the exercise of power was by definition disciplinary and subjectifying. In this political and ideological context, questions concerning the content, meaning, and normative implications of various kinds of mediation and agentive action were analytically shelved.[16]

With global-level transformations (sometimes glossed as "globalization") said to be presiding over the ideological and institutional unbundling of the Westphalian "triune of territory, state, and nation"[17] as the privileged site and scale at which power and sovereignty are imagined, institutionalized, exercised, and studied, the intellectual climate appears once again to be changing. With the links between states and markets, bodies and territories, identities and nations increasingly unstable, we are now witnessing "the return of the broker"[18] in both everyday life and in scholarly attention. Indeed, notwithstanding theoretical lack of interest in brokerage, recent years have seen a proliferation of ethnographic and historical work chronicling the myriad ways in which the paradoxes and inequities of democracy (postcolonial and otherwise) continue to be managed, mitigated, mobilized, and otherwise mediated—hierarchically arranged in patronage relations,[19] organized and channeled by party systems,[20] pacified with welfare schemes,[21] subjugated with physical or structural violence,[22] governed and governmentalized with technologies to appease and discipline subject populations,[23] or negotiated and bargained through "instrumental" uses of the political rights of franchise[24]—and have debated the extent to which these myriad forms of political brokerage exhibit both continuity and departure from longstanding patterns and relations of socioeconomic, structural, and ritual authority, and "differentiated citizenship."[25] Of course, citizenship has always been differentiated in myriad ways the world over, but distinctively so in postcolonial contexts[26] and perhaps especially so in cities. Thus, at the heart of contemporary discussions about contemporary urban life is the figure of the broker, who bridges material, institutional, legal, or informational gaps[27] and whose existence reveals the "blurred boundaries"[28] between societies and states.[29]

In the Indian context, scholarly debates about "brokers"[30] have largely been concerned with the normative question of whether political mediation either reproduces or destabilizes established structures of authority. On the one hand, mediation is characterized as a holdover from feudal times, when local leaders are said to have "constitute[d] a link between the sovereign and the people."[31] Others, on the other hand, have emphasized how contemporary forms of political brokerage do not only (or necessarily) shore up older patterns of authority but can work to challenge these structures as well.[32] Even when challenging entrenched structures of authority, however, political mediation is described with deep ambivalence, as a morally fraught (and frequently violent) sphere of activity bound up with criminality and political-administrative distortion—what Jeffrey Witsoe[33] describes as the "democratization of corruption."[34]

If writings on political brokerage have thus been largely concerned with the normative implications of broker-mediated practices of "corruption" for idealized notions of state and citizenship, scholarship on economic brokerage has been similarly interested in what such practices mean for our privileged theories and understandings of economy, especially the functioning (or nonfunctioning) of national or global markets, the fate of labor, and the role of states and other regulatory bodies in fixing or improving economic growth or national welfare (however defined). The idea that national citizenries made up of enterprising and creative self-starters can both enhance national welfare and advance global development through innovative pursuit of profit, personal risk taking, and self-making has become an important focus of both scholarly inquiry as well as global development discourse and policy making—especially urban policy making—in recent decades. Recent years have seen a wave of popular and scholarly writing on "entrepreneurialism," a valorized ethic of self-making thought to characterize the contemporary global era.

Indeed, the intrepid entrepreneur is celebrated in contemporary business school and development policy circles as the hero of late modernity: taking advantage of the reconfigured business environment and the availability of resources under global capitalism, the entrepreneur enlists the market in creating new sorts of social, economic, spatial, and personal mobilities and possibilities; in so doing, the entrepreneur is said to obviate entrenched hierarchies and to defy socioeconomic exclusions. And yet at the heart of the entrepreneur idea itself sits a tension: on the one hand, the entrepreneur is imagined and celebrated as a solitary and mobile risk taker, embodying a rugged and masculine brand of American-style individualism.[35] Yet at the same time, empirical work and development policy research show that risk-taking entrepreneurialism is not a property of individuals but is instead an intersubjective practice enabled by particular institutional and sociocultural configurations and networks. Although individualist accounts applaud the scaling back of state-regulatory regimes for unleashing entrepreneurial spirit (theorized as a property of agentive individuals), critical scholarship has thus called attention to the structural conditions—socioeconomic relations and institutional contexts—that enable some individuals to thrive while thwarting the efforts of others.[36]

Celebrations of entrepreneurialism have thus been critiqued for obfuscating entrenched and deepening inequalities of class, status, and power, and for ascribing socioeconomic successes born of preexisting structural endowments and class advantages to bootstrapping individualist heroics. In order to successfully enlist markets in challenging exclusionary social structures and hierarchies through enterprise and entrepreneurialism, critical scholarship suggests that what is needed is not some individual personality predisposition toward risk taking but (and on the contrary) strong, state-backed policies to mitigate and socialize risk: planning regimes, positive rights frameworks, public services (water, power, sanitation, and transport), and social programs for education, health care, and social security—the very sorts of state-directed policies and programs, in other words, that market-forward celebrators sometimes charge with having stymied entrepreneurial energies. Critical scholarship has suggested that the redirecting of state resources and policy regimes (either ideologically or in practice) away from these sorts of (modernist, statist, social democratic) redistributive and risk-sharing social programs for (national) citizens, and instead toward investments in infrastructures and institutional frameworks designed to attract and enable circulations of global capital, has simply subsidized (and given free rein) to the already empowered while abandoning the structurally disadvantaged.

Indeed, at the core of these debates is the question of apportionment and management of risk in the institutionally in-flux context of late modernity. Current-day transformations are unmasking the pretentions of territorially bounded nation-states to exercise control (even in theory) over lands, borders, people, and resources. In this context, renewed attention has similarly been drawn to various noninstitutionalized (or unofficially institutionalized) and nonstate geographies and socialities of trust: kinship systems, religious networks, trade diasporas or NGOs, and civil society actors, for instance. In this context "trust" has been theorized as kind of resource—even characterized in economic terms as an endowment, or form of "capital"[37]—that business school and development industry experts point to as the "missing link"[38] that can bridge "institutional voids"[39] and enable valued processes such as business success, ease of mobility, access to knowledge, social aspiration, and entrepreneurial striving.

For example, Harvard Business School professors Tarun Khanna and Krishna Palepu argue that it is the precise relationship between entrepreneurs and intermediaries that distinguishes developed markets from emerging ones: in developed markets, "the requisite information and contract enforcement needed to consummate transactions"—things such as market information, a judicial system that will enforce contract laws, a transparent regulatory environment—are provided by "specialized intermediaries." What are termed emerging markets, by contrast, are defined by what they call "institutional voids"; in the absence of specialized intermediaries, "individuals are prevented by absence of information, contracts, funds, and what-have-you from coming together."[40] Although plenty of "informal intermediaries" might exist in these institutional voids (say, individual local moneylenders), the professors argue that these are not "functional substitutes" for specialized intermediaries because they operate on "an uneven playing field": they exploit informational and power asymmetries in pursuit of personal gain, deal in adulterated goods, and lend money at usurious rates of interest.[41] It is precisely this situation of "low trust" that is theorized to yield entrepreneurial opportunities for those who manage to cultivate a "trustworthy" reputation. But what counts as an institution, and what counts as individual action—and to whom? In practice, this tidy analytical divide collapses: the professors' advice for cultivating the trust needed for "winning in emerging markets" (which is the title of their how-to book) hinges precisely on an ability to capitalize on the very "informal" networks that they disparage as potentially exploitative: "You do need local expertise to be able to identify who to partner with and not to partner with," they write, their corrective phrase *do need* acknowledging that the empirical need for "local expertise" runs counter to received entrepreneurial orthodoxy. Needless to say, the business school professors describe these theoretically unacknowledged but practically much-needed local experts as "deal brokers."[42] *Bombay Brokers* takes as its ethnographic point of departure this paradox of the necessary-yet-suspect character of such "local expertise."

Ethnography in the Interregnum

Khanna and Palepu are not alone in their preoccupation with these matters of trust. Social theorists across the political spectrum have emphasized the shifting location of trust in our contemporary world;[43] the unbundling and reconfiguring of sociopolitical, legal, and economic arrangements and institutions are understood to inject new kinds of risk (material-economic, environmental-climatic, business-transactional, socio-spatial, and moral-ethical risks) into everyday life, even in highly industrialized states where things such as contract law have generally been considered predictable and reliable. The current conjuncture is increasingly characterized as one of global economic and political crisis: on the one hand, with financial upheavals, economic stagnation, and vertiginous inequality presenting profound ideological and practical challenges to the market-forward orthodoxies that have governed international economic institutions for the past half-century,[44] observers have begun asking not whether but how global capitalism "will end."[45] Meanwhile, the worldwide intensification of antiestablishment ("populist")[46] political challenges is feared to portend the "end of democracy"[47] as the hegemonic basis of international political order and stability.

Amid so much talk of crisis, a number of scholars have used the Gramscian notion of "interregnum" to describe the political present.[48] Gramsci famously borrowed the term *interregnum* from Roman law, where it marked an unusual situation in which—following the death of a king and the absence of any appointed successor—the legislative authority (i.e., the senate) found itself without an executive. In this situation of "interregnum" the Roman senate was empowered to act as "interrex" (temporary sovereign) for a limited period (exactly five days) until a new king could be appointed.[49] Gramsci borrows the Roman term but upends its meaning: whereas the Roman interregnum describes a situation where authority of the senate persists notwithstanding an empty throne, Gramsci's use describes the inverse: "If the ruling class has lost its consensus, i.e., no longer 'leading' but only 'dominant,' exercising coercive force alone, this means precisely that the great masses have become detached from their traditional ideologies, and no longer believe what they used to believe previously."[50] Interregnum, in Gramsci's terms, describes a "crisis" situation wherein the sovereign retains coercive power but in the absence of any legitimizing authority.

Crisis talk looms large in popular and scholarly writings on contemporary Indian cities, and especially so in writings on Mumbai. As literary critic Ulka Anjaria notes, contemporary representations of urban India (scholarly, literary, cinematic) tend toward either of two narrative genres: either "a celebratory plunge into the capitalist globalized future" or "a nostalgic lament for a lost cosmopolitan past." The former genre—exemplified in the business school writings of Khanna and Palepu discussed above or the popular and scholarly work of market-forward economists and journalists such as Columbia

University's Jagdish Baghwati and Arvind Panagariya[51]—foregrounds the transformative promises that globalization holds for urban India: "Globalization has given the Indian underground a new energy[, and] an unfettered and liberal India is breathlessly absorbing everything, all the influences the world has to offer," writes Delhi-based business journalist Palash Krishna Mehrotra in a breathless collection of essays celebrating the aspirational upwardly mobile youth of urban India. "The old walls are crumbling," Mehrotra concludes, and young India "is in gobble mode."[52] Mumbai-focused iterations of this globalization story narrate the socio-material transformations of industrial, working-class Bombay into aspirational, consumption-oriented Mumbai, alternately applauding or grieving the re-deployment of formerly industrial urban spaces and structures (erstwhile home to Mumbai's storied textile industry and its lively working-class Marathi culture) now as globally branded shopping and dining destinations for urban elites.[53] All the while, the dramatic and rapid transformations of the city's built fabric feature in a myriad of cinematic representations of Mumbai,[54] which is home to the world's by-far most prolific film industry, globally known as "Bollywood."[55]

Alongside these triumphant accounts of millennial Mumbai in transformation runs a parallel narrative of urban crisis. "The city is seen as in decline," Anjaria writes, "from its cosmopolitan colonial history in the nineteenth century to the rise of Hindu chauvinism and rampant capitalist development in the 1990s, culminating in the Shiv Sena–influenced decision to change the name of the city in 1995."[56] Famously dubbed the "Maximum City" by internationally renowned journalist Sukhetu Mehta, contemporary Mumbai boasts a population somewhere between 18 million and 23 million for the metropolitan region (estimates vary wildly). But by any measure, the city is a staple of development-industry reports on the world's "largest" (most-populous) cities,[57] and it is consistently characterized as the world's by far most densely and dangerously overpopulated conurbation by a very large margin.[58] Meanwhile, Indian census enumerators report that 60 percent of Mumbaikars live cheek by jowl in city *slums*, where basic infrastructural services such as municipal water supply are described to be both legally tenuous and practically unreliable.[59] Mumbai's slums and popular neighborhoods feature as the backdrop to popular and scholarly accounts of the city's storied underworld and its tortuous connections with global terrorist networks and plottings (which, needless to say, provide endless Bollywood fodder) as well as to the city's rough-and-tumble political class.[60] And indeed, Mumbai is home to one of India's longest-established ethno-nationalist popular-political movements—the Marathi-nativist Shiv Sena party—which presided over the ethno-religious riots that rocked Mumbai in 1992–93 and which honed contemporary idioms of political theatricality long before the country's contemporary administration.[61]

Yet, unlike Gramsci's reading of interregnum from interwar Europe—which foregrounds a teleology of crisis and normative valence of morbidity (or "monsters")[62]—the view from Bombay appears somewhat different. Although a generation of subaltern studies scholarship has found analytical purchase in Gramsci's description of power without authority—"dominance without hegemony"[63]—the ethnographies in this book reveals that contemporary Bombay is neither in a state of imminent crisis nor overrun by monsters;[64] rather, the myriad everyday crises and contradictions of city life are managed, mitigated, and metabolized by a myriad of brokers. We take this proliferation in contemporary Bombay of people and practices characterized as brokers and brokerage as an invitation to explore the domains of activity that do not fit neatly into privileged and empowered categories through which power and authority are theorized and institutionalized. Probing the interregnum ethnographically—dwelling in the gaps that brokers are said to bridge, following the faults and failings that fixers are said to fix—compels rethinking some of the key canonical formulations and conceptual distinctions by means of which contemporary scholarship has tended to explain and explore contemporary social, economic, and political life: categories such as states and markets, citizens and sovereigns, cities and hinterlands, nations and territories, rights and wrongs.

IN A PROVOCATIVELY titled essay, "Welcome to the Seventeenth Century," Charles Tilly describes how throughout much of human history, trade and enterprise—particularly long-distance trade and long-term enterprise—have depended on temporally enduring and geopolitically far-reaching social and political networks: "Under various names such as trade diasporas, lineages, and sects, such networks combine strong ties, considerable extent, many trials, and significant barriers to entry or exit."[65] Tilly suggests that the "historically exceptional overlap of trust networks with economic organizations and governmental institutions" that has characterized the past four centuries may well be coming to an end.[66] Yet historiography from South Asia raises the question of whether Tilly's "overlap" ever began in the first place;[67] long-distance, boundary-exceeding networks have played a central role in modern history, not least in aiding the ascent (to take one prominent example) of the British East India Company: enabling the trading firm's transformation into a colonial power and then facilitating the concomitant transitions to capitalism and industrialization over the course of the nineteenth century. Indian Ocean historians have highlighted the central roles played in that heady period by an array of (often Bombay-based)[68] intermediaries—*shroffs* (money changers), *dubashes* (translators), *dalals* (commodity brokers), *sarangs* (labor recruiters), *marfatiyas* (wholesalers), *muqaddams* (tax collectors), *thikadars* (contractors), and *arhatiyas* (financial brokers and moneylenders)—in facilitating and consolidating these world-historical shifts.[69] The spatial concentration of such people and practices in nineteenth-century Bombay reflects that city's location (territorial, institutional, ideational)[70] at the confluence of the seismic global processes and shifts characterizing that particular historical moment.

Bombay Brokers is similarly interested in the array of intermediary activities populating this historical moment: the practices that overflow the normative conceptual categories and institutionally empowered frames. Whereas the global present is witnessing the renewed salience of myriad forms of mediation—in enabling capital and commodity circulations and facilitating access to material and financial resources, global markets, infrastructural services, public goods, and various kinds of institutionally backed rights and entitlements—we have seen that popular and scholarly debates over the significance and implications of these proliferating forms of mediation have failed to change with them, devolving instead into age-old (and remarkably insistent) oppositions between free will and determinism, structure and agency, continuity and change.

This book pushes past these theoretical and philosophical impasses in three interconnected ways. First, *Bombay Brokers* argues that it is not the existence of mediation that is new, but rather the form and content of those mediations that have changed. Although a generation of scholarship—postcolonial and otherwise—has established the thoroughly mediated character of both everyday city life and of the modern state form, recognizing that sociopolitical and economic life (urban and otherwise) is always already mediated allows us to shift the analytical focus away from the figure of "the broker" as such—away, that is, from the question of whether "brokerage" is to be celebrated or condemned—and instead to the ethnographically more interesting question of how and why particular mediating practices are so salient and contested at this particular historical juncture in this particular place.[71]

Second, *Bombay Brokers* refuses the "methodological nationalism"[72] that (still) underpins so much contemporary scholarship on contemporary politics and economy. Rather than beginning our inquiry within the territorial confines and conceptual/methodological frameworks of the nation-state—to the exclusion and obfuscation of other locations, directionalities, and scales—we approach ethnographically the question of how multi-scalar ("global") connections and flows are brought into being through what Anna Tsing describes as the "sticky materiality of practical encounters,"[73] as well as through affective regimes of "potentiality and emergence" that Hansen and Verkaaik term "urban charisma."[74] This book takes the "sticky materiality" and "charismatic potentials" of Bombay brokerage as an empirical point of departure for exploring how boundaries (political regimes, territories, institutions, laws, and norms) are constituted by the very movements and mediations that such activities paradoxically appear to exceed.

Finally, in foregrounding the material dimensions of the practices glossed as "brokerage" and the embodied character of the expertise that animates those practices, the ethnographies explore the distribution of agency among not only human but also nonhuman "actants."[75] Building on the insights from "new materialist"[76] scholarship, we thereby eschew a classic, humanist conception of the agentive, self-authoring, intention-driven subject and instead consider the dispersed, nonhierarchical, materialized character of "agency." Attending to the distributed character of agency allows us to pose as an ethnographic question what brokerage is or does.

Our conceptualization of "brokerage" thus takes a cue from the work of social theorist Michel Callon. Drawing on Goffman's theory of "framing," Callon points out that any coordinated social action, negotiation, or transaction necessarily "presupposes a framing of the action without which it would be impossible to reach an agreement, in the same way that in order to play a game of chess, two players must agree to submit to the rules and sit down at the chessboard which physically circumscribes the world within which the action will take place."[77] Framing is an always-incomplete project, Callon points out, because objects and activities cordoned off within some frame (conceptual or material) are organized by an array of socially and materially embedded elements (objects, ideas, and people) whose actual relationships necessarily "overflow" the boundaries of a frame; the irreducible materiality of the world means that the myriad elements cordoned off by some attempt at framing some situation (a labor contract, a land transfer, a film shoot, a claim to community belonging) are "simultaneously involved in other worlds from which they can never be wholly detached." This phenomenon is understood by mainstream economics, where the afterlives (or rather "paralives")[78] of these relational ties are referred to as "externalities." A common example of market externality is industrial pollution: when toxic waste discharged by a manufacturing plant into a local river affects the health of local residents, then these health costs—which were not taken into account when setting the price of the industrial good—would be considered market externalities. Market externalities are unavoidable because relations necessarily exceed any attempt at framing (hence the need to frame in the first place). And these relationships are of course materialized such that "something must overflow." It is these material objects and flows that simultaneously produce and overflow the boundaries of any given "frame" that Callon calls "intermediaries."[79]

Bombay Brokers builds on Callon's formulation, focusing ethnographic attention on category-exceeding intermediary objects and materials, as well as (and more crucially for our purposes) on the people who make it their business (often quite literally) to manage, mitigate, and maneuver along the routes that intermediaries (say, propane cylinders) travel. These people perform the morally fraught but socially necessary work of transgression, translation, and transborder navigation that Callon calls mediation: a "theory of action in which what counts are the mediations and not the sources."[80] It is this "theory of action" that we propose to call brokerage, and the virtuoso performers of such actions whom we call brokers.

The remainder of this introduction focuses on two domains of framing and overflow in Bombay and on the concomitant mediations (i.e., brokerage) that these frames and flows produce and inhabit. Reflecting the extant literature earlier discussed, the first domain pertains to what's framed as political, the second to what's framed as economic. Empowered framings of the political are evidenced in pervasive moralizing discourses about "corruption"; those pertaining to economy inhere in everyday talk about "value." In Bombay the fraught relations between the official categories—the laws, policy frameworks, and (more or less) institutionalized norms that seek to govern the city—and the real-time socio-material practices that overflow those categories are frequently glossed in the moralizing language of "corruption." This "corruption" discourse is therefore a good place from which to begin to explore the shifting and contested framings—legal, institutional, ideational, and material—that so much moralizing talk holds to be "corrupted."

"Corruption"

On December 26, 2007, following an especially active season of state-led slum demolitions (part of millennial Mumbai's efforts to give the city a "world-class makeover"),[81] residents of the recently bulldozed popular neighborhood of

Mandala in Mumbai's eastern suburb of Mankhurd delivered a bank check to the office of the chief minister of Maharashtra. In the letter that accompanied the check (which was jointly authored with Mumbai-based housing activists), Mandala residents requested that the chief minister officially transfer to them the parcel of state-owned land on which their now-flattened neighborhood had been situated. The letter referenced an intriguing legal precedent for this official transfer request: the government, the letter pointed out, had recently handed over a swath of primely located state-owned land to one of the city's largest property developers—at the token price of only 40 *paisa* per acre (less than USD $1 per acre). The land gift (as it essentially was) had earlier been home to groups of indigenous people (so-called tribals), but—citing the city's need for affordable housing—the land been acquired a decade earlier by the State Development Authority at that same paltry price: 40 paisa per acre. The state's at-cost transfer to a large property developer of this vast swath of expropriated tribal land was made on the condition that the land be used to construct affordable housing. Mandala residents, citing this example, sought to outbid the developer/tycoon, calculating the amount of their own check at a slightly higher per-acre rate. As Mumbai housing activist Simpreet Singh explained, "If [land] can be given to [the developer,] then why not to [Mandala residents]—and that too at a higher price?"

The check-and-letter stunt was of course not actually expected to result in the requested land transfer (although that would presumably have been a happy outcome); rather, it was part of a broader effort to draw public and media attention to the hypocrisy of a city that would criminalize and evict the urban poor from state-owned territories while using law and policy to give outsized land gifts to politically connected builders, all in the name of antipoverty housing initiatives.[82] What's more, as the activists would go on to point out, while the developer failed to build anything remotely affordable on his vast tract of public land, Mandala's housing stock truly is affordable. Indeed, the publicity stunt took place in conjunction with a legal petition filed by Mumbai housing activists against this particular developer, who turned out not to have constructed the promised affordable housing upon which the land transfer was premised. Instead, the developer had created a fairyland township of gated enclaves whose intended occupants were clearly those who—in the words of the High Court judge who ruled on the petition—could afford to buy "Bentley and Ferrari."[83] "How can you build palaces on land allotted for affordable housing?" asked the incensed Justice Dattu. "What is happening in this Country?" The court's outraged ruling—which punctuated a countrywide "anticorruption" wave sweeping India in 2011–12—may have made headlines, but it resulted merely in a token, finger-wagging fine.[84] Yet that it did so at all is notable, the activists' check-and-letter maneuver having thrown into relief—under the bright lights of the news media—the absurdities and contradictions of what was being carried out under the conceptual auspices and institutionalized policy frameworks of "world-class development," "affordable housing," and "antipoverty" programs. Calling attention to the material overflows of these conceptual and institutionalized frames (to use Callon's terms), the housing activists' attention-grabbing bank check revealed the inherent contradictions and routine transgressions of those frames. In so doing, the media-savvy strategists capitalized on the broader "anticorruption" climate of that particular moment.

Indeed, in a classic formulation Joseph Nye defines *corruption* as "behavior which deviates from the formal duties of a public role (elective or appointive) because of private-regarding (personal, close family, private clique) wealth or status gains."[85] In line with this definition, corruption has conventionally been theorized by social scientists and policy makers in terms of boundary transgression: the term is used to describe the breaching of presumed divides separating public from private, lawful from unlawful, rationality from traditionalism. Scholarship has focused on the adverse effects of corrupt actions on social and economic outcomes (e.g., underdevelopment and inequality), on declining social and political trust and legitimacy, and on the subversion of the broader public good by the pursuit of individual gain. In the postcolonial context, as discussed in the previous section, corruption debates have largely been concerned with the extent to which such subversions either reproduce or unsettle established and institutionalized structures of authority.

In other words, an understanding of corruption as exceptional, deviant, indeed corrupting action presumes the existence of distinct phenomena that map onto these concepts: a unified and coherent state, for instance—one that is distinct from society and thereby amenable to subversion of its public purposes by private actors who violate its laws and undermine its projects. Yet a generation of scholarship has firmly established the falsity of this presumption, demonstrating instead how, as Timothy Mitchell explains, the ostensible distinction between states and societies "must be taken not as the boundary between two discrete entities, but as a line drawn internally within the network of institutional mechanisms through which a social and political order is maintained."[86] In this context the question of whether the so-called corrupt mediations of brokers ought to be read as sign and substance of democracy (however conceived) or of its inverse appears to run aground on conceptual terms, presuming the prior existence and coherence of things like state and society, citizen and subject—things that are empirically in formation through the very mediations that are supposed to threaten them.

Indeed, a growing number of theorists have noted that conventional understandings of corruption as exceptional, deviant, indeed corrupting behavior are insufficient for making sense of the everyday character of so much of what is described as "corrupt."[87] One strand of scholarship has thus trained attention on the discourse of corruption, showing how the disdain with which the "corruption" epithet is hurled testifies to the internalization of a particular state idea: the notion that state employees ought to work not for their own good but for the good of a broader public.[88] Yet as noted above, this corruption discourse testifies to a more basic belief in the empirical existence of a coherent state (corrupted or otherwise) that is distinguishable from society in the first place.[89] Another approach has turned an ethnographic eye to the everyday practices that people describe as corrupt. In his work on "ordinary corruption" among street hawkers and the police in Mumbai, for example, Jonathan Anjaria shows how "power . . . works more through moments of contingency than through a systematic rationality of rule."[90] In Mumbai, claims to land, built spaces, and material infrastructures are bound up with a myriad of often opaque and contradictory rules and policy frameworks that render city residents and businesses perilously exposed to the political whims and administrative vagaries carried out under the rubric of "law enforcement." This is especially (but by no means exclusively) the case for the 60 percent of city residents (including half of Mumbai's police force) that the 2011 census reported to be living in "slums."[91]

In the context of scams and scandals of unprecedented scale, corruption talk indexes and inhabits "new terrains of struggle" against forces of dispossession and expropriation.[92] The heated conflicts over urban-development-related land claims and expropriations in Mumbai—especially the revanchist slum eviction and "redevelopment" exercises that are part and parcel of Mumbai's "world-classing" efforts—are a powerful optic, as Doshi and Ranganathan have written, into the relationship between material and discursive dimensions of struggles over land and urban resources. High-profile demolitions and spectacular scandals like these are the bread and butter of anti-corruption activism and political ideology in contemporary Mumbai. In the first decades of the millennium, normative critiques of "corruption" fueled the formation of a new national-level political party—the Aam Admi Party

(Common Man's Party)—and loomed large as well in Narendra Modi's stunning rise to power during India's 2014 general election.

Bombay Brokers is shot through with stories of crime and corruption, of squatters and slums, of illegality and informality, of fakes and forgeries. Yet flying low to the ethnographic ground, we encounter material that is not entirely legible to the tidy moralities of either state-backed thieving on the one hand and headline-grabbing exposé on the other. The ethnographies reveal instead how discourses of corruption, illegality, and informality often have recursive relations with the very processes and practices that they profess to describe.

For an example, we can return to Rasheed and one of his tea shops. The small structure in which Rasheed's establishment is housed sits at the edge of a popular neighborhood where Rasheed lives with his brother's family. The neighborhood is known simply as "Transit Camp," so called because it was built by the state housing authority (MHADA) in the mid-1980s to "temporarily" house residents of condemned buildings while their homes were being reconstructed. After in-transit residents moved into their new buildings in the late 1980s, the block of single-room concrete structures was not demolished according to MHADA's original plan for the "temporary" settlement; rather, in a city woefully short of low-income housing stock, Transit Camp found a ready crop of new tenants. Rasheed himself (at that time a resident in Mumbai's film-famous "Slumdog" neighborhood of Dharavi) sought the help of a local politician (for whose election the politically active young Rasheed had energetically campaigned) in acquiring two adjacent rooms in Transit Camp, one for himself and another for his brother; the brothers promptly knocked down the dividing wall, transforming the two tiny spaces into a single, modest flat. Yet because Transit Camp was not envisioned as permanent housing stock, there existed no policy framework delineating the tenure status of new residents such as Rasheed, who simply pays a monthly "rental fee" (as he puts it) in exchange for permission to reside in the not-so-temporary-after-all transit camp. And given the vagary governing Transit Camp's built space as well as current residents' status there, the neighborhood is treated for service provision and infrastructure purposes (water, sewerage, and garbage collection) according to municipal policy frameworks pertaining to "slums."

To complicate matters further, Rasheed's Transit Camp tea shop is not actually situated in one of the concrete MHADA-built structures that make up the camp's residential housing stock. Rather, the tea shop is housed in a later-built structure, situated at the edge of Transit Camp and adjacent to a gas station. The tea shop was constructed in 1991 by a now-elderly fellow who, like Rasheed, hails from the smallish city of Nagaur in the North Indian state of Rajasthan. The fellow, whom Rasheed simply refers to as "Chacha" (Uncle), had set up shop shortly after the petrol pump was opened in order to prepare tea and snacks for truck drivers stopping to fill up their tanks. Chacha held documentary proof of his tenure on the tea-shop plot since 1991 in the form of a ration card bearing his name and the shop's address. This is a crucial piece of documentation for residents of Mumbai neighborhoods treated as slums, given a policy framework in contemporary Mumbai that ties eligibility for compensation in the event of a demolition to current residents' ability to provide evidentiary proof that their tenure in a given structure predates a (constantly changing) slum-rehabilitation eligibility "cutoff date."[93]

With the security afforded by the proof-of-address documents for his tea shop-cum-residence at the edge of Transit Camp, Chacha ran a brisk business for twenty years. In 2011, however, Chacha began thinking about plans to retire to his Rajasthani hometown of Nagaur. Retirement presented a dilemma: Chacha had no children to whom to pass his shop, and selling the business was not an option because according to Mumbai's slum policy framework (at that time), whoever purchased the business (and the structure housing it) would not inherit Chacha's cutoff-date-meeting evidentiary proofs, meaning that the new owner would not have the requisite documentation necessary to obtain municipal water connections, propane subscriptions, or compensation in the event of eviction.[94] It was in this context that Rasheed approached Chacha with an idea: Rasheed proposed to lease the tea shop from Chacha, to whom he would pay a one-time deposit as well as a monthly rent payment. Rasheed and Chacha drew up a contract stipulating that when Chacha dies, the ownership of the structure will be transferred to a religious trust in Nagaur. Rasheed and his sons—who would retain indefinite tenancy rights—would continue making the monthly rent payments to the trust. The "contract," of course, was not legally binding because the tea shop's official status itself is ambiguous. But the contract was witnessed and countersigned by a few mutually trusted Nagori friends and relatives. And as a bonus, the Nagori trust—which is connected to a mosque—would provide Chacha (who owns no property in Nagaur) accommodation, food, and care for the duration of his retirement.

When Rasheed's chit-fund turn came around, he used the cash to refurbish and expand the tea shop, renovating the storage area behind the structure (which abutted a drainage ditch) into a seating area for customers. To accommodate the additional clientele, however, Rasheed needed to double his weekly propane allocation. This presented another problem because the ambiguous tenure status of the shop meant that there was no clear procedure by means of which Rasheed's establishment could procure a commercial license that would permit him more propane; Rasheed's repeated efforts to obtain a commercial license for the tea shop had been unsuccessful. Chacha had long managed without a license by keeping the scale of his operations small and making small weekly payments (*hafta*) to police constables who frequented for tea while on patrol.

The expanded space and increased propane deliveries to Rasheed's shop drew the attention of city officials, however, and the increasing hafta payments began to threaten the financial viability of his business. In this context, one of Rasheed's friends—a police constable from the nearby station and a tea-shop regular—had an idea: the constable filed a case against Rasheed for operating his tea shop without a license. Rasheed then presented to the court all the documentary evidence of his repeated efforts to obtain a commercial license; given constitutional "right to life" provisions, Rasheed explained, a sympathetic judge might order that he finally be issued a commercial license. Rasheed smiled as he recalled how he had told the judge, "Sir, I'm doing this work to fill my stomach and to feed my family; I've applied for a license, but it was denied. Please give me a license to do my business legally because that's what I want to do." The judge agreed, directing Rasheed to first pay a modest fine for operating without a license and then ordering the municipality to award him a commercial license. "There's no way to apply for a license," Rasheed shrugged, "but the court can order one."

At the time of this writing in 2019, Rasheed's license is still pending with the municipal corporation. Meanwhile, city life goes on, and Rasheed's business is bustling.[95] The opening nearby of a high-end residential complex and shopping center directs a growing stream of taxis past his tea shop; drivers stop for snacks and wait for customers in the shade of Rasheed's little shop, sharing news and stories, making friends and deals. And in the meantime, while he waits (and waits) for his court-ordered commercial license to be issued, Rasheed procures the propane he needs to make tea and fry *pakodas* by forging and maintaining relations with a range of people—at the company warehouse, the local police station, the political party offices—the very relations, in other words, that were instrumental in his bid to "become legal," as Rasheed put it.

Although "corruption" talk tends to fixate on the money that is sometimes enlisted in this relational work, cash transfers do not always or necessarily attend such work (recall that my propane arrived at cost). But more importantly, even in instances where cash does change hands, the meaning of the money inheres first and foremost in the relationship that cash articulates and inhabits. Indeed, as Ratoola Kundu writes in her profile of a "social worker" named Nirmala who enlists money in arranging the anthropologist's meeting with a group of commercial sex workers, "Money alone would not have gained us access. . . . It was [Nirmala's] relationship with these women that led them to speak with us." Meanwhile, back at Rasheed's tea shop a few months after filing the case, Rasheed's police friend received happy news that—with the "help" of a local politician with whom Rasheed has long been associated—the constable's long-pending request for an official transfer to a closer-to-home beat had finally been approved. While the transfer request may or may not have been cash-backed, to speculate with anticorruption crusaders on the presence or absence of cash would be to miss the point. Whereas moralizing talk about the "corrupt" character of brokerage invariably involves talk about money, such cash-mediated relations are of a piece with the longitudinal, material-relational work by which law-legible ("legal") claims are articulated.

Through Rasheed's story, discursive framings of some activity as legal or illegal, formal or informal, are revealed to be ideological-practical effects and socio-material achievements rather than neutral descriptions of some prior relation to law or policy. The expertise and resources that many of the people profiled in these pages wield is precisely concerned with material, practical, and semiotic practices of producing legality and legibility to law or policy (to "become legal," in Rasheed's words) of diverse domains of practice, everything from building construction, land claims, infrastructural service provisioning, business ventures, and the production of official data and state-sanctioned reports. It is thus not simply the case that the boundaries between categories are blurred; such a notion obviously presumes the prior existence of the very things between which margins might become misted. Rather, what ethnography reveals is that the appearance of stability and coherence of things such as state, law, and identities of all kinds is invariably a temporally distal outcome of the very sorts of mediations that are held to be corrupting of those same formations and framings.

Just as probing "corruption" talk with ethnography destabilizes received wisdom about the modern state—about laws and legalities—upon which so much popular and scholarly writing on political brokerage is premised, so tracking discourses about the questionable "value" of certain activities presents an ethnographic challenge to conceptual tropes and framings of economy. In Bombay we see how disparaging talk about brokers is invariably bound up with disparaging talk about the money paid to brokers as fees, yet also how the subject of such moralizing money talk is not confined to the conflation of broker fees with "bribes"—the notion, that is, that whatever fees the broker is paid pass (in part or whole) into the hands of duty-deviating state officials. Whereas in such cases the fee-commanding broker is disparaged as a mere conduit for what are presumed to be lawbreaking, "corrupt" actions of others, we see as well that money-related moral critiques of brokerage are also leveled at the broker's services in their own right, calling into question the value of the expertise, labors, and services performed.

"Value"

In April 2018 I spoke with Pankaj Kapoor, founder/owner of the Mumbai-based real estate consultancy firm Liases Foras: a self-described specialist in "nonbrokering." Liases Foras seemed to be the only "nonbrokering" firm in Mumbai (or in India, or anywhere else as far as I could tell), yet given the scope and diversity of its client base—from State Bank of India to Deutsche Bank, from Godrej Properties to the Maharashtra State Housing and Development Authority—the idea of nonbrokering seems to resonate in Mumbai. Eager to hear more about this remarkable concept and branding strategy, I had appealed to a mutual acquaintance to ask Pankaj to speak with me. Pankaj is a busy man (hence the appeal to a mutual acquaintance to broker the meeting), so when we sat down for our interview, I got right to the point: "What's nonbrokering?"

The question seemed to please him: "My background is in marketing," Pankaj began affably, "so I understand these things." Pankaj told me about a book he had read in graduate school that had left a particularly strong impression: Jack Trout's *Positioning: The Battle for Your Mind*. "Take the example of cold drinks." Pankaj summed up his major takeaway from Trout's book: "At one time, there were only two major competitors in the industry—Pepsi and Coke. But then along came 7-Up! They called themselves 'the un-cola.' So like that, I came up with 'nonbrokering.'" Fair enough, I pressed, but what's so bad about brokering such that Liases Foras would want to differentiate itself in this particular way? After all, I pointed out, notwithstanding all the grumblings about brokers and dalals in Mumbai, real estate brokering seems to be the anomalous variety (not only in Mumbai but globally) whose practitioners somehow get a pass. Pankaj explained that the difference between brokering and nonbrokering has to do with the precise way that payments are calculated:

> When someone gives a job to a consultant, he's generally not only asking for advice; he also wants the consultant to facilitate the transaction. Real estate is all about transaction. There are two parties to a transaction, and then there's the middleman—the broker—who takes a commission. The commission is paid only after the transaction takes place because the fee is linked to the success of the transaction. A consultant working for commission won't give the true price; his advice will be suited to his own bias. But at Liases Foras we don't do transactions. We charge only fees, no commission. So in that way we give unbiased advice on real estate based on our research.

Pankaj's suspicion of brokerage, in other words, is not about the money per se (his nonbrokering services command fees as well) but rather is about notions of "bias" and distortion. The doubts stem from the way in which different sorts of labor are valued and from the relationship between that presumed value (or lack of value) and the ticket price of the services on offer. Pankaj maintains that the fees commanded by a consultant whose payment is attached to the details of a transaction is by definition compromised because the broker's personal interest (in maximizing his own commission) will lead him to misrepresent a property's "true price." The advice offered by the transaction-facilitating broker, in other words, is suspect because rather than adding value, the broker is suspected of distorting "true price" in order to eat a piece from the middle of the value chain. By contrast, Pankaj describes the fees commanded by Liases Foras's services as payment for value-adding service: what Pankaj calls "unbiased advice."

Moralizing suspicions about whether some work either adds or eats value index the opacity and transience of contemporary global regimes and norms of value production; contemporary critiques of "brokerage" are generated from within these existing ideologies and normative frameworks. But what are these contemporary ideologies and frameworks? At one level, Pankaj's disdain for the work of "transaction" recalls classical liberalism's characterization of what John Locke famously described as the rent-seeking nature of "brokers." Lockean liberal thought justified the accumulation of wealth only when that wealth accrued from "productive" activities: labor in land (the creation of "property") or the accumulation of materialized products of such productive labor (the free exchange of property). Economic activities that were not productive in such ways—the work of bankers, scribes, and traders, for instance—were disparaged as parasitical "brokerage." Wealth accumulated through such activities, classical (seventeenth-century) Lockean thought insisted, was not justified by natural law and thus ought not to be protected by positive law either. Andrew Sartori has characterized the ascent and transformation of liberal thought over the course of the nineteenth century as "a form of political argument" in which the quarrel-inciting contours were born of the sweeping changes of that particular historical era. Philosophical debates of that time reflect what Sartori characterizes as an anxious "grappling" with the moral dangers and empirical contradictions that nineteenth-century thinkers sought to navigate: new regimes of wealth accumulation, the rise of industrial capitalism, expanding geographies of imperialism, and attendant violences of land expropriations. Suspicions of certain forms of economic activity reflect uneasy intellectual efforts to reconcile the normative and empirical contradictions of that particular historical era.[96]

Pankaj's hand-wringing over the labor of "transaction" thus appears at once familiar yet strange: familiar in its suspicious disparaging of "brokers" yet strange because Pankaj's typology of brokering and nonbrokering does not map onto Lockean liberalism's normative presumptions of justifiable wealth as rooted solely in a labor theory of value, property, and right.[97] What normative principles of value (or its lack) are implicit in contemporary disparaging talk about certain forms of labor and expertise?

In thinking through this question, it is helpful to turn to another word whose moral valence has undergone a dramatic shift since the nineteenth century: *dalal*. In contemporary Bombay the words *dalal* and *dalali* are generally used in disparaging terms to mean pimp (and the act of pimping), either literally or figuratively.[98] Yet the term *dalal* did not always carry the pejorative connotation that it does in contemporary Bombay. Historically, Dalal was (and indeed remains) a western Indian surname—along the lines of Shroff (money changer) or Dubash (translator)—that simply described an occupation: Francis Steingass's nineteenth-century dictionary defines *dalal* as "auctioneer, broker; a road-guide";[99] another period translation gives the meaning of *dalal* simply as "agent between buyer and seller."[100] Indeed, while Locke expended much intellectual energy sorting valuable, property-producing labor from the parasitical activities of traders and brokers, by the nineteenth century, liberal political economists were keenly interested in the value that could be generated by trade. Economic philosopher John Stuart Mill (who, like his father, the economic philosopher James Mill, worked closely with the British East India Company and wrote extensively in defense of the British colonial project) was famously enthusiastic about the potential societal gains to be had from taxing the "unearned increment": increases in land value that accrue to proprietors even without labor or capital expenditures.

The ambivalent valence that *dalal* would come to assume can be traced—at least in part—to institutional changes attending the project of nineteenth-century colonial state making. Understandings of trade shifted dramatically in that period, as historian Johan Mathew demonstrates, from "transactions between individuals or firms to transactions between states."[101] In this context, moving goods in and out of port cities such as Bombay (indeed, Bombay looms particularly large in Mathew's account) meant navigating increasingly complex procedures of passing through customs; in this context, Mathew writes that "firms started hiring clearing agents whose expertise was in managing customs formalities."[102] These customs agents were often recruited from the communities of dalals and muqaddams (village chiefs and revenue officers): people who commanded the necessary knowledge and practical expertise in actually existing trade practices to facilitate the commensuration and valuations among heterogenous goods and a myriad of currencies. While the expertise of dalals and muqaddams was thereby enlisted in official customs procedures, their newfound location inside customs offices simultaneously positioned exchange agents and commodity brokers to exercise discretionary judgment in their valuations of goods in accordance with their expertise in commensuration and familiarity with established principles of trade. Their long-established relations with particular firms and trades were of course the very skills that landed the brokers inside British customs offices in the first place. And yet this Janus-faced position—mediating between "official procedures" and actual trade and commensurations practices that overflowed those procedural frames—meant that dalals and their valuations were objects of invariable suspicion by colonial administrators. Meanwhile, the founding of Bombay's stock exchange, along the aptly named Dalal Street in 1874 (so named after Parsi sharebroker Rustomji Dalal), signaled as well the centrality of such practices—of brokering and arbitrage—to capitalist development in the region.[103]

In contemporary Mumbai, *dalal* is almost invariably used in a disparaging sense. Sometimes it is used literally to mean pimp: "Kam se kam koi randi ki dalali nahi karta" (At least he's not out pimping some whore), shrugs Bollywood actress Kareena Kapoor in her role as a straight-talking Bombay sex worker in the 2004 film *Chameli*. But more often the use is figurative. As Sanjeev Uprety notes (discussing the epithetical use of *dalal* in the Nepali blogosphere), "To call someone a dalal is to say that such a person (or a political party) is functioning as a pimp, helping the foreign nations to rape or loot mother Nepal."[104]

Bombay Brokers takes the ambiguity that surrounds so much moralizing talk in Bombay about brokers and dalals as an invitation to ethnographic inquiry. Anxious efforts to sort "valuable" knowledge and labor from that which is "parasitical" (or "corrupt") are themes that run through the accounts. For example, we see in Llerena Searle's profile of Kaushal, a Delhi-born, Brazil-based real estate investor struggling to enter the Bombay property market, that abstract "property" doesn't exist at all prior to the mediations of local "brokers" (Kaushal's word), whose expertise in "land agglomeration" transforms land into "investable parcels and global assets." Although Kaushal was initially dismissive of the expertise of local "partners," the would-be Bombay investor quickly learned that entering the Indian property market—and perhaps the Bombay market in particular—required imitating these local practices by building "chains of intermediaries." Kaushal began working with "numerous local 'brokers'" to help him identify desirable parcels and to negotiate terms of purchase with proprietors. "Such intermediaries were necessary," Searle writes, "because they have the kind of local knowledge and political connections that Kaushal didn't have"; It was in learning the value of local knowledge of which he had initially been dismissive that Kaushal learned to act 'like an Indian developer.'" Kaushal proudly rehearses his lesson: "If you take land and make a project, there are thousands willing to invest."

Back at Liases Foras, Pankaj is of course well aware that "investable parcels and global assets" do not exist before his "unbiased research" represents them as such. As my conversation with Pankaj drew to a close, I asked him: "Do your clients ever try to convince you to facilitate transactions?" Pankaj laughed. "Of course they do! They try every day. Especially when we work for the government." The state government, Pankaj explains, is one of Liases Foras's regular clients. "After we give them advice, they always say 'We want you to help us with plans for this or that project, or to select developers or buyers for projects.'" In fact, in most cases, Pankaj reflects that "clients ask us to sell their properties for them. But we refuse. Because if we start doing brokerage, then we would invalidate the credibility of our own valuations." In other words, clients trust Pankaj to facilitate their transactions—land acquisitions for projects, tenders for developers—precisely because of Pankaj's refusal to do so. In this context the discursive work of disparaging "brokerage"—that is, of denying the value of the very expertise that will invariably be necessary (as Kaushal learns) in facilitating any eventual transaction—is part and parcel of how Liases Foras's product ("unbiased advice") acquires its own value.

Pankaj's disavowal of the value of the local expertise upon which the functioning (even existence) of the property market is premised (expertise that Kaushal comes to recognize as essential to the production of "investable parcels and global assets") points to the central line of inquiry animating this book: What are the various forms of knowledge and expertise that are framed as valuable and legitimate, and by what legal-institutional or discursive mechanisms? And what forms of labor are treated as morally suspect, accused of eating from the middle of the value chain?

This line of investigation can be disaggregated into a few parts: first, what kinds of expertise are important enough (perhaps even necessary) to other, more legible or legitimate forms of social, political, or economic activity such that they command their own price? With Kaushal, for instance, we see that the knowledge of even where to go about finding potentially available land (let alone how to go about negotiating with landlords) is a highly valued resource for which investors are ready to pay a price. It is perhaps the particularity of Kaushal's Wall Street training that leads him initially to misrecognize the value in such expertise—to describe local experts in India as "not that smart." Only upon learning the value of "sending 'brokers out in a *dhoti*'" is Kaushal able to see (let alone enter) the property market at all.

The second part of the question concerns the normative presumptions that animate these value-creating activities, as well as the moralizing critiques that are leveled against these activities and those who perform them.[105] This calls attention as well to the matter of currency (pun intended)—to the question, that is, of the material form in which accrued value is measured, stored, and moved, as well as the temporality of those circulations of stored value. In the profiles we see how much of the moralizing talk about brokerage involves the introduction of money—conceived of as a single measure of value—into social spheres previously and/or normatively governed by other moralities or logics of valuation.[106] By rendering comparable—that is, measurable by equivalent units of value—objects and relations that were previously governed by other logics or systems of value, these systems and moralities are held to deteriorate.[107] Indeed, we see in the profiles forms of knowledge and labor that are expected not to be available or exchangeable in monetary terms but instead to be governed by other logics:

of "public good," "social work," or "democratic accountability." It is the presumed undermining of these other moralities—embodied in the cash fees and payments—that invites the condemnation of certain forms of labor.

Reading Yaffa Truelove's profile of Dr. K alongside Sangeeta Banerji's profile of a nonelite "paid agent" named Shazia reveals the striking overlap in the domain of practice and expertise on offer by the two self-described "social workers." Dr. K disparages the practice of accepting fees for services, citing "the fee and accompanying 'bribes'" as the key distinction between his own "social work" and the "corrupt" activities of people who value "profits above helping the community." Yet as the ethnography reveals, the difference between the two domains of practice inheres not in the existence of transactions but rather in the currency in which the transactions take place: whereas Shazia's expertise is valued, stored, and moved using banknotes, Dr. K uses the currency of (nonmonetary) "barter." The elite social worker points to the nonmonetization of his services as evidence of the distance between his social work and the "cash-fueled 'corruption' exchanges" of "paid agents," but the normative implications of this categorical refusal are uneven. Shazia's services are (echoing Simmel's famous formulation) "freely"[108] available to anyone who can pay, yet Dr. K's altruistic efforts are on offer only to the particular people with whom he happens to be acquainted: neighbors, servants, friends of friends. The ethnographies thus reveal the Janus-faced character of money, which appears to both democratize access to social services while also commercializing that access, thereby obviating entrenched hierarchies (caste, community, gender) while threatening to push services out of the reach of those who can't pay.

And yet the profiles also reveal a spuriousness to this distinction between cash and other material forms of stored value. In Sarthak Bagchi's profile of a political party worker named Mishra, for instance, we see how money is only one among many forms of "gift" that is put into circulation at election time—demonstrating that the exchange-gift binary breaks down. This brings us to the third part of the question on the attribution of value, which concerns the temporality of convertibility and exchange. In the profiles we see how the currency of cash works much like any other gift or currency of exchange in producing enduring relations of debt and obligation. In Tarini Bedi's profile of the caterer/caretaker known as Muna, we see how "'currency' . . . took many forms; it was distributed, circulated, shared, and paid back as money, food, favors, interest, and opportunity, all duly delivered through care associated with the kitchen." Indeed, as Bedi points out, the "monetary value . . . of the catering business" was less important to Muna than was the "value of the other kinds of capacities" that the business facilitated, in one instance enabling her to find employment for a neighbor. In Bagchi's profile we similarly see how the value of money is not reducible to the number printed on the note but rather inheres in the longer-sighted social relations that money's movements both trace and produce. The meaning of election-season money inheres less in a note's exchange value than in its semiotic character: the cash has value not only because it can later be used to buy things (shoes or pencils) but also because the cash note comes from Mishra himself. The banknote gift is both a communicative action and a material instantiation of the strength and durability of the ties connecting Mishra to broad networks' power, authority, and resources.

Although Mishra's own signified strength is part of what gives this gifted money its value, we see paradoxically how Dr. K–style conflation of cash with commoditization is part of Mishra's own moral universe as well. Mishra insists that "gifts and cash do not profess to 'buy votes,'" but he continues to blame "both voters and leaders for making elections more 'commercial' over the years." The multiplicity and contradiction among money's multiple moral registers are bound up with the incongruous temporalities that these circulations of election-season cash inhabit: the short-term temporality of purchase and the enduring character of political relations.

Bombay Brokers attends to interconnections among these four lines of inquiry into the attribution of value—the content of valorized knowledge and labor, the materiality of the currencies in which value is stored, the temporality of exchanges that become the object of moral critique, and the presumptions upon which those critiques are based—in order to shine light onto the fraught domains of framing and overflow that our Bombay brokers index.

Fraught Domains

The book's thirty-six profiles fall into six thematic domains: development, property, business, difference, publics, and truth. These six themes did not precede the writing of the profiles; rather, they emerged over a two-year period of grappling with the ethnographic material itself. In order to explain how we arrived at these six themes, it will be useful to briefly outline the process by means of which this project came into being.

Bombay Brokers was conceived over dinner with a friend in Bombay, sometime in January 2017. At some point, the conversation turned (as it often does in Bombay) to stories of the remarkable creativity, skillfulness, and sometimes sheer chutzpah of our research participants. I had been telling a story about a "plumber" named Sunny, whose expertise in procuring official water connections for households without residential documents had recently been at the heart of a high-profile hydraulic debacle in the eastern suburbs, one that had (at long last) compelled policy makers to rethink the rules governing water supply in popular neighborhoods.[109] My friend responded with their own story, about a fellow whose labors were similarly necessary yet fraught. And so I got to thinking: what if we gathered as many Bombay ethnographers as we could manage and asked each one to write a profile of some such person: someone who is not the protagonist of our research in Bombay (the official "water engineer" or the "film director") but rather that person who always seems be hanging about, the one who—even if we can't quite make out what they actually do for a living—nonetheless appears to be indispensable to whatever we are seeking to understand (how movies get made, how buildings get built)?

A few months later I sent around a series of emails to everyone I could think of who had an active research project in Mumbai, explaining the idea and inviting them to write a short character sketch. For many of us, the people about whom we have written are not only key actors in the processes and practices that our research seeks to understand, but they have also been central to our own efforts to learn about those same processes. Ethnographic encounters are invariably (and necessarily) bound up with the shifting and provisional relations of power and positionality that run through the sites and spaces where we produce knowledge: relations that facilitate our access to those spaces, condition our perceptions, and inform our interpretations. The relationships that we have forged through the research process, in other words, are of a piece with the relational worlds upon which our research attentions are trained. These interpersonal intimacies are thus foregrounded in many of our profiles: attention to the social relations by means of which knowledge is produced is what ethnographers refer to as "reflexivity." Rather than "claim the power to see and not be seen, to represent while escaping representation," reflexivity insists that the ethnographer account for the embodied, materialized, real-time research encounters by means of which knowledge is produced.[110] Given the centrality of these social relations to the ethnographic enterprise, my email invitation to contribute proved remarkably fertile; indeed, many authors responded by noting that the real challenge would be to settle on only one such person about whom to write.

On receipt of the drafts some months later, I created a shared electronic folder to which all the authors had access and then grouped the authors into clusters of threes and fours according to what seemed potentially productive overlaps, intersections, or tensions in the various profiles; the goal of the clustering exercise was to invite authors whose characters interface with similar domains of practice, institutional frameworks, political networks, or territorial scales to ask pointed questions of one another's profiles, as well as to gain insights into their own characters by virtue of the perspective that another profile might afford. The idea for the author clusters was to think together about these ethnographies in order to gain insight into the broader processes, contradictions, and gaps that the work of their profiled person bridges and brokers. In addition to these long-distance clustering and feedback-giving exercises, we convened five in-person *Bombay Brokers* authors' workshops (in Boston, Leiden, Göttingen, Oslo, and Bombay) in order to think collectively about the questions animating the project: What is the broker brokering? What is the fixer fixing? Whence the gaps that need bridging? The six themes emerged through these conversations.

Each of the six themes has a long genealogy and established theoretical tradition, yet we see how the material in the profiles destabilizes the epistemological and normative presumptions upon which received formulations and framings hinge. Focusing ethnographic attention on the material-practical content of the expertise that Bombay brokers wield brings into focus the porosity of these discursive framings; we see how the busywork of brokerage is enlisted in producing and maintaining the conceptual boundaries of these valorized categories.

Part I features people who mediate the contradictions of "development" in Mumbai, where the fantasy of becoming a so-called world-class city has captured the imaginations of a generation of urban policy makers. The characters in this section wield a range of resources and expertise by means of which the territory and built fabric of the city are materialized and transformed under the auspices of development—and especially redevelopment—of the city's heterogenous and "unplanned" territories: its popular neighborhoods, small-scale workshops, "informal" industries, and (above all) its "slums." The expertise wielded by the people populating this section is highly embodied, and the skills employed and deployed are born of intimate involvements with the myriad materials that the city comprises: materiality whose irreducible excesses invariably exceed the tidily institutionalized "world-class" developmentalist visions and policy framings that would govern Bombay.

While the people profiled in part I are experts in mediating the contradictions born of efforts to materialize "development," those in part II work at producing and legitimating claims of access to the city's built fabric, claims

of access that are generally articulated in a privileged idiom of "property."
Contestations over access, use, and distribution of land are some of the most
contentious in contemporary Mumbai—as in cities worldwide; as in the
world more generally. The five people profiled in part II are experts in navigating the contradictions and contestations among competing practices and
claims to urban resources (land, space, and infrastructures), and we see in
the ethnographic material that "property" takes its place as just one idiom (if
an institutionally privileged one) among many claims-making practices that
are both legitimate and empowered in the city. The ethnographies reveal the
gendered, racialized, and classed conflicts and contestations over the (re)
production of various forms of hierarchy and differentiated access made in
the name of "property rights."

The domain of mediation and expertise explored in part III pertains to the
world of "business" (*dhanda*). The seven character profiles show how ideas
and practices of "doing business" animate projects of self fashioning and
world making. Rather than presuming the meaning and morality of "doing
business" or the value of "labor" or "consumer goods," we see how value is accrued partially through the material-discursive work of differentiating business from hustling: *dhanda* from *tapori*. In this context the people profiled
put markets to work toward a myriad of sometimes-conflicting goals. And
we see as well the heterogenous temporal horizons of these value-creation
projects, and by extension the heterochronous character of the markets and
movements that such projects bring into being.

Part IV is about the tireless work of differentiation that characterizes Bombay life: the (re)production, contestation, and reconfiguration of
myriad forms of difference and belonging. This is the work of navigating
and mediating the contradictions of a myriad of crosscutting hierarchies:
articulations and spatializations of identity and distinction. The profiles
demonstrate attempts to cordon off and delimit domains of belonging and
propriety (whether in terms of the fraught inclusivity of "citizenship" or the
myriad forms of gendered, casted, communal, sectarian group-ness) in the
context of these intersecting and counterposing forms of difference/differ-
entiation. The expertise of these people is thus in the material technologies
by means of which gender, caste, religion, regionalization, and nationality
are produced, represented, and contested: how, when, and to what ends.

The six people featured in part V are experts in publicity. This section
explores the social imaginaries and material technologies that are enlisted
in the production and representation of publics. The characters profiled call
attention to the shifting practices, tools, and techniques of mediation and

self making, and demonstrate how these labors animate new kinds of collective subjectivity and identity. The profiles demonstrate the importance of taking seriously the theatrical dimensions of urban life, demonstrating quite powerfully the recursivity in Mumbai between life and its representations, and calling into question the presumed divide between onscreen and offscreen lives.

Part VI features people who are experts in verification and authentication. The six ethnographies explore situations calling for investigation, where this need for investigation indexes the anxieties and instabilities animated by society-level changes. The ethnographies in this group demonstrate a range of situations that require investigation and explore the contested terrain of constituting "verification": what forms of knowledge are deemed "true" (when, where, and by whom), and what is the value of this "truth"? The profiles show how practices of verification—about landholdings, social identity, or personal character, for example—are enlisted in efforts to inflict harm and/or produce value. The ethnographies demonstrate the coexistence of multiple, incompatible "truths," such as in the imperative to reconcile the imperative of equal-before-the-law proceduralism with the equally real existence of political power and the authority to sidestep legal equality in the service of various forms of hierarchy: caste, class, community. The profiles thus explore fraught questions concerning who has access to what kind of knowledge and when and how various "truth" accounts ought or ought not to be made "public" or put into circulation.

Each of the six parts is prefaced by an analytical introduction that brings the ethnographic particularities of the individual pieces into conversation with one another, drawing out common themes, unpacking the overlaps in material-practical expertise, and discussing some of the broader context in which these particular practices have become so simultaneously crucial and contested. The introductions therefore have a twofold function, first in teasing out common themes and second, in so doing, working to guide readers in recognizing certain signposts as they are encountered in the rich ethnographic material. For this reason it is suggested that interested readers consider revisiting the part introductions a second time after having read the profiles.

A FEW HOURS AFTER Rasheed delivered my propane cylinder, my cell phone rang. It was Kranti's mother, calling from her home in the suburbs: "I heard you had a gas cylinder delivered," she began. "Yes," I answered, a bit nervously. "Why . . . did someone complain?" She clarified: "Mrs. Patil from across the courtyard rang me up." She paused and then continued: "Your friend who brought the cylinder," she began haltingly, emphasizing the word *friend*, "do you think he might be able to send one to me as well . . . ?" I breathed a sigh of relief and rang up Rasheed.

Notes

1. Bombay's name was officially changed to Mumbai in 1995 when (following a bloody season of politically orchestrated rioting) the Marathi-nativist Shiv Sena assumed control over the Maharashtra state government (for an illuminating discussion of the city's renaming of Mumbai, see Thomas Blom Hansen, *Wages of Violence: Naming and Identity in Postcolonial Bombay* (Princeton, NJ: Princeton University Press, 2001). However, this "before-and-after" story elides the nomenclatural complexities of the contemporary city. Many people continue to use *Bombay*, especially (but neither completely nor exclusively) Urdu-speaking Muslims, portions of the political left, and the city's intelligentsia. Many people will use *both* names—sometimes alternating according to the language (or accent) in which they are speaking: *Mumbai* when speaking Marathi, *Bombay* when speaking Urdu, Hindi, or English. What's more, because *Bombay, Bambai, Bumbai,* and *Mumbai* exist along multiple spectra of vowel and consonantal sounds, it is not always clear (and perhaps intentionally so) exactly which name is being used. This nomenclatural heteroglossia is reflected in the book's profiles.

2. The maps on pages 13–14 show the locations of various places mentioned through this book.

3. Unless otherwise noted, names throughout the book have been changed.

4. This particular conversation took place in Hindi, a language whose Bombay variation includes the English-origin words *allow, manage,* and *risk* (riks).

5. The idiom of *practice* has been taken up by anthropologists in recent decades as a way to navigate some of the impasses among phenomenology, structuralism, and materialist strands of Marxism, and to draw attention to dimensions of human activity that cannot be abstracted to thought and language. Our use of the word *practice* in this book draws on both Heideggerian and Wittgensteinian strands of practice theory and emphasizes three interrelated things: first, our accounts demonstrate that patterns of human activity are neither given by— nor add up to—a coherent body of rules, regularities, or normative justifications (externally given or otherwise); practices are not given by a coherent body of semantically articulated presuppositions, nor are they prior to or separate from the mediations of language. Following on this point, the ethnographies demonstrate that there is no useful distinction to be drawn between (so-called) *discursive* and *nondiscursive* forms of practice. Rather, our accounts reveal how language itself is a social practice that entails "rich practical and perceptual engagement with our surroundings" and that involves "complex bodily skills" (Rouse 535). Third, our

conceptualization of practice rejects presumptions of mind-body autonomy—and the distinction between "natural" and "social" worlds upon which such presumptions hinge—that inform some strands of practice theory. Instead, the material in this book demonstrates how social practices are "embodied, and the bodily skills through which they are realized are intimately responsive to the affordances and resistances of their surroundings" (Rouse 536). For discussion and elaboration of these points, see Webb Keane, "Perspectives on Affordances, or the Anthropologically Real," *Hau Journal of Ethnographic Theory* 8, nos. 1–2 (2018): 27–38; Webb Keane, "A Minimalist Ontology, with Other People in It," *Hau Journal of Ethnographic Theory* 8, nos. 1–2 (2018): 45–47; Joseph Rouse, "Practice Theory," in *Handbook of the Philosophy of Science*, vol. 15, *Philosophy of Anthropology and Sociology*, ed. Stephen Turner and Mark Risjord (Amsterdam: Elsevier, 2006).

6. These are the questions that were posed to the authors when inviting them to write contributions.

7. Here we take a cue from Appadurai's important insight that "things can move in and out of the commodity state" (Arjun Appadurai, *The Social Life of Things: Commodities in Cultural Perspective* [Cambridge: Cambridge University Press, 1988], 13).

8. The relationship between price and value is discussed later in this introduction.

9. Our approach to exploring these multi-scalar shifts thus shares analytical and methodological overlap with what anthropologist Anna Tsing terms *friction*: "the awkward, unequal, unstable and creative qualities of interconnection across difference." In her study of "global connections," Tsing demonstrates ethnographically how dynamics generally glossed as "globalization" (the seeming universalization of things such as "science," "capitalism," or "politics") are actually brought into being through the "sticky materiality of practical encounters" (Anna Lowenhaupt Tsing, *Friction: An Ethnography of Global Connection* [Princeton, NJ: Princeton University Press, 2004]).

10. Bipan Chandra's *The Rise and Growth of Economic Nationalism in India, 1880–1905* (New Delhi: People's Publishing House, 1966) is exemplary of this genre.

11. Dipesh Chakrabarty, *Habitations of Modernity: Essays in the Wake of Subaltern Studies* (Chicago: University of Chicago Press, 2002), 5.

12. Whereas Cambridge University historian Anil Seal's pioneering work *The Emergence of Indian Nationalism* focuses rather narrowly on the high-caste and foreign-educated character of indigenous elites, historian Sumit Sarkar notes that subsequent work of Cambridge School historiography "disaggregated the category of 'elite' into locality-based 'patron-client' linkages or 'factions,' equally animated by selfish interests" (Anil Seal, *The Emergence of Indian Nationalism: Competition and Collaboration in the Later Nineteenth Century* [Cambridge: Cambridge University Press, 1968]; Sumit Sarkar, "Nationalisms in India," in *India and the British Empire*, ed. Douglas M. Peers and Nandini Gooptu [Oxford: Oxford University Press, 2012]). For a summary of these debates, see Dipesh Chakrabarty, *Habitations of Modernity: Essays in the Wake of Subaltern Studies* (Chicago: University of Chicago Press, 2002), chapter 1.

13. Mysore Narasimhachar Srinivas, "The Social System of a Mysore Village," in *Village India: Studies in the Little Community*, ed. McKim Marriot, 1–35 (Chicago: University of Chicago Press, 1955).

14. Sydel P. Silverman, "Patronage and Community-National Relationships in Central Italy," *Ethnology* 4, no. 2 (1965): 172–89.

15. Jonathan Spencer, *Anthropology, Politics and the State: Democracy and Violence in South Asia* (Cambridge: Cambridge University Press, 2007).

16. Johan Lindquist, "Brokers and Brokerage, Anthropology of," in *International Encyclopedia of Social and Behavioral Science*, 2nd ed. (Amsterdam: Elsevier, 2015).

17. Zygmunt Bauman, "Times of Interregnum," *Ethics and Global Politics* 5, no. 2 (2012): 49–56.

18. Deborah James, "The Return of the Broker: Consensus, Hierarchy, and Choice in South African Land Reform," *Journal of the Royal Anthropological Institute* 17, no. 2 (June 2011): 318–38.

19. Anastasia Piliavsky, ed., *Patronage as Politics in South Asia* (New York: Cambridge University Press, 2014).

20. Stuart Corbridge and John Harriss, *Reinventing India: Liberalization, Hindu Nationalism and Popular Democracy* (Cambridge: Polity, 2000); Yogendra Yadav, "Electoral Politics in the Time of Change: India's Third Electoral System, 1989–99," *Economic and Political Weekly* 34–35, no. 21 (August–September 1999): 2393–99.

21. Partha Chatterjee, "Democracy and Economic Transformation in India," *Economic and Political Weekly* 43, no. 16 (April 2008): 53–62; Joop de Wit, *Poverty, Policy and Politics in Madras Slums: Dynamics of Survival, Gender and Leadership* (New Delhi: SAGE, 1996); Tariq Thachil, *Elite Parties, Poor Voters: How Social Services Win Votes in India* (New York: Cambridge University Press, 2014).

22. Thomas B. Hansen, *Wages of Violence: Naming and Identity in Postcolonial Bombay* (Princeton, NJ: Princeton University Press, 2001); Akhil Gupta, *Red Tape: Bureaucracy, Structural Violence, and Poverty in India* (Durham, NC: Duke University Press, 2012).

23. Akhil Gupta, "Blurred Boundaries: The Discourse of Corruption, the Culture of Politics, and the Imagined State," *American Ethnologist* 22, no. 2 (May 1995): 375–402; Partha Chatterjee, *The Politics of the Governed: Reflections on Popular Politics in Most of the World* (New York: Columbia University Press, 2006).

24. Chatterjee, *The Politics of the Governed*, 40–41.

25. James Holston, "Insurgent Citizenship in an Era of Global Urban Peripheries," *City and Society* 21, no. 2 (2009): 245–67.

26. Chatterjee, *The Politics of the Governed*; Mahmood Mamdani, *Citizen and Subject: Contemporary Africa and the Legacy of Late Colonialism* (Princeton, NJ: Princeton University Press, 1996).

27. G. R. Reddy and G. Haragopal, "The Pyraveekar: 'The Fixer' in Rural India," *Asian Survey* 25, no. 11 (1985): 1148–62; Jeffery Witsoe, "Corruption as Power: Caste and the Political Imagination of the Postcolonial State," *American Ethnologist* 38, no. 1 (February 2011): 73–85.

28. Gupta, "Blurred Boundaries."

29. C. J. Fuller and Veronique Bénéï, *The Everyday State and Society in Modern India* (London: C. Hurst, 2001).

30. In the Indian context, the figure of the "broker" is also referred to as an "intermediary," a "fixer," a "dalal," and a "middleman." See R. Véron, S. Corbridge, G. Williams, and M. Srivastava, "The Everyday State and Political Society in Eastern India: Structuring Access to the Employment Assurance Scheme," *Journal of Development Studies* 39, no. 5 (2003): 1–28; C. Jeffrey, "Democratisation without Representation? The Power and Political Strategies of a Rural Elite in North India," *Political Geography* 19, no. 8 (2000): 1013–36; S. Jha, V. Rao, and M. Woolcock, "Governance in the Gullies: Democratic Responsiveness and Leadership in Delhi's Slums," *World Development* 35, no. 2 (2007): 230–46; Reddy and Haragopal, "The Pyraveekar"; J. Parry, "The 'Crisis of Corruption' and the 'Idea of India,'" in *The Morals of Legitimacy*, ed. I. Pardo (New York: Berghahn, 2000); Witsoe, "Corruption as Power"; P. Oldenburg, "Middlemen in Third-World Corruption: Implications of an Indian Case," *World Politics* 39, no. 4 (1987): 508–35.

31. Reddy and Haragopal, "The Pyraveekar," 1151.

32. Hansen, *Wages of Violence*; Craig Jefferey, *Timepass: Youth, Class, and the Politics of Waiting in India* (Stanford, CA: Stanford University Press, 2010).

33. Jeffrey Witsoe, "Everyday Corruption and the Political Mediation of the Indian State: An Ethnographic Exploration of Brokers in Bihar," *Economic and Political Weekly* 47, no. 6 (2012): 52.

34. This ambivalence toward brokerage contrasts sharply with celebratory accounts of what are characterized as *direct* forms of "insurgent" political claims making, material appropriation, or "occupation" that are theorized as democratizing "alternatives" to relational (that is, brokered) forms of "client patronage." See, for example, Solomon Benjamin, "Occupancy Urbanism: Radicalizing Politics and Economy beyond Policy and Programs," *International Journal of Urban and Regional Research* 32, no. 3 (2008): 719–29; James Holston, *Insurgent Citizenship: Disjunctions of Democracy and Modernity in Brazil* (Princeton, NJ: Princeton University Press, 2008).

35. In their discussion of how market reforms in India have enabled "the rise of Dalit entrepreneurs," for instance, Kapur, Babu, and Bahn argue that "a combination of grit, ambition, drive and hustle—and some luck" have enabled some structurally disadvantaged and socially excluded individuals "to break through social, economic and practical barriers," thereby remaking not only their own lives but also challenging powerful social-political structures and exclusionary nationalist ideologies (Devesh Kapur, D. Shyam Babu, and Chandra Bhan, *Defying the Odds: The Rise of Dalit Entrepreneurs* [New Delhi: Random House India, 2014]).

36. John Harriss, *Depoliticizing Development: The World Bank and Social Capital* (London: Anthem, 2002); Barbara Harriss-White and Elisabetta Basile, "Dalits and Adivasis in *India's Business Economy: Three Essays and an Atlas*" (Haryana: Three Essays Collective, 2014).

37. Robert Putnam, "Bowling Alone: America's Declining Social Capital," *Journal of Democracy* 6, no. 1 (1995): 65–78.

38. Christiaan Grootaert, "Social Capital: The Missing Link?," World Bank report, April 1998.

39. Tarun Khanna and Krishna G. Palepu, *Winning in Emerging Markets: A Road Map for Strategy and Execution* (Cambridge, MA: Harvard Business Review Press, 2010).

40. Tarun Khanna, *Trust: Creating the Foundation for Entrepreneurship in Developing Countries* (Oakland, CA: Berrett-Koehler, 2018), 64, 225.

41. Khanna, *Trust*, 64, 225.

42. Khanna and Palepu, *Winning in Emerging Markets*, 64–65.

43. For example, see Anthony Giddens, *Modernity and Self-Identity: Self and Society in the Late Modern Age* (Stanford, CA: Stanford University Press, 1991); Charles Tilly, "Power: Top Down and Bottom Up," *Journal of Political Philosophy* 7, no. 3 (1999): 330–52; Francis Fukuyama, *Trust* (New York: Simon and Schuster, 1997).

44. Some of these institutions have themselves begun voicing concerns about the threats to political instability posed by the vertiginous inequality over which they have presided and have themselves begun (gently) advocating for increased social spending (Rune Møller Stahl, "Ruling the Interregnum: Politics and Ideology in Nonhegemonic Times," *Politics and Society* [May 2019]: 2).

45. Wolfgang Streeck characterizes the collapse of the global order in terms of a "post-capitalist interregnum" (Wolfgang Streeck, *How Will Capitalism End? Essays on a Failing System* [London: Verso, 2016]).

46. William Mazzarella, "The Anthropology of Populism: Beyond the Liberal Settlement," *Annual Review of Anthropology* 48, no. 1 (2019): 50.

47. David Runciman, *How Democracy Ends* (London: Profile, 2018).

48. "The crisis consists precisely of the fact that the old is dying and the new cannot be born," writes Gramsci in an often-cited passage of *Prison Notebooks*; "In this interregnum a great variety of morbid symptoms appear." Chantal Mouffe uses "interregnum" to characterize contemporary "period of crisis" in which the contemporary "populist moment" unfolds; economic sociologist Wolfgang Streeck characterizes as a "post-capitalist interregnum" the ideological and material challenges to the contemporary global order; Zygmat Bauman characterizes the unmaking of an "old order" based on a Westphalian "triune" of territory, state, and nation as one of interregnum (Chantal Mouffe, *For a Left Populism* [London: Verso, 2018], 15; Streeck, *How Will Capitalism End?*; Zygmat Bauman, "Times of Interregnum," *Ethics and Global Politics* 5, no. 1 [2012]).

49. Philippe Theophanidis, "Interregnum as a Legal and Political Concept," *Synthesis* 9 (fall 2016): 110.

50. Gramsci, cited in Theophanidis, "Interregnum," 111.

51. See Jagdish Bhagwati and Arvind Panagariya, *Why Growth Matters: How Economic Growth in India Reduced Poverty and the Lessons for Other Developing Countries* (New York: PublicAffairs, 2014).

52. Mehrotra, cited in Ulka Anjaria, *Reading India Now: Contemporary Formations in Literature and Popular Culture* (Philadelphia: Temple University Press), 63.

53. The decline of Mumbai's textile industry is generally narrated as result of some combination of technological innovation, neoliberal gentrification, and ethnic politics. See Neera Adarkar, ed., *The Chawls of Mumbai: Galleries of Life* (Delhi: ImprintOne, 2012); Darryl D'Monte, *Ripping the Fabric: The Decline of Mumbai and Its Mills* (Oxford: Oxford University Press, 2003); Gyan Prakash, *Mumbai Fables* (Princeton, NJ: Princeton University Press, 2011). For a critical engagement with these nostalgic narratives, see Maura Finkelstein, *The Archive of Loss: Lively Ruination in Mill Land Mumbai* (Durham, NC: Duke University Press, 2019).

54. See, for instance, Vikramaditya Motwane's film *Trapped* (Phantom Films, 2016). For a scholarly account of the Mumbai film industry, see Tejaswini Ganti, *Producing Bollywood: Inside the Contemporary Hindi Film Industry* (Durham, NC: Duke University Press, 2012).

55. Although Bollywood's profitability is second to America's Hollywood (Bollywood's earnings are merely 10 percent of the American film industry's), in terms of number of films produced, Mumbai is unmatched: in 2012 it produced more than 1,600 films against America's 476 (and China's 745) (Niall McCarthy, "Bollywood: India's Film Industry by the Numbers," *Forbes*, accessed November 29, 2019, www.forbes.com/sites/niallmccarthy/2014/09/03/bollywood-indias-film -industry-by-the-numbers-infographic/#f7a0a602488b.

56. Anjaria, *Reading India Now*, 61.

57. Claire Burke, "500 Years in 59 Seconds: The Race to Be the World's Largest City," *Guardian*, March 21, 2019, www.theguardian.com/cities/2019/mar/21/500 -years-in-59-seconds-the-race-to-be-the-worlds-largest-city.

58. Elzy Kolb, "75,000 People per Square Mile? These Are the Most Densely Populated Cities in the World," USA *Today*, July 11, 2019, accessed November 29, 2019, www.usatoday.com/story/news/world/2019/07/11/the-50-most-densely -populated-cities-in-the-world/39664259.

59. See the glossary for an account of Mumbai "slums" and their enumeration.

60. Vikram Chandra's novel-turned-Netflix-series *Sacred Games* (New York: Harper Perennial, 2007) is exemplary.

61. For sensitive and compelling accounts of the Shiv Sena's rise to power in Mumbai, see Hansen, *Wages of Violence*, and Atreyee Sen, *Shiv Sena Women: Violence and Communalism in a Bombay Slum* (Bloomington: Indiana University Press, 2007).

62. Slavoj Žižek uses a different translation of Gramsci's statement in his book *Living in the End Times*, in which the phrase *morbid symptoms* is replaced with "monsters" (Slavoj Žižek, *Living in the End Times* [New York: Verso, 2011], 249).

63. Drawing on Gramsci's formulation, South Asia historian Ranajit Guha—a foundational thinker of the "subaltern school" of historiography—calls this "dominance without hegemony" (Ranajit Guha, *Dominance without Hegemony: History and Power in Colonial India* [Cambridge, MA: Harvard University Press, 1998]). Jean and John Comaroff later reversed the formulation, insisting that colonial power actually tended to be a matter of hegemony without dominance (Jean Comaroff and John L. Comaroff, *Of Revelation and Revolution*, vol. 1, *Christianity, Colonialism, and Consciousness in South Africa* [Chicago: University of Chicago Press, 1991]).

64. However, it depends on who you ask.

65. Charles Tilly, "Welcome to the Seventeenth Century," in *The Twenty-First-Century Firm: Changing Economic Organization in International Perspective*, ed. Paul DiMaggio (Princeton, NJ: Princeton University Press, 2001), 201.

66. Tilly, "Welcome."

67. Indeed, Tilly's "overlap" was only ever a reality for certain classes of people in the West as well.

68. For a recent account of nineteenth-century Indian Ocean traders and brokers in which Bombay looms large, see Johan Mathew, *Margins of the Market: Trafficking and Capitalism across the Arabian Sea* (Oakland: University of California Press, 2016).

69. Key works in this extensive literature include C. A. Bayly, *Rulers, Townsmen, and Bazaars: North Indian Society in the Age of British Expansion 1770-1870* (New Delhi: Oxford University Press, 2002); Amalendu Guha, "The Comprador Role of Parsi Seths, 1750-1850," *Economic and Political Weekly* (November 1970): 1933-36; Mathew, *Margins of the Market*; Ghulam Nadri, *Eighteenth-Century Gujarat: The Dynamics of Its Political Economy, 1750-1800* (Leiden: Brill, 2008); Asiya Siddiqi, "The Business World of Jamsetjee Jejeebhoy," *Indian Economic and Social History Review* 19, no. 3-4 (July 1982): 301-24; Lakshmi Subramanian, *Three Merchants of Bombay: Business Pioneers of the Nineteenth Century* (New Delhi: Penguin Books, 2016).

70. Territorially as the sole deep-water port on the subcontinent's western shore, institutionally as the seat of British colonial power in West India, ideationally as the locus of the Indian nationalist movement.

71. Here we take a cue from anthropologists Johan Lindquist, Joshua Barker, and Erik Harms, who have proposed focusing ethnography on what they call "key figures" (along the lines of Raymond Williams's "keywords"), with the idea that "key figures" can shine important light onto "the ground," against which a particular figure acquires meaning. "Figure and ground," they write, "form a composition that shift in relation to one another when located in time and place. As such, this composition becomes capable of communicating something larger than itself" (Joshua Barker, Erik Harms, and Johan Lindquist, "Introduction to Special Issue: Figuring the Transforming City," *City and Society* 25, no. 2 [2013]: 160). *Bombay Brokers* takes up this provocation and invitation to attend to "figures as real people" as way of opening up new ways of thinking "the ground." Joshua Barker, Erik Harms, and Johan Lindquist's book *Figures of Southeast Asian Modernity* (Honolulu: University of Hawai'i Press, 2014) served as something of an inspiration for the current work.

72. Manu Goswami, *Producing India: From Colonial Economy to National Space* (Chicago: University of Chicago Press, 2004), 4. Goswami defines *methodological nationalism* as "the common practice of presupposing, rather than examining, the sociohistorical production of such categories as a national space and national economy and the closely related failure to analyze the specific global field within which specific nationalist movements emerged."

73. Tsing, *Friction*, 1.

74. Thomas Blom Hansen and Oskar Verkaaik, "Introduction—Urban Charisma on Everyday Mythologies in the City," *Critique of Anthropology* 29, no. 1 (2009): 8, 22. In their influential formulation, Hansen and Verkaaik characterize the "complex realization of properties or potentialities of people and their environment through actions and events" as "infra-power."

75. Bruno Latour, *Reassembling the Social: An Introduction to Actor-Network-Theory* (Oxford: Oxford University Press, 2005), 54.

76. Following Coole and Frost, we use the term *new materialisms* broadly, including the vast body of work inspired by Latour's "actor network theory" and Deleuzian notions of "assemblage" (without attempting to reconcile the debates among them). (Diana Coole and Samantha Frost, "Introducing the New Materialisms," in *New Materialisms: Ontology, Agency, and Politics*, ed. Diana Coole and Samantha Frost [Durham, NC: Duke University Press, 2010], 1–43).

77. Michel Callon, "An Essay on Framing and Overflowing: Economic Externalities Revisited by Sociology," in *The Laws of the Markets*, ed. Michel Callon (Oxford: Blackwell, 1998), 250.

78. Indeed, as William Mazzarella (personal communication) points out, "Externality is not subsequent to the model-salient features of the situation."

79. Callon, "An Essay," 256–57.

80. Callon, "An Essay," 267.

81. For discussion, see Lisa Björkman, *Pipe Politics, Contested Waters: Embedded Infrastructures of Millennial Mumbai* (Durham, NC: Duke University Press, 2015).

82. As housing activist Simpreet Singh notes, the goal of these sorts of efforts is to "show the scandal of Mumbai's development . . . to create suspense and shock. . . . It's the only way" (quoted in Sapana Doshi and Malini Ranganathan, "Contesting the Unethical City: Land Dispossession and Corruption Narratives in Urban India," *Annals of the American Association of Geographers* 107 [2017]: 1, 187).

83. Jaspal Singh Naol (Jal), "Hiranadani's Special Leave Petition Dismissed by the Supreme Court Upholding HC Judgement," March 30, 2012, http://socialactivistjal.blogspot.com/2012/03/hiranadanis-special-leave-petition.html.

84. "MMRDA formed a six-member committee in 2007, and on the basis of its report, slapped a penalty of Rs1,993 crore on the developer in 2009. The amount was subsequently reduced to Rs304 crore, and then to Rs89 crore in January 2010. . . . In August, justice Sawant gave a clean chit to the developer, following which Niranjan Hiranandani filed a plea seeking dismissal of the PILs pending for the last three years" (Kanchan Chaudhari, "HC: Will Hiranandani construct low-cost homes in Powai?" *Hindustan Times* Mumbai, December 16, 2011).

85. Joseph S. Nye, "Corruption and Political Development: A Cost-Benefit Analysis," *American Political Science Review* 61, no. 2 (1967): 417–27.

86. Timothy Mitchell, "The Limits of the State: Beyond Statist Approaches and Their Critics," *American Political Science Review* 85, no. 1 (1991): 77–96. For some key anthropological works in this genre, see Veena Das and Deborah Poole, *Anthropology in the Margins of the State* (Santa Fe: School of American Research Press, 2004); C. J. Fuller and Veronique Benei, *The Everyday State and Society in Modern India* (New Delhi: Social Science Press, 2012); Gupta, "Blurred Boundaries."

87. For example, Jonathan Anjaria, *The Slow Boil: Street Food, Rights and Public Space in Mumbai* (Stanford, CA: Stanford University Press, 2016); Beatrice Jauregui, "Provisional Agency in India: Jugaad and Legitimation of Corruption," *American Ethnologist* 41, no. 1 (2014): 76–91; J. P. Olivier de Sardan, "A Moral Economy of Corruption in Africa," *Journal of Modern African Studies* 37, no. 1 (1999): 25–52; Jonathan P. Parry, "The 'Crisis of Corruption' and 'The Idea of India: A Worm's Eye View,'" in *The Morals of Legitimacy: Between Agency and System*, ed. Italo Pardo, 27–55 (New York: Berghahn Books, 2000).

88. Parry, "The 'Crisis of Corruption' and the 'Idea of India.'"

89. Gupta, "Blurred Boundaries."

90. Anjaria, *The Slow Boil*.

91. See the glossary entry for *slum*.

92. Sapana Doshi and Malini Ranganathan, "Contesting the Unethical City: Land Dispossession and Corruption Narratives in Urban India," *Annals of the American Association of Geographers* 107, no. 1 (2017): 183–99.

93. The slum-rehabilitation eligibility cutoff date looms large in contemporary Mumbai—and therefore also in the profiles. See the glossary entry for *slum*.

94. A government circular in 2012 addressed this problem by allowing transfer of ownership of slum structures; for extended discussion, see Björkman, *Pipe Politics, Contested Waters*; Lisa Björkman, "The Engineer and the Plumber: Mediating Mumbai's Conflicting Infrastructural Imaginaries," *International Journal of Urban and Regional Research* 42, no. 2 (March 1, 2018): 276–94.

95. Or at least it was until the 2020 COVID lockdown.

96. Andrew Stephen Sartori, *Liberalism in Empire: An Alternative History* (Berkeley: University of California Press, 2014), 232.

97. Pankaj's nonbrokering services involve neither labor in land nor free exchange of property but rather the giving of advice.

98. The Hindi/Urdu/Marathi word *dalal* comes from the Arabic words *dallāl*—which means something like "a person who offers things in an auction"—and *dalāl*—which describes the act of flirting with a woman. Although the connection between the two etymological origins of the Hindi word—agent and flirtation—is unclear, Arabic language scholar Khaldoun Almousily (personal communication, 2019) offers that the contemporary Hindi valence of *dalal* as "pimp" could be the result of a historical conflation of the two Arabic words: "the auctioneer could be offering a woman."

99. Francis Joseph Steingass, *A Comprehensive Persian-English Dictionary, Including the Arabic Words and Phrases to Be Met with in Persian Literature* (London: Routledge and Kegan Paul, 1892).

100. Horace Hayman Wilson, *A Glossary of Judicial and Revenue Terms and of Useful Words Occurring in Official Documents Relating to the Administration of the Government of British India, from the Arabic, Persian, Hindustani, Sanskrit, Hindi, Bengali, Uriya, Marathi, Guzarathi, Telugu, Karnata, Tamil, Malayalam and Other Languages. Compiled and Published Under the Authority of the Honorable the Court of Directors of the East-India Co* (London: W. H. Allen, 1855), 121.

44   LISA BJÖRKMAN

101. Mathew, *Margins of the Market*, 166.

102. Mathew, *Margins of the Market*, 164.

103. It is unclear why the designation *muqaddam* did not take on the pejorative sense of *dalal*. In contemporary Bombay, *muqaddam* seems to be used in a rather banal sense to indicate various sorts of mid-level supervisor. In the Municipal Corporation's Department of Hydraulic Engineering, for instance, the term is used to describe the senior-most nonengineering staff position, reporting to the junior engineer (Distribution) (Björkman, *Pipe Politics, Contested Waters*, 234). Yet "dalal" was among a number of professions undergoing a shift in moral valence in late nineteenth-century Bombay. Between 1864 and 1921, the Bombay Census reclassified the occupation of "prostitution" from the category "luxuries and dissipation" (alongside "bracelet dealer," "musician," "photographer," and "toymaker") to a new category termed "unproductive occupations" (L. J. Sedgwick, *Census of India 1921*, vol. 9, *Cities of the Bombay Presidency*, part 1 (Report) [Poona: Yeravda Prison Press, 1922], accessed May 29, 2019, https://archive.org/details/in.gov .ignca.31069/page/n77). These sorts of changing census classifications, historian Ashwini Tambe notes, provide insight into the "formation of colonial categories and the social valence they carry" (Ashwini Tambe, *Codes of Misconduct: Regulating Prostitution in Late Colonial Bombay* [Minneapolis: University of Minnesota Press, 2009], 116).

104. Sanjeev Uprety, "Pimps, Paranoia and Politics: Narratives of Masculinities and Femininities in the Nepali Blogosphere," in *Media as Politics in South Asia*, ed. Sahana Udupa and Stephen D. McDowell (London: Routledge, 2017), 63.

105. This question connects to the earlier discussion of the obfuscating discourse of "corruption."

106. Theorists of money from Marx to Simmel have emphasized money's particularity as an object of exchange that renders "everything quantifiable according to one scale of value" (Bill Maurer, "The Anthropology of Money," *Annual Review of Anthropology* 35, no. 1 [2006]: 20). "It is in the nature of a general-purpose money," Bohannan (1955) writes, "to standardize the exchangeability value of every item to a common sale" (cited in "Introduction: Money and the Morality of Exchange," in *Money and the Morality of Exchange*, ed. Jonathan Parry and Maurice Bloch, 13 [Cambridge: Cambridge University Press, 1989]).

107. The effects of this "great transformation" (Maurer, "The Anthropology of Money," 19) on sociocultural life have been both celebrated and condemned: on the one hand, money's "qualityless" quality has been feted for "freeing" people from oppressive gender, caste, or other hierarchical institutions; on the other, this same qualitylessness has been cast as amorality, with money accused of undermining and disembedding other sociocultural institutions, relations, and moralities. "If modern man is free," Georg Simmel (1907) writes, "—free because he can sell everything and free because he can buy everything—then he now seeks . . . in the objects themselves that vigor, stability and inner unity which he has lost because of the changed money-conditioned relationships that he has with them" (cited in Maurer, "The Anthropology of Money," 23).

108. Georg Simmel, *The Philosophy of Money*, ed. D. Frisby (New York: Routledge, 2004).

109. Björkman, "The Engineer and the Plumber."

110. Timothy Pachirat, "The Political in Political Ethnography: Dispatches from the Kill Floor," *Political Ethnography: What Immersion Contributes to the Study of Power* (Chicago: University of Chicago Press, 2009): 143–62.

PART I DEVELOPMENT

Rachel Sturman

THE DECADES FOLLOWING India's liberalization-era policy shifts that began in the 1980s witnessed distinct efforts at all levels of government (central, state, municipal) to remake Mumbai as a "world-class city," often citing the model of Shanghai, Hong Kong, or Singapore. This commitment has involved a vision of a transformed city, marked by a dense multinational business and finance sector, luxury housing, and a sanitized experience of the street, oriented toward sensory enjoyment and consumption by a cosmopolitan elite. This vision has also been taken up by many from among the city's new middle class, who have actively organized civic associations aimed at "urban beautification," focusing on issues such as slum removal and clearing footpaths of pavement dwellers and hawkers.[1] The policy frameworks that have accompanied this set of urban imaginings have at once sought to leverage and to empower private capital. Echoing much-broader global cosmopolitan visions of development via economic liberalization, Bombay's boosters have sought to enhance conditions for business, real estate, and private investment as a means of generating wealth, and they have turned to "public-private partnerships" (PPPs) to expand private finance and to execute what were earlier considered areas of governmental responsibility.[2]

"Development" in this context thus references the idiom of the real estate and construction industries, of urban planners and policy makers, as well as of NGOs and transnational institutions aiming to transform the lives of the urban poor. Although the mandates of development NGOs and transnational agencies clearly extend beyond the focus on urban building examined here (including both urban and rural health, education, empowerment of women and girls, economic uplift, and the like), for the past several decades the aim of addressing urban poverty has concatenated around the issue of housing, lending particular salience to this subset of development priorities within the city.

These broad shifts in global capitalism have presided over a fever of construction activity and demand for construction labor that is similarly global in scale. The demand for construction labor and expertise draws rural migrants to Bombay, even while propelling existing city residents overseas, especially to the Gulf states, where they find work as laborers, contractors, technicians, and engineers. Meanwhile, in Bombay's popular neighborhoods, new and old aspirations for high-rise, middle-class living intersect in sometimes-complimentary/sometimes-contradictory ways with builders' appetites for "slum redevelopment," whose policy framework has offered an economical way for Bombay builders to obtain coveted *transferrable development rights* (TDRS).[3] "Slum redevelopment" in fact links all three "uses of the idiom of "development," tying real estate opportunities to the provisioning of housing for the poor through a city-level policy framework that seeks to ultimately eradicate such settlements from the urban center. Slum redevelopment in turn both hinges upon and generates dense networks of connections among city residents, NGOs, the municipal corporation (BMC), the *Slum Rehabilitation Authority* (SRA), and private builders. In this context the expertise of the people profiled in this chapter consists in materializing the city's built environment—physically bringing the fabric of the city into being.

Given both the broad-scale dynamics and the close-to-the-ground knowledges that are shaping building and dwelling in the city, the experts examined in this section are skilled in operating in the interstices and mediating contradictions of urban development laws and policies. Understanding existing legal and regulatory frameworks, they turn these to use in order to enable building to happen. On one level, legal instruments, codes, and regulations define the terrain of the possible. But in the dynamic world of building construction, both law and possibility are shifting and flexible. Building regulations (the necessity of licenses and permits, limits on building in slums, etc.) render many forms and contexts of construction illegal or unauthorized, but they also generate what have become standardized work-arounds (fixed payments and methods) as the means of getting things done, creating new opportunities for those positioned to realize them.

Moreover, these urban navigations are occurring in a context in which the law itself is continuously being remade. Various interested parties and a dynamic, unpredictable economy have led to changes in key elements of the SRA and TDR policy and regulatory frameworks over time, requiring experts to remain knowledgeable about a shifting legal landscape. The impact of such changing legal frameworks is nowhere more apparent than in the mobile designation of informal settlements as "slums," a shift that has rendered vast numbers of city residents vulnerable to the whims of dispossession and expulsion. Likewise, within these settlements those who have proof of residence prior to a certain date are granted rights and entitlements that later residents (or those with no such evidence of residence) are not. The arbitrariness and profound power of such legal designations generate a variety of means of action, as several of these profiles show. In a context where much of the landscape of construction across the socioeconomic spectrum is lacking proper permits or is in violation of some building code, law, or planning regulation, the designation of certain structures as "unauthorized" (i.e., lacking the proper permits or licensing) enables police to demolish them, even if they may not have been "illegal." At the same time, both unauthorized and illegal structures have been regularized through the payment of a fine, making the process of converting illegal to legal simply a minor additional outlay incorporated into the cost of the project. In this way, not only is the distinction between unauthorized and illegal blurred in popular perception, but the boundaries of law themselves become protean, for some.

Equally, these ethnographies highlight individual striving and the entrepreneurialism that is so characteristic of the present moment.[4] Such efforts may have a much longer history, but they are currently being identified and sometimes celebrated as marks of a contemporary vernacular capitalism, as seen in the recent celebrations of "*jugaad* innovation"[5] and in the new status accorded to Dharavi (previously notorious as "Asia's largest slum"), now heralded as a model at once of agentive "self-help" by the poor and of effective use of urban space (high-density built environment, proximity of living and work space, efficient and low-cost materials, low levels of waste, etc.).[6] In this environment these experts in development turn their enjoyment of risk and their facility with the "rules of the game" of circumventing formal law into the means of making urban space.

Concomitantly, their expertise centers on both mobilizing and creating a sense of the local: of local knowledge in a context of global actors, of familiarity in unfamiliar and potentially dangerous contexts, and ultimately of the making of locality itself, as at once a materialized place and a sense of space and place. Such projects involve the mobilization of a variety (even a jumble) of translocal resources: international NGOs and their discourses, finance capital, migrant sensibilities, actual materials of construction, and so on in the creation of the physical and the ideational space of the locality. The ethnographies in this section detail some of the ways in which a claim to the local can be mobilized as an asset to build trust in an industry that depends upon it. More generally, these actors frequently depend on relational skills, on the ability to make connections, and on making those connections productive and profitable. They are people who excel at communicating with diverse audiences, building trust as they reach across social contexts.

Prasad Khanolkar's profile of Mehmoodbhai, the "toilet operator," highlights some of the ethical complexities that the context-crossing work of development entails. In an environment where transnational agencies, local and national governmental projects, and local NGOs have come to focus on "informal settlements," and especially on the issue of "slum sanitation," Mehmoodbhai created a "model toilet block," a project that went beyond utility to become an object of aesthetic enjoyment and that seems to embody all that translocal agencies dream as a success story. Mehmoodbhai played a key role in liaising between the local residents of the informal settlement (of which he was a part), NGOs, and municipal officials in the Slum Sanitation Program (SSP), organizing the residents into a community-based organization (CBO) in order to get the toilet block built, and continuing to interact with NGOs, their donors, and the municipality to ensure its success. The relationships and expertise he has cultivated have made him a crucial local figure whose aid is sought by residents for all manner of bureaucratic needs. At the same time, as Khanolkar details, his ability to leverage his role—and the toilet itself—to advance the success of his vision has created disgruntlement among some of his would-be competitors as well as ethical accusations against him. These competing narratives reveal the seams that Mehmoodbhai's story—but also his expertise—rendered seamless. On the one hand, Mehmoodbhai's ability to smoothen relationships and to generate cash and consensus across local and translocal scales—the work that brought his "model toilet block" into being—remains somewhat submerged in his own account. It is through the less successful struggles of his competitors that we can see the range of knowledge and skill involved in the work of development. At the same time, and on the other hand, Khanolkar's profile leaves us with a sense of the way that appealing examples of small-scale heroism such as Mehmoodbhai's remain embedded within political struggles for control over resources, struggles in which control over the narrative forms a crucial part.

Similarly concerned with building processes and aspiration in popular neighborhoods, Tobias Baitsch's profile of Imran, a self-described "contractor," highlights the myriad resources and forms of expertise brought to bear in enabling small-scale construction, remodeling, and vertical expansion in the so-called slum neighborhood of Shivajinagar. Like many similar neighborhoods, Shivajinagar has never been officially classified as a "slum" under the provisions of the Maharashtra Slum Areas Act, but it is nonetheless "treated as a slum" for policy purposes.[7] This practice has implications regarding ways in which residents can make claims to municipal services as well as for the kinds of building that can be authorized in the area—for example, limiting vertical construction to fourteen feet and defining what kinds of materials can be used for construction. Imran's business operates within this single neighborhood, but his work involves activities ranging from materials procurement to overseeing workers to aesthetic design to management of legal and regulatory enforcement, and beyond. He is, Baitsch writes, "the central actor through which all links run." This in turn means that the work of contracting not only "makes building possible" but also extends beyond "designing buildings" to designing processes and practices that mediate relations between state actors and urban dwellers. As Baitsch describes, this involves a kind of flexible control, an ability to keep "myriad actors and materials at bay or at hand." Imran made use of existing family connections within the neighborhood to initially secure his position, and he developed his skills on the job through a process of learning by doing. In this business of enabling people to materialize aesthetic sensibilities and housing dreams, the ability to work with, through, and around the law forms a key component of the contractor's skill. Where arbitrary legal rules (such as the height limit) hamper building, the contractor manages relations with the police that at once signal regulatory enforcement and ultimately allow the construction to occur. For example, in the building and destruction of what Baitsch terms the "symbolic wall," the contractor builds a short vertical extension upon an existing structure that signals to the police the intention to build a second story; he then coordinates with the police a planned (and documented) demolition of this wall. After this demolition, building the additional story can proceed. Thus, in an environment where legal status and the prevailing regulatory regime depend upon contradictory and sometimes absurd determinations of whether a neighborhood is treated as a "slum," contractors and police engage in their own forms of absurdist theater that fulfill the needs of each. These complex methods of legal and institutional navigation form a crucial component of Imran's work.

A related skill proves definitive for Dalpat in Lisa Björkman's ethnography. Dalpat, trained as an engineer, does the critical work of securing licenses from the municipality for all the various facets and stages of the construction process. Through the chance opportunities opened up by a particular moment when liberalization led many engineers to move to the private sector, creating an unprecedented shortage of engineers within the municipality, Dalpat and his brother initially found jobs within the BMC. In later moving to the private sector, where he took a job as a site engineer with a real estate construction firm, Dalpat skillfully used established connections within the BMC to facilitate the work of private builders. As Dalpat describes, his expertise lies in his ability to secure permissions in contexts where—given the material and institutional contradictions governing Mumbai's built environment—permissions are "impossible." Dalpat's work involves monetary transfers to be sure, but more importantly it involves relational skills and a mastery of the at once extralegal, opaque, and yet regularized means of getting things done. As Dalpat moves between ever-larger private companies involved in high-end real estate projects, his salaried work is increasingly tied to the informal earnings of municipal bureaucrats and real estate barons alike. And as in the popular context described by Baitsch, in this elite context the work of building also depended upon an ability to navigate and bend regulatory regimes as needed. Moreover, as Björkman's ethnography of Dalpat makes clear, both elite and "slum" builders have become intertwined with the recent and current planning instruments, the development plans for 1994–2014 and for 2018–34, which seek to incentivize private development of housing for displaced (or to-be-displaced) slum dwellers by linking such SRA building with private development rights to build luxury towers for private sale. If elite building and popular building are structurally linked, with the production of each dependent upon the other, both also share a similar complex orientation toward legal and extralegal norms.

Grasping extralegal norms particular to this environment remains crucial to getting things done, especially things that are "impossible," but Dalpat also recognizes, even valorizes, laws and regulations. Ironically, but inevitably, it is the existence of the regulatory regime that generates the entire ecology of interactions aimed at circumventing it—that is, the expertise of people like Dalpat. But Dalpat's acknowledgment of the need for law does not derive from a self-serving appraisal of its role in generating his work. Rather, he views regulations—for instance, those governing private connections to municipal water mains—as socially valuable while simultaneously valuing and enjoying his own extraordinary capacity to get things done when there is no legal framework to accomplish them. Dalpat doesn't pass judgment on the particular projects of his employers that his work makes possible, focusing instead on the need for his skills. It is the lack of straightforward means to accomplish the work of building development that justifies the exceptions he is able to achieve, and also what generates the pleasures of this work. Indeed, all of the profiles in this section suggest an enjoyment of the work: the way that it requires and mobilizes their particular skills and expertise, the ways in which they have made themselves valuable or necessary, the ways in which they have been able to materialize the "impossible."

If family relationships played a key role in enabling Dalpat and Imran to gain access to the terrains of their work and to operate successfully, the idiom of family is integral to the construction labor subcontracting work of Janu, presented in Uday Chandra's account. As a rare woman operating in the area of labor subcontracting, Janu mobilizes both her gender and fictive kinship relations through the term *didi* (older sister). As the model of the older sister, Janu is positioned as both someone who has been through what newly recruited rural, and especially tribal, teenagers are now experiencing and someone who will serve as their temporary protector. She is close enough to their age and experience to be relatable and is also an elder who can be counted upon. She also draws on her local and personal knowledge of the needs and concerns of the migrants, as one whose personal experience mirrors their own. At the same time, in providing labor for builders and building contractors, Janu maintains and manages connections to employers, in part by effectively evaluating which recruits will be suitable for what kind of labor. She also manages the behavior of her recruits on the work site, even when she is not physically present. In this context as well, the familial idiom facilitates Janu's intervention. Workplace and broader social control thus get recast as quasi-familial guidance and care. Indeed, according to Chandra, a general model of familial seniority, learning, and obligation pervades the workplaces of Janu's charges, as her earlier recruits take on the role of teaching the new arrivals. Such modalities operate through the power of informal norms. Although Janu's work is legal, she also positions herself and her recruits into a familiar and valorized ethical frame.

Janu appeals largely to preexisting social norms, using those norms to frame perceptions of her own work, which might otherwise be perceived as nonnormative, if not transgressive, for a relatively young woman. A more extended evocation of and play with such norms emerges in Lalitha Kamath's ethnography of the making of urban space on the city's periphery. Kamath's account presents Bunty Singh, a complex figure who rose from humble origins as a taxi driver to become one of most prominent builders in Sanjaynagar, at the "frontier" of Vasai Virar, at the edge of the Mumbai Metropolitan Region (MMR). As in Björkman's presentation of Dalpat, for Bunty Singh the opportunity presented by a particular historical moment or event—in his case, the eviction and displacement of large numbers of informal settlers from other parts of the MMR as part of urban "beautification" projects in the early 2000s—proved crucial to his success. At the margins of municipal reach, where the state was largely absent, Bunty first bought land from agriculturalists and sold it to those arriving in a state of desperation in the area. He then began building chawls to house these new arrivals, and with that undertook broader processes of urban development: laying out not just building plots but also water and drainage lines, building schools, and more. All of this was described as "illegal" because it involved a change in land use from agricultural to other purposes, but in Bunty's view it was nonetheless "development." In the absence of a functional state administration, Bunty became an expert in navigating and manipulating nonstate-based rules, norms, and modes of operation. At the same time he cultivated good relationships with politicians and political parties that would serve as important allies and resources. Furthermore, he took on an expansive role in community development, mediating disputes, sponsoring community festivals, and eventually building a lavish temple. Bunty's success was thus premised on visibly sustaining existing community norms and working within them to enhance his honor and reputation. His "social work" was integral to his status work but also involved an implicit and sometimes explicit critique of the state. It was illegal but nonetheless recognizably ethical, meeting the needs of the poor while the state was at best ineffectual and frequently worse.

In his visibility and popular heroism, Bunty and his associates drew upon familiar visual and narrative tropes from Bollywood gangster films, adopting styles that "connote power and wealth that is laced with violence." This image of virile power in turn enhances his aura as a man who rose from humble beginnings to one who can readily achieve "the impossible." This gangster style is mobile, available for various types of appropriation, but in this context it situates Bunty Singh in the local: his style embodies and is appropriate to this frontier zone on the margins of the state, and his "development work" has been crucial to creating the locality as such. And yet, as Kamath concludes, the frontier zone of open-ended possibility and danger that enabled Bunty Singh's rise ultimately posed an obstacle to his goals of middle-class respectability: living in a "tower" and sending his children to English-medium schools. Such a challenge he could meet only by leaving the locality that he had made and that in turn had made him.

Bunty Singh's embeddedness in local norms and ideals, his direct involvement in the making of place, and his popular visibility contrast sharply with the final profile in this section, Llerena Guiu Searle's account of Kaushal, who uses a thin claim to local knowledge to bolster his position in global real estate markets. A Non-Resident Indian who had grown up in Delhi and attended an Ivy League university in the US, Kaushal had pursued real estate investment opportunities on a global scale but turned to India both as a place of upcoming opportunity and one that held some personal—if vague—attachment for him. Kaushal, like other foreign real estate investors, decried his reliance on Indian developers and other middlemen whose knowledge was crucial to securing developable land parcels but who took large fees for their time and expertise. Seeking to circumvent but also position himself as equivalent to these Indian developers, Kaushal thus became involved in the work of land-parcel agglomeration himself. Searle speculates that he was able to use his status as both an insider and an outsider to these markets to his advantage. Drawing upon his upper-caste Delhi upbringing and familial connections to Delhi real estate markets, alongside the global sheen of his Ivy League credentials and fluency with New York finance capitalism, he also benefited from his distance from local strongmen and their political struggles. As Searle argues, "The work of moving capital is the work of making chains of intermediaries—from farmer to developer to investor—that can transform Indian land into investable parcels and global assets." In this work, Kaushal "served as a central link in a chain of 'investment partners' that he was constructing." Kaushal's claim to the local remained thin and indeed ultimately depended in part on his ability to mobilize his cosmopolitanism, but he was nonetheless able to recast himself meaningfully for different audiences, always attempting to work the profit margins. Kaushal continued to rely on a variety of intermediaries, but he also benefited from being able to operate as a link in the chain himself. Not his visibility, in this case, but his ability to traverse distinctive ecologies of capital enabled his success. Moreover, as not only

Kaushal but also in some ways each of these figures demonstrates, local and global are not oppositional terms: constructing locality involves an eclectic selection and integration of translocal or global styles, sometimes including cosmopolitan fantasies of the local.

The work of the people profiled in this section on development is particularly attuned to the needs and possibilities of the current moment, when actors of all sorts are working across multiple scales. Agents and middlemen from a variety of social strata have long played these kinds of roles, often garnering elite disdain and popular animosity in the process, with evidence from western India dating back to at least the early colonial era and likely before.[8] Moreover, modes of operating that came to characterize the "License & Permit Raj" of the Nehruvian era and beyond seem in many ways to continue to operate under the neoliberal state.[9] But certain types of knowledge, expertise, and skill have found particular relevance and value in the present: the ability to recognize the existence of, and possibilities generated by, new kinds of actors, such as NGOs and CBOs, as in Mehmoodbhai's toilet project; tactical precision in managing the material flows of people and things, as in the work of Imran; the ability to portray oneself as both inside and outside of a given collectivity, and indeed to speak the specialized languages and address the particular needs of multiple actors, as we see with Mehmoodbhai, Kaushal, or in the affect work of Janu; similarly, skill in navigating legal regimes and in using both the categories of governmentality (such as project-affected persons, or PAPs) as well as pragmatic physical action (building walls, digging for pipes) to create new conditions of possibility, something out of nothing, as emerges in the profiles of Dalpat, Bunty Singh, and to some extent Imran. At the same time, perhaps distinctive to the present is the ambivalence surrounding the activities of these figures, who on the one hand may seem to undermine the idealized functioning of state and market and on the other hand seem to embody precisely the forms of entrepreneurship that are currently being imagined as a societal good. "Development," tied to a model of unidirectional historical progress achieved by removing barriers to individual enlightenment, economic opportunity, and societal advancement, turns out to be produced in practice through precisely the forms of mediation that the concept decries. In this context, such moral ambivalence may be read in part as a longing for a political-economic ideal, fantasized as having been realized elsewhere and as itself integral—along with the activities that it judges—to sustaining a contemporary moment characterized by dynamic, contingent, and unpredictable powers of maneuver.[10]

Notes

1. Jonathan Anjaria, "Ordinary States: Everyday Corruption and the Politics of Space in Mumbai," *American Ethnologist* 38, no. 1 (2011): 58–72; Leela Fernandes, *India's New Middle Class: Democratic Politics in an Era of Economic Reform* (Minneapolis: University of Minnesota Press, 2006); Asher Ghertner, *Rule by Aesthetics: World-Class City Making in Delhi* (New York: Oxford University Press, 2015).

2. Lisa Björkman, *Pipe Politics, Contested Waters: Embedded Infrastructures of Millennial Mumbai* (Durham, NC: Duke University Press, 2015); Malini Ranganathan, "Paying for Pipes, Claiming Citizenship: Political Agency and Water Reforms at the Urban Periphery," *International Journal of Urban and Regional Research* 38, no. 2 (2014): 590–608.

3. See the glossary for a discussion of transferrable development rights.

4. Nandini Gooptu, "Introduction," in *Enterprise Culture in Neoliberal India: Studies in Youth, Class, Work and Media,* ed. Nandini Gooptu (London: Routledge, 2013), 1–24; Craig Jeffrey and Stephen Young, "*Jugad*: Youth and Enterprise in India," *Annals of the Association of American Geographers* 104, no. 1 (2014): 182–95.

5. Beatrice Jauregui, "Provisional Agency in India: *Jugaad* and Legitimation of Corruption," *American Ethnologist* 41, no. 1 (2014): 76–91.

6. Roma Chatterjee, "Slums and the Global City: Housing Plans in Dharavi, Mumbai," in *Cities in South Asia,* ed. Crispin Bates and Minoru Mio (London: Routledge, 2015), 84–97; Colin McFarlane, "The Entrepreneurial Slum: Civil Society, Mobility, and the Co-production of Urban Development," *Urban Studies* 49, no. 13 (2012): 2795–2816; Navi Radjou, Jaideep Prabhu, and Simone Ahuja, *Jugaad Innovation: Think Frugal, Be Flexible, Generate Breakthrough Growth* (San Francisco: Jossey-Bass, 2012).

7. For discussion, see Björkman, *Pipe Politics.*

8. C. A. Bayly, *Rulers, Townsmen, and Bazaars: North Indian Society in the Age of British Expansion, 1770-1870* (Cambridge: Cambridge University Press, 1983); Neil Charlesworth, *Peasants and Imperial Rule* (Cambridge: Cambridge University Press, 1985); Sumit Guha, *Beyond Caste: Identity and Power in South Asia, Past and Present* (Leiden: Brill, 2013); David Hardiman, *Feeding the Baniya: Peasants and Usurers in Western India* (Delhi: Oxford University Press, 1996).

9. Stuart Corbridge and John Harriss, *Reinventing India: Liberalization, Hindu Nationalism, and Popular Democracy* (Cambridge: Polity Press, 2000); Francine Frankel, *India's Political Economy, 1947-2004: The Gradual Revolution,* 2nd ed. (New York: Oxford University Press, 2006); Sunil Khilnani, *The Idea of India* (New York: Penguin, 1998).

10. Rosalind Morris, "The Mute and the Unspeakable: Political Subjectivity, Violent Crime and the 'Sexual Thing' in a South African Mining Town," in *Law and Disorder in the Postcolony,* ed. Jean Comaroff and John Comaroff (Chicago: University of Chicago Press, 2008), 57–101.

1 **BUNTY SINGH** BUILDER OF DREAMS

Lalitha Kamath

BUNTY SINGH IS ONE of the oldest builders operating in Sanjaynagar, the Wild West frontier of Vasai Virar, a city on the periphery of the Mumbai Metropolitan Region. The evolution of Bunty—from builder to distributor of favors, dispute resolver, upholder of moral codes, cultural patron, and temple builder—reflects the truly stunning range of expertise that builders in the young edge city of Vasai Virar must display to succeed in a part of the city where development is predominantly informal and state-provided services are largely absent.

Bunty's own explanations for his myriad specializations are tied to what he calls "doing development." Bunty's cousin Tunku Singh, who joined the business in 2008, powerfully conveyed the sense of what Tunku and Bunty described as their social service to the "public"—and to the poor. Until 2009, Tunku explained, the *shasan* (public administration) was absent. When there was nothing there, it was they who built neighborhoods and laid the gutter lines and water pipes; it was because of them that there was "development." Everything in Sanjaynagar might be "illegal," Tunku explained, but this doesn't mean it's not "development."

The story of Bunty's beginnings as a builder powerfully captures the sense of responsibility that drives this work of "development"—work that he is quick to contrast with the quite-different way this same word is used by state actors. For Bunty, "doing development" often involved cleaning up the messes created by the state in the name of "development." Bunty started his working life as a teenager, driving a taxi in the largely rural and uninhabited expanses of Sanjaynagar. A turning point in Bunty's fortunes came with the sweeping slum evictions of the early 2000s, which displaced tens of thousands of people who had been living within the boundaries of Sanjay Gandhi National Park in Mumbai's western suburbs. In response to a court case filed by environmental activists, a revanchist court decision declared these dwellings to be "encroachments." The Bombay Municipal Corporation's deputy commissioner—a man named Khairnar, who was widely known as Bombay's "one-man demolition army"—presided over demolitions that displaced an estimated 50,000 huts (more than 200,000 people) from the park.[1] Desperate for shelter, many of the evicted boarded the Mumbai local trains and fled to Sanjaynagar, drawing on kinship networks already established in that area. Aspiring builders such as Bunty bought agricultural land from the local landowners, and using chalk they drew lines across fields. These 10-by-20-foot "plots" were then sold to evicted migrants who started building their own homes. Bunty evocatively described the situation prevailing in Mumbai at that time as a *bhookamp* (earthquake) that Khairnar had unleashed through the demolitions. Although Mumbai's middle classes celebrated Khairnar for ridding the city of "encroachers," in Bunty's estimation this was a humanitarian disaster, one that was mitigated only by people like him, who took up the work of resettling the flood of displaced families. "Money did not matter," Bunty explained. "We sold land for very little because people needed homes."

From selling land, Bunty soon moved on to building *chawls* (tenements) to house new populations seeking to settle in Sanjaynagar. For Bunty, his work as a "builder" is intertwined with what he calls "social work": builders must not settle people, he explains, if they cannot take care of them. Thus, on seeing that the children of new arrivals needed schools, Bunty has built schools. He has resolved disputes that have arisen in his chawls. Bunty has catered to different communities' cultural expression and entertainment by sponsoring music and dance programs for his *bhoomi pujans* (ground-breaking ceremonies) or during festivals such as *Holi, Chhath puja,* and *Janmashtami.* He has even built others' careers through his patronage of the arts—letting his brightly colored office be used on weekends by musicians to conduct

FIGURE 1.1 Patchwork development in the "no development" zone. Used courtesy of Lalitha Kamath, photographer.

FIGURE 1.2 One-room tenement housing for workers. Used courtesy of Lalitha Kamath, photographer.

meetings for shows. A common theme of the Bhojpuri music featured in these concerts is its powerful rendering of migrant memories of "home" in the village while also referring to the new "home" in the city. A Bhojpuri musician who has benefited from Bunty's patronage has recounted how as Sanjaynagar expanded and Bunty's stature has risen, the nature of the shows and the community they have fostered has also changed. Earlier, there used to be only a harmonium (keyboard instrument) and a *dholak* (type of drum). Now there is an orchestra, dancers, and a sound system and speakers. Thus, the scope of Bunty's patronage activities has expanded from its earlier focus on building-related cultural activities, now encompassing an annual concert every January, on which Bunty spends hundreds of thousands of rupees and which is attended—his followers boast—by at least 25,000 people. By creating such cultural spaces, the musician explains, Bunty not only enlarges his network of followers but also benefits the local tenants and contributes to building the social fabric of community. Bunty's broad range of operations and his farsightedness demonstrate the responsibility and sense of authority he enacts through the work of "doing development"—work that involves the production of not only built forms but also social space in a context where the state does not sponsor such development activities.

Undoubtedly, Bunty cannot be pegged as just a builder. Equally clear is that his know-how and success as a builder hinged on his numerous other abilities and activities. Knowledge, networks, and reputation were vital to his success in building operations in Sanjaynagar, which is delineated in the city's development plan as a "no development" zone and yet functions as the heart of the city's informal construction industry. The buildings that mushroom here are mostly absent the necessary official documentation and permissions. Further, as a newly incorporated area, the legal status of permissions previously given in village areas may be uncertain now. In this context, most construction activity in Sanjaynagar is characterized by residents and the municipality as "illegal"—a term commonly used as shorthand for a range of violations, from those in which the occupant has no valid title to the land, to those built on agricultural land that is not permitted for urban use, to those in which the building is not compliant with the city's building regulations. Buildings in Sanjaynagar are characterized by one or more type of "illegalities," so it was widely acknowledged that land disputes could not be settled through recourse to the law but rather negotiated through a series of widely accepted, well-structured ways of working that had evolved based on need and context, and had sedimented through practice and precedent. Bunty's success as a builder rested on his skill at deciphering this alternate

FIGURE 1.3 *Chawl* along main Sanjaynagar road. Used courtesy of Lalitha Kamath, photographer.

system of rules and skillfully manipulating the authority it wielded, in the niche area of building construction, to get results that were favorable to him. This tacit knowledge was extremely important in the volatile and continuously under-construction building landscape of Sanjaynagar.

Being a builder in this terrain required always keeping an ear to the ground and nurturing relations with a wide network of landowners, party workers, and politicians. Keeping on the good side of landowners afforded Bunty key information about the buying and selling of land: when, where, and by whom. To do this he employed various strategies: for instance, he is reported once to have purchased a piece of land but to have allowed the former owner to continue farming it until Bunty decided to develop, thereby building goodwill and trust. Maintaining strong connections with party workers and politicians was vital for keeping up with the latest news regarding changes to the development control rules and regulatory practices of the Vasai Virar City Municipal Corporation (vvcmc), knowledge that could affect the legal standings of Bunty's buildings and/or could be enlisted in the settling of land disputes. In the event of a dispute, Bunty was acutely aware about which of his extensive networks of contacts he could appeal to, and the authority they might command, while also considering how to strengthen his own material claims. Once, for example, Bunty had sold a piece of land that later turned out to have a second claimant. Both asserted ownership to the plot, so Bunty enlisted the help of local party workers and politicians to resolve the issue. In these sorts of situations, builders such as Bunty not only relied on their good contacts among both ruling and opposition parties to win their case but also sought to wield their own reputations—for serving the public interest, rather than their own, and intimidating those who might go against them—to support their cause. The double-edged nature of this reputation—for both generosity and violence—was crucial in striking and furthering deals in their business.

Sanjaynagar is a risky place to live and work, stated Bunty, and the ability to thrive here requires safeguarding one's reputation for social service alongside the performance of hypermasculinity, violence, and "illegal" acts. On the surface, reputations for service and violence may seem to be in conflict, but they are actually deeply intertwined. It is in straddling these spheres of social work and *goondagardi* (strongmanship) that Bunty revealed a particular genius. Bunty's reputation and its continuous enactment were essential to him. He described the dangers he faced when *media-goondas* blackmailed builders like him if they discovered news that portrayed him or his buildings unfavorably. Once, when one of his tenants was caught using her flat as a safe house for criminals and their stolen loot, the news got out despite Bunty paying off a lot of people in an attempt to hush it up. Bunty evicted the tenant but recalled that "the next thing I hear, she is telling everybody I raped her. How can I raise children here? Men can work all their lives to build their *izzat* [honor], but women can tear it apart in a minute." The importance of the pursuit of izzat to Bunty is clear, as is the constant danger of it being eroded by the uncertainties inherent in the business of construction in Sanjaynagar and by this kind of accusation, which held precipitous risks for his *mardangi* (manliness). And mardangi was the linchpin of his reputation in the male-dominated environment of Sanjaynagar.

Indeed, the world of Sanjaynagar is distinctively gendered. In Bunty's mental map of the area, women seemed to be easily divided into "decent" women who should, ideally, stay out of Sanjaynagar and whose honor their menfolk needed to protect, and those who were not "decent." Bunty implicitly named the latter sort of women as the cause of many fights in his buildings that he then had to step in to resolve. For both kinds of women, their place was seen to be the private space of the home, whereas men were seen as aiding the building of the city, performing the crucial public roles of "builder" and "social worker." Sanjaynagar's public spaces are consequently overrun by young men, constantly on the lookout for opportunities to better themselves, keen to endear and attach themselves to powerful people like Bunty. Builders are exclusively men, dominating the landscape through the performance of a distinctive masculine demeanor: crisp white clothes, thick gold chains and rings, flashy phones, and large cars. These are motifs that have been reinforced by Bollywood's depiction of gangsters and politicians, and connote power and wealth that is laced with violence. Bunty's cousin Tunku, who works with him, epitomizes such a persona. Tunku's knowledge of guns, his formidable physical presence, and the notoriety gained from his six-year stint protecting one of Mumbai's feared mafia dons have proved valuable currency to Bunty in a business that requires a constant show of mardangi and valor, and the enhancement of one's reputation for goondagardi.

Bunty has emerged from within a space of possibility where the state is largely absent in delivering public services but is very much present in the form of building and land-related rules and regulations that must continually be negotiated if Sanjaynagar is to grow and endure. However, the state is not the only locus of power in Sanjaynagar. Indeed, there is no singular, clear authority in Sanjaynagar, where laws are suspended or unevenly applied, and where many things are possible but also potentially destructive. It is the ability to negotiate and navigate the offices and officers of the state and political parties and to bend them to his interests that defines Bunty Singh's authority. The social and spatial mobility of Bunty's life trajectory and everyday work demonstrates the possibilities inhering in his world to transgress various social, moral, and geographical boundaries and to make the seemingly impossible possible.

I witnessed such boundary-crossing potentialities one winter night in 2015, when I attended the annual musical performance sponsored by Bunty. The concert was held in a flat, undulating stretch of land in the interior of Sanjaynagar: paddy fields that were not yet developed, fringed by rising hills and a star-studded sky. As I entered, the first thing I noticed was a large, conspicuously new and brightly colored temple—built by Bunty, I was told. On one side was a stage where the musicians sat, in front of which were rows of red plastic chairs surrounded by large crowds pressing close. In another far corner, preparations for dinner had already begun, with large cooking vessels placed on firewood stoves and kilos of rice laid out on mats on the floor.

Two of Bunty's followers came to meet me. They pointed to the temple, the Kashi Vishwanath Dham, and said that every year during the festival of Mahasivaratri, Bunty Singh organizes a *mahabhandara* (grand feast for devotees) at the end of the spectacular musical performance. The feast is in celebration of Shiva's birthday as well as of the day that Bunty laid the cornerstone of the temple. "He doesn't take a single rupee from anyone for this," they told me. "This is for God." Although Bunty is a "simple" man whose business isn't large, his benevolence is magnificent, they assure me. "Do you know the story behind the temple that 'our Bunty Bhai' [our brother Bunty] has built?" Awe and pride were on their faces as they recounted the story: "One night, Bunty went to relieve himself in the field, and suddenly a snake appeared to him in front of the *bargad* (banyan) tree. Then Bunty saw a small Shiva *ling* under the stone where the snake had appeared. He picked it up, and the snake appeared to him as if in a dream, saying, 'Mai tera bahut kuch karoonga, tum mera kar de' [I will do many things for you if you build a temple in my honor]. This is how the idea of building a temple to honor Shiva was born." The fragrance of *biryani* (a mixed rice dish) wafted through the air and in the foreground the sensuous, earthy lyrics of the song. But both men were unaware, completely immersed in their story.

The second man now picked up the story where the first had left off. After his encounter with the snake, Bunty embarked on a pilgrimage to the North Indian city of Banaras in service of his goal of constructing a temple in this spot. It was from the ancient, holy city of Banaras that Bunty brought all the material used to construct the temple. In fact, the very vessels in which food was being prepared for tonight's performance were those in which the idols for the temple had been carried to Mumbai from Banaras. I looked at the temple with new eyes. It stood testimony to Bunty's journey from taxi driver to "developer" of dreams—a tangible expression of the aspirations and ability of this "simple" man to make things happen, to build a temple that is rumored to have cost Rs250 million and that the Snake God himself had blessed with abundance.

Bunty Singh's temple embodied the myths and dreams of this young and restless city and of the spirits and souls animating its hidden, seemingly unknowable spaces—spaces not readily captured by words like *urban* or *rural*, *city* or *village*. I felt the phantasmic and powerful aura of the temple and the Snake God that inhabited it, and by extension that of the man who had built it. The temple instantiated the generative possibilities of this space on the city's edge, a space that enables a gestation and rebirth that are perhaps more difficult in the more central regions of Mumbai, where possibilities of negotiating access and exchange are often foreclosed.

A few years ago, however, Bunty moved out of Sanjaynagar to a high-rise residential tower in a "better" locality. He said he wanted his son to go to a good English-medium school and to learn "good values." "Sanjaynagar is not a place to live a respectable life," he explained. Now that he was a man of some means, the very fluidity and provisional possibility that had enabled his meteoric rise seemed to be an obstruction to his stability and upward social mobility. Middle-class life seems to be at odds with the very stratagems that enabled its achievement.

Note

1. Eighty thousand residential structures were identified in the park, out of which 33,000 were deemed eligible for relocation because the residents could prove their habitation in the area prior to 1995 under a special scheme of the state government. See www.nivarahakk.com/slum-movement-national-park.php.

2 **IMRAN** HOUSING CONTRACTOR

Tobias Baitsch

RESIDENTS OF THE NEIGHBORHOOD where Imran lives and works refer to him as a "contractor." Imran builds houses in Shivajinagar, a large and growing *slum*[1] neighborhood near Govandi station in Mumbai's M-East Ward, where rising aspirations keep pace with climbing incomes.[2] The settlement is home to at least 250,000 people residing in somewhere around 50,000 individual structures. More than anything else, it is the need for space that fuels a demand-driven urban development and rapidly transforms the built environment. Imran estimates that about 300 contractors like him are active in the neighborhood, which in most cases is also the place where they live. My research suggests that taken together, Shivajinagar contractors build or repair at least 3,000 structures annually.[3] At this rate—with the neighborhood's entire building stock replaced and renewed every twenty years—there is no shortage of work for contractors like Imran. Indeed, contractors are central actors in Mumbai's urban transformations. Yet their work generally does not involve actual physical construction; rather, the work of "contracting" is the work of making construction possible.

I MET IMRAN THROUGH MY RESEARCH on low-income housing production in Mumbai; the period of my fieldwork coincided with his initial steps toward becoming an independent contractor. In this context Imran and I learned together about the complexities of local construction and about what it meant to be a contractor. At that time Imran was about twenty-two years old, had graduated from twelfth standard with a degree in commerce, spoke fluent English, and wanted to continue studying toward a degree in economics. Notwithstanding Imran's wish to continue his education, his father pushed him to start working with his cousin Salim (a contractor in his own right) in order to acquire some work experience. A booming construction industry had opened lucrative and promising careers for many smart and savvy local boys, and Imran's father believed that his son must not miss the opportunity to ride the wave.

Imran's father's early career (as a supermarket salesman in the Gulf) had afforded his family of four a comfortable life in a two-room flat located in an apartment complex near Shivajinagar. Nevertheless, the family maintains close relationship with the neighborhood of Shivajinagar, where Imran's father grew up and where the familial center of gravity lies. The family is well established in the local community, and Salim's father is a man of some political clout in the neighborhood. Although neither Salim nor Imran openly engages in local politics, their businesses are bound up with Salim's father's politically inflected social and business networks, which laid the foundation for Salim's successful engagement as contractor.

Learning the job from scratch, Imran started his career working as junior site manager for his cousin. This privileged entry into the contracting business spared Imran the long and (physically) demanding career of the tenacious few who manage to move up the ladder from manual construction work, to build their reputations through practice and experience, and to eventually become independent contractors. As site manager, Imran was Salim's on-site eyes and ears, tightly connected with his cousin by the ubiquitous cell phone, through which Salim would guide and instruct Imran's work of overseeing and coordinating the on-the-ground construction process. Imran spent his days moving between the different construction sites, ordering building material, monitoring workers, and making sure that the work was executed correctly. And even when no particular direction was necessary, it was Imran's on-site presence that compelled the workers to do their job. Thereby, Imran's relationship with the workers oscillated between jocular familiarity and high-handed imperiousness. He joked amicably with workers, explaining to me that one has to take care of them and treat them well. Liberal with *chai*

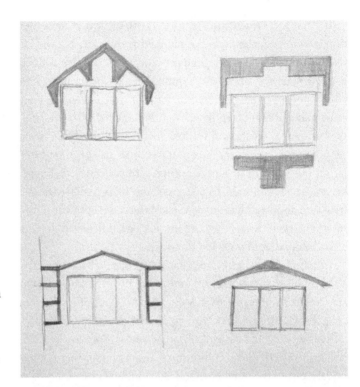

FIGURE 2.1 My proposal sketch for a *chajja* design. Used courtesy of Tobias Baitsch, photographer.

FIGURE 2.2 Reference photo from a Berlin building. Used courtesy of Tobias Baitsch, photographer.

FIGURE 2.3 Imran's Berlin-inspired trademark chajja design. Used courtesy of Tobias Baitsch, photographer.

(tea) and kind words, Imran was much friendlier than his cousin, who was often reluctant to allow his workers even short breaks. Yet notwithstanding Imran's easygoing attitude, he takes his work seriously. With the help of a tiny notebook, he kept track of who was working on which construction site and for how long. These notes established the laborers' daily wages, calculating expenses and serving as a basis for price negotiation. When I first met Imran, he had little knowledge of construction. However, he learned quickly on the job and became well-versed in procedural, technical, and design questions. A year after joining his cousin's business, Imran had become Salim's only site manager and gradually took over most of Salim's responsibilities.

Imran was particularly eager to add sophisticated and intricate embellishments to his buildings: an elaborate color scheme, for instance, or fancy tiling and upmarket stonework. I learned more about his aesthetic sensibility and appreciation of adornment after returning to Switzerland, when I received a message from Imran asking for help with *chajja* (window eave) design for his newest construction site. The first drawings I sent in return to

Imran's request were apparently too elaborate; a somewhat worried Imran responded: "Plzz sir . . . send me easy chajja design . . . I'm not that level contractor." While my proposals were not technically complicated, they nonetheless remained incomprehensible to Imran, who was untrained in reading "architectural" drawings and unfamiliar with my go-to mode of conveying ideas. In a second attempt I sent Imran a photo of a facade I had taken during a recent trip to Berlin. This went over quite well, and in the months that followed a modified variation of this design became Imran's design trademark. Nowadays, multiple houses in Shivajinagar boast similar Berlin-inspired decoration. Indeed, it is common among the ambitious contractors in Shivajinagar to have some sort of distinguishing feature. Imran and Salim's designs mark their houses as their houses—for example, through the form of a particular window grill, a decorative shape of the parapet, or, in Imran's case, an "internationally" inspired chajja design.

Although Imran's "foreign contacts" might be rather peculiar in the area, the transnational character of design ideas in Shivajinagar is hardly unique. Ideas travel easily and quickly nowadays: returning labor migrants from the Gulf bring new inspirations and pictures of how to live and express "the good life." Internet access to sites such as YouTube contributes to spreading and diversifying housing dreams. In this context, contractors are eager to satisfy their clients' cravings for expressive decoration. Such adornment can be interpreted as a will to shape the built environment according to aesthetic imaginations about the good life. These houses reflect the social and economic position and express the ambitions of residents and contractors alike. At the same time, contractors' claims of "authorship" point to the emergence of a professionalizing market, where distinction between competitors is established, among others, through design. In that sense, Imran's appropriation of a particular chajja design marked the moment when he became a proper contractor with his own signature and taste. Imran regularly accompanies his clients on visits to local tile shops and advises them on how to select coloring themes. He is known locally for his keen sense of "highlighters": decorative tiles of different colors, patterns, or images of fruits, dolphins, and deities. His preference for elected design mirrors those of the clientele to whom he is catering: the upper crust of Shivajinagar's residents.

As the word *contractor*[4] suggests, people like Imran are contracted by house owners to (re)build or remodel a building. By these "contracts," contractors enter into relations with clients full of potential and actual conflicts. These arrangements between client and contractor are in most cases agreed upon orally, but written contracts increasingly complement and make precise such mutual understandings about the houses to be built. Such contracts might take different forms, such as oral, written by hand in a notebook, printed and duly signed, or exchanged over mobile phone. Imran refers to several sample contracts to establish a new version with every client. Often thorough regarding technical questions, they remain relatively mute on other dimensions of the agreement. For example, they do not touch on questions of land tenure. The contracts are limited to building questions and make explicit and formal what is common practice in the construction of houses in Shivajinagar. Besides a time frame and (of course) a price, the contracts specify the future house with all its characteristics: volume and functional properties, structural and technical properties, and design features. Such written agreements are accompanied by multiple oral accords. In a context characterized by strong social control, these agreements often form the starting point for further negotiations and are rarely implemented literally. Written contracts form just one element in the ongoing negotiation process that shapes the construction of a house. Houses are designed as and when they are built, and contracts therefore tend to be quickly outstripped by the progress of construction.

The relationship between contractors and their clients is rarely without disputes and differences over services agreed upon: quantities and qualities (not) delivered and (not) paid or delays are among the many reasons for disagreement. "It is important to have a contract," explained one of Salim's clients to me. "Almost always there is a problem with the contractor." Although a contract represents some sort of assurance to the client, its value for the latter in case of a serious dispute is questionable. Rather, the expertise and also the social position of the contractor tip the balance in his favor; house owners often describe (with some fatalism) being fooled, yet they put up with the consequences and rarely seem truly dissatisfied. Such dependence on the contractor's benevolence and the many uncertainties involved in housing production underpin this practice of "formalizing" relations through written contracts.

For owners, housing transformation is a complicated and high-stakes matter. In the contracts, the house owner's obligations are limited to paying the agreed sum and making design choices such as choosing tiles and painting colors within a given budget. In practice, however, things were often quite different. Despite the trust that owners must place in the contractor, clients closely followed the construction process and were often present on site, sometimes more often than the contractor himself. In addition to the cost of the house, owners often forgo income from their own work and invest much of their own time staying on site in order to ensure that the design meets their requirements.

Apart from the investments in time and money, there were several other activities that Imran's clients generally performed during the construction process. For example, it was often the clients themselves who would water the newly constructed brick walls for several days, in order to ensure the proper setting of the mortar and thus the strengthening of walls. House owners were generally more than happy to execute this crucial work themselves. Beyond that, clients had little to do with laborers, with officials, or with disputes concerning ill-wishing community members or interfering neighbors. The delegation of responsibility to contractors is far-reaching. For instance, when one neighbor lamented to a client that excess water from the wetting of the walls was seeping into her house, the house owner advised her to direct her concerns about the damage to Imran.

For his part, Imran is responsible for everything involved in the construction process, including potential social or technical complications. He "adopts" each house-to-be for the time of construction, so it is common that municipal officers on "rounds" or curious passersby would inquire about the contractor rather than about the "owner" of a house under construction. Imran's contracts usually make this issue explicit: "Municipality, Police, Councillor and others will be handled by us." This single line describes the relations among all actors potentially involved in the construction of the house and, in particular, their relation to the contractor as the central mediator. Although Imran takes upon himself most responsibility for this mediating work, he also makes himself indispensable. As a contractor, he is the central actor through which all links run: the procuring of materials, laborers, and technical expertise; the handling of official paperwork; the negotiation of building regulations; the keeping in check of potential extorters; and the managing of complaining neighbors. To navigate the social, technical, economic, and political waters of housing production, Imran relies on a tightly knit network of construction specialists. A plethora of masons, metalworkers, plumbers, electricians, plasterers, labor contractors, and so on form a highly efficient system of subcontractors. As a contractor, Imran is a central link in this network, engaged by house owners for his expertise in bringing together all of the myriad resources (material, technical, sociopolitical) necessary to get a house built. Indeed, Imran and Salim make it a point to maintain excellent relationships with local politicians and administrative bodies, of which other contractors occasionally also make use. In turn, they almost always rely on labor contractors[5] to procure skilled workers from the local *naka* (crossroads where day laborers gather). Illustrating the contractor's central position, Imran's contracts conceal this complex reality. For instance, laborers are not even mentioned and are only implicitly present by way of technical description, and further third parties appear only as passive actors to be "handled." In contrast, the municipality, police, and councillor are explicitly mentioned, demonstrating their obvious importance and making clear that they need to be successfully managed.

One striking example of how to "handle" municipal officers is what I've elsewhere referred to as the "symbolic wall":[6] a wall constructed by the contractor, the sole function of which is to be promptly destroyed by the municipal authorities. In Mumbai's slum neighborhoods, municipal rules permit building or rebuilding only within a fourteen-foot limit, a restriction that presents a regulatory obstacle to the (re)construction of Shivajinagar's multistory houses. Given the pressing need for living space, this height restriction for structures in popular neighborhoods is among Mumbai's most contested building regulations.[7] Taller houses are not only a necessity to create more space but also a question of (thermal) comfort, and last but not least reflect the residents' aspirations. In Shivajinagar and other areas of Mumbai, a practice has emerged whereby contractors who plan to exceed this limit will construct a wall of three-and-one-half feet on top of the first slab. Hinting at a future window opening, the "symbolic wall" signals to the municipal authorities the intention to build a second story. As a reaction, the municipality issues a notice demanding structural modification. Then the contractor contacts the municipal officer responsible for the area, inviting him to fulfill his duty by destroying the offending wall. Invariably backed by cash payments, the demolitions are carried out in a very careful way in order not to demolish any other parts of the building. The officers then sign the notice and take a picture proving they have fulfilled their enforcement duties. After this, the contractor proceeds to build the second story, and the officers are safe from accusations of complicity, having evidence that they carried out a demolition.[8] The destruction of the symbolic wall is meticulously timed and coordinated, one of the few events during the construction process that always happens on the predicted day and within the hour indicated by Imran.

The creative and pragmatic work of contractors fulfills Mumbai's housing dreams, making the production of nonelite built space possible, not only with respect to aesthetics and technical soundness but more fundamentally with the constraints of restrictive and contradictory building regulations

FIGURE 2.4 The "half window" in the "symbolic wall" indicates a future second story. Used courtesy of Tobias Baitsch, photographer.

and limited resources. Contractors' expertise hinges upon their ability to keep the myriad actors and materials at bay or at hand, and to assemble, mediate, and coordinate actions and flows of information and materials. Mastering processes such as the symbolic wall, they design not only buildings but also processes and practices of urban transformation, opening up possibilities for more colorful (quite literally) urban futures.

Notes

1. Shivajinagar has never been officially declared as a "slum" but is treated for policy and administrative purposes as such. For extended discussion, see Lisa Björkman, *Pipe Politics, Contested Waters: Embedded Infrastructures of Millennial Mumbai* (Durham, NC: Duke University Press, 2015).

2. The name *Shivajinagar* is used here as a shortcut to designate a cluster of settlements that developed around and along with the resettlement colony of this name.

3. A comparison of the built-up environment in 2011 and 2014 indicates that every year about 6 percent of the building stock undergoes major remodeling or is completely reconstructed. Tobias Baitsch, "Incremental Urbanism: A Study of Incremental Housing Production and the Challenge of Its Inclusion in

Contemporary Planning Processes in Mumbai, India" (PhD diss., Swiss Federal Institute of Technology Lausanne, 2018), 153–57. However, phases of increased construction activity are of a cyclic nature, and three years later, in 2017, Imran complains about a sluggish dynamic in the local building sector.

4. *Contractor* is the locally used word to describe people such as Imran.

5. See Uday Chandra's profile of Janu (chapter 6).

6. See also the writings of Matias Echanove and Rahul Srivastava, "Dweller and Slum Dweller," in *Mumbai Reader* 13, ed. Rahul Mehrotra and Pankaj Joshi (Mumbai: Urban Design Research Institute, 2013), 329–43, as well as Masoom Moitra et al., "Shivaji Nagar: Homegrown Neighbourhood," URBZ User-Generated City (blog), September 1, 2012, http://urbz.net/page/15/.

7. The application of the fourteen-foot rule to construction in Shivajinagar is highly contentious, not least because the neighborhood is not officially a "slum." See Björkman, *Pipe Politics*.

8. Echanove and Srivastava estimate that at least 10 percent of housing cost is spent on these sorts of cash payments. Matias Echanove and Rahul Srivastava, "Shivaji Nagar Govandi—Mumbai," 2013, www.flickr.com/photos/urbzoo/sets /72157641098143633.

3 **DALPAT** MANAGER OF SERVICES

Lisa Björkman

"DID GUPTA SIGN your permissions form the other day?" I posed the question to Dalpat once we were seated at a small cafe a few blocks from the Municipal Corporation's head office, where we had both spent the morning waiting to meet a senior municipal water engineer, a fifty-something man named Gupta. Dalpat smiled, "Of course—no problem." Dalpat was the "manager of services" for one of Mumbai's largest real estate developers. He's the guy whose job it is to secure all the requisite "service approvals" needed from the Municipal Corporation offices over the course of a construction project ("Fifty-two approvals are needed just in services!"). Dalpat's domain includes permissions for everything from water taps for construction laborers living on-site to sewerage connectivity for completed projects. Gupta was a regular in both our schedules in those days—for very different reasons—and Dalpat and I had grown chummy over the months, passing the time during our long waits outside Gupta's busy office, chatting about his work, about my work, and about the surprising overlaps between the two. "But . . . if there was 'no problem,'" I pressed, "then why did you need to see a senior engineer?" Dalpat explained that it was because the water connections for which he sought approval were for a project that didn't have an occupation certificate (OC).

And this was because the no-objection certificates (NOCs) that Dalpat had secured at the project's outset were for only a nineteen-story building; his completed building had twenty-three floors.

I asked Dalpat how he convinced Gupta to approve the water connections; after all, it had been only three days since the news media had reported on a Water Department decision to cut off all water connections to buildings not having occupation certificates. Dalpat explained that "at first [Gupta] said no, but then I said that look, the building is part of an SRA [Slum Rehabilitation Authority] project." That is to say, the twenty-three-story residential tower had been constructed on land freed up by the demolition of a "slum" neighborhood whose dis-housed residents were given allotments in mid-rise tenement blocks that were part of this same project. Because they are part of the same project, permission to connect the twenty-three-story high-end residential tower to the municipal water grid was linked to that of the Slum Rehabilitation Scheme tenements. Dalpat explained how he told Gupta, "If you don't give water, then the corporators [elected municipal councillors] will scream, and the public will be at your doorstep. You're the water department, after all."

Eventually, Gupta approved the water connections to all the buildings as "HG connections." I asked, "What's HG?" Dalpat responded with something unintelligible. "What?" Unintelligible. "Sorry?" Dalpat took my notebook and wrote "Humtraine Ground." Humanitarian ground. I asked Dalpat whether he knew the meaning of the English word *humanitarian* (although our conversations took place largely in Hindi, Dalpat was reasonably comfortable in English). He shook his head; no, he wasn't familiar with the English word. But he went on to explain the HG policy under which Gupta had granted the connection. This policy allows consumer water connections to residents of constructions not having the mandatory OC because of some or another irregularity: excessive consumption of *floor space index* (FSI), for instance, or violation of some zoning regulation. These are common conditions in Mumbai, Dalpat explained, affecting most new constructions, especially those built in conjunction with SRA projects rehousing "slum dwellers" and "project-affected people" (known in Mumbai as "PAPs") displaced from various infrastructure-upgrading projects throughout the city. Dalpat tells me that every building on which he's worked since joining the building industry in the 1990s has upper floors that were not included in the building proposal.

But why do builders build extra floors onto the slum-rehabilitation tenements of an SRA project instead of just on the free-sale component where the profits are actually made? Dalpat explained that builders earn incentive development rights of an area equivalent to the FSI constructed in the SRA buildings. Allotments for the additional rooms in SRA buildings are sold on the "free market," meaning that, by some means or another, the names of families who were not actually displaced by the slum-rehabilitation project will be included in the list of surveyed households slated for "resettlement." In this backdoor way, Mumbai's working-class housing stock is being augmented: extra slum-rehabilitation housing is a cost-effective way for builders to earn lucrative development rights that can then be used in conjunction with higher-end residential or commercial projects. Both SRA and free-sale buildings invariably consume more than the allowable FSI, Dalpat explained, and both resettled slum dwellers and new home buyers generally move into their new building blissfully unaware that it has not been granted an OC and will likely never meet the requirements for the OC's procurement. It is because of the "innocence" of the new residents, Gupta later explained, that water connections are given on "humanitarian grounds." In other words, builders construct overly large SRA buildings, match the FSI in the free-sale component of a project, and use the threat of political mobilization among the urban poor as a means to secure approval for water connections. Unlike regular water connections, however, HG connections are granted at only half the per capita daily supply of a regular water connection. Untold numbers of city residents—slum dwellers and otherwise—are thus systematically and officially allocated only half the amount mandated by municipal rules governing daily water supply.

I ASKED DALPAT TO EXPLAIN for me how he goes about getting service approvals. For instance, the approval he finally got from Gupta the other day, what did this actually entail? He explained: "First I tell the executive engineer in the head office what it is I want and give him my proposal. Then he sends the proposal to the ward-level engineers." The engineers at the head office need information from the ward-level engineers regarding "present connectivity in the area"—the size and position and pressures of the mains, for instance. The ward engineer writes his notes and then sends them back to the head office. Then a senior engineer in the head office makes an official proposal (or else signs Dalpat's version, depending on the project) and gives it to Dalpat, who then waits outside Gupta's office in order to get final approval from the HE—the city's chief hydraulic engineer. Gupta was an executive engineer who at that time reported directly to the chief hydraulic engineer. "Gupta acts very strict—he gives various conditions, tells me I have to do this or that," Dalpat explains, "and then eventually he signs the form." I ask, "Do you also give money?" Dalpat gives me an incredulous look: "Yes. Of course. Everyone has to be paid." "You pay a lump sum to a senior engineer who then distributes it downward?" He answers, "No, no, nothing like that; there's no internal discussion among the engineers. Money is sent to each engineer individually." He explains that his work depends upon his personal relations with individual engineers. That's why the company hired him.

We finish our tea and head back to the Bombay Municipal Corporation (BMC)—he too has a meeting scheduled with Gupta. Dalpat walked in a few minutes before me, fifteen or twenty minutes earlier (so that our acquaintance might not become a topic of conversation among the staffers). When I arrived, a staff person greeted me and waved me into Gupta's office. I walked in, and Gupta smiled warmly, waving for me to sit down . . . right next to Dalpat. I sat down nervously without looking at Dalpat. "Okay," Gupta nodded to Dalpat, saying it a bit gruffly, and with some finality—acknowledging, it seemed, whatever it is that they had just discussed. "Thank you, sir," Dalpat responded with an easy smile, getting up to leave without looking at me.

DALPAT WAS BORN IN SINDHI CAMP, in the eastern suburb of Chembur, where his Sindhi parents resettled following the partitioning of India and Pakistan in 1947. Then, when Dalpat was around four years old, his parents moved the family to the suburb of Thane. "My father didn't want us to grow up only in a Sindhi neighborhood," he explained. "He thought we'd never advance, we'd never get ahead." Dalpat studied in a Sindhi-medium public school in Thane until class ten, after which he joined the English-medium college, where he and his elder brother studied for degrees in civil engineering. On their graduation, the brothers found positions in BMC. He recalled that there had previously been "stiff competition" to join the municipal corporation as an engineer, but with the building boom in the Gulf in the 1980s, "all the engineers in Bombay ran off to Dubai." He and his brother simply "walked in" and were given posts as junior engineers in the Municipal Maintenance Department: working on roads, storm-water drains, desilting. Dalpat worked for eight years in the Maintenance Department, but because he had only completed his "graduation"—and not his engineering diploma—he was stuck as a junior engineer. "It would take a long time to get any promotion," he explained, so he and his brother decided to diversify into the private sector: Dalpat would join a private contracting company that could bid on Municipal Maintenance tenders.

Dalpat joined a small Thane-based contractor as an engineer, and Dalpat's brother, still in the Municipal Maintenance Department, helped him to make successful bids on tenders. "There was no money given," Dalpat explained; he didn't have to pay anything to get the contracts. Because his brother was friendly with the clerks who managed the various tenders, his brother was able to glean which companies were likely to give "good fights." Looking at these companies' past projects, Dalpat and his brother could estimate what the other contactors were likely to bid. Dalpat would then bid a little lower.

Beginning in 1992, public concern about the "shoddy work" of municipal contractors inspired a new rule that contractors bidding more than 15 percent below official estimates would have to pay the "marginal money"— that is, the difference between the official estimate and the contractor's bid—up front as a security deposit. "The bids were so low," Dalpat explained, "that the municipality was afraid that the contractors would run off with the money." And indeed, this was often the case, particularly in the case of desilting tenders, where no one came to check whether the contracted work had ever been done at all. By 1995, the "marginal money" rule had put his small contracting firm out of business.

In 1995, out of work, Dalpat joined a small builder as a site engineer doing "vertical constructions." He stayed with this company for ten years ("It was good work!"), but when the owner died without an heir to take over, the company folded. So in 2005 Dalpat went to Dubai, taking a job with a firm owned by a Pakistani-origin Emirati. "We had language in common," Dalpat recalls, "but the guy was a crook." The fellow had "somehow overlooked" taking Dalpat's passport on arrival in Dubai, which turned out to be a stroke of luck. After a few months, when his employer—realizing his error— demanded Dalpat's passport, Dalpat in turn demanded a contract, which needless to say he still hadn't been given. When his employer presented the contract, the salary was only half what he'd been promised. When Dalpat refused, his visa was canceled and he headed back to Bombay.

Dalpat stayed "two weeks" in Bombay, procured another visa, and headed straight back to the Gulf, having joined another company—this time an Indian-owned venture. "They were just doing maintenance and repair work, but they wanted to construct buildings," Dalpat explained. "And they needed a civil engineer for licensing purposes." The boss had "good contacts with the sheiks"; they just needed an engineer. So Dalpat came for the interview, applied for his Emirati contracting license, and stayed on. "They were just doing general maintenance, and I made them into builders!" But these guys ended up being crooks as well, Dalpat explained; the salary on which they had agreed was meant to be complemented by a "partnership"—a profit-sharing arrangement. But when he received his contract, the "partnership" component was left out. The boss said that "we'll work it out informally," Dalpat recalled, but after six months, when he raised the issue again, his boss pretended that the conversation had never happened. Dalpat left, disillusioned with Dubai; in the end his stint in the Emirates lasted less than a year.

It was on his return to Bombay in 2006 that he took his first position with a Bombay builder: a Thane-based company that I'll call Company A. "I didn't know how much to ask for salary," Dalpat recalled with a laugh, "because I didn't know the industry." He asked only a paltry sum for a person of his position, "and they were of course thrilled because it was very cheap." He stayed a few years working as a site engineer but resigned when the firm shifted its offices farther south in the city. "It was too far," Dalpat recalled. "The petrol costs were high, and my salary was too low, so I applied for a job at a different builder." "But why didn't you ask your boss for a salary increase?" "They could have asked me why I was leaving and offered me more money," Dalpat said, "but they didn't . . . they didn't care." In any case, he was fed up. "I found out I was earning less than the foreman. Why would I stay?"

When he entered negotiations with a second company—Company B—he asked for double his previous salary. "They said, 'Why are you asking so much?' I said, look, that's what I'm asking; you can take it or leave it." He explained, "I knew that their licensing section was weak, and my licensing background was front and center on my application. I knew they'd hire me for licensing, and that's what they did." He laughs, adding that "they even gave me money for petrol."

Dalpat's brother was by that time a Maintenance Department sub-engineer in the eastern suburbs, and this connection facilitated the licensing work. Dalpat explained the way it worked: he would "search out" the names of the four or five engineers in a position to grant the needed permission. Then he would tell their names to his brother, who would invariably have worked with one of them in some department over the years. "Then I would meet with that engineer and just mention, 'Oh, you worked with my brother in this or that department in that year!' That's all it takes." By the time Dalpat had joined Company B in the "licensing section," his brother's son had also joined the BMC as a Maintenance Department engineer. Dalpat grinned broadly, adding that "this is a really plush post. He makes only five *lakhs* [500,000 rupees] per year from BMC, but unofficial earnings are at least 25,000 [rupees] per day." I asked him how much he made in addition to his salary. He looked at me blankly. "Me? Nothing! Who would pay me? I just pass the money."

I ASKED DALPAT, "Tell me something—when I was in Gupta's office with you the other day, clearly you both knew how things would turn out in the end: he'd sign your form, and you'd send him money. But even though you both know this, you don't speak directly. Rather, he asks you to 'do this and that and this and that, fill forms. . . .' Why the *natak* [acting]?" "It's not natak," Dalpat demurred. "We have to go through proper procedure." "But if you're going through the proper procedure, then why the money?" By way of explanation, Dalpat told me a story.

Last month he went to the water department's head office to get a layout approved for a very large residential development. He just needed an approval for the final connection to the BMC network; the towers were already complete. A senior water-supply planning engineer sanctioned the layout, giving him approval to connect to a 300-mm belowground distribution main. But when they unearthed the distribution main to which the engineer had given permission to connect, that main "wasn't live." So Dalpat approached a friend—an assistant engineer (AE) at the ward level—and asked him what to do. "That engineer, he said, 'Look, just dig around a little; there's a feeder main under that road somewhere.'" So they dug around, and eventually they stumbled upon a 1400-mm diameter main. "It must be over a hundred years old!" Dalpat laughed. "It's an original trunk main, a cast-iron main. And it was continuously pressurized—24 hours per day!" His friend the AE told him to just go ahead and connect it. "This is totally not allowed according to municipal rules, but he let me do it." Dalpat explained how they made a cross connection with three valves, and when they opened up the main, "water was everywhere, the pressure was so strong!" But they did it; they made the connection. "But see, because the configuration was technically disallowed, it was never recorded on the water department's survey sheets—which in any case have not been updated in decades.[1] "Those valves are not on any map," Dalpat explained, "and no one above the AE knows about the configuration." Instead, in order to supply water to the development, the AE just "manages the *chaviwallas*"—meaning that he'll pass some money to the valve operators who are tasked with the daily opening and closing of Mumbai's more than eight hundred daily-operated valves.[2] "If the engineers in the head office come to know, what will happen?" Dalpat shrugs. "What can they do? Maybe they'll ask for some money, that's all." As a gesture of appreciation to the AE who helped him figure out the arrangement, as well as to enable all the work of "managing" the valves that the configuration will require in the future, Dalpat passed his friend some money. "The payments aren't much; it's just a bonus, just to say thanks." I ask how much he sent. "For that work? Twenty thousand rupees maybe." Why so little? "It's not as if the engineer has done anything illegal or anything. It was no big risk for him. So the money is just a token of thanks. For being cooperative."

I asked Gupta as well about these sorts of cash transfers, and he explained similarly that this money works less like a payment—or a "bribe"—but rather as a "bonus" (he used the English word) for an engineer who has been helpful and cooperative. Like Dalpat, Gupta used the English word *cooperative*. Most engineers are "very cooperative," Dalpat explained, because they know that if they do not process some particular work, the approval will likely be obtained in any case by some other avenue. An uncooperative engineer would thus not only lose out on his "bonus" but more crucially would also be left ignorant (and over time increasingly so) of vital information about the distribution system. This kind of hydraulic illiteracy would quickly render an engineer less and less able, as one engineer put it, to "manage well" and "solve problems" down the line.

WE MEET AT HIS FAVORITE Sindhi place in Sion for lunch. Dalpat walks up grinning like a mischievous child caught with a bag of candy before dinner. He's excited, proud: "Look!" He unfurls the building plans for which he's just gotten approval: a hundred-story residential tower to be constructed in an ecologically fragile zone—an area where development is officially restricted. He lets me take photos of the water department's "no-objection certificate," on which the engineer has written that municipal water availability in the area is "nil."

Dalpat seems elated by this particular victory, and I ask him to explain: "What do you like so much about this work?" He thinks a moment and then says, pensively, "It's about getting an impossible task accomplished." He uses the English word *impossible*. It's "fun," he explains (using the English word *fun*), because it's "impossible." But what's fun about it? "Because it's a challenge. It's about being able to make things happen—impossible things. I can do impossible things because I know how to talk to people." The fun isn't about the final product—the building, the water connection, the money. "Of course there is the recognition from my boss and in the office; that's all nice too," he says. "But the work I do, no one else can do it!" I ask him for an example, and he returns to the story about the trunk main: "It's impossible to connect to a trunk main! Both because it's not allowed but more importantly because it's technically extremely complicated." I ask, "But don't you worry that it might have negative hydraulic effects on the network as a whole?" He shrugs. "It's just one connection. I mean, the rules have to be there because if everyone connected like that—to the trunk main—then if something went wrong, then the city wouldn't get water. It's a trunk main!" He laughs loudly, gleefully, incredulous at his own audacity and ingenuity and success. "So it's not that the rule is wrong. It's a good rule. But it's also good that I was able to get around the rule because now we have good water and also there's no problem with the system. So the fun was in getting that done."

He continued, again pensively: "Anyone who needs anything from the BMC, they come to me. Because I have good relations with everyone. My boss knows that. He doesn't know exactly what I do, or how things get done, but he knows I can get anything done. Before, when I was doing civil engineering, that wasn't satisfying at all. I hated going to work. Now I love going to work in the morning! I meet with everyone, I figure things out, and then . . . things happen! It's very satisfying." "More satisfying than actually building big buildings?" I asked. "Oh yes!" he responded, "much more."

Notes

1. For discussion, see Lisa Björkman, *Pipe Politics, Contested Waters: Embedded Infrastructures of Millennial Mumbai* (Durham, NC: Duke University Press, 2015).

2. The valve operator is a key mediator in Mumbai's hydraulic landscape. See Björkman, *Pipe Politics*.

4 **MEHMOODBHAI** TOILET OPERATOR

Prasad Khanolkar

Forgive the trickster and the tribe will be happy, but kill the trickster and the tribe will be ruined.—DAVID HECHT AND MALIQALIM SIMONE, *Invisible Governance: The Art of African Micropolitics*

"COULD YOU TELL ME ABOUT any one object in your neighborhood that you find beautiful?" I asked Siraj, a resident of Toba Tek Nagar[1] in Mumbai's eastern suburbs. Siraj answered without pausing: "Our toilet."

Built in 1998, the toilet in Siraj's neighborhood was one of the first to be built under the Slum Sanitation Program in the slum settlement of Toba Tek Nagar. The new toilet replaced an older one that was built in the 1980s, using the discretionary funds allocated to elected municipal councilors under the Slum Improvement Program: a state government initiative dating from 1971 that had sought to "improve" the city's "slum" settlements by investing in basic infrastructures such as water and sewerage. But the old toilet in Toba Tek Nagar had been in a state of constant disrepair almost since its commissioning. For starters, the facility had only eight seats (four for men, four for women) in a neighborhood of at least fifteen thousand residents. Secondly, the toilet block was connected not to the city's sewerage system but to an overburdened belowground septic tank. To make matters worse, the facility was built as a load-bearing structure on reclaimed marshy land and had therefore (unsurprisingly) begun to sink slowly into the ground, further reducing the capacity of the septic tank. Needless to say, toilet sludge and its putrid odors regularly overflowed into the neighborhood.

Furthermore, in the absence of municipally provided water and sewerage infrastructure, local residents were forced to depend on private tankers and truck operators to supply water and to periodically pump out and cart away the sludge. These were huge expenses for most local residents. Every few years, just before a municipal or state or central government election, residents would deposit letters and file petitions with different politicians, requesting the rebuilding or repair of the toilet, requests that sometimes resulted in some patching and a tanker or two of free water but never in a lasting solution. The old pink toilet had thus come to represent a circular time of "development" governed by electoral politics among residents.

Then, in 1997, the Slum Sanitation Program (SSP) was launched by the Mumbai Municipal Corporation as part of a broader umbrella initiative known as the Bombay Sewerage Disposal Project (BSDP). Funded by the World Bank and the Maharashtra government, the BSDP aimed to strengthen Mumbai's sewerage infrastructure. The implementation of the SSP was recommended by the World Bank as a mandatory condition for funding the BSDP. The SSP aimed to address four key areas: providing "sustainable" sanitation facilities in Mumbai's slums and connecting them to wider city sewerage networks, reversing "clientelistic" relationships between politicians and slum residents by changing the older "supply-based" model to a "demand-based" model, encouraging community participation by involving nongovernmental organizations (NGOs) and community-based organizations (CBOs), and instituting a new financial model in order to foster a sense of "ownership" among slum residents and help them maintain and operate toilets without external funds.[2] To institute the last goal, the SSP mandated an initial household contribution of INR 100 per individual (around USD $2.50 in 1997) or a maximum of INR 500 (USD $12.50) per family. In return, these individuals or households were to be provided a family pass for a minimal yearly cost of INR 120 (USD $3). The SSP also required participation of at least 50 percent of households in order to ensure financial sustainability of any project.

The new SSP toilet in Toba Tek Nagar is an aesthetically striking structure—a sharp contrast to the old, dilapidated toilet that it replaced. The new toilet is built with a raft foundation whose reinforced concrete piles travel thirty feet below the ground to find stability in the hard rocks below the marsh. The building's surfaces are carefully and attentively adorned: the outsides are clad with rough off-white ceramic tiles and the inside walls with glossy gray, brown, and off-white tiles. Furthermore, the sludge is disposed into the septic tank and from there into a *nalla* (stream) using an ad hoc pipe that was absent in the plumbing drawings submitted to the municipality. The toilet boasts metered electricity and billed water connections, although a suction pump purchased using residents' contributions is used to offset the low-pressure municipal water supply. The presence of these different elements helps the residents avoid dependence on discretionary funds of local politicians. However, this did not mean that the toilet was built without the municipal councillor's involvement; on the contrary, she was invited as the guest of honor for the toilet project's *bhoomi poojan* (ground-breaking ceremony). In addition, a black granite tile with the councillor's name engraved in golden letters was installed at the toilet's entrance. In seeking the councillor's blessings for their toilet, the residents wanted to ensure that they would be able to seek her support on other issues.

A cast-iron staircase at the back of the concrete structure leads up to a terrace, which is used by residents for various non-toilet-related activities (tuition classes, tailoring classes). The terrace floor is decorated with colored ceramic tiles and lined with potted green plants. A small channel around the edge of the terrace floor carries rainwater to the underground water-storage tank. The tank is connected to a metered municipal water connection, out of which pressurized water flows between 6 and 8 a.m. each day. Mehmoodbhai— the new toilet's caretaker as well as the head of the CBO that operates and maintains it—or Mehmoodbhai's son Sajid switches on the electric pump that lifts the water from the underground tank into the overhead tank.

A short, stout man with a cropped beard, Mehmoodbhai migrated from Muzzafarnagar, in the North Indian state of Uttar Pradesh, to a slum settlement in the South Bombay neighborhood of Byculla in 1972. He was then relocated by the municipal authorities to Toba Tek Nagar in 1975 following Emergency-era slum demolitions and evictions in Byculla. Mehmoodbhai's office is located up on the terrace next to the overhead tank. He resides with his wife and with his son, daughter-in-law, and their two children in a two-room structure at the other end of the terrace. Mehmoodbhai had played a key role in getting the SSP toilet built: he organized the residents to form the CBO; liaised among the residents, the NGO, and the municipality; and, more importantly, gave up his own house to make space for the new toilet. His old house, he told me, had been situated just next to the old pink toilet. Rather than being relocated by the new toilet project (whose footprint would be much bigger than the old one and thus would occupy the land on which his house was situated), Mehmoodbhai opted to take on the role of the caretaker, which provided his family a rooftop home. In recent years, Sajid has taken over as the caretaker while Mehmoodbhai attends to the family's vegetable stall in the wholesale market in Navi Mumbai and is also actively involved in organizing a body of SSP-related CBOs at the city level.

Access to the new toilet works like this: older residents—those who can provide documentary proof that their tenure in Toba Tek Nagar precedes the *cutoff date* of January 1, 1995[3]—can avail of a prepaid monthly pass that costs INR 500. Residents who have taken up residence in Toba Tek Nagar after 1995 can purchase monthly prepaid toilet passes as and when they are able to provide documentary proof of residence (electricity bills, power-of-attorney certificate, children's school fee receipt, water-supply bill, etc.). Allowing post-1995 residents to purchase monthly passes was a unique feature of Mehmoodbhai's toilet; this was not a part of the SSP program, which explicitly excluded post-1995 residents. Newer migrants living as subtenants (and who therefore will generally not have documentary proof of residence in their own names) are not provided a monthly pass. They pay INR 2 (USD $0.025) per visit. These renting tenants are mostly single men—many recent migrants from North India—who have found employment in manufacturing workshops in Toba Tek Nagar. They form the largest group of "pay-per-visit" clients, and income from their "visits" is the primary income source for the maintenance and upkeep of the toilet.

While Toba Tek Nagar's resident renters must pay a retail (per-use) charge to use the toilet, relatives of pass-holding residents visiting from outside Toba Tek Nagar are allowed to use the toilet for free. For Mehmoodbhai, it is a matter of pride when these outside visitors express their awe of the beauty and cleanliness of "his" toilet or become envious of their relatives who are its members. During one of our many conversations, Mehmoodbhai explained some renovation plans to me while arranging the tile pattern for the outside walls on his desk: "I want the inside tiles to be glossy and those on the outside to be rough. It will give the toilet a natural look from the outside and a posh look on the inside. . . . I also want to install speakers—you don't see that often, right?" I agreed and suggested he could play songs. "Not songs," he insisted, but "news, melodies, and instrumental music. It will help people relax while using the toilet." He wanted the toilet to be not just pleasurable for use but also a spectacular object: an object of everyone's attention. Every year, Mehmoodbhai celebrates World Toilet Day. The toilet gets covered with colorful lights, music is played on hired speakers, and a chief guest—a well-known builder, a senior municipal official, or a local politician, for instance—is invited. The toilet becomes a space for a festival and the festival a space to develop affiliations with prominent actors in urban development.

Over the years, Mehmoodbhai's SSP toilet has become renowned in international development circles as an instance of slum-sanitation "best practice." Photos of award ceremonies, certificates from international organizations, travelogues of international conferences, newspaper cuttings, and photographs of visits by NGOs, researchers, and foreign visitors are all archived on his computer, on the walls of his office, and on social media. Mehmoodbhai has used the celebrated SSP toilet as a conduit to develop strong relations with different actors, including municipal bureaucrats and myriad national and international development agencies. For instance, he allows specific NGOs to showcase "his" toilet to international donors as "their" best-practice model in order to attract more funding. In turn, Mehmoodbhai calls upon these NGOs when he needs funds or favors. A few years after the toilet was built, Mehmoodbhai set up a citywide NGO to coordinate among different cities' slum-based CBOs and the city municipality. Furthermore, given his affiliations and knowledge, residents from Toba Tek Nagar come to him for help in navigating all manner of bureaucratic procedures: getting themselves onto the government's "Below Poverty Line" list, resolving issues of contested land occupancy, obtaining municipal water and electricity connections, or leveraging Mehmoodbhai's contacts in various government offices for timely completion of paperwork. Mehmoodbhai tells me that he assists the residents in whatever way he can and does not expect anything in return. Mehmoodbhai thus expressed surprise and disappointment when the NGO refused to fund his renovation plans. He recounted how he responded by politely refusing to allow his toilet to be showcased to the NGO's donors.

Nizambhai, another toilet operator in Toba Tek Nagar, has a somewhat different story to tell about Mehmoodbhai's toilet. According to Nizambhai, Mehmoodbhai is a *kamina*—a trickster—who had fooled local residents who were unable to afford the initial contribution toward the toilet to sign up for the program anyway. Mehmoodbhai had convinced them, Nizambhai explained, by offering to pay their part of the initial contribution. But once the toilet was built, Mehmoodbhai had refused to hand these residents their family passes and demanded per-visit payments until they repaid him for the initial contribution. Furthermore, Nizambhai continued, Mehmoodbhai had never actually owned a house next to the old toilet; it was a story he made up to justify his residence on the roof of the toilet block.

Residing at the other end of Toba Tek Nagar, Nizambhai also has a toilet story. Having migrated from a village in western Maharashtra to a slum settlement in Mahalaxmi during the droughts of 1970–73, he too relocated to Toba Tek Nagar during the Emergency-era demolitions. The neighborhood was without much in the way of infrastructural services in those days, Nizambhai recalled, so he and his neighbors had worked closely with local politicians and government officials to gain some basic services: an access road, electricity lines, bus routes, and so on. A few years later, he left his job as a private security guard and began working with a local NGO that had recently set up an office in the settlement. As months passed by, Nizambhai grew frustrated with the NGO's narrow scope of work, which was limited to health and education. He began organizing informal waste pickers and textile workers in his free time. Eventually, he quit the NGO and started his own organization with a few friends, most of whom earned their incomes by renting out additional floors of their houses to local tenants and recent migrants.

For their first project, Nizambhai's new NGO had applied for an SSP contract to oversee the community awareness and community organization component of the program. Nizambhai's plan was to obtain a SSP contract that would enable his NGO to continue working in Toba Tek Nagar, but the municipality assigned it instead to work in another part of the city. Despite the disappointment, the NGO took on the work in these localities and built relationships with municipal officials, local politicians, contractors, and local leaders in those areas. A few months later, drawing on the relationships with municipal bureaucrats and contractors that he had forged through his work with the SSP, Nizambhai managed to divert funds from a failed SSP project to build a twenty-four-seat toilet in a newer (post-2000) area in Toba Tek Nagar that lacked any toilet facilities. On completion, the toilet block was handed over to Nizambhai's organization for operation and maintenance on a five-year lease. This arrangement occurred outside the ambit of the SSP, but Nizambhai operated his toilet according to the SSP rules. A few months later, Nizambhai fell into ill health and became less involved with the NGO. Without his leadership, the organization foundered, but Nizambhai himself continued to operate the toilet block by SSP rules—and to collect dues from its users.

A few years later, Nizambhai was approached by an NGO that had recently been awarded an SSP contract to build a toilet in the neighborhood where Nizambhai's (non-SSP) toilet was located. The NGO wanted to demolish the toilet that Nizambhai managed and to build in its place a bigger, forty-seat SSP toilet. The NGO, like many involved in the SSP, also ran a private, for-profit construction company that had been awarded the contract to construct SSP toilets. The NGO and its associated construction company, needless to say, had much to gain (in the form of international development funds and contract awards) from demolishing and rebuilding Nizambhai's toilet. After a few informal exchanges, a face-to-face meeting was organized at the local youth center between the NGO, the contractor, and Nizambhai. After some initial disagreement, Nizambhai, who was in need of money, agreed to "sell" the toilet for a price that included its cost of construction and his expected income over the next three years.

Meanwhile, seeing the success of Mehmoodbhai's SSP toilet, Kasim, a youth-group leader in an adjacent neighborhood, decided to initiate a similar project in his locality. He identified an empty site for the toilet with the help of Abdulbhai—Kasim's mentor, who had earlier been in the business of reclaiming land. All the requisite paperwork had been successfully completed over the next few months, and the process of excavating for the new toilet block had started. But the very next day, a group of "old" (i.e., pre-2000) residents intervened, halting the excavation and voicing their opposition to the toilet project. The old residents claimed that they had been the ones who (along with local politicians) had reclaimed the land in the first place, and on that basis they demanded a part of the land for themselves. The matter was taken to a neighborhood community center, and respected local leaders—religious leaders, primarily—were invited to mediate. *Maulvis* (religious scholars) were invited to give their blessings, and a Quran was placed on the stage to ensure a peaceful meeting; politicians, municipal officials, and NGOs—as "outsiders"—were excluded from the negotiations. The meeting was peaceful, but it concluded without the participants having reached any agreement. That very night, an anonymous group of men attacked Kasim in front of his house.

The attack had shaken Kasim, but Abdulbhai's continued support brought the situation to a standoff; any move would almost certainly court violence. As tensions rose, the toilet project was stalled. The elected councillor did not intervene because he had struck a deal with the old residents for a share in the houses to be constructed on the disputed piece of land; the maulvis couldn't be called upon to intervene because they had a deal with the municipal councillor for the construction of a new mosque in the area. A few weeks later, gossip began circulating in Toba Tek Nagar that the news of violence over a piece of land had reached the municipal office. The ward officer, Abdulbhai told me, was planning to send a team to verify the paperwork of all residents located around the toilet site; it was feared that this survey might lead to demolitions of many of the houses built after 2000. Religion, land, money, and power, Abdulbhai explained, are intricately intertwined in

Mumbai and have engulfed everyone. The toilet operators traverse these multiple worlds, identities, relationships, and ethical positions without being engulfed by any particular one. It is along the paths of such traverses that the city gets built. However, this movement involves a tragic play that often results in uncertain outcomes.

Notes

David Hecht and Maliqalim Simone, *Invisible Governance: The Art of African Micropolitics* (Brooklyn: Autonomedia, 1994), 77.

1. The name of the settlement has been changed. I have borrowed the name from Sadat Hasan Manto's short story "Toba Tek Singh," which revolves around a Sikh protagonist's desire to stay in his village of Toba Tek Singh in Pakistan and his refusal to be sent to India based on his religion. The story ends with the protagonist lying flat in the no-man's land between the two countries.

2. R. N. Sharma and Amita Bhide, "World Bank Funded Slum Sanitation Programme in Mumbai: Participatory Approach and Lessons Learnt," *Economic and Political Weekly* 40, no. 17 (April 2005): 1785.

3. See the glossary entry for *cutoff date*. When the SSP program was initiated, the eligibility cutoff date was January 1, 1995. This date has been modified twice since then. In 2014 the Congress Party–led government extended it to January 1, 2000, and in December 2017 the Bharatiya Janata Party–led state government passed a resolution in the cabinet to extend it to January 1, 2011.

5 **KAUSHAL** LAND AGGLOMERATOR

Llerena Guiu Searle

I MET KAUSHAL at a real estate conference in Mumbai in the fall of 2006. He was about thirty-five years old, with a mop of salt-and-pepper hair, sharp features, and a penchant for knit ties in muted solid colors. We exchanged business cards and chatted over coffees in an upstairs lounge at the Taj Mahal Palace Hotel during one of the many networking breaks at the conference. We ran into each other again at a Credit Suisse–sponsored after-party that evening. As we perched on couches on an outdoor terrace, surrounded by suspended *diyas* (oil lamps) and eating shrimp canapés, Kaushal told me more about his life.

Kaushal grew up in Delhi, attended an Ivy League university in the United States, took time off to follow the Grateful Dead, and later became an investment banker. He left investment banking for IT consulting but then realized he didn't like managing people and decided to switch to an "asset-based" industry: real estate. He felt that on Wall Street a lot of "really smart guys" compete over a very small territory of moneymaking; in real estate, he realized he could make money in relatively noncompetitive small markets buying unsexy assets. (His reasoning about industries was based on a hierarchy of "smartness": small real estate markets were uncompetitive, he felt, because local real estate developers in the US were not that smart.) His first break came buying up some seventeen thousand low-end housing units in Florida that were rented mostly to Latinx residents; he then moved on to projects in São Paulo, Brazil.

He had come to India the year before, scouting out real estate deals for an investment fund he had started. Kaushal was not from Mumbai; he hadn't lived there, and he didn't necessarily plan to buy any land or to invest in any real estate projects there. But as he chased deals internationally, Mumbai became an important node in a global landscape of business locales. Kaushal used a five-star hotel in Mumbai as his base of operations in India. He flew in and out of Indian cities, arriving in the morning and leaving by the evening, in his search for deals. Mumbai was a place to make important connections, to pick up pieces of industry information, and to survey the competition. Indeed, as we talked at the party, he pointed out people he knew from New York.

I got the sense talking with him at the Credit Suisse party that Indian real estate was just one investment possibility among many that spanned the globe. He and another young investor we chatted with (a young Marwari man who went to university in Bombay and then worked for a financial firm out of New York) discussed with equal fluency real estate in New Jersey, São Paulo, Miami, and Australia. Their conversation also strayed to investment opportunities in server farms, telecom, and Indonesian palm oil plantations. Their conversation seemed to epitomize a worldview in which anything could be made into an asset and few barriers restricted capital movements.

However, Kaushal had his reasons for looking into Indian investments, and they seemed to require a lot of work from him, contradicting my impression of instantaneous capital flows. Kaushal did have family in Delhi, and his status as a Non-Resident Indian helped him to secure land deals and navigate local bureaucracies. More than ties of nationality or kinship, though, India promised meteoric economic growth. Many of the investors I met had their own calculus for determining where to invest; Kaushal's metric was the rate at which India's wealthiest people were increasing their wealth, which he calculated to be 24 percent per year (or approximately three times the GDP growth rate), compared with only 9 percent in the United States.[1] Rising incomes (for the wealthy—he noted that India's poor were growing their income at less than GDP) augured well for luxury real estate sales and thus for growing his own capital.

Economic growth made India exciting—globally, the place where the action was. (Other investors I spoke with called India the "flavor of the month," reflecting an awareness of how quickly growth could stagnate and investor interest could turn elsewhere.) Kaushal claimed that he liked living in Brazil (where his wife and young child still lived) but that he felt he could not miss being in India now. He compared the India of 2006 to the late 1990s dot-com boom in the US or to China in 1994, and then waxed eloquent about India's emergence from a dark period of colonization into the limelight of capitalist growth. His voice tinged with pride, he said he would regret not taking part in India's rebirth: "I would kick myself."

If Kaushal's approach to Mumbai tells us something about the city's function as an international business hub and about his thoughts regarding India and investor sentiment in 2006, his approach to real estate investment also illuminates the way the industry worked in 2006–8. It was an intensely personal business, in which investors like Kaushal spent their time building networks of people, links in a chain of capital accumulation that Kaushal hoped would stretch from investors in the US through land in India. This work began at the conference we attended. Kaushal claimed that if you didn't attend, people would think you weren't "in the market." He also insisted that you had to have your "feet on the ground" in India, to do things in person. Making personal connections continued after the after-party: Kaushal called me the following day from his room at the Intercontinental to continue our conversation, as he did every other person he had met at the conference the day before, diligently making his way through the business cards he collected.

Foreign real estate investors knew that the closer they got to land deals themselves—the fewer intermediaries they used and more risk they took on—the more profit they could make. It was industry common knowledge that most of the risk in Indian real estate lay in the process of buying up small parcels of land, agglomerating them into a site large enough for new construction, and getting permits for development. Many things could go wrong in this highly political process: individual farmers could refuse to sell, other people could claim to own the land you thought you had purchased, permits could prove impossible to get, or the land could prove too costly to develop. Few investors had the cultural competence, freedom of action, or "risk appetite" to get involved in this business, partnering instead with Indian developers who had already amassed "land banks" and who charged investors a hefty premium for construction-ready land parcels.

Kaushal was the exception who proved the rule. As a small-time player, he hoped to limit the amount of equity he had to invest in a project without relying on debt; thus, he was looking for small but profitable projects.

However, a lot of Indian developers told him that if they saw the kind of opportunity he was looking for, they would do it themselves, without a foreign investor partner. Instead of working with developers who already had land in place or projects underway, then, Kaushal got into the business of land agglomeration himself.

Buying up Indian land required building networks of intermediaries. Kaushal worked with an international property consultancy to do feasibility studies on land he was considering, and he hired numerous local "brokers" to help him identify properties, vet deals, and negotiate with farmers. Such intermediaries were necessary because they have the kind of local knowledge and political connections that Kaushal didn't have; they enabled him to extend his reach, socially and geographically. By sending "brokers out in a *dhoti*" (sarong) to talk to farmers, as he reported he did, Kaushal overcame his lack of local cultural competency and disguised his interest with the aim of keeping prices down and increasing the profitability of deals. Once he had a deal in place with landowners, he hired an Indian developer, basically as a builder.

Although I do not know how he managed the actual land purchase and permitting, I assume that Kaushal was able to "take out the risk" because he was both an insider and an outsider. His close contacts in Indian real estate (his maternal uncle was involved in land dealing in Delhi), his social and cultural capital as an upper-caste Delhiite conversant in New York financial worlds, and his status as a Non-Resident Indian, which would allow him to buy property (though, importantly, not agricultural land), were assets that he could call on to forge some connections, primarily with corporate real estate consultants, developers, and other financiers. But this social positioning marked him as an outsider when he negotiated deals in Bangalore, where he seemed to have several projects going. He claimed that outsider status was a boon: because he was not directly connected with any of the established local real estate players, farmers trusted him not to use thugs to muscle them out of their land. Although he used the local connections he forged to obtain land-use conversion permits and permits for his projects, I think that he bypassed land ownership regulations through the way he set up his companies, giving farmers equity shares in the real estate projects he would build on their land in lieu of straightforward land payments. He claimed that farmers also appreciated this approach, although it involved careful cultivation of trust.

The value that Kaushal offered came not from him inserting himself into an existing value chain so much as attempting to create one. Kaushal claimed that his approach was very different from the "big funds" (IStar Financial, Blackstone, Credit Suisse, Deutsche Bank, Lehman Brothers, etc.), which, constrained by bureaucracy, substituted the kind of "on-the-ground" negotiation and network building that he did with "throwing money at projects." He also claimed to be nimble in the face of the quickly changing regulatory environment and the whims of local politics. I told him that—notwithstanding notions of a hierarchy of smartness in which local knowledge features toward the bottom—he was acting just like an Indian developer. He said, "Yes! There's a wall of capital coming once you've taken out the risk. If you take land and make a project, there are thousands willing to invest." The conference where we met in Mumbai was a chance for Kaushal to interest those "thousands willing to invest." He hoped to offer the "big funds" investment-ready projects with land and permits in place and "bring them in on" his deals as secondary sources of funding to amplify the investments he made with his own capital. Kaushal also planned to continue this work in the US, setting up a team of people there to help him drum up capital from individual investors. In this way he served as a central link in a chain of "investment partners" that he was constructing, one that he hoped would stretch from New York to various construction projects on the outskirts of India's largest cities.

The work of moving capital is the work of making chains of intermediaries—from farmer to developer to investor—that can transform Indian land into investable parcels and global assets. In making such chains, Kaushal offered partners the potential of profit. His projects—like so many at the time—were speculative, based on his fantasies about the Indian economy and his belief in his ability to "unlock value" in Indian land. Some—like the Indian developers who told him they would rather develop projects on their own—did not believe in Kaushal's "value proposition." Others, like farmers promised a share of the future development proceeds, did. Either way, there was no guarantee that Kaushal's land agglomeration attempts would prove profitable. His value project, like so many others, was a gamble.

Some gambles proved ruinous, and some chains of intermediaries proved ephemeral. Certainly, Kaushal turned out to be elusive. I met with him three or four times in 2006–7, but then he stopped texting me. We only ever communicated by phone or text, so when his phone stopped working, I couldn't track him down. Internet searches of his name or the company name on the business card he gave me have turned up nothing over the years. Unlike the big-name developers, he did not name projects after himself—indeed, if his strategy was successful, he would profit from remaining in the background, arranging deals for other, bigger players to claim—so I couldn't track him down through his projects. I will never know. Did he get buildings constructed? Did he cash out and move on to some other industry or a comfortable early retirement? Did he lose his money in the financial crisis of 2008 that caused so many foreign investments to sour? Although many of my informants have been difficult to trace over the years as they moved from company to company in a quickly growing industry, there have been several like Kaushal who simply disappeared. They are indicative of an industry constructed from quickly shifting partnerships and alliances, cascades of holding companies registered offshore, and *benami* (anonymous) transactions. Kaushal's disappearance remains an enigma, but one I've come to think of as representative of Indian real estate and international finance.

Note

1. I don't know how inflation figured into his calculations.

6 **JANU** SISTER-SUPERVISOR OF MIGRANT CONSTRUCTION WORKERS

Uday Chandra

IT IS A CHILLY evening in late February. Thirty-odd teenage men and women are awaiting a train on the main platform at the busy Rajkharsawan station in the erstwhile princely state of Seraikela in southeastern Jharkhand. The train, which started in Kolkata more than six hours ago, will take them to Mumbai over a day and a half. From afar, there is nothing to separate this Mumbai-bound group from the rest. But if you come closer, you cannot miss the rotund figure of Janu explaining to the group what will follow.

Janu, whose real name is Sonam Purti, was once like these teenagers (most of whom—like Janu—belong to the Ho tribe) waiting with a mix of eagerness and trepidation to go to Mumbai. Today, she is their *sirdar* (boss) as she directs them to board the train and then sit together inside the compartment. In Mumbai she will also be their *didi* (older sister) as she guides them through the intricacies of life on a construction site. Two decades ago, Janu also worked on a construction site until she had developed enough contacts and courage to chart a new career as a labor recruiter. In this new role she visited their villages, mobilized her contacts accumulated over the years, and explained to potential recruits what livelihood options and wage rates were on offer in a faraway megacity.

The long train journey offers a preview of Janu's relationship with the group. She has food for everyone: *roti* and *sabzi*, and packets of biscuits for later in the journey. Inside the train, she is ready to answer every question that crops up: Where are the toilets? How long until the next station? Is it okay to lie down between the doors of the compartment? There are always first-time travelers, Janu tells me, and she is particularly patient with them. Inevitably, someone asks: What is life in Mumbai like? Or: How did you feel when you went to Mumbai for the first time? Janu has stock answers to these questions. To the first question, she replies: You'll find out for yourself. To the latter question, she says: Just the same as you do. Everyone giggles in response, but this is no inside joke. It is the nervous laughter of those who await unknown pleasures and dangers.

Without Janu, all of the travelers would need to make their own individual arrangements to travel to Mumbai and find work there. There are brave, foolhardy, or desperate souls who accept the risks involved in such an adventure, but they are the exceptions that define the rule. Mumbai is, for them, a city of dreams, and the Hindi and Bhojpuri films made in the city make it seem particularly alluring.[1] But Kolkata, Patna, Delhi, and Hyderabad are nearly as common as destinations to find short stints of work to supplement rural farm and nonfarm incomes back home in the villages. For their part, contractors in the city prefer paying an advance to someone who can vouch for a gang of workers to the daily hassle of rounding up freelance laborers. The latter is much too costly and cumbersome relative to the ease of doing business with a handful of known labor recruiters with deep networks back home. Every recruiter I encountered had worked previously as a construction worker, and even though Janu stood out as a woman in a predominantly men's club, she connected with former acquaintances and bosses in exactly the same way as her male counterparts did. For new migrants in Mumbai, not only is the time and effort spent finding work minimized if one seeks out the help of a *didi* or *dada*, but the likelihood of finding work in the city at all is vastly greater. Janu, in other words, brings together those who need workers and those who seek work. Without someone like her, with extensive knowledge and contacts at both ends of the labor migration process, Mumbai or, for that matter, any metropolis in India would come to a standstill.

Janu has already worked out plans for each member of her group. One of her old contacts in the city, Pyarelal, had connected her with a construction site owned and managed by Tata Housing, part of the renowned Tata family conglomerate, in a suburb located between the Mulund salt pans and the new express highway on the eastern edge of the city. Once built, there will be six towers, labeled A to F, each with at least forty floors of two- and three-bedroom luxury apartments. Each new worker is assigned a role based on gender and prior experience (if any). Sheela and Phulmani, for instance, will learn how to mix cement with sand and water before supplying the mixture to male workers on each floor in each tower at the construction site. Ram Dular and Masihdas, on the other hand, will learn how to build brick walls according to their supervisor's instructions. There are other tasks that will not be available to the group, such as plastering walls or installing marble tiles on the floors of apartments. These are regarded by contractors and workers alike as specialized tasks for those with experience, so newcomers are not expected to undertake them. Most construction workers will not progress to specialize in plastering or tiling because only a small number of such jobs are available at any site and opportunities to up-skill are exceedingly limited.

Janu has a certain invisible, almost spectral, presence on the site. Older, more experienced workers typically take newcomers under their wing and teach them the basics as well as the finer points of the trade. But this is not a randomized process by any means. Not only are there ethno-linguistic boundaries within the workforce, but there are also fictive kinship structures that connect the likes of Janu to different individuals and groups on a construction site. Those whom Janu had brought in earlier feel an obligation toward those who have just arrived. This obligation is often expressed in the idiom of *ehsaan chukaana* (repaying a debt incurred earlier). A few notorious individuals are denounced regularly as *ehsaan-faramosh* (ungrateful) for their failure to repay their past debts. They include the likes of Dimple, who left Janu's group to chart her own career in the city, and Vijay, who was much too inebriated after work to consider his obligations to anyone. New arrivals, in turn, are expected to show the appropriate forms of deference and patience on and off the site. Uppity or arrogant newcomers are swiftly rebuked and shown their place in the pecking order. Many *bhais* and *behens* (brothers and sisters) dot the social landscape of a construction site as well as the adjoining workers' quarters. On-site romances add fresh wrinkles to both kin relations and Janu's management of her wards, but they are much too commonplace to be discouraged altogether. Norms of deference vary by gender, age, and on-site experience, and violations of these norms, however rare, can have serious consequences for individuals. Persistent rudeness or cheekiness, for example, led to ostracism and then dismissal from work in every case I followed. It is not only through speech acts that a familial structure is produced and maintained among gangs of construction workers, but also through the everyday practices of kinship relations that emanate from their common reference point: Janu.

Janu is not present at the site or even in its vicinity at all times. She has her own rented room a safe distance away on the other side of the railway tracks. If someone needs her, they call or send a message to Janu's mobile. Indeed, her basic Nokia phone is almost always ringing or beeping, and any conversation with Janu is invariably punctuated with multiple calls and pauses to check her inbox. She is always at hand to answer any questions or solve any problems. The group that just arrived with her from Rajkharsawan is one of several groups she must tend to. All her *bachhe* (kids), more than one hundred of them at the time of this research, hail from rural districts in Bihar and Jharkhand. They speak variants of Hindi that are mutually intelligible as a lingua franca of sorts. They stick together on each site, often sharing meals, rooms, and cooking, cleaning, and *puja* (ritual worship) responsibilities in an unfamiliar city. When someone needs her, she is available for them as their didi; maternal responsibility toward younger siblings is very much the norm for her at home as it is at work.

Janu visits each construction site on designated days and times during the week. The not-so-infrequent problems with on-site supervisors or security personnel require deft diplomacy and special visits. Someone reporting to work in the morning drunk will not be tolerated, for instance. Misbehavior of this sort typically requires an intervention by Janu, whether by tough talking or by sending a repeat offender back home. Vijay, mentioned earlier for his drunkenness after work, often tested the limits of what was permissible on-site. Reeking of alcohol on some mornings, he had received at least two threats of suspension or dismissal from work, and a third one was certain to end in termination of his employment. Confrontations involving anyone from her group are particularly testing. Site managers and contractors in Mumbai expect the likes of Janu to handle those they bring with them. They will not get involved in unpleasant situations that they cannot handle on their own. In Vijay's case, Janu got involved to ensure that he was not dismissed without warning and, at the same time, rebuked him harshly. In general, she detests such situations for their sheer unpleasantness, but none of the parties involved view her as merely a labor subcontractor. As the most senior member of her fictive kin group, she is expected to resolve disputes speedily and firmly. It is rare but not impossible to witness Janu slap someone accused of stealing money or harassing a female worker. For instance, Phulmani accused two male peers of her cohort of leering at her and then attempting to grab her arm. Janu summoned the two men, who stood silently with their heads down as she scolded them using the choicest abuses. No further action was needed in this case, and Phulmani later told me how grateful she felt to "Janu didi" for her prompt and decisive intervention. Usually, such a familial approach to conflict resolution works out satisfactorily for all concerned. Otherwise, it is Janu's responsibility to send any errant souls back to their villages.

Beyond work and its problems, Janu remains the focal point of the everyday lives of her fictive kin from rural Bihar-Jharkhand. Initially, Janu (or someone she deputes) takes newcomers around to see the sights and sounds of Juhu's Chowpatty beach, the busy by-lanes and bazaars of Dadar, or the imposing mix of Indo-Gothic and Indo-Saracenic buildings in the old colonial city. Soon they learn to take local trains to new destinations, whether alone, as couples, or in small groups, and experience Mumbai's varied cityscapes for themselves. The fictive kinship of the workplace invariably shapes a migrant's journey through the city, but there is much time and scope for an individual to chart his or her own course over even short periods of time. Similarly, when someone falls ill or gets injured, Janu must take care of the matter. On-site doctors are the primary source of medical advice, but occasionally second or even third opinions are necessary, and it is Janu's task to find suitable medical assistance promptly. When a number of her bachhe were down with dengue fever, they recall, it was Janu who paid for their medical expenses and who later submitted receipts to seek compensation from the contractor or manager on a site. On that occasion, she also successfully lobbied housing site officials to take steps to prevent mosquitoes from breeding in pools of stagnant water after monsoon rains. On the rare occasions that someone is unfit to work for a long period of time, they are sent home with an assigned companion on the next available train. In the absence of any state-sanctioned or employer-provided medical insurance for migrant workers, Janu steps forward to become, if needed, the difference between life and death.

Besides the physical well-being of her fictive kin, their spiritual well-being is also Janu's responsibility. To begin with, she appoints someone from her kin group as a surrogate priest. A person with the necessary talents is found and then taken from site to site to perform pujas. For special days in the ritual calendar such as *chhathh puja*, Janu negotiates extra days off work for fasting and worship. Specific individuals at each site are authorized by Janu to act as guides for their kin members. Prearranged meeting points enable different groups to mingle as part of a larger kin group, which is itself a microcosm of the tens of thousands who gather by the seaside on *chhathh*. Pilgrimages to make offerings to, say, Jivdani Mata in the suburban area of Virar demand their own special arrangements. Rarely, if ever, does the burden of travel fall on an individual worshipper, whose ritual practices are visibly public and invariably group affairs. Last but not least, sowing and harvest festivals as well as regional festivals such as Karam and Maghe Parab for Hos require trips back home for specific durations of time. For those from Bihar, Holi or Dussehra are the typical occasions to head home for a week or two. Migrant workers pay for their own travel expenses, but Janu usually helps them book tickets and apply for leave beforehand. As long as Janu is taking care of their ritual needs, her kin need not worry about accumulating *paap* (sin) or failing to stock up on *punya* (merit).

In retrospect, one may wonder how Janu manages to do so much for so many. "I don't know how I do all this," she often wonders aloud, especially as a woman in an overwhelmingly male-dominated line of work. It is a physically demanding role that cannot be fulfilled by even middle-aged (let alone elderly) men (and women), who would struggle to cope. Janu is no different from male *sirdars* in this regard, and she, too, will retire at some point in the not-too-distant future. "Five or six more years," she says, is the most she can imagine continuing in this role. In addition to a large and growing number of contacts at both ends of the migration process and two decades of construction-related experience, the deeply personal role that she plays as didi to her fictive kin creates its own everyday demands. It is not enough to know many contractors in Mumbai; there are, after all, male counterparts who know at least as many, if not more. The key to Janu's success is arguably the multifaceted personal relationship she forges with migrant men and women who have followed her own journey from the distant villages of Bihar and Jharkhand to the metropolis of Mumbai. Indeed, there is a distinctly gendered character to the authority she exercises over her ever-expanding kin in the city. She is certainly a caregiver in ways that male sirdars are not, but she consciously avoids cultivating a maternal persona that might create a generation gap with her migrating kin. As she put it to me once, a didi can care for her younger siblings, but she can also guide them in ways that parents cannot. Janu is, after all, a role model for those she brings with her to Mumbai. As migrant lives are scaffolded in malleable new kin networks that revolve around the big-sisterly figure of Janu, the multiple roles that she plays in these lives respond to different challenges faced by migrants inside and outside work. By fulfilling her varied responsibilities as didi to her kin, Janu is able to command their respect and emerge—in their eyes, at least—as a model migrant in Mumbai. She is also a potential trailblazer, especially for women migrants. It would hardly be surprising if one or more of them follow in her footsteps as a sirdar a couple of decades later.

Note

1. See Kathryn Hardy's profile of Anil Prakash in chapter 26.

PART II PROPERTY

Lisa Björkman

WHILE THE PEOPLE PROFILED in part I are experts in "developing" land and infrastructure in Mumbai, those in part II work at producing and legitimating claims of access to that built fabric, claims that are often characterized in terms of "property."[1] The processes, practices, and resources marshaled in making ("developing") and in claiming land are often indistinguishable: making land is a form of claims making—not only in a Lockean-liberal sense (where the mixing of labor and land is said to create "property," rights to which are protected by positive law) but also in a performative sense that the material-practical work involved in actualizing access to land simultaneously endeavors (sometimes successfully, sometimes less so) to legitimate those same claims. The profiles in part II demonstrate the vast array of claims-making practices and legitimating idioms within which the institutionally and ideologically empowered language of "property right" finds its rightful place as one among many.

In this way, the ethnographies in part II unsettle some of the key categories, canonical formulations, and conceptual distinctions by means of which access to land and space in Mumbai (as in the world more generally) are often explored and explained: binaries such as property and theft, legal and illegal, private and public, formal and informal. It is empirically unten-able, the ethnographies demonstrate, to abstract as formal the conceptually privileged, normatively valorized, institutionally empowered, and legally legitimated idioms and practices that are legible to liberal property rights and then to cordon off as exceptional those idioms and practices that are il-legible to this orthodoxy. Such conceptual efforts to disentangle rules, proce-dures, and institutions from socio-material contexts and everyday practices of claims-making tell us little about how access to land and infrastructures is achieved and legitimated in practice of what rights and rules do or mean in various contexts, and of how and where "stateness" (however conceived) is encountered or conjured. The profiles reveal, for instance, that even when claims seek to enlist a language of "rights," such rights talk often happens in conjunction with—or even subsequently to—other idioms of claims-making, idioms such as "community" (Vevaina), neighborhood "character" (Kundu), "public good" (Vachani), and "eligibility" for compensation in "development"-related displacements or expropriations (Kundu, Banerjee).

In this context, where effective claims are made through myriad comple-mentary and competing idioms and practices, Yaffa Truelove's profile of a "middle-class social worker" who—upon vowing not to do any "illegal work" finds himself without any clear path do to any work at all—is particularly re-vealing and a good place to start. Truelove's profile opens with an account of a former Bombay Municipal Corporation physician named Dr. K, who finds himself facing a moral quandary: after his personal connections prove effec-tive in bringing municipal attention and resources to bear on his housing so-ciety's broken footpath, Dr. K finds himself in demand by his neighbors, who wish him to enlist those same connections in opposing a planned municipal road that is slated to slice through their swish society, eat into their park-ing lot, and deprive the society of their boundary wall. This time, however, when Dr. K approaches his municipal contacts, he learns some unpleasant news: both the parking lot and the boundary wall have been constructed in flagrant violation of the city's development plan. This situation, writes True-love, finds Dr. K "lodged between conflicting moral codes"; his disavowal of any "illegal work" leaves the self-described "social worker" without any clear path of action.

Although Dr. K describes his footpath situation in binary terms ("personal" versus "public" interest, "legal" versus "illegal work"), the predicament is more complex than such dualisms suggest. Contrary to the presumption inher-ent in Dr. K's explanation for his inaction (i.e., that he "does not do illegal work"), Mumbai's development plan doesn't actually have the status of law, meaning that activities falling outside its scope are not "illegal." Yet however not-illegal Dr. K's parking lot and boundary wall may have been, absent an unambiguously procedure-given path forward in resisting the planned road, Dr. K decided not to take any action at all. Truelove's profile concludes with the social worker waiting for a request that is legible to the categories by means of which Dr. K sets his moral compass.

Conceptualizations of claims-making practices via these binary categories (legal/illegal, personal/public) reads any practice not immediately legible to their orthodoxy as "corruption." Indeed, the corruption idea looms large in popular and scholarly discourses about urban development and planning in Mumbai (as elsewhere in India),[2] where multiple and often contradictory regulatory frameworks give rise to a heterogenous terrain of land access and claims-making practice. Illegible to ideological-conceptual tenets, such practices are held to pose an existential threat to the liberal state and to reveal the deep-seated "corruption" at its heart. When Lalit Vachani's profile introduces us to septuagenarian "anticorruption activist" Ashok Ravat, for instance, the latter is "armed" with a well-worn copy of *Commentary on Development Control Regulations for Greater Bombay, 1991.* "If the Mumbai development plan is the holy grail that must be tracked and followed scrupulously," Vachani writes, then "the guidelines provided by the DCR are for Ravat much like the holy book guiding the earnest and devout initiate." Ravat devotes much of his time to policing and protecting the city's open spaces—especially his beloved Shivaji Park—from the creeping intrusions of "shadowy corporations and corrupt corporators," as well as from the "aggressively competing political parties" whose ever-louder, ever-longer political rallies and party-backed religious functions began (especially in the 1990s) to crowd out cricket and to drown out conversation.

Indeed, Ravat reserves a special disdain for politically backed intrusions into public space, particularly those of the religious variety, such as temples and shrines, which, because of their political backing and popular support, are a "favored form of encroachment." Ravat leads Vachani on a tour of some of Shivaji Park's particularly egregious invasions, notably the sprawling Shree Udhyan Ganesh Mandir temple complex, which has steadily expanded its footprint since the 1960s. Because the temple trust has the backing of the city's ruling party, Ravat explains, the temple itself was "authorized and recognized" by the municipal authorities. But notwithstanding this "authorization," Ravat insists that the complex remains "illegal": the land is reserved in the development plan for a "recreation ground." Although Ravat's characterization of the structure as "illegal" is—like Dr. K's description of the footpath—not entirely accurate, it remains the case that the building is situated on state-owned land that the city has designated as open space for general use. Which is to say, in approving the temple's building plans, one department of the Municipal Corporation gave the go-ahead to a project that subverted the authority of another department. The temple itself is thus a contradiction: its construction was simultaneously approved and yet unauthorized; its construction was not illegal, but its existence on that particular plot of land violates Mumbaikars' rights of equal access to a municipal recreation ground.

But whatever its legal status, the Shree Udhyan Ganesh Mandir's evident safety from the bulldozer appears to have little to do with such matters, as comparative evidence from the nearby Kali Mata Mandir demonstrates. Kali Mata is both "unauthorized and illegal," Ravat explains: illegal because of the "recreation ground" reservation in the development plan and unauthorized because—unlike Shree Udhyan Ganesh Mandir—Kali Mata's backers never bothered to submit plans and seek construction permissions from the Municipal Corporation. The Kali Mata temple's legitimacy comes from elsewhere, neither from law nor from official authorization but rather from the fact that the temple is "extremely popular." With "popularity" and political backing of the temple outflanking regimes of rights, development plans, and official authorizations, we see that Ravat's legal activism has little purchase.

The temples dotting Shivaji Park—the power and authority of whose political backers render the structures so impervious to legal action and activism—demonstrate as well how the production and instantiation of authority to claim land is also bound up with the practical work of effecting and actualizing these very sorts of material claims. To be certain, the temples are resilient because of the authority already wielded by the political networks that back them, but at the same time, the profiles in this chapter demonstrate how political power in Mumbai is constituted and consolidated through these very sorts of spectacular, brazen, real-time displays of material authority. The profiles demonstrate a wide range of contexts in which adeptness in mediating the dense fields of power, knowledge, and influence necessary to access land and resources in Mumbai—to have potholed roads repaired (Truelove), garbage removed (Vachani), water pipes pressurized (Truelove), buildings built and destroyed (Banerji), police raids averted and invited (Kundu), and subsidized inner-city housing made available (Vevaina)—works to instantiate the very sociopolitical relations and networks upon which the effectiveness of such authority ultimately hinges.

In Sangeeta Banerji's profile, for instance, we meet Shazia, resident "social worker" and party-affiliated *karyakarta* of the "unauthorized neighborhood" of Bhim Nagar. Shazia's expertise is in the procuring of documents—things like survey slips, for instance, that would provide residents both a measure of protection from the bulldozer and proof of eligibility for compensatory alternative accommodation in the event of a demolition. We also learn that Shazia is a building contractor and a landlord, the owner of some half-dozen Bhim Nagar structures that she rents out. We meet Shazia in Bhim Nagar, in the hours before a demolition, and we see her frenzied efforts to mobilize her sociopolitical contacts and connections to avert the impending destruction. Shazia's efforts prove futile; the strength of her political connections are outflanked by those of a higher-ranking politician determined to demonstrate—by means of this demolition—his superior strength to make (or unmake) effective claims to land.

Banerji's profile of Shazia shows us that the production of Bhim Nagar's built fabric is bound up with the production of the political authority of the very people who are later responsible for bringing destruction upon that same fabric. The neighborhood's elected representatives, Banerji tells us, had initially supported (and protected) Bhim Nagar's booming construction industry; it was by means of this increasing housing stock that Bhim Nagar's voter rolls also grew. The evidenced ability of politically affiliated area "contractors"[3] to produce and protect this newly built space—and to issue documentary proofs of address to new residents—earns the confidence of the area's growing number of voters. But when opposition-party contractors like Shazia—a North Indian Muslim in an area politically represented by the Marathi-nativist Shiv Sena party—begin to steal market share, a tussle over shrinking profits ensues between the two high-ranking Shiv Sena politicians, the most senior of whom brings the bulldozers to the neighborhood.

The spectacular three-day destruction spree wrought by the senior politician (a member of Parliament [MP]), Banjerji explains, seeks to signify— through real-time performance—the MP's capacity to supersede the power of his co-partisan junior (a member of the State Legislative Assembly [MLA]) to protect structures built by the latter's cadre of contractors. In so doing, the MP's destructive display of force worked to carve a path (quite literally) for his own "loyal cadre" to enter the Bhim Nagar construction industry: to build and sell homes, and then to provide residential address proofs (and of course voter registration cards) for families taking up residence in the growing neighborhood. The destruction of the neighborhood was thus an act of political theater, one in which not only the police, the municipal bulldozers, and the officers of the district collector were made to play their parts but also one in which the built fabric itself was enlisted in this spectacular display of the capacity to act, and to act decisively. The MP's demolition not only demonstrated (quite viscerally) his own authority but simultaneously demonstrated his capacity to override others' efforts to perform their own authority by saving the neighborhood from destruction. This sort of political spectacle works by actualizing and materializing the organizers' capacity to mobilize and move various offices and officers of the state. Indeed, while this particular instance of political theater involved the municipal bulldozers, riot-ready police, and clipboard-wielding officers, the spectacle of destruction indexes the MP's ability to mobilize the offices of the state more generally, a demonstration in real time of his practicable expertise.

But echoing a theme that runs throughout this book, we see as well that the meanings that onlookers (and unwitting participants) attribute to such performances are unstable, open to multiple interpretations and normative evaluations. The careful spreading of rumors ensures that Bhim Nagar residents are well aware of whose power is on display during the days of destruction (the MP's power to destroy, the MLA's powerlessness to protect), yet this does not result in a clear consolidation of the Shiv Sena MP's authority in Bhim Nagar. On the contrary, we see how—in conjunction with a senior opposition party leader, a former MLA affiliated with the National Congress Party (NCP) who would go on to seek reelection—Shazia and her opposition-party higher-ups take advantage of the internal Shiv Sena tussle, as well as the anti-migrant, anti-Muslim exclusionary discourse in which the destruction was sought to be legitimated. Shazia is herself a North Indian migrant (and a Muslim), and her reputation for wielding networks powerful enough to build houses and (usually) to keep them standing allows her to gather an impressive crowd of a thousand Bhim Nagar residents, who accompany the opposition-party politician to the office of the district collector.

Although the NCP rally that Shazia helps was one among a number of such events that took place in the aftermath of the Bhim Nagar demolition, it was not clear to anyone present why the neighborhood had been suddenly demolished nor what might compel the collector to convince residents to rebuild and stay put. Such matters were the subject of much speculation, and political leaders set to work trying craft a compelling narrative according to which they themselves could claim credit. Thus we see how following the NCP meeting with the collector, the opposition-party politician announces that he had personally negotiated an agreement whereby

Bhim Nagar's newly dis-housed would be considered proactively eligible for resettlement housing as "project-affected persons" in conjunction with an upcoming infrastructure project, a project already poised to take over much of the state-owned land on which Bhim Nagar is situated and that would thereby displace its current residents. In the weeks following the demolition, we see Shazia and other opposition-party karyakartas hard at work (in conjunction with the former MLA's explicitly pro-migrant pronouncements) assembling documentary "proof of eligibility" for inclusion in the upcoming metro project and compiling a list of the eligible Bhim Nagar residents to present to the collector. All of which is to say that although the Shiv Sena MP brought the bulldozers to the neighborhood in a theatrical display of his personal capacity to either provide or deny access to land (and to supersede the power of both his co-partisan MLA and the opposition-party-affiliated builders and social workers such as Shazia), it is Shazia who steals the show.

Like Dr. K, Shazia describes herself as a "social worker," and also like Dr. K, much of her work consists of producing and processing documentary proofs of identity and address.[4] For both the elite and the slum-dwelling "social worker," the disjunctures between official rules governing "residence proof" and the actual ways in which people inhabit the city are bridged through the forging and leveraging of sociopolitical relations with offices and officers of the state. However, popular discourse in Mumbai would characterize the nearly identical work of these two people in contrasting terms: *Shazia lives in an unauthorized neighborhood, so her work involves liaising with politicians in order to break laws and make illegal claims to urban land and resources; Dr. K is a law-abiding elite professional who lives in a legally, planned, high-end residential compound, so his work involves liaising with state officers so that they will follow laws and not engage in corrupt activities fueled by cash payments from people like Shazia.* Yet the ethnographies of Shazia and Dr. K do not map onto this notion—in other words, that Shazia's work is to break the law while Dr. K's work is to enforce it. Rather, we see in the profiles how things like laws, policies, and regulations are not (only/necessarily) a point of departure but rather/also an outcome of these sorts of interventions. This point recalls my own essay in part I, in which we saw Dalpat the "manager of services" work together with city engineers to provide municipal water access for residents of unauthorized upper floors of a new high-end construction in Mumbai—water connections made on somewhat euphemistic "humanitarian grounds." Although the existence of these upper-floor residences in the elite residential complex is—much like Shazia's Bhim Nagar homes—"unauthorized" by the municipal offices, Dalpat's resources and resourcefulness render residents' claims to municipal water legible to law and policy.[5] Similarly, in Shazia's profile we see how the demolition of "unauthorized" structures in Bhim Nagar resulted in the production of a new policy framework whereby the dis-housed could be rendered eligible for compensation as "project-affected persons." Shazia's work—much like Dalpat's hydraulic mediations on behalf of residents in high-end residences like Dr. K's—is to articulate these access claims into regimes of law and policy, to render their lives and claims legible to empowered discourses and institutional frameworks.

Notwithstanding the striking similarities in the content of Shazia and Dr. K's practical expertise, we see that Dr. K takes pains to distance his (avocational) "social work" from what he describes as the "cash-fueled" "corruption" of those who—like Shazia—take fees in exchange for offers of help: "Social work is the work you can do without any self-interest or money," Dr. K insists.

Although Dr. K maintains that it is the fee that distinguishes public-spirited "social work" from "self-interested" profiteering of "paid agents" (or "*dalals*"), this tidy distinction also collapses under ethnographic inquiry. We see how just like Shazia, Dr. K depends for his work on his connections to high-ranking officials and politicians: in seeking to have a potholed road repaired, he rings up a powerful elected official who might provide a quick fix. That is, rather than put in a regular request to the Municipal Corporation to fix the road—a request to which overburdened maintenance engineers might take months to respond—Dr. K instead enlists personal connections to a politician to "speed up" the process by using discretionary funds. Dr. K achieves rapid responses to his requests for infrastructural repair work by means of the authority (and implicit threat) inhering in a call from a high-ranking politician.

Politicians are responsive to Dr. K, Truelove explains, because of long-standing relations of exchange and transaction. In one instance, Dr. K "barters" an arrangement whereby a politician uses the various resources at his command—persuasion, money, moral authority, threat of force—to bring resources to a popular neighborhood, in exchange for which the neighborhood renames itself after the politician. Dr. K's relations of mutual benefit with politicians, in other words, allow him to have his personal requests for work float to the top of the general pile, but without having to offer the cash gifts of "speed money" like the "paid agents" from whom he is so keen to distance himself. For both Shazia and Dr. K, in other words, work is accomplished by leveraging relations of exchange that encourage the differentiation of individual requests from the general pile. The difference is that Shazia's services are available to whomever will pay. Dr. K, by contrast, who deals in "barter" rather than in banknotes, might offer his services for free, but his services are available only to people with whom he is already personally acquainted. The varied forms of "capital" by means of which each social worker engages the state and the municipal bureaucracy thus call attention to how class and education figure within a broader range of powers and urban resources.

Ratoola Kundu's profile of yet another self-described "social worker," named Nirmala, echoes the insight from Banerji's profile of Shazia that although cash might be helpful or necessary in facilitating various kinds of work, this does not mean that such work is reducible to money. Kundu's profile begins with a behind-gated-doors conversation with a group of commercial sex workers in Mumbai's infamous red-light district of Kamathipura. The meeting had been arranged by Nirmala, whose long-standing relationships with these women were forged over the decades that Nirmala had spent as a "health worker" in Kamathipura—providing medicines and arranging doctor visits for sex workers, as well as procuring the identity documents that such visits require. Nirmala's work hinges upon the "trust" she has cultivated over the years. This trust is more necessary than ever these days, Kundu explains, because of the creeping assertiveness of a moralizing "middle-class sensibility" that "dreams of 'cleaning up' Mumbai," alongside an increasingly powerful "developer" lobby that has its sights set on Kamathipura. There are many, it seems, who are eager to evict Nirmala's clients from their places of work and residence, and to make the land available for high-end "development."

Notwithstanding this "trust," Kundu notes that Nirmala paid the madam in cash for allowing Kundu and her assistant to conduct the interviews. As Kundu explains, in Nirmala's world, social trust is not the opposite of cash payment (as Truelove's Dr. K and Banerji's NGO worker Anjuman Bhai would have it) but rather its complement and even precondition. Without "relationship," as Nirmala calls it, there would be no way to pass the cash, and the interviews wouldn't have been possible at all.

Recent transformations in the sociopolitical and institutional environments that have rendered the homes and livelihoods of Kamathipura's resident sex workers ever more precarious have rendered Nirmala's reserve of social trust valuable not only to her clients but also to those who would like to see them evicted. Although Kundu's profile opens with a skeptical Nirmala scoffing at the prim proprieties of a college-going Kamathipura resident dreaming of the day when a "redevelopment scheme" might rebuild Kamathipura "as a block of tidy new apartments and shops," by the end of the profile we see that Nirmala is ecumenical in her visions for Kamathipura's future. On the one hand, she insists that redevelopment would not only wreck livelihoods and displace longtime residents but that such efforts to "sanitize" the area of sex work would also cleanse Kamathipura of the very character that renders it such a vibrant and valuable location in the first place. Yet only two years later, Kundu finds Nirmala in the office of an area developer who has sought the social worker's help in gaining the "community support" necessary to "demolish and rebuild" Kamathipura with high-end shops and residential towers. Notably, Kundu expresses little surprise that Nirmala helps the developer with his project; it is Nirmala's ability to nimbly navigate "contradictory commitments," Kundu explains, that comprises the social worker's expertise. Capitalizing on the "trust" that Nirmala wields, the developer is able to bypass recalcitrant landlords and negotiate with the tenants directly. For the developer this means greater profits, while for the women it means a larger share of the spoils: brand-new flats in a brand-new tower. And for Nirmala, the social worker whose livelihood depends upon both parties believing she is on their side? A commission most likely . . . but one modest enough to ensure that, when it's all said and done, her reservoir of trust remains intact.

The contradictory position that Nirmala so deftly inhabits regarding the proposed redevelopment project in Kamathipura is echoed in Leilah Vevaina's portrait of Farhad, a legal activist and self-described "troublemaker." Farhad is a member of Mumbai's Parsi (Indian Zoroastrian) community, which is among the wealthiest in Mumbai, not least in terms of their extensive landholdings. Parsi assets in Mumbai are managed by the Bombay Parsi Punchayet (BPP), of which Farhad is a "general member." While the official mandate of the BPP is to manage these assets for the benefit of all "beneficiaries"—that is, all Parsis—recent years have seen much dispute over who is to be considered "Parsi" as well as over precisely what "benefits" ought to be made accessible to which "beneficiaries." In this context of debate and disagreement among Parsis over access and distribution of community resources, Farhad has made a habit of taking the BPP to court.

When we meet Farhad, he is shaking hands affably with a group of elderly, low-income Parsi women. The women are residents of BPP-owned "widow *chawls*" that count among the more than three thousand "heavily subsidized" trust-owned flats. The women are completely dependent on the BPP's charitable programs, and their pitiable appearance speaks to the motivation behind Farhad's efforts to help. "Our community is so rich," he tells Vevaina, "but so many—especially the aged—are left behind." Although

Farhad is not a lawyer by profession, Vevaina (herself Parsi) points out that the Parsis are a famously litigious bunch, and Farhad's relatively elite background and education afford him enough "legal-ease" to be able to enlist the courts in various efforts to extract resources from the BPP on behalf of low-income Parsis. But these efforts at intra-community redistribution of assets hinge upon not challenging this elite community's claim to such a wildly disproportionate share of land in Mumbai, where 60 percent of the population resides on 6 percent of the land.

Using the courts is not a particularly new strategy among Parsis seeking "to secure their minority rights," but there are two ways in which the suits filed by our self-described "sue maker" in contemporary Mumbai differ from those of historical Parsi "nuisance makers": first, Farhad enlists the courts not to make claims against the state (colonial or otherwise) but against his own community elites. The second difference concerns the effect of these claims, which, "much like the growing strength of the shareholder within the shareholder revolution," work to shore up "the strength of the trust beneficiary." Farhad's work—like that of all the characters profiled in part II—thus inhabits a contradiction: the idiom of community is enlisted in making particularistic (even individual) claims against that same community, revealing a "community" shot through with internal conflicts and disagreements about its own identity and boundaries. Making legal claims against the BPP works to both produce and reaffirm the existence of the "Parsi community" as a whole, while simultaneously empowering the claims made in the idiom of the individual "beneficiary." Part II ends here, with Farhad, and with the contradictions and uneasy mediations among parts and wholes, individuals and communities.

Notes

1. The author wishes to acknowledge (without implicating) Srimati Basu's contributions to this introduction.

2. See the discussion in this book's introductory chapter.

3. See also Tobais Baitch's profile of Imran in chapter 2.

4. Dr. K reports that "at least 80 percent" of his voluntarism involves the processing of identity documents and residence proofs for his middle-class friends and neighbors (personal correspondence).

5. While both types of structures are "unauthorized," Bhim Nagar's structures face the additional challenge that the owners of the structures (Shazia, for instance) are not the owners of the land; the state is. But in Mumbai, this situation is hardly unique to low-income, so-called slum neighborhoods, as the profile of Ashok Ravat demonstrates.

7 DR. K MIDDLE-CLASS SOCIAL WORKER

Yaffa Truelove

ON AN ORDINARY DAY of his retirement, Dr. K sits near the guard station of the housing society where he lives, a gated set of thirteen high-rise buildings in Mumbai's western suburbs. A former high-ranking health officer of the Bombay Municipal Corporation (BMC), he spends his free time waiting to perform what he describes as "everyday social work." When a neighbor approaches him one afternoon to complain about unsafe potholes in the nearby municipal footpath, it is just the sort of work that he eagerly anticipates. The footpath in question had fallen into disrepair and was proving to be a danger to the society's residents, who took frequent spills in potholes while walking home. Opening his black book, which contained the numbers of key politicians and political authorities, Dr. K jumped into action. He called the local ward officer at the BMC, whom he knew well from his prior job. In fact, Dr. K himself was one of the officials who had signed off on one of the ward officer's earlier promotions. His connection with the officer produced quick payoffs, as she arranged for the potholes in question to be filled with tar in a matter of days.

Dr. K's quick success with the footpath elevated his reputation in the housing society for "social work." Following the pothole victory, Dr. K's neighbors requested his help in opposing the construction of a planned public road that was slated to cut through the compound. The building of the road would require the demolition of the society's parking lot, as well as the adjacent wall and walking area outside their residences. Many of the society's residents were staunchly opposed to the planned road, citing concerns of security (removing the wall and building the road would allow "anyone to enter the area") and of convenience (the road would take up some of the space currently used for parking residents' vehicles). However, when Dr. K approached the BMC with the society's concerns, he was left with an unpleasant discovery and, even worse, a moral dilemma: the residential parking lot and an adjacent wall were in violation of the city's most recent (1991) development plan. Rather than a parking and walking path, the development plan envisioned an open road cutting through the housing society. While Dr. K personally identified with his fellow neighbors' concerns, persuading officials to violate urban plans and codes fell outside the moral boundaries of what he considered "social work." While recognizing that the city's design for the area "is a nuisance to us," he ultimately conceded that the road "is in the plan, and it is convenient to the [greater] public." Lodged between conflicting moral codes and with no easy work-around, Dr. K took the rare decision to abstain from action. He advocated neither for residents of the society nor for the planned road. Rather, Dr. K justified his inaction, articulating one of the core principles and guiding tenets of his everyday social work, simply stating that "I don't do illegal work." He returned to his seat at the guard station, waiting for the next social work "case" to come his way.

The Materials and Networks of the Middle-Class Social Worker

In the top drawer of a wooden cupboard in his flat, Dr. K keeps some of the most important yet seemingly mundane tools of the trade: his stationery, with his name and credentials as a retired BMC health officer embossed in blue; his business cards, which also indicate his voluntary position with the Mumbai Police as a "special executive officer"; his stamp and ink pad, which allow this information to be quickly and uniformly communicated on any bureaucratic paperwork that he processes. These objects work to encourage action and "cooperation" from various actors in the city positioned to respond to this or that request, including state bureaucrats, local politicians, municipal engineers, and the police. Bringing together these ecologies of people and objects, Dr. K is able to facilitate some of the vital requirements of city life: obtaining things like identity cards (*Aadhar* [biometric identity] cards, ration cards, voter registration identification) as well as resolving municipal matters such as the removal of rubbish, the fixing of broken water pipes, or certifying life and death.

However, the most effective of tool of all, by Dr. K's reckoning, and deployed through all of his different social work activities, is his name. Dr. K enjoys wide recognition among key political actors in Mumbai, including local members of the Legislative Assembly (MLAs), high-ranking municipal bureaucrats, and officers of the Indian Administrative Service (IAS). His strongest and most responsive connections are with the Bombay Municipal Corporation, where he worked for twenty-five years until retiring more than fifteen years ago. Dr. K's work in the BMC extended far beyond narrow matters of "health governance" to include a wide range of activities, not only at the municipal level but also at a regional and even occasionally national level: he has been involved in deciding locations for Mumbai cemeteries and maternity wards, in administering the 1991 and 2001 household censuses, in deciding on promotions of BMC officers, and even in collaborating with the World Health Organization and Doctors Without Borders on nationwide polio-eradication initiatives. Even fifteen years after his retirement, Dr. K tells me matter-of-factly that "everyone [in the BMC] knows Dr. K."

Dr. K's bureaucratic responsibilities during his years at the BMC put him in direct contact with some of Mumbai's most famous (and sometimes infamous) personalities: there was the day he met the film star Amitabh Bachchan while administering the 2001 census in Bachchan's Juhu bungalow (a photo of which Dr. K proudly shares with visitors). He worked closely on another occasion with Uddhav Thackeray (leader of the Mumbai-based Shiv Sena party) and Uttar Pradesh Governor Ram Naik on new regulations regarding birth certificates. Dr. K also has long-standing relationships with some of Mumbai's most powerful real estate developers, including the directors of K. Raheja Constructions, whom he met while conducting health inspections for some of the developer's restaurants. Subsequently, Raheja agents asked Dr. K to make personal introductions to various BMC engineers needed for gaining approvals. This relationship, Dr. K explains, enabled him to also ask his own favors of the developer in return: a few months later, he approached Raheja with a request that the company provide construction jobs to young men from the nearby *jhopadpatti*. Dr. K had become acquainted with these young men during his daily walks through the neighborhood adjacent to his house, and they had repeatedly asked Dr. K if he could connect them to employment opportunities. When Raheja's agents reached out to Dr. K for municipal introductions, Dr. K wasted little time in cashing in the favor.

Despite his political connections, Dr. K insists that he does not form party alliances. For instance, while he worked closely with Shiv Sena leaders during his tenure at the BMC, he is quick to point out that he has taken decisions that have also gone directly against Shiv Sena directives. For example, during his tenure at the BMC he endorsed the placement of a *dargah* (Muslim shrine) on land that the Shiv Sena had sought to use for a Hindu cremation ground. Dr. K's decision went directly against the wishes of the elected Shiv Sena municipal councillor. Indeed, while frustrating the councillor's aspirations, the decision ultimately worked inadvertently to strengthen Dr. K's connections to the current elected MLA (known locally as the "bhai of Malad")[1] of his own constituency. The MLA—who belonged to a different party—turned out to be the son of the man who had petitioned for the dargah in the first place. Such fortuitous and often unpredictable connections, which often reveal themselves only over time, are what Dr. K relies on to move papers, officials, bureaucracies, and police: the things that are necessary to accomplish "social work."

Defining Everyday Social Work

Dr. K tells me that he's a direct descendant of Bombay's "early freedom fighters" and that for this reason, "social work is in my blood." I ask him what he means by the term *social work*, and he explains: "Social work is the work you can do without any self-interest or money." Social work, he adds, is "work for the community." Brought up in a one-room flat in the South Bombay neighborhood of Colaba, Dr. K says he learned how to conduct political dealings by following his older brother's example. His brother ran a medical clinic in Colaba, where as a young man Dr. K would spend hours observing his brother's practice. It was in this clinic that he learned about the everyday problems of Colaba's poorer residents who came to his brother for treatments and simultaneously complained of broader public health issues in the neighborhood, particularly lack of access to potable water. Dr. K noticed his brother becoming increasingly involved with politics in order to address patients' public health concerns, eventually negotiating a "barter" of sorts between the water-scarce jhopadpatti and the local MLA: the politician would see to improvements in their water services in exchange for which area residents would rename their neighborhood with the MLA's moniker, as the "Geeta Patkar Colony" (now called Geeta Nagar). "I learned from my brother how to tackle [negotiate with] all these people," Dr. K recalls, referring to the tricks of the trade needed for persuading politicians and other key political authorities in the city.

Dr. K draws a firm distinction between *his* everyday social work and the activities of those whom he calls "paid agents": people who work "more formally." "Paid agents," Dr. K explains, are people who (unlike him) take a fee for helping residents with time-consuming tasks such as attaining government identity cards (such as PAN [permanent account number] or Aadhar cards) or assembling documents necessary for life in the city. Some "paid agents" work out of small neighborhood shops while others simply stand outside government offices offering help in pushing paperwork. It is the fee and accompanying "bribes," Dr. K explains, that distinguishes him from those others who are devoted to "profits above helping the community." Indeed, taking or giving money in the form of bribes is described by Dr. K as the "opposite of social work," a distinction echoed by a number of Dr. K's neighbors with whom I spoke. The moral economy within which Dr. K and other members of his middle-class housing society characterize "social work" is counterposed directly with what they describe as the cash-fueled "corruption" exchanges within which "formal agents" ply their trade.

Dr. K maintains a distance from those agents who pocket or use money for their work and instead relies on mutual relations of exchange—for instance, with official political figures. His high-level connections at the BMC enable him to bypass dealing not only with "formal agents" but also with political party workers and *karyakarta*s, whose low-level political positions and informal connections might otherwise be useful in accomplishing social work, but whose practices include what he considers more morally questionable acts such as taking or giving money. However, even government higher-up officials can have their unsavory sides, and Dr. K has to tread carefully. Within his matrices of exchange, if Dr. K comes to know that one of his key contacts is engaged in criminal activity—for example, is facing accusations of violence or rampant corruption—he proceeds with caution, either avoiding the person altogether or else weighing what is being offered (for example, jobs for the poor young men or the granting of ration cards) against the "hazard" of dealing with political figures who might eventually (and perhaps violently) retaliate.

Undergirding each of Dr. K's social work interventions is a carefully cultivated ability to sift through the complex, overlapping layers of state agencies (at the municipal, state, and central levels) to identify which agency and tactic will best serve the day's work. Rather than seeing the state as either a singular entity or a finely calibrated hierarchy, he instead identifies particular actors, practices, and spaces of political malleability at differing levels needed to orchestrate particular effects. This deftness often produces a quick solution to what are mundane, yet seemingly intractable, everyday problems of predominantly middle-class residents. In addressing his society's infrastructural complaints—for instance, a long-standing, deep pothole in the road that had been injurious to cars and people alike—Dr. K contacted the "bhai of Malad," the earlier-mentioned MLA. On this occasion, Dr. K's municipal contacts had not been available during his in-person visit. By turning to the MLA as a next step, Dr. K calculated that this politician's discretionary budget (which can be put to use to directly fund infrastructural fixes) and ability to pressure the BMC through differing channels would provide the quickest fix. In such cases, Dr. K's first line of action is to turn to his black book of numbers, dial the MLA directly, and pay an in-person visit (usually the same day). The end effect is not only a solution but also a "speeding up" of the work of the state itself, getting rapid responses by routing his request through a high-ranking politician instead of offering "speed money" like the "paid agents" from whom Dr. K distances himself. In this case the MLA called his own contacts at the BMC, and days later a team was sent to fix the road. At the same time, Dr. K deployed a different tactic when faced with the challenge of arranging for the removal of a long-standing rubbish pile from a construction site near his own daughter's flat in the suburb of Kandivali. In that instance, Dr. K determined that an immediate meeting with the BMC ward officer—during which he mentioned his personal relationship to the BMC commissioner—would be the most effective. By the following afternoon, the garbage pile troubling his daughter had vanished.

Alongside these two strategies—calling a politician to intervene or making a personal visit to the municipality—Dr. K sometimes uses his own stamp. For instance, when friends or neighbors are thwarted in efforts to confirm their identity or local address (required for everything from Aadhar and voter registration cards to passports and pension payments), Dr. K's stationery and stamp can do the trick. For example, when a new resident named Mr. Cheda from Delhi moved into the housing society, Dr. K's name and stamp were instrumental in resolving Cheda's problems with getting an Aadhar card. Dr. K recounts that without this mandatory ID, Cheda was struggling to accomplish basic tasks as a new transplant to the city, such as opening a bank account. When Cheda applied for the Aadhar card on his own, he did not have a lease or bill in his name for providing a "proof of address." This was the case because Cheda was living in his son's flat and thus had no lease, deed of ownership, or bill that linked his own name to the residence. Instead, Cheda improvised and asked a retired judge to write a letter on his behalf that attested to his residency in the society, hoping that this judge's credentials would persuade the municipality to grant his address verification. When the judge's letter was torn up by a municipal officer at the P-Ward office (having fallen outside the parameters of the Aadhar accepted document list) and the entire application subsequently rejected, Cheda turned to Dr. K for help. In this case, Dr. K simply handwrote a note on his stationery (with his stamp and credentials) confirming the identity and address of Cheda, attesting to his firsthand knowledge of the "citizen in question." As Dr. K's name was known at the P-Ward office (by both the municipal commissioner and other office workers) where the application was submitted, this letter did the trick. To Cheda's great relief, the application was quickly accepted and the card shortly arrived at his new home.

For residents of the nearby jhopadpattis, who occasionally approach him with requests for help for help getting Aadhar, election, or ration cards, Dr. K also readily assists with such handwritten letters. Dr. K lends his physical presence only in particular state offices and in more complex scenarios, he explains—cases in which dropping the name of a high-ranking figure is needed in order to provide critical leverage ("Of course I am happy to talk to the municipal commissioner, whom I used to work closely with") and generally in instances when other strategies have failed.

Dr. K's social work requires delicate maneuvering between state institutions (such as the BMC and the offices of MLAs) and wider nets of middle-class society. However, this maneuvering sometimes lands him in ethical dilemmas. Perhaps his most difficult judgment calls are less about whom to contact, and through what techniques to get work done, but rather whether residents' own wants and desires stack up against what the city and state should ethically and morally offer its inhabitants. Whereas election cards and pension checks fall into a code of straightforward entitlements of citizenship, many requests—footpath repair, boundary walls, parking spaces, and other built forms that have a more complicated relationship with the city's myriad (and often contradictory) urban laws—pose moral hazards for Dr. K. Faced with these difficult cases, Dr. K sometimes chooses to remain in his seat at the entrance to the housing society, abstaining from what could be considered lawbreaking and morally compromising action, and waiting eagerly for his next case to find him.

Note

1. *Bhai* is a colloquial expression that means both "brother" and "don."

8 **ASHOK RAVAT** SHIVAJI PARK'S SENTINEL

Lalit Vachani

"OH, you must talk to Ashok Ravat—he's the man who saved Shivaji Park."

I had just begun a visual ethnography called *Maidan Histories and Stealth-scapes*[1] that looked at the daily use and the transformations over time of an exemplary public space: Shivaji Park in the Dadar area of Bombay.

I approached Shivaji Park as a site where different groups (Hindu nationalist political parties and their rivals, cricket and football clubs, advanced locality managements (ALMs)/resident welfare associations and citizens groups, to describe a few) coalesced and clashed over competing definitions of the ideal *maidan* and, ultimately, of the ideal city and citizen. I saw Shivaji Park as a microcosm of urban social relations in the city of Mumbai, where the intersections of business, politics, religion, recreation, and sport have shaped the expanding city and its shrinking public spaces.

I was particularly interested in the history of maidan use at Shivaji Park. Famously known as the crucible of Indian cricket, Shivaji Park was also central to the growth of regional political parties and in giving primacy and pride of place to the *marathi manoos*. The Maharashtra Samjukta movement used the spaces of Shivaji Park as its launching pad, and the vast expanses of the maidan were central to the mobilization practices

FIGURE 8.1 Ravat talks to other members of the WECOM Trust. Used courtesy of Lalit Vachani, photographer.

and the politics of the Shiv Sena in the late sixties and onward. Shiv Sena supremo *Bal Thackeray* was cremated there amid much fanfare, and today at the very center of the maidan is a memorial that marks his political legacy.

In the 1980s and 1990s the park became a battleground between aggressively competing political parties wanting to use the site not merely as a recreational space for sport and leisure-time socialization for the Mumbai citizenry, but rather for political rallies. In 2008 this conflict reached crisis proportions, and residential life in Shivaji Park became particularly hellish, with well more than a hundred days dedicated to round-the-clock political and religious functions involving the use of loudspeakers at the expense of sports and other recreational activities.

This is when Ashok Ravat intervened on behalf of the residents of Shivaji Park. Using the newly introduced noise-pollution regulatory guidelines, Ravat's Walkers Ecology Movement Trust (WECOM), along with the Awaaz Foundation, filed a joint public interest litigation (PIL) appealing for the Shivaji Park Maidan to be declared a "silence zone."

In its interim order, the Bombay High Court ruled in favor of the plaintiffs—the NGOs—and against the defendants—the BMC and the police—in finding that Shivaji Park should be declared a "silence zone." It decreed that all public events at the maidan should be limited to four days each year, along with strict monitoring of loudspeakers for noise decibel levels.

The court decision was hailed as a huge victory for the nascent open-spaces movement by environmental and middle-class residential welfare groups. It also made Ravat quite famous as a Right to Information Act (RTI) expert and anticorruption crusader fighting to bring an errant bureaucracy in line by using legitimate tactics of legal redress.

When I do meet Ashok Ravat, he is armed with a humongous tome with yellowing, dog-eared pages that he occasionally leafs through to syncopate our conversation: *Commentary on Development Control Regulations for Greater Bombay, 1991* (DCR). If the Mumbai development plan is the holy grail that must be tracked and followed scrupulously, the guidelines provided by the DCR are for Ravat much like the holy book guiding the earnest and devout initiate.

Ravat, who is seventy-seven, comes from a family of real estate developers and took to the family business as a teenager. As an insider, he witnessed the transformations in the industry post-Emergency as builders began to manipulate the rules, bribe politicians and bureaucrats, encroach on land, and develop illegal projects. Disillusioned, Ravat gave up on the family business and turned to full-time activism. He has headed several voluntary organizations related to environmental protection and consumer and civic rights: Mumbai Grahak Panchayat (Mumbai Consumers Council), All India Bank Depositors Association, Citizens Forum Block G/North Ward, and the Shivaji Park ALM.

Over the course of his professional career, Ravat has become an expert in matters pertaining to property management and taxation, and he has diversified his interests to include RTI activism and legal interventions in the form of the PIL to safeguard open public spaces in the city. When he's not keeping constant vigil over his beloved Shivaji Park, he works toward reclaiming and greening other parks and gardens in South and Central Mumbai. He also works with the Moneylife Foundation, giving lectures and master classes on how to file RTI applications and on property tax management.

Ravat takes me on a quick tour of Shivaji Park and its neighboring RG, PG, P&G.[2] He warms up to his favorite subject of research and environmental activism: the modes of "encroachment" on Mumbai's parks and maidans by shadowy corporations and corrupt corporators working in cahoots with the BMC.

Ravat is particularly incensed at the appropriation of open, public space in Shivaji Park by religious interests and temple trusts that have the backing of powerful political lobbies.

FIGURE 8.2 "The Sentinel of Shivaji Park." Used courtesy of Lalit Vachani, photographer.

At the Kali Mata Mandir, which he calls an instance of an "unauthorized and illegal" construction on a recreation ground, Ravat points out that no construction plan was ever submitted to the BMC. The Bengali priest there confirms a haphazard process of growth with different deities being installed by different individuals over the years, all with the blessings of Kali Mata. The temple is extremely popular with the Bengali community in Bombay and unlikely to face any threat of demolition.

Shree Udhyan Ganesh Mandir occupies a huge tract of land in Shivaji Park. Its origins as a temple also follow what one might describe as the Ram Janambhoomi mode of encroachment, as it is reminiscent of the placement and sudden appearance of the Ram Lalla idols at the site of the Babri Masjid in 1949. As Ravat told me, "In the sixties a small idol of Ganesh mysteriously appeared under a *peepul* tree. It began its amoeba-like growth and soon developed into a concrete structure. With the backing of political parties, this temple complex was eventually authorized and recognized by the Municipal Corporation." Ravat points out that the structure might have been authorized but is still illegal because it has been sanctioned on a recreation ground, which is not permissible.

When I next visited the temple, it had been demolished in order to build a much larger complex. According to Ravat, this renovation was completely illegal as well: the plans for expansion had not been sanctioned or approved by the BMC. Over subsequent visits I filmed the building of sections of the grand temple with subtle and incremental concrete protrusions extending into the Shivaji Park maidan, much to Ravat's chagrin.

Building a religious shrine in order to capture public space appears to be the most favored form of encroachment. In a PIL filed by Bhagvanji Raiyani's NGO, Janhit Manch, more than eight hundred small temples were found to have been constructed illegally on footpaths in Mumbai. The high court ordered the demolition of these temples, which was duly carried out by the BMC. At least 50 percent of these temples then reappeared, having been illegally reconstructed at the same spot a year later.

Desai Maidan in the Mahim neighborhood of Mumbai is an instance of encroachment and appropriation of a playground by changing the contours of its land use. The playground was being used temporarily by the BMC as a dumping ground for garbage. Ravat and his colleagues from Citizens Forum Block G North Ward filed an RTI application and discovered that a builders' group had earmarked this land for an SRA (Slum Rehabilitation Authority) scheme that they hoped to develop soon. The builders' lobby had also paid the slum dwellers and had promised them housing elsewhere. But they were unable to begin construction on this SRA scheme because of an injunction filed by CitiSpace[3] that prevented any construction activity on public open space.

I visit several other parks, gardens, and maidans with Ravat and his friend Nagesh Kini. At Datta Mandir Maidan, Ravat shows me how an elected representative's fund (in this case, a corporator or municipal councillors' fund) is used to build a gym and how this is then used to create private interest in a public playground.[4]

Ravat and Kini are particularly pleased about the reclamation and the rescue of the Dhote Udyan garden in Mahim "from the clutches of drug peddlers who ruled the park in the 1990s." The garden is now a heritage site with a sunroom, a children's corner, and a yoga area replete with very strict rules about what you can eat or drink, when you can visit, and how walkers must comport themselves, with particularly strict adherence to one-way walking.

As architect and urban planner Prasad Shetty told me, "You can tell how 'public' a public space is by the number of do's and don'ts in the rules and regulations that determine entry to the park, and by telltale signs such as fencing, the presence of a guard, etc." Shetty pointed out that the semiprivatization of the Oval Maidan in South Mumbai created a precursor template for the systemic control of several other parks and gardens in the city.

Our meetings begin to have a pattern. On each of my trips to Bombay, I make my pilgrimage to Shivaji Park and begin by meeting Ravat. On each occasion, we have a conversation and a brief update on video. We then drive in his car and revisit the same parks and gardens, where I film and try to capture the incremental and stealthy encroachments on open public space, all under the watchful eye and the eager supervision of Ravat. In the process I learn from him the nuanced ways in which land-use regulations are manipulated by stealth to acquire land for building and sale as I add to my visual archive about transformations in urban public space.

For whom does Ashok Ravat mediate, and whom does he represent? To my mind, he represents a swath of interests ranging from the small-building resident to the ALM volunteer, the open-spaces-movement activist to the outraged RTI petitioner seeking redress through the legal grid of the public interest litigation. Ravat recognizes that the PIL is expensive, cumbersome, and slow and that it can be used only occasionally for larger issues. But he also believes that even the potential and possibility of its implementation are useful in keeping rampant encroachment and construction in check.

Ashok Ravat and the Open-Spaces "Movement"

Over the course of my many visits to Mumbai, I meet several of Ravat's friends and colleagues who provide voluntary service to their local ALM[5] and are active within the self-styled open-spaces "movement" that seeks to reclaim parks and gardens in a belated attempt to green Mumbai.

Unlike Ravat, with his single-minded focus on using the DCR rule book in curbing the powers and the reach of corporations, politicos, and local-level bureaucrats in their incremental aggrandizement of public space, a number of these individuals tend to target "other bodies" and individuals that they deem unfit for passage and perambulation in their narrow conception of what constitutes an ideal public space.[6]

Whereas Gaurav spoke to me about the drug pushers, the alcoholics, and the necking couples frequenting the park and the terrible influence this might have on his children, Madhukar was intent on exposing "the menace of prostitute couples." As he tells me, "Normal couples are bad, but prostitute couples are the worst—you can make out the prostitute couple by looking in their eyes."

Tasneem spends her time placing potted plants at strategic points on her street. Although the ostensible aim is to green and beautify the neighborhood, Tasneem says the real reason is so that hawkers may not encroach on public space, a process that RTI activist Krishnaraj Rao referred to as "reverse encroachment": "If I don't encroach, someone else will. So I better be the first to do so."

Tasneem is quite oblivious to the capture of public space by her very own potted plants as a form of encroachment. Her pet peeve is the *pav bhaji* seller who sets up shop every morning at the end of her street, and she is determined to have him thrown out.[7] I do not have the heart to tell her that this is unlikely to happen when I discover that this vendor has been around Shivaji Park for much, much longer than she has and that he enjoys the patronage of the Maharashtra Navnirman Sena (MNS) and Shiv Sena politicians who live around the block and who gratefully devour his superb food every weekend.

But the most venomous form of "othering" and upper-class prejudice is on display on December 5 and 6, which are two of the four official days when political and public events are permissible at Shivaji Park. On *Mahaparinirvan Diwas*—the death anniversary of Babasaheb *Ambedkar*—hundreds of thousands of *Dalits* congregate to the Chaityabhoomi in Dadar to pay homage to their beloved leader. In the process they must pass through and meet at Shivaji Park, and, in effect, they take over the maidan.

Each year provides a cycle of routine predictability: the setting up of food stalls and free food delivery by Dalit philanthropic organizations and political parties;[8] a lack of garbage-disposal infrastructure and waste mismanagement by the BMC, resulting in the littering of the streets with food by Dalit consumers; the ritualized venting of upper-caste bile at the "stench and the filthy streets" and, by extensional logic, the "uncivilized and unclean bodies"[9] that dare to inhabit an upper-middle-class residential public space and the performative reproduction of bourgeois revanchist rhetoric. Finally, redemption and praise for the BMC as *their* Dalit sanitation workers clean up after the event and render the Shivaji Park streets spick-and-span less than twenty-four hours after the "invasion."

Over the course of these few days in early December, most of the residents of Shivaji Park take the opportunity to leave their homes to escape what they describe as a Dalit "infestation." Many of those who remain behind claim to do so only because they fear that burglaries and robberies will take place in their homes in absentia.

But Ashok Ravat demurs. He always makes it a point to stay behind and has a completely different take on the crowds that throng Shivaji Park on December 6. As I film him walking past the jostling, friendly, excitable milling crowds joyously chanting *Jai Bhim*, I discover that there is a bit of the resident ethnographer in Ravat as he shows me the reinvented tradition of

FIGURE 8.3 Ashok Ravat at the beach *pooja* on Mahaparinirvan Diwas (December 6). Used courtesy of Lalit Vachani, photographer.

the simple, individualized Dalit *puja* (ritual worship) of incense sticks, flowers, and *diyas* (oil lamps) that takes place on the beach.

As Ravat asks admiringly, "Isn't it amazing that 600,000 people come here over these two days? Look at them waiting their turn, standing in line. Look at their discipline. And there is never a single incident of theft or a single crime that is reported. And look at the crowds, the sheer numbers who have come to pay homage to Ambedkar. Can any other dead leader in India be so beloved by his followers?"

Notes

1. My thanks to Peter van der Veer and the Max Planck Institute for the Study of Religious and Ethnic Diversity, and to Dagmar Coester-Waltjen and the Lichtenberg-Kolleg at the University of Göttingen, for their support.

2. A favorite acronym with Bombay's open-space activists, architects, and builders, it refers to "recreational grounds, playgrounds, parks, and gardens."

3. CitiSpace (Citizens Forum for the Protection of Public Spaces) is the umbrella organization that provides logistical and legal support to ALMs in their quest for reclaiming public open space.

4. This is an instance of what one might call "legal encroachment" or the "follow one regulation so as to flout another regulation" maneuver that underpins the stealthy takeover of open public space.

5. Mumbai citizen partnerships with civic bodies such as the Municipal Corporation of Greater Mumbai (BMC), these ALMs are neighborhood voluntary organizations entrusted with solid-waste management, sanitation, and environmental protection, and are similar in function, orientation, and scope to the RWAS (residents welfare associations) that are active in Delhi and other Indian cities.

6. Amita Baviskar's concept of *bourgeois environmentalism* perfectly captures the inherent violence in this drive to control and privatize public space (Amita Baviskar, *Uncivil City: Ecology, Equity and the Commons in Delhi* [New Delhi: SAGE Publications Pvt. Limited, 2019], III).

7. CitiSpace began its campaign politics for a cleaner Mumbai with its drive to evict hawkers. For a fascinating account of the CitiSpace crusade against Bombay hawkers, see Jonathan Anjaria, *The Slow Boil: Street Food, Rights and Public Space in Mumbai* (Stanford, CA: Stanford University Press, 2016).

8. The fact that every single political party (including the Hindu nationalist ones) feels compelled to pay obeisance to Ambedkar on December 6 is evidenced by gargantuan billboards that dominate the landscape of the Dadar area. This does not preclude the passing of casteist remarks and racist abuse against Dalits by the well-to-do residents of Shivaji Park.

9. See the Chaityabhoomi/Shivaji Park sequence in Anand Patwardhan's *Jai Bhim Comrade* for an exposé and indictment of upper-class prejudice against Dalits (Anand Patwardhan, *Jai Bhim Comrade* [India: Film South Asia, 2011], 199 min., English, Hindi, Marathi).

9 **SHAZIA** PROOF MAKER

Sangeeta Banerji

I MET SHAZIA for the first time in Bhim Nagar, just as the District Collector's bulldozers were about to arrive. The whole settlement was abuzz with rumors; primary among them was that about fifteen hundred households were to be demolished that day. Although the people of Bhim Nagar were more than familiar with the anxiety of the process of demolition, having been subject to it six times now, the atmosphere today seemed very Kafkaesque. No one knew how, when, and why the notice of demolition had been delivered to this settlement. On all other occasions, the people of Bhim Nagar had been allowed to stay put and eventually rebuild. That day, however, no one could tell us why, but the threat of complete displacement loomed large. In the midst of this situation, many people were trying to mobilize resources: making phone calls to officers, trying to coax information out of the patrolling policemen by offering them tea, or making incessant calls to the elected officials. Shazia's endeavor that day seemed to somehow stand out, highlighted by the fact that she was the only woman doing so. She spoke fast, so fast, and with an unmatched energy that almost prevented me from keeping up with the inquiries that she made of the officials. Swiftly yet steadily, she made her way to the end of the settlement and started reassuring the residents of those tenements that even if the bulldozers did destroy their homes that day, she would make sure that they had some shelter, a plot of land where they could lay their belongings. This is when I was told that she was the local social worker or *karyakarta* of the Nationalist Congress Party in Bhim Nagar.

This was the first time I met Shazia; my introduction into this community was through Anjuman Bhai, one of the conveners at the M-Power[1] project in the Tata Institute of Social Sciences. Anjuman Bhai had started a small community space where the children of Bhim Nagar could come to receive tutoring for the various subjects taught in Bombay Municipal Corporation (BMC) schools. Along with this work of bringing education opportunities to his community, as one of the first residents of this precarious settlement he is actively working toward bringing piped water to Bhim Nagar as a part of the Pani Haq Samiti.[2] He is perhaps one of the kindest people that I have encountered in Mumbai, always caring for the people who surround him. He was the one who made a frantic call to me that morning, informing me of the impending doom that was to befall Bhim Nagar. Powerlessly, he, like all others, was forced to stand by and watch as the demolition machines arrived. In this atmosphere of despair, I saw these very different personalities: the humble Anjuman Bhai and the boisterous Shazia discussing strategies about what needed to be done to avoid the demolition. I heard Shazia reassuring Anjuman Bhai, saying, "Aap ghabraiye mat, ham kuch upaay zaroor nikalenge" (Don't worry; we will find a way). She was referring here to her political connections, which she believed could be mobilized in some way to avoid the demolition that day. However, as soon as she left, Anjuman Bhai skeptically commented to me, "Aa gaye dalal dekho"[3] (Look, the *dalals* have come). Why, I wondered, was Anjuman Bhai so disdainful about someone who—like him—was trying to help avert this demolition?

The patrolling policemen arrived first, clearing the path for the bigger vehicles. Then came three large police trucks full of cops, both male and female, dressed in their riot gear. Close on their tails were three SUVs carrying officials with clipboards. No one from any media outlet came to report on the plight of these people that day, but there were cameramen employed by the office of the collector to record the proceedings of the demolition as evidence of action. As the officials and the camera crew set up, three bulldozers and a truck full of demolition workers arrived, giving the impression that perhaps the entire settlement was slated for demolition rather than, as was more common, just a few errant or token structures.

The rumored reason for the demolition—recounted to me in similar terms by both Anjuman Bhai and Shazia—was that there had been a quarrel

FIGURE 9.1 Bhim Nagar after the demolition. Used courtesy of Sangeeta Banerji, photographer.

between state-level and central-level elected representatives (the member of the Legislative Assembly [MLA] and the member of Parliament [MP]), within each of whose districts Bhim Nagar fell. The two politicians were both members of the Shiv Sena party, but this had not stopped the MP from filing an official complaint against the MLA citing the rapid rate at which "encroachments" were growing in Bhim Nagar, which stretched along the wall of the adjacent National Armament Depot. The rumor held that the MLA—who was currently campaigning for reelection in the upcoming 2019 state assembly elections—had "lost control of his dalals," people who (like Shazia) had been busily extending the borders of this precarious neighborhood both vertically and horizontally. The "dalals" were responsible not only for the creation of a new and affordable housing stock, Anjuman Bhai explained, but also for the consolidation of votes. The process is one in which caution and discretion must be maintained: palms must be greased, threats neutralized, intimidation tactics deployed against those who would otherwise seek to intimidate—those who might, for instance, complain to the authorities about "unauthorized construction" and thereby bring destruction upon the neighborhood.

In the aftermath of the demolition, trying to make sense of what had happened, I prodded Anjuman Bhai to explain why he had referred to Shazia using the disparaging word *dalal*. In response, he told me a bit of history. Shazia had initially started out also as a karyakarta, he explained, helping people gain access to documents—election cards, permanent account number (PAN) cards, Aadhar (biometric identity) cards, and ration cards—in exchange for a small fee. Then, as her political and bureaucratic connections grew, Shazia began dealing also in "slum survey slips": crucial pieces of "documentation" that were particularly hard to come by in Bhim Nagar because the most recent slum survey was conducted in the year 2000, which is before most of Bhim Nagar even existed. But having documentary proof of enumeration within this survey (i.e., the *survey slip*) is key to warding off demolition in unauthorized settlements such as Bhim Nagar. Anjuman Bhai claimed that the slips that Shazia was providing were all *farzi* (fake): most of Bhim Nagar was built after 2010 and could not possibly have been there during the slum survey. Residents who were working hard to solidify their claims in this settlement bought into this false promise of stability that Shazia was providing at a high price: 25K–30K rupees. With the profits from her fake survey slip business, Shazia had begun investing in Bhim Nagar's real estate market, building housing stock and renting out homes to newcomers to whom she also provided farzi documents. It was this brazen entrepreneurialism of local karyakartas like Shazia that was thus held to be responsible for the bulldozers that rolled through Bhim Nagar that day. Shazia was trying to rescue people from the bulldozers not because she *cared* about people, Anjuman Bhai explained, but rather because those people were her tenants; the houses slated for demolition were her investments. It was this combination of profiteering and flimsy promises of protection from the bulldozer inhering in the fake documents that sat at the root of Anjuman Bhai's disdain for Shazia, prompting him to refer to her not as a karyakarta or social worker (words he uses to describe himself) but rather as a dalal.

I recalled that during the demolition, Shazia had been frantically urging people to get their documents out: "Banvaya toh tha, dikha do sahib ko ki ham yehaan 2000 ke pehle se rehne wale hai" (I know you have documents saying that you have been living here since before 2000; show them to the officer!). She knew that they had documents because she had helped make them. But while most of the residents held documents like those provided by Shazia, these had proven useless in the face of the wrath of the MP.

Nearly a third of Bhim Nagar was razed to the ground in a demolition exercise that lasted three days. Only at the end of the third day, when the bulldozers had crushed approximately seven hundred homes—rendering at least four thousand people without shelter—did the MLA show up. Addressing a gathering of those dis-housed, he assured Bhim Nagar residents that the bulldozers would not return the next day and explained that he had not come to the rescue sooner because he was "punishing those who in their greed had forgotten common decency." Muslims and North Indian migrants, he explained, had "invaded" land that rightfully belonged to *Marathi Manoos*. "Common decency?" Anjuman Bhai explained that behind this anti-migrant diatribe was the fact that Shiv Sena–affiliated karyakartas had been losing out in the business of neighborhood construction to those affiliated with other parties—people like Shazia. Outflanked by builder-karyakartas affiliated with the other parties, cash-strapped Shiv Sena karyakartas had sought to reduce their construction costs by cutting out of the profit-sharing circuit the offices of the party higher-ups. The lack of "common decency" about which the MLA raged was simply the "common decency" to share profits with those in power—that is, with the MLA and the MP. In retaliation against the MLA's disloyal karyakartas, the MP had begun to cultivate a new cadre of builders in Bhim Nagar; the demolition spree was part of an effort (the story went) to open a path for this new, loyal crop of karykartas to enter the construction sector. The MLA's speech that day— and his tirade against "North Indians and Muslims"—was part of an effort to shore up his flagging reputation by claiming *credit* for the demolition, thereby reassuring both his karyakartas and area residents, who would of course be voting in the upcoming assembly election, of his own power and authority.

Although Shazia of course knew the subtext of the MLA's tirade against Muslims and North Indian migrants, it hit close to home in any event. Like many of the people who lost their homes during the demolition, she is both Muslim and North Indian, the fourth child among nine siblings. Her father had provided a meager income to their family by driving bullock carts. At the young of age of fourteen, her marriage was arranged to a boy from a neighboring village. Painfully remembering her lost childhood, she tells me that "my mother-in-law used to make me do all the household work and was abusive on multiple fronts." Frustrated by these living conditions and by the general absence of any livelihood in their village, she and her husband moved to Mumbai when Shazia was eighteen, taking up residence on a pavement in Wadala. This is where she had her first child and started a family. This is also where she had her first run-in with the complex workings of the bureaucracy in Mumbai. She had been assigned a temporary ration card that she wanted to make permanent, so—on the introduction of a neighbor—she had approached someone whom she'd been told might help with this work. But this man, Shazia recalled, demanded an exorbitant sum in exchange for access to essential state services—a sum that, needless to say, she could not afford. It was at this point, Shazia recalled, that she vowed to learn for herself how to work within this opaque bureaucracy, not only for her own benefit but in order to help others.

Shazia's career as a karyakarta began with the devastating floods of July 2006, during which she lost her home. By then, Shazia had been pregnant six times and had borne two children. Through yet another neighbor, her family took up residence near Bhim Nagar, where she first came into contact with the National Congress Party (NCP). She soon met the local MLA, Nawab Bhai, while he was visiting the area after a particularly dramatic bout of rain. Nawab Bhai had come to reassure the residents that he would work toward providing security of tenure and improving infrastructural services in Bhim Nagar and the adjoining areas.

It was at this time that Shazia decided to put her primary school education to good use by doing regular rounds of local bureaucratic offices to help people from her locality apply for various documents. From her small home, she started a business of helping people gain access to documents, bringing legibility to people. She told me that her success in this business was dependent on her ability to be patient and to be respectful toward the officers in charge. But familiarity with the official process is less than half the job, she explained. It was also important to have the right contacts: "Nawab Bhai ke naam ke saath, yeh pata hona ki kab aur kiske pass jaane se kaam ho jayega hamare line mein bahut zaroori hain." [Alongside being able to drop Nawab Bhai's name, knowing who and when to go to get the job done is the key to this work.] She told me that she had some guidance from people within the party, yet most of her skill was acquired from hands-on experience. She is also one of the karyakartas, I learned, who has a reputation for *not* duping people once she has taken an advance payment for a job—a reputation that has been reaffirmed by many people as exceptional among those described disdainfully as "these dalals."

Over the week following the demolition, I had the opportunity to see Shazia in action. Within days of the demolition, she gathered a thousand people—all dressed in NCP flags and hats—to accompany a high-ranking politician (the area's former MLA, Nawab Bhai) to the collector's office to lay claim to their land.[4] Shazia explained the situation in Bhim Nagar to the officers while other residents and I waited and listened for the politician to negotiate with the collector on behalf of those who had been rendered homeless. With the help of a thousand-person-strong crowd, the politician extracted a promise from the officer that the displaced would be allowed to stay on the plots where their homes had stood until some form of resettlement plan was decided upon. The officer explained that the demolition had been carried out as a part of a "routine action of encroachment removal." The settlement could stay for the time being, but the officer explained that it would have to be removed in conjunction with an upcoming Metro (transport) project—displacement by which, needless to say, would render all residents eligible for resettlement housing as "project-affected persons." This information came as a great relief and gave hope to the people.

Over the following weeks, on the instructions of Nawab Bhai, Shazia and her "*chelas*" (helpers), as she called them, took up the task of assembling the documentary proof of eligibility for resettlement under the Metro project to present to the collector. The former MLA insisted that all of Bhim Nagar—Muslims, North Indians, Marathis, Bengalis, Tamilians—would be equally eligible for resettlement. According to Shazia, this promise of inclusivity would provide Nawab Bhai an edge over the incumbent Shiv Sena MLA in the upcoming assembly election.

It was in conjunction with this promise that I had the opportunity to watch Shazia do her work. Dozens of people gathered—documents in hand—around Shazia, who scrutinized their papers before adding their names to a list of households that had lost their homes in the recent demolition but were eligible to resettled as part of the upcoming Metro project. Intrigued by the array of documents on display that day, I asked those gathered how they had managed to actually procure these documents in the absence of any clear legal standing according to any current slum policy in Mumbai. One of the residents in line told me that he had procured his documents through Shazia: "I don't know how I would have been able to get any of the documents without her help. When we go to any government officer, they take one look at us and turn us away or keep making us run around in circles."

I was puzzled to see Shazia asking a hundred-rupee fee (around $2) from each resident accounted for on her list, something that had not been mentioned in any of the meetings with party leaders that I'd attended. "These dalals do this," Anjuman Bhai had quipped. Later, when I asked Shazia about the payments, she explained that of course these things cost money . . . but her work is not reducible simply to money. Officers will not do work for just any stranger with a few hundred rupees! Rather, she explains, the relationships and social networks that she has forged over her many years working as a karyakarta make her work possible: "You really have to know who to approach in these offices," adding that "whenever I am unable to get something done, I directly call the party office, and they sort out things. And of course," she shrugs, "Gandhij is always helpful."[5]

When Shazia showed me the list of eligible families, I noticed the names of many members of her own family: her brother-in-law, her sister-in-law, a cousin, and herself. I recalled Anjuman Bhai's words from the day of the demolition, that Shazia didn't care about people, only about the houses that she owned. Indeed, Shazia was the owner of at least five houses that had been demolished. But that day, as she sat sifting through and gathering documents to help people gain security of tenure, it seemed that Anjuman Bhai's assessment hinged on a false distinction between caring for herself and caring for others; rather, Shazia's "interest" and that of her neighbors were inextricably intertwined.

Notes

1. Policy advocacy project at the Tata Institute of Social Sciences.
2. Pani Haq Samiti is a neighborhood coalition working toward getting piped water supplies to their communities.
3. See the introduction and glossary for discussion of the term *dalal*.
4. See Sarthak Bagchi's profile on Mishra in chapter 27.
5. As Mahatma Gandhi's image appears on Indian rupee notes, "Gandhiji" here refers to cash.

10 **NIRMALA** KAMATHIPURA'S GATEKEEPER

Ratoola Kundu

IT WAS A HOT summer afternoon in 2015. My research assistant, Shivani, and I were waiting by a tailor shop in a congested alleyway lined with video parlors, motorbike repair shops, and ramshackle workshops that spilled onto a road lined by crumbling buildings plastered with B-grade film posters. Nearby, a few women milled about, standing, sitting, and occasionally exchanging a few words with the passing men. The women were dressed conspicuously, and their faces were heavily made up; they were looking for clients. Soon it would be evening, and the streets would become busier and more raucous. The apparent ease that these women displayed distinguished them from the others who hurried past, often with children in tow, gazes averted. Several passersby cast curious glances in our direction. An unspoken code seemed to hang in the air, one into which Shivani and I didn't fit. We shrank back as a half-clothed drunken man ambled past us, vomited into the open drain, and passed out in the street. The tailor, perhaps sensing our discomfort, mercifully offered his rickety bench and two cups of tea.

As he went about fixing a fancy *zari* (lace) border onto a blouse, he narrated the history of Kamathipura, one of the largest red-light districts in Asia. We prodded him on, mentioning that we were university researchers

interested in the socio-spatial transformation of Kamathipura.[1] A few of
the women from the street corner—perhaps out of curiosity, perhaps out of
boredom—joined us. An older-looking woman chimed in: "Woh zamaana
alaag tha" [Times have changed]. In earlier days, she recalled that rich and
poor patrons alike would "pour their money on the girls," and the *attar* (per-
fume) shops and tailor shops would flourish. Cars would line up in front
of the well-established *kothas* (brothels). The eateries, *daaru* (liquor) stores,
and tea shops would remain open all night. The kothas would be filled with
the sound of *mujras*: music and dancing. The cinema and theater halls were
always full. Today, Kamathipura's shine has worn off. The rich clients have
long deserted the neighborhood; the buildings have become dilapidated.
The traditional kothas have closed. Factories have replaced brothels.

Through the crowds, a woman—slightly out of breath—appeared. It was
Nirmala, dressed as always in a staid *salwar kameez* and a crisply starched *dupatta*, her large *bindi* and blood-red *sindoor* firmly in place on her forehead.
It was a carefully cultivated look that set her apart from the women on the
streets, an armor protecting her from the gaze of the men who frequented
the area. Before she could reach us, a woman from the opposite street corner
accosted her. We faintly caught the words: "behen . . . hawaladar . . . dhanda
kharab . . . dawa" (sister . . . police . . . business destroyed . . . medicine). A
few minutes later, after calming the distraught woman and pausing to speak
to others in the group, Nirmala finally reached our spot. She greeted us with
affectionate hugs and promptly ushered us out of our little refuge.

We had met Nirmala quite by chance a few months earlier, at a research
workshop organized by the Mumbai NGO Partners for Urban Knowledge,
Action and Research (PUKAR).[2] One of the groups presenting research comprised young, middle-class, college-educated, paraprofessional women from
Kamathipura. They had chosen to study the ways in which the negative social perceptions of Kamathipura left lasting impacts upon its residents. The
group claimed that although commercial sex work was restricted to only
a "few lanes" within the neighborhood, the stigma clung to Kamathipura
as a whole, affecting long-term residents who had nothing to do with sex
work. They said, "Kabhi kisi ka shaadi rukh jaaati hain, ya toh naukri mil-
naa mushkil ho jaati hain" [Getting married or getting a job was difficult for
residents once they revealed their address]. Real estate developers insisted
that no one would willingly buy an apartment in a red-light district.[3] This
group clearly wanted to dissociate themselves—socially and spatially—from the
people, places, and practices that they believed gave their neighborhood an im-
moral character. During the presentation I had noticed a woman standing in

FIGURE 10.1 Bar dancers in the balconies. Used courtesy of Ratoola Kundu, photographer.

the corner. Her demeanor suggested some ambivalence about the presentation. When we approached her, she introduced herself as Nirmala, a "health worker" who had worked in Kamathipura for close to two decades; she was eager to talk. Nirmala strongly believed that the brothels were central to Kamathipura's very identity and history. Developer-driven efforts to "sanitize" the neighborhood would displace the sex workers and strip them of their livelihoods.

Thus began the friendship and collaboration that had brought us to Kamathipura that sweltering afternoon. Nirmala pointed to what at first glance looked to be shuttered, decrepit, and uninhabited buildings. These, she explained, would come to life at night as brothels. We walked through a lane where on one side there were *chawl*-type structures, many of which looked to be used as warehouses for construction material. On the other side were four-story buildings in various stages of disrepair. Several young women were hanging around on the tiny balconies of these buildings. These were the quarters of the "underground"[4] bar dancers. It became very clear that Nirmala had developed a unique relationship with the neighborhood and was acutely tuned in to its tacit rhythms, flows, and spaces. As we wove our way through the busy lanes, Nirmala displayed her intimate knowledge of the neighborhood. Now and then, women would greet her warmly, either by her name or as "*didi*" (elder sister). Local policemen addressed her respectfully as

"Nirmala ji." She pointed to an innocuous-looking, middle-aged fruit seller with a cart of semi-rotting bananas, casually mentioning that he was one of many men in the neighborhood who "kept watch" over the girls—some of whom had been forced or trafficked into prostitution—so that they could not escape.

On Thirteenth Lane, in front of an extremely dilapidated three-story building housing a small shoe factory on the ground floor, Nirmala exchanged a few words with a swarthy-looking man of indeterminate age, wearing a torn vest and a *lungi* (sarong). He led us up a steep staircase, past rooms where men were stitching *chappals* (slippers). On the second floor, he unlocked a heavily padlocked and grilled door, leading us into a small dark room with shuttered windows. I could barely make out the shabby furniture, a tattered carpet, and frayed, heavy curtains in the dim light. The door inside the room opened, and six heavily made-up women entered. They were brothel-based commercial sex workers, some of the few who remained in Kamathipura today. On Nirmala's request, they had "agreed" to talk to us about their lives and about the ways in which their livelihoods had been affected by the changes in the neighborhood. This was a minor feat, given the layers of secrecy and surveillance through which the brothel owners and sex workers operated.

Nirmala introduced us and then left the room with one of the women, presumably the "madam." However, the man made no effort to leave. The other women responded with varying degrees of eagerness and wariness. At first we stuck to the scripted questions that Nirmala had insisted upon. Two of them were Bengali, and (because I know Bengali) I struck up a side conversation with them. Although they remained taciturn about details of their profession, they were more open to talking about the intense poverty that had driven them to this work. They scoffed at the idea that Kamathipura might turn into an upscale neighborhood, yet they agreed that most of the brothels had been hit hard by the AIDS epidemic. They also mentioned that the constant influx of migrant sex workers who operated on the street corners for much less money was cutting into their *dhanda* (business). Our questions met with uncomfortable silence only when we wanted to know about the landlord or about the intensity of police raids on brothels in the last few years. Clearly, some things were not to be discussed. One of the other women got up and went to call the leader, perhaps sensing that we had deviated from the script.

On the way out, Nirmala handed a hundred-rupee note to the man. Maintaining this "relationship" with the "gatekeeper" was one of the many ways that Nirmala maintained her access to the women working and living in these extremely guarded environments. Nirmala explained that he likely played a number of complex roles: watchman, cleaner, bouncer, pimp, go-between for the ladies and the landlord. The madam exercised control over the everyday working of the brothel and managed the clients; liaised with the police and the landlord; and ensured that the sex workers were fed, clothed, and received medical aid. She was simultaneously "protecting" and ruthlessly extracting her pound of flesh. Nirmala had also paid her in cash for accommodating our unconventional request of "interviewing" the sex workers. Although access to the women and their stories clearly commanded a price, money alone would not have gained us access. It was clear that our meeting had been facilitated by Nirmala—that it was *her* relationship with these women that led them to speak with us.

"Yeh ladies log mujhe bohut trust karate hain" [These ladies trust me a lot], said Nirmala. Indeed, in a locality where trust appears to be in ever short supply, trust was an important if ephemeral resource, and Nirmala's networks within the community were sought after by many. Trust is of primary importance in organized sex work, given that the law is ambiguous and several powerful stakeholders are engaged in various facets of the trade. The police are complicit in the everyday goings-on of the brothels, as are landlords, local politicians, residents, and so on, all operating on a certain level of "trust." However, this is at best an extremely tenuous arrangement. Deep-seated suspicion oscillates against trust (forged through years of working together). Dependence upon social workers for access to medicine and identity documents may quickly turn sour, given that commercial sex work takes place on the fringes of legality.

Although Nirmala wasn't a resident of Kamathipura (she lives in a small, one-bedroom house in the far-flung northern suburbs of Kandivili with her two teenage children and unemployed husband), her affectionate demeanor and her purported connections to various NGOs and local charity organizations seemed to grant her an insider's privileged status in an extremely complex and hostile environment. Nirmala claims, as a Nepali woman herself, that she was moved by the plight of the women in Kamathipura and drawn to the work of Asha Mahila Sanstha: a nonprofit providing health care access to sex workers and headed by a former sex worker of Nepali origin. Nirmala's identity enabled her to break into the closely guarded circles and garner the trust of the many Nepali migrant and trafficked sex workers. But at the same time, her very embeddedness has exposed her to dangers. On several occasions she has been mistaken to be a sex worker by the predatory police and the pimps. In those situations she has had to vociferously claim and prove that she is a "social worker" and a woman of "good repute" in order to escape them.

As a health worker in the early nineties, she had been instructed to "befriend" female sex workers. Her initial efforts had met with skepticism, indifference, and even outright refusal. But the AIDS epidemic took a heavy toll on the sex workers, and the ensuing socio-material reconfiguration of Kamathipura's brothels was contingent upon a number of conditions. The number of sex workers in Kamathipura dwindled drastically. The landlords, clients, and residents turned against them. This emboldened the women to seek help, building new networks of trust and exchange, particularly with NGOs. This made it easier for Nirmala to bypass the multiple barriers encircling access to sex workers. The empathy shown by Nirmala toward them, and her ability to help them with accessing medicines and negotiating with the police when everyone else seemed to be withdrawing, opened up a window for her to become embedded in this emergent landscape.

In the present conditions, Nirmala's range of networks and services has grown manifold, given the ever-increasing threats to commercial sex workers. In addition to pressures from private developers is the growing assertion of middle-class sensibility and "morality" that dreams of "cleaning up" Mumbai, ridding its central districts of "pollutants" and remaking itself as a "world-class" city. This volatile mix has meant ever-more-frequent police crackdowns on brothels, increases in *hafta* payments, rising real estate costs, and a shrinking customer base. In this context, Nirmala's established networks amount to a repository of trust, and she is constantly called upon to find ways to mediate and mitigate the contradictions, dangers, and opacities that pervade Kamathipura's sex industry.

Nirmala reveals that with the socio-spatial environment constantly in flux, her relations must constantly be renegotiated and renewed. She struggles to maintain her trust networks and demonstrate her legitimacy, never taking these for granted. She has been labeled a *khabri*—a police informant—in some of the brothels she has had access to, which squarely places the blame on *her* when the police conduct raids to rescue underage girls. Nirmala's former NGO colleague had accused her of *setting kaarna* [having cut a deal] with the police to make quick money on the side by informing them of the whereabouts of trafficked victims. She tells us all this with obvious anguish: "Mujhe in ladkiyon ki pet me laath maar ke ghotala nahin karna" [I do not want to snatch away their livelihoods by earning through dishonest means]. Yet Nirmala expresses ambivalence about her work, describing her disillusionment with the government's HIV/AIDS interventions and her increasing involvement with "prevention of trafficking." These different commitments index the contradictory moral-ethical and practical situation that Nirmala constantly performs and inhabits, highlighting her Janus-faced relationship to the idea of commercial sex work itself.

Nirmala has been renegotiating her position in the neighborhood through the multiple connections and positions she has cultivated with emerging NGOs. She proudly displays the awards and honorary certificates that she has received from various "charity" and "human rights" organizations (many acting as fronts for political parties). But NGO affiliation can be a double-edged sword. Nirmala described with much disgust how she found out that a local *karyakarta* linked to one of the charity organizations she worked for leveraged her name in order to collect rations from grocery stores, keeping for himself foodstuffs that were earmarked for destitute sex workers and their dependent children. Indignant, Nirmala told me, "Mereko zarurat nahin kisi NGO ka, mein khud yeh kaam kar sakti hu!" [I don't need help from any NGO; I can do my own work!]

IN 2017, a year after we had finished writing up our research report, Nirmala rang me up out of the blue (and sounding rather urgent), inviting us to meet her in Kamathipura. We were a bit confused because she gave the address of a local, small-time real estate developer's office in the heart of the middle-class residential quarters of the Andhra community! Shivani and I had earlier interviewed the developer for our research on Kamathipura's stalled redevelopment projects. He had called on Nirmala in his effort to garner "community support" to demolish and rebuild a large section of the neighborhood, which would be reborn as a block of tidy new apartments and shops. The new development was to be renamed "Balajinagar," erasing any traces of the "stigma" that the name Kamathipura might conjure up. The developer was shrewdly interested in acquiring information on the inhabitants, layouts, activities, and tenancy status in the cluster of buildings where brothels continued to operate. However, such information was hidden behind multiple (and potentially perilous) barriers of entry. Given that Nirmala possessed the tacit knowledge and "easy access as well as entry" to the buildings, it seemed that the developer wanted to begin negotiations with the tenants and madams directly, bypassing the absentee landlords.[5] Having seen the recommendation letter that I had provided to Nirmala a year earlier, the developer had suggested that she involve us as well, insisting that our participation would lend his plan credibility and gain the trust of the inhabitants in the negotiations. We declined as politely as we could.

The developer's proposal recalled my first meeting with Nirmala at the PUKAR workshop when she had criticized the group of young neighborhood women for undervaluing Kamathipura's history. But here was Nirmala, strategically inserting herself into the redevelopment dynamics that sought to erase the very character and history of Kamathipura, to replace the neighborhood's kothas and chawls with a block of "towers" about which I'd earlier heard her express only disdain. Did her active participation in the developer's plans surprise me? Did the comfort with which she straddled apparently contradictory commitments in Kamathipura unnerve me? Given what I had learned about the complexity, precarity, and volatility of the world in which Nirmala operated, and how tenuous that the relationships and alliances with the marginalized community could be, the deftness with which she navigated these tensions left me far more intrigued and impressed than surprised.

Notes

1. Kamathipura is one of Mumbai's oldest neighborhoods, laid out across a grid of fourteen lanes of densely packed tenement housing in the heart of the city. Originally inhabited by Kamathis, construction migrant laborers, the area became a "designated zone" for prostitution during the colonial period. Since then, the area has been associated with filth, poverty, crime, congestion, immorality, dirt, and disease—a tolerated aberration. The number of sex workers fell from 50,000 in 1992 to 1,600 in 2009 (BMC survey). The rest of the population in the neighborhood comprises diverse communities and occupations.

2. The aspiration of the Mumbai-Based Partners for Urban Knowledge Action and Research (PUKAR) is to create "barefoot researchers"—that is, to train young people from the city's marginalized communities and neighborhoods to ask tough questions and produce knowledge that they can then use to engage productively in public debates about the city.

3. Several state-led official plans to redevelop Kamathipura, given the extremely old and congested buildings in desperate need of repairs and lacking basic urban infrastructure, have failed in spite of the neighborhood's well-connected location in the heart of the city. Private developers have acquired a few properties and erected modern towers, but redevelopment has proven to be a complex proposition given the sheer density of the neighborhood, the layers of tenure claims and counterclaims, and the lack of unity among landlords.

4. In 2005 the ethno-moralist Maharashtra government issued a blanket ban on all dance bars, citing exploitation of women. The ban was challenged in the higher courts, which found it to be unconstitutional, but the government refused

to issue licenses. Some dance bars functioned clandestinely. About 75,000 women bar dancers lost their livelihoods.

5. Many of the buildings are governed by the archaic Rent Control Act, which meant that landlords lost interest in even collecting the rents or doing repairs. The buildings became dilapidated, yet tenants refused to move out without rehabilitation packages. In some cases the premises would be sublet, and in other cases there would be an informal sale of the building through the pagdi system— a locally evolved workaround whereby Bombay landlords and tenants circumvent the city's archaic rent control laws in a way that enables flows of cash necessary for building upkeep and also allows for a more fluid rental housing market. The system works like this: the landlord of some flat in a rent-controlled building offers a cash payment to the existing tenant in exchange for that tenant vacating the flat. The cash is by the incoming tenant, who makes a lump-sum payment to the landlord equivalent to some proportion (85 to 90%) of the flat's estimated hypothetical market value (that is, were the flat not in a rent-controlled building but rather able to be sold on the "free market"). As per pagdi system convention, the lump-sum payment is then divided between the former tenant and the landlord at a 35/65 ratio. After moving in, the new tenant continues to pay the "controlled" nominal monthly rent to the landlord, but effectively the new "tenant" has become a partial "owner." The prevalence of the pagdi system in Bombay makes it exceedingly complicated (perhaps impossible) to pin down ownership rights in/of any particular building.

11 FARHAD "SUE MAKER"

Leilah Vevaina

FARHAD WAS A RETIRED dentist I met during the Bombay Parsi Punchayet (BPP) trustee election of 2011. This trust is one of the most prominent Parsi (Indian Zoroastrian) charitable trusts in Mumbai and considers itself the "apex" trust of Parsis in India.[1] As part of my fieldwork, I had attended almost every election meeting of every candidate, amounting to several per week over a few months. Most took place in the *maidan* (outdoor open area) or community hall of a *baug* (housing colony) during the evenings so that younger Parsis with jobs could attend after work hours. However, most of the audience remained the elderly and retired members of the community, with younger Parsis often walking past to their homes or standing in small groups at the back of the audience only for a few moments before they left. After seeing Farhad at several meetings, I approached him, and we began to discuss trust politics and community affairs. Although he had run for trusteeship in the past, he was now resigned to be a "general member," but with a knowing grin, he also informed me that he was "active" in other ways.

Farhad lives in Godrej Baug near Malabar Hill, the recently built housing colony that abuts the Tower of Silence funerary ground. He is a trustee of the Bhikabehram Well near Church Gate. We agreed to meet there; he visits the site almost every day. The well is just off the main road at the southern end of Cross Maidan and has been open to passing travelers since 1725. As we meet and he takes me around the small site, he greets almost everyone by name and inquires after Parsis he has not met before. The well used to be open to the public, but after heritage renovations the trustees had recently enclosed it within a wall with a new sign. Non-Parsis may now take water only from a tap from the outside. Upon seeing my slight disappointment that the well was now cordoned off, Farhad noted, "We Parsis must protect our assets . . . people were throwing things inside [the well]."

As Farhad took me around the space, he greeted several older Parsi women sitting together with their heads covered, fanning themselves. Their clothes looked worn, their blackened teeth and cloudy eyes betraying their need for more care. Farhad shook all their hands with both of his, nodding his head as if to reassure them of something. "I am helping them with some claims to the Punchayet," he said, explaining that they lived off the Punchayet's welfare programs and within another trust's widow *chawls*.[2] "Our community is so rich," Farhad continued, "but so many—especially the aged—are left behind."

Speaking to some in the community about Farhad elicited many nods that yes, he is very active in community affairs. Others reacted with a palm to the forehead and a hiss in exasperation. Farhad is aware of his reputation as a troublemaker, one earned through the myriad lawsuits he has filed against the Parsi Punchayet. "They are there to serve not to rule," he exclaims, and he is proud of being known as one of the "watchdogs" of the fund. The BPP trust has a multitude of funds and properties that it manages, and according to its deed, all Parsis are its beneficiaries. The BPP has been a communal organization since the seventeenth century and has taken various organizational forms. In its current incarnation it is a public charitable trust that manages welfare funds, scholarships, medical care, much charitable housing, two fire temples, and Doongerwadi, the Tower of Silence funerary ground in South Mumbai. The BPP further serves as the umbrella trust for other Parsi trusts in India.[3] However, the definition of who the BPP counts as a Parsi has sparked much controversy over the decades.[4] With the aid of other beneficiaries, and sometimes on their behalf, Farhad has filed more than forty lawsuits against the Punchayet over the decades. With one finger pointing in the direction of the Punchayet office close by on DM Road, he says, "promise breaker," and then, pointing at himself with his thumb, "sue maker."

Farhad files suits on behalf of other beneficiaries who have less legal knowledge, money, time, or perhaps inclination than he. He initiates the suit along with his compatriot, who is a lawyer. But it is Farhad who is the main conduit of the suit, bringing together the beneficiaries and coaching them through the case. The BPP, like any other trust, is composed of trustees who manage the property and funds for Parsi beneficiaries, who may partake in them. But unlike other trusts, the BPP has grown over the years into a large bureaucracy and, since 2008, one with *elected* trustees. The most critical assets that the BPP manages are trust housing and sacred space. Though managing only two fire temples in the city, the Punchayet is the manager of the Doongerwadi funerary grounds, which has been a site of ritual and identitarian controversy for decades.[5] In terms of housing, the BPP manages more than three thousand flats, all heavily subsidized, with rents and leases dramatically below market rate for their respective locations. Even while Parsis are demographically declining, there remains a long waiting list for flats in Mumbai. Parsis, and only Parsis, may fill out an application for housing, which is evaluated by the trustees under a merit-based rating scheme. In order to encourage Parsi marriage and population growth, the BPP gives newly married couples of childbearing age priority in housing applications. The scheme itself and the criteria of evaluation have inspired a few beneficiaries to take the BPP to court, and Farhad has often been a party to these suits.

For instance, Farhad was party to the suit known as the "104 case," wherein 104 Parsi applicants for Punchayet trust housing appealed on the grounds that they thought others had received flats out of turn. Most of the 104 applicants were quite poor. Farhad, along with the Alert Zoroastrian Association (AZA), appealed to Maharashtra's charity commissioner and created enough publicity about the case that eventually the Charity Commission assigned a retired high court judge to oversee all the allotments. Farhad's role was to gather aggrieved beneficiaries and explain the process to them. Much of his method relies on relating what rights they actually have in terms of the trust and encouraging them to push back against the trust's misbehavior. While the case was partially successful, in the end many of the 104 did not actually receive flats because they no longer qualified under the scheme, either being too old or having found other housing.[6] What the case brought to light was that there were many aggrieved beneficiaries who could link up with people like Farhad, who had the will and legal knowledge to fight these cases.

Although Farhad is neither a lawyer nor a lay expert in trust law, he has enough legal knowledge—or what I have elsewhere called "legal-ease"[7]—to gather beneficiaries with complaints and then put together the necessary paperwork and procedures to file a lawsuit with a lawyer friend of his. He tells me that often the suits do not go very far, but they have the effect of causing enough nuisance that the parties reach some agreement out of court. In interviews with the Punchayet, which has legal counsel on staff, they described the money and energy that go into appearing at court dates, filing papers on time, and then just persevering through the glacial pace of the Indian court system. Farhad explains this to the beneficiaries: they must stick with the case, even though they might not see results or redress quickly. His most recent cause has been to support a petition against a multimillion-dollar charitable gift to the Parsi General Hospital for a cosmopolitan wing.

In 2017 a very wealthy Parsi family from Hong Kong, Pervin and Jal Shroff, with roots in Mumbai, offered to donate $22.5 million (Rupees 160 Crore) to the Parsi General Hospital to build an entire new wing to serve as a cancer ward, with the newest and best medical equipment. According to the wishes of the donors, the ward would be cosmopolitan—that is, open to all communities. Part of the profits of the new wing would be given to the main, Parsi-only hospital for charity patients. The trustees of the hospital were very open to this gift, for the hospital had been in arrears for years. Farhad and other conservatives were strongly against the idea of the traditionally Parsi-only hospital being opened up to non-Parsis, as well as fearing that the new wing would give priority to paying patients at the expense of charity patients. He worriedly asked me in early 2018, "How do we make sure that the poor can walk in [to the hospital] tomorrow?"

Farhad used his visits to the well as a pulpit and even published letters in a few Parsi periodicals asking for reassurance from the trust that charity patients would still be a priority. The hospital trustees were dismayed that Farhad and his lawyer had stirred up so much fear and suspicion about such a huge beneficial gift to a hospital that was financially in dire straits. Although Farhad was initially disappointed that the deal for the hospital went through, he remarked to me that he still had his eye on things and that he would make sure that the hospital honored its mandates to favor Parsi and charity patients. In fact, months later, the donors, who were surprised and upset about the backlash, made an announcement that if all the legal matters and complaints were not settled, they would withdraw their large donation. In an open letter, they wrote, "God willing the project will have your and the community's support; if NOT we tried our best, and can only apologize that we failed."[8] As of spring 2019, the project was still delayed, but the Shroffs have not rescinded their donation.

Farhad's work reveals much about the state of the trust-beneficiary relationship among Parsis today. But in getting into the details of this relationship—and what insights might be gleaned from attention to Farhad and his lawsuits—it will be helpful to first take a slight detour through the broader legal-political context and conceptual terrain within which charitable trusts exist and take on meaning.

Trusts are similar to corporations. Like corporations, they are instruments of common property, have perpetual succession (in that they survive beyond the natural lives of their founders), and are attributed some form of legal personality.[9] But there are important differences as well. Trusts are bound by their deeds and original objects and, in cases of charitable trusts, by the laws governing charities. Corporations are organized under chartered bylaws and may shift these under certain circumstances. Corporations and trusts manage generated income and profits differently as well: a public trust must deposit its income into its corpus and is allowed only certain expenditures, whereas a public corporation is bound to distribute its profits among its shareholders. Shareholders are active and interested members of a corporation and share the tax burden of the dividend income. The beneficiaries of a public charitable trust, by contrast, may choose to receive and enjoy the trust's assets and obligation but need not; they have no burden of duty or responsibility within this relationship.

These similarities between trusts and corporations call our attention to the dramatic shifts in the goals of public corporations—beginning in the United States in the 1980s—away from production and employment and toward increasing share price. Often described as the "shareholder revolution," value was no longer produced by providing services and sustained employment, but now by increasing stock price for stockholders, who were the "real" owners of the company.[10] What can be gained by thinking about these broader processes concerning the shareholder revolution in corporate practice through attention to actors like Farhad? Much, I believe: not only are trusts and corporations sister or cousin organizational forms of common property, but the analogy also sheds light on how value within these forms has shifted in contemporary times.

Indeed, even though beneficiaries of the Bombay Parsi Punchayet may choose to enjoy the funds and services that the trust provides, they need not, and there are scores of Parsis who perhaps interact with trusts only when they visit the *agiary* (fire temple) and others who perhaps have nothing to do with Parsi communal life. But a great many Parsis interact with trusts on a daily basis as their landlords or through welfare, education, and medical programs. There are several large Parsi trusts, but the BPP is the largest and is also considered by many to be the most dysfunctional, eliciting complaints within the Parsi media and often within the courts. Sharafi has shown that since the nineteenth century, Parsis have not only been frequent litigants in courts but have also disproportionately served as lawyers and judges. She claims that Parsis chose to secure their minority rights by pushing through the colonial (and postcolonial) legal system rather than fighting against it.[11] I will add to her insight that this has much to do with the lack of centralized or ecclesiastical authority for the community as well as the very ubiquity of instruments such as trusts in Parsi lives.

Farhad initiates these sorts of lawsuits, which have the effect of shoring up the strength of the trust beneficiary, much like the growing strength of the shareholder within the shareholder revolution. One reason that beneficiaries sue the BPP so often is because of a move to elect BPP trustees that many actors like Farhad were keen to introduce. Before 2007, trustees were nominated from among the wealthy who were themselves donors to this trust, as is common practice. Controversy had brewed at the turn of the twentieth century about trusteeship becoming heritable, but for the most part trustees were the privileged members of old merchant Parsi families. The trusteeship was an honorable, unpaid, prestige position, with many trustees serving on several other trusts as well, many of them eponymous family trusts. By the 2000s, many nonelite Parsi trust beneficiaries began to complain that the BPP was becoming an all-powerful, opaque organization that served as their landlord, the guardian of their sacred space, and the de facto leader of all the other small Parsi settlements in India. For instance, many felt that the majority of the trustees had become too conservative about issues like intermarriage, promoting evictions of these couples from trust housing. Others felt that the trustees were overstepping their purviews and making decisions that should be left to priests.

It was in this context that a leading Parsi lawyer spearheaded the case for universal adult franchise (UAF) in 2007 in front of the Charity Commission, an arm of the Bombay High Court. He argued that because the BPP was such a strong and influential organization, it was time that its beneficiaries had a say in who ran it. So, since 2008, also after much litigation, trustees have been elected by adult Parsis who have registered to vote in BPP elections. This has greatly elevated the status of the beneficiaries, who overwhelmingly supported UAF for the BPP trust.

By the time I began my fieldwork in 2011—less than five years from the inception of universal adult franchise—most people were already decrying the system. While the first election succeeded in nominating six new trust-ees, there was a cost, both literal and figurative. Elections now require high levels of campaigning, with great deals of money for advertising and many volunteers able to reach out to Parsis all over the city. One former trustee, a successful Parsi real estate developer, is said to have spent millions of rupees on his campaign.[12] While Farhad had run for trustee, he explained that he was not surprised that he lost: "I didn't have a fortune to spend, and I didn't have a name." After the first set of elections, every candidate stressed the need for regulations on campaign spending and events, but once candidates are elected, no limits are enforced. Parsis are no longer very active in Mum-bai municipal politics, but they have certainly accepted the relationship be-tween cash and electioneering.[13] All the election meetings I attended were followed by a gratis hot meal or a meal box given to all those who sat through the speeches. Trustees still receive no salary, yet they do gain prestige and power in the community. Most Parsi priests make meager incomes from ritual performances, and many depend on the Punchayet for their housing as well as income subsidies. Therefore, many priests completely defer to the wishes of the majority trustees in matters such as shunning those who have intermarried or those who prefer more heterodox rituals.

The special election in 2011, where I first met Farhad, was called because one of the current seven trustees had abruptly resigned, alleging that he had been marginalized by the other trustees and could no longer function under such conditions. The two replacement candidates, while both running as traditionalists, had very different platforms and profiles. One was from an "illustrious" family known for its philanthropy, and the other was a more conservative middle-class community activist whose spouse was already a trustee.

While the BPP has often been taken to court over its long history, in the past litigants were mostly from either the wealthy or from those in the legal profession.[14] In recent years, however, with the aid of interveners like Far-had, more and more lay Parsis have been successfully suing the Punchayet and other trusts either for their entitlements or for overreach by the trust into religious affairs. The UAF scheme has further shored up the strength of the beneficiary through elections but has also injected a whole new avenue of rent seeking into the role of the trustee. Therefore, the UAF gives more Parsis a "say" in how their communal assets are governed, but it has also created a perception of rampant corruption within the trust. This in turn has turned a retired dentist like Farhad into a champion of poorer Parsis who wish to challenge the trust.

Notes

1. Parsis are Indian Zoroastrians from the ninth century BCE to the seventh century BCE who migrated to India from Iran. Their early settlements were in Gujarat until successful ties with colonials brought many of them to Bombay. One of the key incentives for their shift to the city was the availability of sacred space and housing, all endowed by wealthy Parsis and held in trust for the community.

2. Chawls are residential buildings with small units and shared toilet and kitchen facilities. They were built to support working-class accommodation and are often found adjacent to factories or mill lands (see glossary entry). There are a few Parsi colonies built in the style of chawls, and they remain heavily subsidized for widows or very-low-income Parsis. Most tenants pay only a ceremonial amount, perhaps a few rupees, for the rent.

3. Jesse S. Palsetia, *The Parsis of India: Preservation of Identity in Bombay City*, vol. 17 (Leiden: Brill, 2001).

4. Currently, the BPP accepts those with two Parsi parents, as well as the children of Parsi men married to non-Parsi women. Growing numbers of intermarriage by Parsi women have brought several challenges to this definition (Leilah Vevaina, "Good Deeds: Parsi Trusts from 'the Womb to the Tomb,'" *Modern Asian Studies* 52, no. 1 [2018]: 238–65; Mitra Sharafi, *Law and Identity in Colonial South Asia: Parsi Legal Culture, 1772–1947* [New York: Cambridge University Press, 2014]).

5. Early in the twentieth century a landmark civil suit, *Petit v. Jeejeebhoy*, was fought over trustee succession and the rights of a non-Parsi woman married to a Parsi to avail of BPP assets as well as internment at Doongerwadi. It culminated in the High Court decision that established the prevailing definition of who is a Parsi.

6. Vevaina, "Good Deeds."

7. Leilah Vevaina, "Trust Matters: Parsis and Property in Mumbai" (PhD diss., New School for Social Research, 2014).

8. Letter from Pervin and Jal Shroff to BPP Chairman Yazdi Desai, reprinted in "Jal and Pervin Shroff Clear the Air," *Parsi Khabar*, November 19, 2017, https://parsikhabar.net/issues/jal-and-pervin-shroff-clear-the-air-on-the-parsi-general-hospital-medanta-issue/16478/.

9. Frederic William Maitland, David Runciman, and Magnus Ryan, *Maitland: State, Trust and Corporation* (Cambridge: Cambridge University Press, 2003).

10. Karen Ho, *Liquidated: An Ethnography of Wall Street* (Durham, NC: Duke University Press, 2009).

11. Palsetia, *The Parsis of India.*

12. I analyze this expenditure and the concomitant effects it has had on the kinds of projects that the trust undertakes in Leilah Vevaina, "Good Thoughts, Good Words, and Good (Trust) Deeds: Parsis, Risk, and Real Estate in Mumbai," in *Handbook of Religion and the Asian City: Aspiration and Urbanization in the Twenty-First Century* (Oakland: University of California Press, 2015), 152–67.

13. Lisa Björkman, "'You Can't Buy a Vote': Meanings of Money in a Mumbai Election," *American Ethnologist* 41, no. 4 (2014): 617–34.

14. Palsetia, *The Parsis of India.*

PART III BUSINESS

Tarini Bedi

A FEW YEARS AGO, during the busy month of Navratri, I overheard a comment made ever-so-casually by the owner of an *atta-chakki* (flour) business in the western suburb of Malad. As she surveyed the long line of customers waiting to pick up the freshly ground flour that would later turn into *puris* (fried bread) for the evening festivities, she proclaimed:

> One thing is true here in Bambai, and that is that no one, not even the poorest of the poor, ever goes to bed hungry at night. The daytime always brings something into your pocket so that you can put something into your stomach at nighttime. The politicians say that Mumbai's language is Marathi. But really, there are only two languages in Mumbai, *dhandha* [business] and *tapori* [hustling], and some days you may do dhandha and another day you will do tapori, but whichever side you choose you will go to bed with food in your stomach. In all of India, only Mumbai is like that.

The essays in part III seem to find their beginnings in this casually stated understanding of Bombay's enduring capacity to enable people to survive and thrive via practices of exchange. This is not to say that Bombay is singularly experienced; the seven essays in this section detail very different ways that people engage in practices of trade and exchange in the making of lives and livelihoods: a surrogacy agent (Deomampo), an e-waste recycler (Taskar), a network of local and global "development" consultants working on water-related issues (Rangwala), a caterer (Bedi), a *dabbawalla* (Kuroda), a fabric trader (Cheuk), and a *tantric* (Björkman). These are people whose labors not only facilitate market exchanges but also bring those markets into being in the first place. As well, these people expand our conceptions of what "doing business" looks like in the contemporary world.

Indeed, for all these people, Bombay is a place of dwelling, but more importantly it is a place where myriad forms of value are produced, extracted, circulated, translated, and consumed. It is where different kinds of markets are created and accessed both literally and metaphorically. However, although dhandha and tapori are generally characterized as antithetical practices of value production and market making, we see from these profiles that any tidy distinction between dhandha and tapori, between licit and illicit trade, and between "productive" labor and racketeering is discursive (and often strategic) rather than empirical. On the one hand, the Mumbaikars profiled in part III move easily through and across these distinctions. The labor that these people perform is central to the production, circulation, direction, redirection, and revaluation of diverse forms of currency. Together, these seven profiles illustrate how ideas and practices of "markets" and "market access" are drawn into heterogeneous projects of world making and value production.

Read together, the profiles invite us to see how markets and prices are rooted in a wide and often inchoate range of activities that might be seen as outside classic liberal understandings of valuation, exchange, and "productive" labor but are nevertheless fundamentally engaged in a variety of value-generating activities, operating at multiple territorial scales. For each of these seven Mumbaikars, their intertwined social, economic, political, material, and spiritual worlds are rooted in something that resembles a closely embraced *agency*. These articulations of agency do not map neatly onto a classical humanist notion, where the individual human actor is an autonomous and self-determining *agent*, nor through a "new materialist" characterization of nonhierarchical and distributed character of *agencies*.[1] Instead, we see how, in performing the material labor of "making a living," people also perform the labor of (re)producing and materializing urban life. In this sense, as the nexus of mediation and materiality, the people profiled in part III might be understood in Appadurai's terms as *mediants*.[2] The seven essays illustrate these connections between mediation and the intersubjective making of lives, where Mumbaikars make lives for themselves while they also make and mediate the lives of others.

Daisy Deomampo's essay on Ramita, a "surrogacy agent," provides entry into some key questions that run through the seven essays. First, who and what produce different forms of value, and how are these values rendered commensurate for exchange? What skills and resources are enlisted in these value-production and commensuration practices? How do these activities encounter and navigate changing institutional and regulatory frameworks at different scales: local, national, global, virtual? What are the differently classed and gendered bodies through which value emanates and/or dissipates? What are the temporal horizons of these value-creation projects, and how might we characterize the heterochronous character of markets and market-access practices? Deomampo's essay tells the story of a former commercial pregnancy surrogate who now works in the business of recruiting, counseling, and caring for other surrogates. Ramita is more educated and indeed more "literate" in medical and institutional procedures than other women in her neighborhood; she therefore becomes a link between the poor women she recruits as surrogates and the broader social, institutional, and legal systems that the world of commercial surrogacy inhabits. These myriad institutions comprise the always-shifting sociomaterial and legal-political context within which Ramita's own capacities accrue value, capacities that are to facilitate the (re)production (quite literally) of life and to facilitate the gendered, racialized, and geographic distributions of labor that reproduction entails.

Aneri Taskar's essay tells us of Muhammad, the owner of an electronic-waste ("e-waste") recycling business who has an eye for how value can be created out of defunct electronic goods. Through the labor of disassembling discarded objects, and the revaluation and exchange of component parts, Muhammad helps bring into being the very markets within which his business is embedded. He makes markets simply by forging relations not only among people but also among different kinds of things and materials. Like Ramita, Muhammad must navigate a changing legal and procedural framework as he attempts to transition from being an *unlicensed* to a *licensed* recycler of e-waste. Here, Taskar reminds us of how much the capacity to produce of one kind of value or "re-value" is tied to the value of land, which remains a fundamental source and sign of value in Mumbai. In the end, Tasker shows us that in the case of Muhammad those who hold land are in the best position to convert that value into other things that support their business.

This focus on land, space, and place is also central to Lubaina Rang-wala's essay on how the material exigencies of survival in the city are par-layed into various kinds of valorized knowledge and expertise. Rangwala's profile demonstrates how efforts to represent urban life and death in terms of quantifiable "water risk" bring global and local knowledge experts into fraught relations of knowledge valuation, valorization, and exchange. We see how linguistic, class, and geographic divides result in the valorization and devaluation of different kinds of knowledge. This autobiographical and self-reflective essay destabilizes the lines between who might teach and who might learn—between subject and object, urban expertise and urban experience—and is therefore a provocative subversion of how to think of "urban problems" not as self-evident pathologies but rather as materially and discursively framed sites for value creation through the marketing of objects and the technologies of redress.

My own essay continues with the theme of urban sustenance, shifting our attention from the transregional geographies and epistemologies of water flow and distribution to the local distributive ecologies of food and fla-vor. Bedi focuses on Muna, a one-stop shop of local expertise and resources who runs the neighborhood out of her kitchen. Muna runs a catering busi-ness that provides employment to several local women. Muna's profile dem-onstrates how the work of "making" food draws in people from all corners of the neighborhood. Through food, which is deeply connected to kinship and maternal care, we see how Muna's catering business facilitates myriad kin and extra-kin connections. The local dimensions of these food-mediated extended-kinship relations are extended outward in Ken Kuroda's essay on Shankar the dabbawala, who transports foods across the city each day. This profile illustrates the connections among different kinds of markets: those who cook, those who deliver, and those who consume. Shankar's role in the circulation of food, and Muna's in its production, together articulate the fun-damental connections among value, care, and kinship. Moreover, Shankar participates in a market of movement where speed and accuracy—the timely delivery of the right meal to the right person—are integral to the creation of value and in the mediation of kinship relations between those who cook the food and those who eat it.

This business of producing value out of complex and growing distances—both epistemological and socio-spatial—through which bodies and materi-als move is a theme that also emerges in Lisa Björkman's essay on Ramji, a Bombay-based tantric whose work is bound up primarily with Bombay-related "business." This profile illustrates the multiple articulations between the "visible and invisible urban orders" of the city—between the material, emplaced forms of urban value (buildings, business, banknotes) and the unseen, translocal forces (financial, vibrational, karmic) that might produce them. The question of the local and translocal character of the forces that animate the production of value through "business" is also explored in Ka-Kin Cheuk's profile of a China-based fabric trader named Deepak. Deepak hails from the town of Ulhasnagar, in the Mumbai metropolitan region, but he now lives in the Chinese city of Keqiao, where his extended-kinship networks play a crucial node in a wide-ranging value chain, the global textile industry. Deepak's specialty is import-export, and he draws from an array of imaginative socio-relational connections—all based in Mumbai—even as the city itself is closed to him as a site of value accrual. We see, in other words, that social relations that are based and territorialized in the social and kinship space of the city are enlisted in global-level production and trade networks, even if nary a sari touches ground in India. Thus, in all these profiles we see how Mumbai labor and expertise enable the accrual of value in myriad ways, not only financial-economic but also spiritual, social, and vital. These people conjure and enlist markets in making a living for themselves, while at the same time generating diverse forms of value and materially sustaining other lives—human and nonhuman—within and beyond city lines.

Indeed, in all the essays the connections between "mediation and materiality"[3] in the production, storage, and movement of value as diverse forms of currency are front and center. We see how values are stored in a wide variety of material forms and flows: as electronic waste for Taskar's e-waste specialist, in fabrics for Cheuk's fabric trader, as food for Bedi's and Kuroda's caterers and dabbawalas, in human life in the case of Deomampo's surrogacy agent, as metal coins conveying extra-monetary value for Björkman's tantric, and through hydraulic flows for Rangwala's "development" consultants. What's more, as Ramji the tantric and Shankar the dabbawalla remind us, there is exchangeable value produced through affiliations with invisible—and even immaterial—forces such as sound and vibration, flows of finance, spiritual "purity" of food, and the ambiguous temporalities of karma and causation.

The profiles in part III demonstrate how particular configurations of expertise and resources acquire and lose marketable value in the context of a rapidly changing world. In Deomampo's profile of the surrogacy agent, for instance, we see how Ramita's agent work acquired enormous value during a period when regulation and social debate over this form of producing kinship lagged behind the actual practices of global surrogacy. We then see how Ramita's particular, Bombay-based skill is devalued as India grapples with the ethics, politics, and regulatory frameworks of the national-level surrogacy industry. In this changing institutional context, we see Ramita move first into and then out of a brokerage "situation."[4] In a similar vein, Taskar's profile shows how an e-waste trader navigates a rapidly changing legal-institutional context that sees his recycled e-waste products lose market value, even while his own expertise in navigating the opacities of that same market acquires value in its own right.

In all the essays, heterogeneous projects of value creation, marketization, and exchange are emplaced in particular locations of the city: Ulhasnagar, Bandra, Nandipur, Juhu, Borivili, Kurla, Saki Naka, Dharavi, Saat Rasta, and Byculla. Each of the characters profiled here finds their lives and practices situated in these particular places, and it is in these situated practices that they mediate the disjunctures and contradictions of heterochronous markets.[5] The vitality of time as a fundamental dimension in the creation and marketization of value is most immediately illustrated in Kuroda's essay, where the primary currency that Shankar the dabbawala holds is the capacity to deliver *tiffins* across different locations in a "squeezed time." For the dabbawala, the blockages of space also result in the slowing down or blockage of time produced by everyday congestion, transportation delays, and road blockages, along with the frequent religious processions, political rallies, and monsoon rains that temporarily destabilize the city. In this sense, time not only has a value in its own right, but it is something that also requires time-consuming labor to navigate. When a "dabba" does not arrive "on time," this very slowness simultaneously deflates the value of the particular dabbawalla who delivered the late lunch box while *augmenting* the value of the dabbawalla service more generally. A dabbawalla disaster thus fuels the market for dabbawala expertise.

The characters in part III thus provoke fundamental questions about the kinds of labor that are valued—when, where, and by whom—and how this value both shapes and is shaped by a multiplicity of urban speeds and rhythms. Each of these people is acutely attuned to the city's multiple and conflicting temporalities, as well as to contingent and often fleeting capacities for individual and collective gain through the ability to arbitrage these temporal conflicts. The conflicts also operate at various scales. For Kuroda's dabbawalla and Bedi's caterer it is the cycle of the day that matters, the rush hour and the mealtimes; for Deomampo's surrogacy agent it is the cycle of gestation and birth; for Taskar's e-waste recycler it is the pace of technological obsolescence; for Björkman's "business energizer" it is a desired future (in this life or the next) of improvement and development animated by the intangible forces of tantra; for the fabric trader it is the rise and fall of the global market and trade on the one hand and the breakneck speed of "fast fashion" and consumer taste on the other; for knowledge experts like Rangwala it is the intersections between the temporalities of municipal water on the one hand and the globally mobile forms of expertise, institutional collaborations, and international travel tours on the other.

The entanglements with space and time mean little if not for the abilities to capitalize on myriad forms of currency, in the material sense in the generation of value, such as old coins, fabrics, and clothing; the ruins of electronic waste; the fecund human body; and the sustaining flows of water and food. Each of the characters in part III sees themselves or is seen by others as generators of different forms of a particular material currency. For example, Ramita is in the business of *life as currency* itself; Shankar and Muna are entangled in the currency of food and the politics of its purchase, production, and circulation. Rangwala and Taskar both provide us with provocative ruminations on how competing forms of currency are produced at different scales. For Rangwala, despite the best efforts of both technocrats and what in contemporary "development" parlance are called "stakeholders," their different understandings of currency function like two ships passing each other in the night. The technocratic focus on "outputs" and "solutions" for water scarcity as sources of value contend with the material hydrologies of piped water in Mumbai. The latter is a field of inchoate and dispersed value generated out of differentials in water pressure, timings of water supply, and the actions of engineers, plumbers, and politicians. For Muhammad, it is his capacity to "revalue" electronic waste that creates the markets enabling washed-up goods to reenter rivers of exchange. While his expertise is integral to how e-waste is set in motion, we see as well how—as the institutional and licensing frameworks in the e-waste industry shift—Muhammad is prevented from immediately converting his expertise into cash. Therefore, the trader's capacity to revalue refuse (indeed, to market his expertise at all) is put on hold. This capacity does not lose value, but rather the materiality in which such value is stored is rendered *unconvertible* until Muhammad becomes a licensed recycler. His story demonstrates how the material forms in which value and expertise are stored matter very much indeed insofar as they enable (or disable) the conversions that render value movable and marketable.

We see in Taskar's profile how efforts to rationalize and technologize "markets" have meant the devaluation (even criminalization) of knowledge-related practices falling outside institutionally privileged spheres. The e-waste recycler is a powerful illustration of how uninstitutionalized ("informal") knowledge is produced not outside but rather from *within* "formal" domains of market exchange. Yet we see how as the e-waste industry becomes increasingly regulated and formalized, Muhammad's low-tech tools and illegible, "informal," increasingly criminalized forms of expertise actually increase in value. This puts Muhammad in a paradoxical situation in which his very ability to enter the "legal/formal" waste-trade market hinges upon his knowledge of the actual material-practical workings of the market, workings that deviate in key ways from the far-removed regulatory frameworks to which his expertise is illegible. Muhammad's expertise in both regimes—in the legal regulatory regimes of the formal "market" and the toxic and informal work of actually breaking down e-waste and bringing it (quite literally) to the market—makes for an extraordinarily valuable skill set.

As both Taskar and Rangwala illustrate, these differently valued kinds of knowledge are also materialized as currency insofar as each amounts to stored value that is later converted or exchanged for something else. Ramji, the tantric in Björkman's essay, illustrates the close connections between karmic and financial currency, and the other unseen energies and vibrations that undergird these. Even more pertinently, perhaps, we see how Ramji conjures big material gains for his clients from smaller material objects of lesser value; the material properties of *yantra* demonstrate the misguidedness of attempting to disentangle one from the other. Indeed, as the profiles of Muna, Shankar, and Ramji illustrate, the distinctions among cash (as a standard measure of value used for exchange), food (as a particular form of use value that physically feeds the body), and "energy" (vibrations) or "purity" of food are often blurred and indistinct. Deepak, in Cheuk's essay, employs a rather ambivalent form of currency: the capacity to mediate a commodity that derives value from its association with Bombay but that generates value through markets and consumers who bypass the city entirely. Cheuk therefore enjoins us to see how new forms of value and new markets are produced as and when others are closed.

If these people tell us something about the storage of value in different visible and nonvisible forms, they also illustrate how this currency is exchanged as cash: the king of currency in Bombay.[6] Cash as a material form of currency appears in exchange for other forms of currency in various places in these essays. Undeniably, cash undergirds both dhandha and tapori (the distinction between which, as we have seen, tends to collapse under the weight of ethnography) no matter what other currencies are encountered along the way. Muna's ambivalent relationship to the ATM machine, Ramji's capacity to mediate between the energetic properties of obsolete metal coins and contemporary paper money, and Shankar's fraught proposition to Kuroda (in which the dabbawala requests a cash payment in exchange for access to his work and world) reveal how cash-based monetary transactions are fundamental to the valuations that enable commensuration and marketization. Other forms of currency, such as food, purity, fabric, and coins, can also be converted into cash. But as we see in Björkman's profile of Ramji, the value of the cash itself exists not in relation to any externally given "standard measure of value" but rather to the particular energetic exchange that some cash transfer seeks to enact: "If ending war is for the good of society," Björkman asks the tantric after he claims to have the powers to avert violent conflict, "why don't you do it for free?" Ramji explains that "the money is also energy—it is the intention of those who want to resolve the matter."

Indeed, there is an intentionality—we might say a futurity—to these conversions and exchange. However, this view to a future has differentiated temporalities that are undergirded by different strategies and practices. In some places, exchanges are kept in abeyance; in others, they are undergirded by promises, aspirations, and faith in the ability to generate either cash or something else of value. Therefore, the "currency" of cash money is omnipresent in the accounts, but the value of the currency is not reducible to the number printed on the banknote, nor is cash the only form of currency that circulates through the worlds of these seven people. Both Kuroda and Taskar describe the moral ambivalence that emerges when the slippage between these multiple modes of valuation are turned on the ethnographer: Muhammad asks Taskar for her assistance as a member of a powerful institution in order to help his business gain accreditation from the state; Shankar asks for money for the work of sharing information about what he does each day for *outsiders* (tourists, students, corporate consultants). This slippage among the various registers of valuation renders cash money morally suspect. In this context, Rangwala's essay is a provocative look at how the framing of "urban problems" by "development experts" is a form of value creation and market making in its own right. These essays thus shine new light on long-standing debates over anthropological ethics—about the encounter of practices of value accrual and exchange in "the field." This is not simply the old question of ethnographic positionality; rather, it is about how the ethnographer is implicated in the production and circulation of value, as well as in the storage, transfer, and redeployment of this "currency"—whether money or monographs—in ever-new markets.

Finally (and to anticipate part IV), these essays on "markets" illuminate how capacities for translation and marketization are mediated through classed, casted, and gendered practices of *differentiation*. Ramita the surrogate agent seems to represent a unique position of value between the poor (who produce children for money) and the rich (who can pay that money). Ramita calls this mediation of monetary transactions for life itself "agent work," thus suggesting how "agency" itself might be rethought. While Ramita's "agency" is seen as operating through her individual body, Rangwala's essay points us to how agency and value might be produced through collectives rather than individuals, and how in Bombay collective forms of urban value creation and urban knowledge intertwine intricately with a myriad of people and things. Muna's currency is her food, which she brings to market through her catering business. However, cash payments are only intermittent actors here as Muna's supplies—and indeed much of the labor she extracts—operate through deferred forms of payment that rely not on any material currency at all but rather on (immaterial) "trust." Yet even without the hard currency, or perhaps precisely because of its absence or invisibility, Muna is able to deploy other forms of value in her exchanges, whether the making of markets or the forging of family. And if in Muna's case payment is deferred, in Ramji's case it is "advanced," used to procure materials for the *yantra*. However, once procured, the value of those material inputs for the yantra lies solely in Ramji's ability to convert that value (through tantra) into his profits for his clients' businesses, profits that can then be turned into cash through market exchanges.

Undeniably, all these projects of value creation are undergirded by very particular forms of labor—labor that, as we have seen, is indispensable to the value chains in which these labors find themselves enlisted. Kuroda's "ethical labor," Bedi's "distributive labor," Taskar's labor of "disassembly," Björkman's ritual labor, Cheuk's labor of commodity circulation, Deomampo's "reproductive labor," and Rangwala's labor of urban "education" are forms of urban expertise and practice that have acquired (and in some cases lost) particular value in contemporary Mumbai, both in animating markets and in creating kinship and feeding friends.

Notes

1. Jane Bennett, *Vibrant Matter: A Political Ecology of Things* (Durham, NC: Duke University Press, 2009); Bruno Latour, *Reassembling the Social: An Introduction to Actor-Network Theory* (Oxford: Oxford University Press, 2005); Isabelle Stengers, *Cosmopolitics I* (Minneapolis: University of Minnesota Press, 2010). See also the discussion in this book's introduction.

2. Arjun Appadurai, "Mediants, Materiality, Normativity," *Public Culture* 27, no. 2 (2015): 221–27.

3. Appadurai, "Mediants."

4. See the discussion in the introduction.

5. Laura Bear, "Doubt, Conflict, Mediation: The Anthropology of Modern Time," *Journal of the Royal Anthropological Institute* 20, no. 1 (2014): 3–30.

6. Appadurai, "Mediants."

12 **RAMITA** SURROGACY AGENT

Daisy Deomampo

ON ONE EVENING, after a long day of interviews with some of Ramita's patients, my translator and I relished a quiet moment in Ramita's home following a feast of delicious biryani. As she sipped her tea, Ramita began to explain the tumultuous year that her family had experienced. In the years since Ramita's sister-in-law, Sumita, initially introduced Ramita to the world of pregnancy surrogacy, the relationship between the two women had deteriorated. Sumita, Ramita claimed, had recently taken away two of her clients—each of whom had undergone embryo transfer—by convincing the two women that Ramita did not properly care for her patients. Ramita explained that after stealing her clients, "Sumita did not even take care of the patients herself; instead, she gave them to another agent for a mere Rs. 1,000–2,000. Do you do that to anyone? She has been defaming my name and calling me a thief for stealing patients' money. Basically, she is jealous of my success." Ramita, eager to set the record straight, concluded by insisting that "everyone here who is my patient recommends my name to another needy woman."

I first met Ramita in early 2010 at her home in Nadipur, an industrial city approximately sixty kilometers from Central Mumbai. At the time, Ramita was in the early stages of establishing herself as a surrogacy agent, eager to gain a foothold in the burgeoning industry of transnational commercial surrogacy. Prospective parents flocked to India from around the globe, seeking commercial surrogacy arrangements, in which a surrogate mother carries and births a child for a paying couple or individual. The highly complex process involves a wide range of actors, including doctors, nurses, psychologists, social workers, travel agents, lawyers, gamete (egg and sperm) donors, and third-party brokers that connect intended parents around the world with fertility clinics in India.

Key to this process are local surrogacy "agents" (as the women call themselves) who are often invisible to commissioning clients. Also referred to as caretakers, recruiters, or social workers, depending on what they do and whom you ask, agents are former egg donors and/or surrogates who recruit potential surrogates and sometimes care for them throughout their pregnancies. In India, surrogacy agents' roles in the complicated process of global surrogacy are central but under-examined.[1] Their work is varied and wide-ranging, with recruitment a central aspect.

Before Ramita became an agent, she was introduced to the world of commercial surrogacy by her husband's sister, Sumita, herself a former surrogate. Even though her husband earned a decent living in construction, it was irregular work, and Ramita knew that surrogacy offered an opportunity to raise their standard of living. Ramita convinced her husband to allow her to try to become a surrogate mother. He eventually agreed, and in 2009 Ramita delivered a child for a North Indian couple via cesarean section.

While the money she earned—1.25 *lakh*—was not an insignificant sum, "it was not enough," Ramita asserted. She kept some of the money for her daughter's education and used some of it to repair her family's home in their village in Maharashtra. But she soon realized that she was uniquely qualified to make a living recruiting potential surrogates. As a former surrogate, Ramita could tell women about her experiences going through the process. As she explained, "Somebody who has the knowledge, who has experience and has gone through it, she will be able to explain it better. There are lots of people who have never done this but want to become agents, because they see the money at the end of the road. But that is not going to help. They need to have knowledge first." Here Ramita not only draws in prospective surrogates by highlighting her own expertise, based on her own experience as a former surrogate. By referring to women as her "patients," she also enfolds women into a discourse of care and medical custody, key to her identity, role, and responsibility as an agent.

When she first started out, she would roam her neighborhood, approaching women to let them know about surrogacy. But by the time I returned to Mumbai for follow-up interviews in 2013, Ramita no longer recruited strangers on the street for surrogacy. Her established reputation as an agent preceded her, and rather than approach women in her neighborhood, she explained, "They come by word of mouth. Most of the patients I have come on their own. Some were told about surrogacy by somebody else." Ramita's experience reflects the ways in which the urban poor attain expertise and professional regard. Indeed, agents such as Ramita do not gain success through traditional educational attainment and conventional professional accomplishment alone; rather, Ramita's reputation, word of mouth, and relational ties offered her the opportunity to obtain expertise and respect in her field.

Yet for Ramita, agent work encompassed far more than recruiting potential surrogates, and her success and expertise as an agent came not only from her previous experience as a surrogate. Ramita was high school–educated and thus capable of navigating the complicated medical procedures and processes involved in surrogacy, a key detail in understanding surrogate care through the lens of governmentality. After a surrogate tested positive for pregnancy, Ramita would celebrate briefly and then take charge of keeping track of her doctor's appointments, hormone injections, and medical treatments. "Agent work," Ramita explained, "means that when we take patients, we have to take care of them completely. Whether she is taking the medicines properly or not, to get her blood test done timely, to get the sonography done. Keep track of her checkups. The people at the clinic inform us of a patient's sonography dates or blood tests, whether they have to come fasting or having had some food; we have to tell all these things to the patient." Clearly, such forms of medical management and surveillance reveal not only the care provided by the agent but also the workings of governmentality and the ways in which power embeds in the very practices of surrogate care.

As Ramita's work expanded and her income grew, Ramita, a quick self-study when it came to gaining business know-how, made investments to improve the efficiency of her work. With her earnings, she was able to purchase a refrigerator outfitted with a padlock, in which she kept all medications. With some of the money her daughter received from a college scholarship (awarded to students from scheduled castes who received top grades), she purchased a scanner and a printer. As a high-achieving Dalit student, Ramita's daughter was eligible for the award, which was intended to support her studies but was ultimately repurposed to improve the overall well-being of the household (not unlike the use of microcredit loans to pay off medical bills or to host weddings). The scanner was an important investment, Ramita explains, that saves her money and time previously spent at copy shops scanning patient profile photos and PAN (permanent account number) cards. Ramita's hard work paid off, and she garnered a reputation for being an effective agent who shepherded many patients through the surrogacy process. As one former surrogate, Salma, explained, "Ramita is first place in terms of deliveries at the hospital."

But, as Salma clarified, "It's not just about numbers. [Ramita] has a good nature; she helps everybody. That's why patients are also happy. She helps those who do not have money; she gives them money, and she does many things for them." For instance, one of her former surrogates, Anjali, became a surrogate so that she could buy a house of her own. Anjali received 2.5 lakh for her surrogacy, yet in Mumbai, where property prices are among the highest in India, it was not enough. Anjali needed a loan to cover the difference, and Ramita acted as guarantor.

Discussing how she feels about her work as an agent, Ramita explains: "I love this work. But it is a lot of hard work. It's not easy being an agent. I don't get work just sitting at home; it takes a lot of work, and it involves running around. Getting them to hospitals, to appointments. When I have patients at multiple centers, I sometimes need help getting them there."

Perhaps this is why Ramita feels some ownership over agent work and has sought to restrict opportunities for other surrogates to also become agents. "All patients would like to become agents," Ramita explains, but she is against this. With a few fellow "senior" agents, Ramita approached Dr. Meera, the primary physician they worked with, and said, "If our patients bring patients, you should not take them. What if every person who had done surrogacy wanted to become an agent? Without knowing, without understanding what they are doing?" Although this clearly limited the possibility of her former surrogates developing their own careers as surrogacy agents, Ramita did not feel it was unfair. Instead, she demanded that her former patients bring potential surrogates to her, rather than to the doctor directly, and she would then share a cut of the earnings with them. In doing so, she strategically carves out her own niche of power by highlighting claims to specialized expertise and knowledge, particularly her ability to not only identify and recruit women for surrogacy but also care for them as they navigate the medical system.

Ramita's social expertise clearly overlaps with the financial aspects of her job: How do agents balance the profitability of surrogacy with social obligations and relationships? What happens when social relationships suffer at the expense of financial incentives? Earlier, we saw how Ramita contrasts her care-oriented work with that of her sister-in-law, whom she accuses of prioritizing profit over patients' health. But it is her reputation for prioritizing patients over profit, she explains, that attracts paying clients in the first place, thus complicating the conceptual separation of profit and care.

Much of Ramita's work is behind the scenes, but her role is crucial in the expansive network of surrogacy actors. Here, a key domain of her expertise stands out: her ability to facilitate the creation of new constellations of kinship as well as "traditional" family arrangements, even as surrogacy renders the very concept of family unstable. Yet although surrogacy clearly demonstrates the power to create new families, how does it affect the agent's own family? What happens when surrogacy arrangements go awry?

For example, Ramita explained how Sumita's brother, Raju, had "brought shame to the family." Although he is married to Kalpana (herself a would-be surrogate), Raju had had an affair with another woman while Kalpana was in the hospital recovering from embryo transfer. The woman stayed with Raju for a week, Ramita explained, insisting as well that Sumita herself was complicit in the affair because she denied that anyone was staying with him. Eventually, Kalpana returned home and found out about the affair. As Ramita reported, "It came to blows," and Raju, Kalpana, and the other woman each in turn made attempts at self-immolation. Even though Sumita had by that time distanced herself from Ramita's family (for reasons described earlier), Sumita's daughter approached Ramita and asked for help. As Ramita recounts, "Whenever it is about money, they come to us. When I reached the hospital, the staff had not even touched him, he was in pain, and they had not begun any procedure. I had recently got money for my share in my father's land, plus I had recently been paid for an ET [embryo transfer], so altogether I paid Rs. 35,000 for Raju and that girl's treatment. They never thanked us and only spoke badly to us." Ramita now avoids Sumita and her family altogether.

This was not the only family drama that Ramita has mediated. Although she worked hard to ensure that her patients' surrogate pregnancies went as smoothly as possible, things did not always go according to plan, and sometimes surrogacies went awry. In 2011 one of her patients, Vadya, became pregnant and experienced a largely uneventful pregnancy. She eventually gave birth to healthy twins: a boy and a girl. The problems started, Ramita explains, when the Israeli couple arrived to pick up the babies. After receiving the results of the mandatory DNA tests needed to prove paternity, the Israeli couple learned that the would-be father's DNA did not match that of the twins'. The twins' DNA did indeed match Vadya's, but it turned out that Vadya had not undergone tubal ligation as was believed, nor did she follow the doctor's orders to abstain from sex around the time of embryo transfer. To complicate matters, Vadya had separated from her husband and had become sexually involved with another man, who, needless to say, was believed to be the genetic father of the twins. The Israeli couple maintained their commitment to parenting the twins and stayed in India for a month, hoping for permission to take them home. However, the Indian government refused to acknowledge the paternity of the Israeli couple, a devastating end for the would-be parents and a particularly poignant illustration of the material complexity of the surrogacy process that the sterile contractarian language of "market" spectacularly fails to capture.

Vadya, meanwhile, had no desire (and little means) to parent the twins herself. "I do not want to keep the children," Vadya told Ramita. "I already have two daughters; how can I also bring up these two?" At that point, Ramita told Dr. Meera's lawyer that rather than put the children into an orphanage, she would keep them herself. "If they don't go for adoption, they will be with me and grow up," Ramita recalled having told the lawyer. Dr. Meera gave Ramita a monthly stipend to help her in looking after them, and Ramita cared for the twins for a full year. During this time, she says, "I did everything for those children. I performed the *Nakshatra Shanti puja*; I did blessings so they wouldn't have problems in the future." Ramita recalls that the twins' fate was a source of great stress for her and her husband: "As the children started to grow up, I thought, they will get used to staying here, and then how will they cope when they leave?"

Shortly after their first birthday, Ramita explained, the twins were split up and adopted by two different families. At this point in our conversation, Ramita tells her son to fetch the computer to show us photos and videos of the twins. "Every time we look at these pictures we feel like crying," she says, and as I look at the photos it is clear how much they cared for the babies. In one video Ramita is lying casually on her side while her son holds and bounces a baby; everyone is smiling and laughing. I asked Ramita whether her experience with the twins had changed her opinions about surrogacy, and she responded that while it had not, she also felt that "there must be some changes made. The doctors are also to blame. When you are doing the ET, you check for everything. But how can you miss this? How did you not know she was already pregnant?"

Eventually, the surrogacy industry did change, though not in the way Ramita hoped. In 2013 the government instituted a visa restriction that limited commercial surrogacy to heterosexual married couples who hailed from countries where surrogacy was already recognized. Then, Ramita explained, surrogacy started to slow down, and she saw opportunities for her patients shrink along with the doctors' international clientele. At the same time, the number of Indian clients rose, with more doctors offering what Ramita called "budget surrogacy" packages. In 2016 the government moved to ban commercial surrogacy altogether. As of this writing, the Surrogacy (Regulation) Bill, 2016, remains to be passed, and the Indian Parliament is still considering the bill. Although policy makers continue to debate the ethics of surrogacy, Ramita's experience highlights the diverse notions of ethics at play. Clearly, Ramita seeks to legitimize her expertise to herself and her clientele, seeking the best care and income possible for her patients and herself, and engaging in the everyday ethics of survival in poverty. At the same time, ongoing debates suggest that Ramita's efforts to build skills and expertise are viewed by the rest of the world as a symptom of exploitation.

While the fate of surrogacy in India remains uncertain, Ramita can feel secure knowing that at least she achieved her main goal of owning a home. As she recounts, through her work as an agent she was able to pay off her loans and save the bulk of the money needed to purchase her family a house. Even this, however, is open to question, as Ramita reveals that her husband insisted that the deed be placed in his name. "I told him to put my name on the papers," Ramita explains, "but he said, how can that be? When the payment was given, he said to put it in his name, and later when the owner came, I asked him why he is not doing the paperwork. He said, 'The paperwork is already done. Didn't your husband tell you?' I asked him in whose name the paperwork is done. He said, 'Your husband's.'"

Note

1. Daisy Deomampo, "Transnational Surrogacy in India: Interrogating Power and Women's Agency," *Frontiers* 34, no. 3 (2013): 167–88.

13 **MUHAMMAD** REVALORIZER OF E-WASTE

Aneri Taskar

"PCB is the most dangerous of all the e-waste items," Muhammad began, presuming from the outset my familiarity with the acronym for "printed circuit board," the breakdown of which constitutes much of Muhammad's business. "The remaining products—copper, plastic or aluminum, for instance—they do not make as much of an impact. Take any electronic item for that matter. Say, a mobile. One of the most dangerous components is the PCB. After that, the battery." After three years of information in bits and pieces, I was hoping Muhammad would share some of the peculiarities of his e-waste recycling business and about the hazardous-waste-disposal sector more generally. My long wait seemed to be turning fruitful on a warm April morning in 2015, as we sipped coffee in a café near his shop. Muhammad was in one of his pensive and conversational moods, and he seemed ready to tell me a bit more. Muhammad had recently made the successful transition into the official, established world of registered e-waste disposers. Perhaps his newfound position of relative security and safety contributed to his willingness to tell me more about the e-waste business and about the less "official" underbelly of the industry in Mumbai, where he had cut his teeth.

Now that his business was firmly on the right side of "law" and "policy," he could comment more openly on what went on on the other side, in the "informal sector." He began: "The problem is that in this industry nobody wants to talk about these problems and the dangers that those of us in the industry face. There are some good people in the industry who are willing to address the problems, but no one really takes these matters seriously. The NGOs, the government—they're all just doing time pass. More people should take interest in it." I smiled at his comment—"More people should take interest"—which I interpreted as a positive commentary on my research. His words also brought back memories of our first encounter a few years earlier.

In the winter of 2011, I began a master's thesis project studying the informal workers engaged in the recycling and disposal of electronic waste, or "e-waste" as it is colloquially known. A new law on e-waste called the "E-waste (Management and Handling) Rules, 2011" was under the interim period of compulsive registration and authorization from the state pollution-control board for the informal disposal businesses like Muhammad's across the country. The new rules would go on to instantiate a new corporate-led regime of waste governance and would thereby put in peril the livelihoods of untold numbers of Mumbaikars employed in informal-sector e-waste recycling.[1] Indeed, until then, electronic waste—like other solid waste in the country—was managed by a complex network of actors engaged in the legally ambiguous work of breaking down obsolete electronic equipment, then reselling, refurbishing, recycling, and disposing of various (and often highly toxic) component materials. Unless people like Muhammad registered their businesses with the pollution-control board by May 1, 2012, the new law would render them all "illegal." It was in this highly fraught context that I was directed to meet Muhammad by one of Mumbai's better-known waste activists: Mr. Rakesh, who suggested that Muhammad might give a "balanced perspective" on the sector and on the promises and problems of the new law.

I met Muhammad at his small shop at Saki Naka, a well-known center of waste processing and scrap dealing in Mumbai. I'm not sure what I was expecting an "e-waste disposer" to look like (popular mythologies about urban informal economies perhaps had me unwittingly expecting someone both grittier and more glamorous), but I was struck by Muhammad's unassuming appearance as well as by that of his shop. Short in stature and dressed in a plain white kurta pajama (his attire on all further visits), he called me into his small office cubicle in an ordinary store, where CCTV cameras followed me diligently. The store was unremarkable, with piles of electronic equipment stashed in a corner, workers shuffling around, and a person poring over records. We sat down, and I explained my purpose of visit and my research.

By this time, I already knew quite a bit about the e-waste industry. Although a small component of solid-waste production, e-waste was becoming a menace for disposal and recycling in the dense urban environments where most e-waste is handled, both in India as well as globally. With a repository of valuable metals and hazardous elements fused into its composition, the materiality of e-waste makes its recycling and disposal a complicated technical process.[2] For instance, a significant amount of gold and copper is recoverable from PCP, but the boards are also full of lead, mercury, and cadmium: substances that are highly polluting and that pose health risks to those who handle them. Despite the hazards, monetary gains from the extraction and resale of precious metals and secondhand sale of equipment outweigh the risks for those who are drawn toward the sector. An industry study from 2016 found that the city of Mumbai produced the largest amount of e-waste in India and that 95 percent of the country's e-waste was managed by the unorganized sector, while local news media regularly reports on the "incorrect" manner in which the unorganized sector carries out the work of e-waste recycling and disposal. The 2016 study advocated stronger legislation.[3]

I explained to Muhammad that I wanted to understand the labor conditions within the e-waste industry in Mumbai, in addition to the workings of the e-waste sector as a whole. How was electronic equipment revalued (and thus resold) or else disposed of through the various stages of repair or recycling? What work was performed at each of these nodes of valuation and exchange, and what were the living and working conditions of the workers who perform this work and expose themselves to the noxious fumes and substances? And how, moreover, did e-waste reach his unit for recycling in the first place?

Muhammad was dismissive of my approach: "You are missing the point. Do not look at where it is *coming* from; it comes from *everywhere*. The links are already made. There are a hundred of ways that e-waste can arrive, but there are only two ways it can then leave." Muhammad explained that it can be disposed either legally or illegally: "The worker is a very small part of the problem. The real problem is the corruption in the government. I am trying to get my business registered as an official e-waste disposal unit, but nobody is taking me seriously because I do not have much money."

We spoke for some time, and he finally conceded that yes, of course, the disposal processes, if not done in a controlled way, were extremely hazardous for the workers. But Muhammad explained that the business wasn't only (or

FIGURE 13.1 E-waste worker removing plastic coating of the wires for metal extraction in Dharavi. Used courtesy of Aneri Taskar, photographer.

FIGURE 13.2 Copper extracted from e-waste set aside at a workshop in Deonar Dumping Ground. Used courtesy of Aneri Taskar, photographer.

even primarily) about disposal; his business was a one-stop shop for disassembly, valuation, resale, and (only then!) removal and disposal. Only materials that couldn't command a price for reuse were "disposed of." Much of the material that passed through his shop was amenable to refurbishing and resale, with about twenty people working under him performing this skilled-labor revalorization.

Muhammad's raw materials come in the shape of old discarded household appliances and devices, which he generally procures from any of the thousands of itinerant *kabadiwalas*: scrap buyers and collectors who make house-to-house collections in Mumbai. Kabadiwalas are also known to sometimes purchase gadgets and old machines from those who scavenge them out of the city's various dumping grounds. Once the machines have been recovered from the dump (or the storage closet) and have made their way into the hands of an informal dismantler, there are at least three levels of dismantling that take place, and which are carried out either by people like Muhammad who are "all in one" or other, smaller vendors who can resell components after dismantling.

First, the dismantler judges the possibility that a machine might be brought back to life and reused in its current form in the secondhand market. If not, then things such as a PCB or a compressor are taken out of the machine to be sold, while the remainder of the machine is picked apart for plastics or other elements. From here, the various gadgets and machines are taken to scrap markets at Kurla, Saki Naka, or Dharavi for disposal to specific businesses, sometimes as a whole or sometimes only specific components such as PCB. These "economies of disassembly" extend the life of the electronic equipment while generating vast employment at the same time.[4]

Muhammad's wide range of expertise came from years of experience in the business. Muhammad entered the e-waste sector as a seventeen-year-old, working as an apprentice repairman in an electronics shop. After years of learning the trade, he started his own venture with a few trusted partners. Once he knew the business and had the contacts, he explained, finding a space for himself within the city's extensive networks and chains of revaluation was relatively easy.

These infrastructures of material recovery and recycling have thus existed for as long as e-waste has been produced and disposed in Mumbai, but they are largely illegible to the new legal framework, in which recycling can be done only in units registered and licensed by the Maharashtra State Pollution Control Board as "collector," "dismantler," and "recycler" units. Muhammad explained that policy makers, NGOs, environmentalists, and various experts have displayed little interest in incorporating experts like him—with their old technologies and established systems—into new regimes of waste governance, preferring instead to repeat platitudes about the hazards of e-waste disposal and the need to eradicate the informal sector. I asked Muhammad: "So . . . under what category would you register your business?" "I don't know, madam," he answered. "I am also trying to figure it out."

Indeed, the new e-waste governance regime's corporate model of disposal was tied to a "policy boosterism"[5] by means of which Mumbai's global aspirations led policy makers to import approaches from "model" countries such as Switzerland. Instead of cooperating with people like Muhammad to enable their practices to meet environmental regulations and health standards, the new rules privileged larger corporate operators, granting permits—thereby formalizing—newcomers while taking business away from existing circuits now deemed "illegal."[6] Muhammad pointed out that yes, some of the processes are dangerous but not at *all* stages. And in any case, at a later stage, air and water pollution was inevitable, whether by formal or informal actors. Other e-waste experts echoed this observation yet remained unwilling to consider informal operators as viable partners in the industry. "You know, the informal sector could be like the foot soldiers for e-waste," one expert reflected in a personal conversation. "The networks are so strong that it could regulate the whole sector very easily." But as Muhammad pointed out, the policy discourse from the beginning framed the existing waste processors as the problem to be eradicated—"informal is bad; formal is good"—rather than approaching Muhammad and his colleagues as a foundation of expertise upon which better solutions could be based.

Before I left, Muhammad agreed that next time he would let me interview some of his workers. But my efforts to contact Muhammad over the following weeks dampened my enthusiasm. My calls went mostly unanswered, and my requests to interview his workers were invariably dodged or deferred. He had other things on his mind: frustrated at his inability to get permission for setting up his e-waste unit from the pollution-control board of Maharashtra, Muhammad was thinking about relocating to another state. Finally, he presented me with a proposal: if I could procure a letter from my university—the Tata Institute of Social Sciences—recommending him to the Karnataka board as a candidate for a licensed "e-waste recycling unit," then he would introduce me to his workers and allow me to interview them. Having no way to fulfill his request, I was at a loss. But his requests became persistent and his calls a constant source of anxiety. I began to avoid him and to explore the e-waste sector through other avenues. In turn, Muhammad began to reframe his requests for help in new forms: "You know I am a good man, doing business in a good way," he offered. "You can join me in my new formal registered company!" I politely dodged Muhammad's numerous requests while remaining sporadically in touch.

Over the following months and years, Muhammad tried desperately to register his business as a formal recycling unit. But he encountered huge obstacles. For instance, the new rules required substantial landholdings in order to set up a formally registered e-waste unit in an industrial area. Muhammad and other small owners of e-waste companies lack the resources to buy land and to introduce sophisticated technology in their units. Thus, older patterns of landholding and landlessness were reproduced by Mumbai's new regimes of "techno-ecological" urbanism:[7] those with landholdings were able to enter smoothly into "legal" circuits of value and valuation and to institutionalize ecological concerns and worker-safety protections. However, those without landholdings (Muhammad, for instance) were squeezed out of the industry, cut off from larger, cleaner, more-secure value chains. What's more, the new regulatory framework meant that unregistered businesses were vulnerable to legal action from previous work, so many operators were reluctant to approach state functionaries to register in the first place. The necessary cost cutting meant that the work became increasingly more hazardous as well.

Unable to register their businesses, Muhammad and his colleagues have found themselves further and further on the wrong side of various new laws and rules. The legal and financial dangers posed by the new criminalization of the sector have only increased the secrecy of trade—making the sector both increasingly dangerous while also less amenable to innovation. Given these dangerous working conditions and environmental hazards, small owner/operators such as Muhammad were understandably hesitant to acknowledge or admit to profiting from the industry. For those who who work with their bare hands in nitric acid to dissolve gold from PCB, the reluctance to speak about the industry is likely less out of moral ambivalence about such hazards than unwillingness to bite the hazardous hand that feeds.

WHEN I MET MUHAMMAD again, a few years later in April 2015, he had recently relocated to the state of Gujarat. The tables had now turned as Muhammad was on the other of the "formal-informal" divide, running a registered e-waste company. His personal characteristics remained much the same. As usual, he chastised me for my lack of knowledge of e-waste sector reforms. And though now a formal operator, he was still a loyalist to the informal-sector economy: "Why is it still all done by the units in Saki Naka?

There is a lot of chori [theft] in this sector." Muhammad explained that the new licensing system had given rise to a whole new world of "leakage." Unregistered processors now needed either the license of some formal-sector company to procure scrap, or else the formal operator simply resold the waste for a profit into the informal sector—where it could be processed more cheaply. Dealers of e-waste preferred to sell to the informal sector, which often yielded a higher price. Informal-sector operators would buy the waste material on the registered license of a formal-sector operator and would then share some part of the profits with them. Audits of the formal-sector companies were planned and orchestrated beforehand, giving companies enough time to be able to show good record keeping. Which is to say: under the new system, the waste is processed exactly in the ways it always did, only now much of the profits are either captured by the "formal" company or else "leaked" in negotiations for the official license. The decrease in revenues has led to cost cutting on the part of the informal operators, measures that, needless to say, often have negative environmental and health consequences.

Toward the end of our conversation in the café, Muhammad hesitantly picked up his phone (which had been ringing for some time) and told a lie: "No, I'm not in Mumbai," he said into the mouthpiece. "I will be back next month." I could sense some tension on the other end of the line, and in the end, Muhammad promised to the person on the other end of the call a meeting next month, when he's "back in the city." Knowing that I had overheard his fib, he offered an explanation: "There is a journalist from a leading newspaper. He is chasing me because he wants to write something on e-waste and is asking me to show him how e-waste is done." Sensing an opportunity, I asked brightly: "So you will show him around next month? Can I come along?" "No!" came his emphatic reply. "Not with him. I don't trust these guys. In the end, they write whatever they want to write. I will show him only the little part that is safe to show." I suppose his emphatic "no!" suggested that he didn't trust me either; I knew too much, and perhaps he feared that I might reveal something (wittingly or otherwise) to the journalist. "You can come later."

Notes

1. Vinay Gidwani and Julia Corwin, "Governance of Waste," *Economic and Political Weekly* 52, no. 31 (2017): 53.

2. Amit Jain, "Global E-waste Growth," in *E-waste Implications, Regulations, and Management in India and Current Global Best Practices*, ed. Rakesh Johri (New Delhi: TERI Press, 2008), 26.

3. "India to Sit on E-waste Pile of 30 Lakhs MT with Mumbai on Top of Heap: ASSOCHAM-Frost & Sullivan Study," Associated Chambers of Commerce and Industry of India.

4. Deepali Sinha-Khetriwal, Philipp Kraeuchi, and Markus Schwaninger, "A Comparison of Electronic Waste Recycling in Switzerland and in India," *Environmental Impact Assessment Review* 25, no. 3 (2005): 500.

5. Rajyashree Reddy, "Reimagining E-waste Circuits: Calculation, Mobile Policies, and the Move to Urban Mining in Global South Cities," *Urban Geography* 37, no. 1 (2016): 58.

6. Ravi Agarwal, "E-waste Law: New Paradigm or Business as Usual?" *Economic and Political Weekly* 47, no. 25 (2012): 16.

7. Vinay Gidwani and Rajyashree Reddy, "The Afterlives of 'Waste': Notes from India for a Minor History of Capitalist Surplus," *Antipode* 43, no. 5 (2011): 1640.

14 **DEEPAK** MAKING MUMBAI (IN CHINA)

Ka-Kin Cheuk

ONE MORNING IN AUGUST 2017, in the Chinese city of Keqiao, I visited the office of an Indian fabric trader named Deepak, who had been born and brought up in the Mumbai suburb of Ulhasnagar.[1] In Deepak's office that morning, a fabric sample caught my attention: with a shining orange as the background color, the fabric was printed with a cartoonish, sari-wearing female figure who pressed her hands together, an image of woman in traditional "Indian" dress. I told Deepak that I was impressed by the beautiful and colorful design and asked about the fabric. Deepak told me that it was his own designer work. He has no professional training in fabric design but became knowledgeable after having worked in textile industries for more than twenty years. Deepak explained that this fabric—like all other fabrics in the city—is manufactured in the Chinese factories nearby. These factories, which are regarded by Deepak as highly efficient, are run on what can be called a make-to-order model: should a Chinese factory accept an order from Deepak, it will quickly make the fabrics based on what Deepak's sample looks like. Within a span of just a few weeks, hundreds of thousands of meters of Deepak's fabrics can be produced, which will certainly fill up a few shipping containers.

Specializing in both production and wholesaling, Keqiao is a vibrant trade zone where over a third of made-in-China fabric is manufactured and traded; about half of this fabric is exported. I asked Deepak where the sari fabrics would eventually be sold. I presumed that they would make their way to sari markets in India, but Deepak explained that no, that they were being sent to the Gulf to serve South Asian markets in Dubai and other Middle Eastern cities where sizable middle-class Indian and Pakistani populations are located.[2] While bearing designs that clearly symbolized and evoked "India," not one of these fabrics had ever touched ground in India, nor would the saris that would be made from the fabric be sold and worn on Indian soil.

Deepak explained, much to my surprise, that he had made this business decision consciously and carefully—that is, not to export his company's Chinese-made fabrics from Keqiao to India. For his business in Keqiao, Deepak relies heavily on the Dubai consumer market, despite its contraction after the global economic crisis in 2007. He had only a few regular buyers in Mumbai; these buyers used to buy fabrics through Deepak's uncle before he quit this trade. A few years ago, one of Deepak's Mumbai buyers refused to pay him after a deal completion. This experience made Deepak rather reluctant to do business with people in Mumbai. Deepak perceived that there is always a high risk to dealing with buyers there, given that they usually do informal business only on cash credit and without proper papers, a common survival strategy for small-scale local businesses to avoid paying taxes in India.

Deepak explains that from his vantage point in Keqiao, the fabric markets in Mumbai are enormously complicated and impenetrable, even more so than the markets in Dubai and elsewhere, notwithstanding the fact that Deepak and his much of his extended family were born and brought up in Mumbai. The Mumbai market is accessible to a small number of Keqiao's Indians, Deepak explains, those who are connected to long-established fabric trading networks in the Mumbai neighborhoods of Kalbadevi, Santacruz, Khotwadi, Dadar, and Dharavi—the wholesale bazaars where loads of made-in-China fabrics are redistributed every day after being exported from Keqiao. Although Deepak knows Mumbai intimately, he explains that he is unable to generate reliable business contacts in these bazaars. In other words, while his Mumbai roots enabled him to establish a transnational brokerage network from scratch, he remains locked out of the city, unable to either produce or sell his fabrics in his hometown.

Deepak was born in a Sindhi family in Ulhasnagar in 1979. Just like many other Sindhi families in Mumbai and nearby areas, Deepak's family has a strong background in business. His paternal grandparents decided to come to Ulhasnagar after Partition in 1947. As Deepak explained, "Just like many other Sindhis, they felt there were more business opportunities here than in other places" in India, despite the fact that they were initially refugees in Mumbai.[3]

Deepak's father started a business trading in building materials in 1970. Before that, he was working in the same industry for Deepak's great-uncle. In fact, most of Deepak's relatives (with a few notable exceptions who work in the government) are active as commodity traders in Ulhasnagar. Despite the family business connections, Deepak's parents sought to raise him at a distance from the family businesses, away from Ulhasnagar and even from the city's Sindhi community more generally. When Deepak was only two years old, he was sent to Andheri and Santacruz to live with his maternal grandfather, who worked for the Indian Railways. This decision was made in an effort to ensure that Deepak would receive a good education; the quality of schooling in Ulhasnagar, Deepak explained, was perceived by his parents as not very good. Deepak completed his education—from primary school until university—in Andheri and Santacruz, where only a few of his classmates were Sindhi. His schooldays exposed him to a much wider world in Mumbai. He never expected to return to Ulhasnagar or to join his father's business. But it was the family business that eventually presented him with an opportunity of overseas adventure. When the opportunity came, Deepak quickly withdrew from his university program and set off for Hong Kong.

Deepak left India in 1997 to join a suit trade business established by his mother's brother in Hong Kong in the mid-1970s. During that time, Ulhasnagar was still an industrial center for a wide range of counterfeit commodity manufacture; the products were often made with low budgets and sold with the mimicking label "Made in U.S.A." standing for "Ulhasnagar Sindhi Association," for the local Sindhis were at the center of this trade.[4] However, the vibrant manufacturing economy in Ulhasnagar was not attractive to aspiring young Sindhis like Deepak, who were eager to move overseas in search of entrepreneurial success. Indeed, few of them could afford the capital-intensive investment that was necessary in Mumbai's manufacturing sectors. Meanwhile, opportunities for working overseas were regularly on offer by Sindhi relatives willing to pay not only salaries but also migration fees and living subsidies. And, of course—and perhaps most importantly—overseas employment also offered the prospect of eventually starting one's own business. Throughout the 1970s, 1980s, and 1990s, Sindhis in Ulhasnagar wanting to try their luck outside of India considered Hong Kong, Dubai, and Bangkok to be the best destinations for business- and work-led migration.

After a brief stint as a trainee in his uncle's tailor firm in Hong Kong, Deepak was sent as the company salesman to Europe, where he set out looking for potential customers for mail-order suits made in Hong Kong— a globally renowned industry that has become a niche economy for the Sindhi minority in Hong Kong since the late 1950s. "The company used to sell tailor-made suits to diplomats, lawyers, and other professionals in Europe. These sorts of people like tailor-made products," Deepak recalled, "so my job was to find them." Deepak felt homesick during the early days of working alone in strange cities. But after a while, he adapted to the rhythm of the job and also began to appreciate the unfamiliar customs and new experiences to which his life in unfamiliar places introduced him. "It was amazing to visit so many European countries!" Deepak told me, reserving particular praise for the "peaceful way" of life that he observed in Scandinavian countries, countries where he felt that he had met "the nicest people in the world."

Although he was beginning to enjoy the traveling, Deepak also came to wonder whether this salesman job, which kept him moving from one city to another, could suit him in the longer term. In 2000 Deepak became engaged to be married to his former classmate Geeta, one of the few other Sindhis in his class. For this reason he had begun to feel that the sojourning life might not work well because it was "impossible for my wife to travel with me all the time" in Europe. Finding a place to settle became a priority for Deepak, and at the same time, he was still eager to develop his business outside of India.

It was a Sindhi wedding party in Mumbai that presented him with his next lucky break. The party was hosted by Deepak's paternal uncle, who had been running a fabric trade business in Dubai since the late 1980s. This uncle invited Deepak to join his Dubai company as a trader and help him forge stronger connections with fabric suppliers in East Asia, especially those in South Korea and China. This uncle convinced Deepak that the position would offer him not just better business prospects but also the stability he sought: Deepak and his wife—and later, their son—could all settle in China.

Deepak's uncle eagerly needed someone to help build a closer link with China. That was because during that time China had been rapidly replacing other East Asian countries as the main manufacturing base for low-cost, mass-produced commodities, including the fabrics that Deepak's uncle used to import from places like Keqiao, where the world's cheapest price for fabrics could then be found.

After short stints—again as a trainee—in Dubai and Seoul in 2004, Deepak was sent by his uncle to a small city called Keqiao. Located in eastern Zhejiang Province, Keqiao quickly became a popular destination for Indian traders like Deepak to establish a new hub for their transnational businesses. Deepak's first assignment in Keqiao was to set up a company office for his uncle. The timing of his relocation to Keqiao, as Deepak explained, was absolutely perfect, just as his uncle's company was shifting its primary area of investment in Dubai from fabric to real estate, given that this was the time of Dubai's housing boom. This afforded Deepak the space to pursue his own business plans in the fabric trade. Deepak was allowed to use the company's existing trade networks in Dubai and the contact information of suppliers in China to advance his own business advantage, while the uncle was too busy in the new property business.

Deepak eventually established his own independent business in Keqiao while maintaining strong and close connections with his former company's office in Dubai, which is now owned by his uncle's son: "My cousin who heads the Dubai office now is my biggest buyer. That cousin also became the owner of that office when he became independent—which happened more or less at the same time. We're still using the same [Dubai-based] company names in our offices, but we're now under different ownerships."

Deepak's main work in Keqiao—like that of other Indian traders in the Chinese city—is to provide intermediary services between visiting buyers (most of them Sindhis from Dubai or other parts of the Middle East) and local Chinese suppliers. Although Deepak and his Sindhi buyers could easily trace their connections with these people back to Ulhasnagar, none of the products they trade are actually made in Ulhasnagar, but rather in China. Indeed, the rapid decline of Mumbai's textile production since the 1980s[5] has made Mumbai, as well as India in general, increasingly reliant on the import of made-in-China fabrics. Demand for fabrics remains strong there, but Deepak has not considered it an option to shift his business focus from Dubai to Mumbai, as he mentioned many times throughout our conversations. Deepak observes that only Sindhi traders who had traded in Mumbai long enough before—at least for a few decades—manage to keep a good level of success in exporting fabrics from Keqiao to Mumbai; despite the success, these traders still constantly complain how difficult it is to deal with people in Mumbai, as they inevitably become less familiar with the local market after having moved to Keqiao.

Deepak's company is neither the producer nor final consumer of the made-in-China fabrics but is made up of traders who earn "commissions" from either or both sides. Deepak spends a lot of time in his office, where his buyers and suppliers meet and discuss the purchase proposal through his mediation. From his office, Deepak tirelessly helps his clients with business negotiations and bargains in the office to reach mutual agreement on fabrics' color, patterns, and production budget before they confirm the order.

As with many other trade offices in Keqiao, there is a large showroom in Deepak's office where piles of fabric samples are on display. Most of Deepak's specialized items are so-called woman fabrics in Keqiao. These fabrics can be considered as only a raw material that needs to be further processed to become garments for women. On most occasions, Deepak is acting as an intermediary, responsible for conveying buyers' requests, such as those about fabric color and production budget, to the Chinese factories; he needs to ensure that the final products meet requirements from the sides of both buying and producing. In other words, Deepak helps place the production order as his buyers wish, and most of his job involves ensuring good quality control during the production. But on other occasions, Deepak will do more work in promoting the fabrics designed by him. His long exposure to the Indian market in Dubai enables him to grasp the kinds of fabrics that are likely to be in demand by South Asian women in Dubai and other parts of the Middle East: soft texture, more stylish design (like the cartoonish Indian figure, which, as Deepak claims, would be accepted as fashionable in Dubai but not in India), as well as bright and colorful motifs. He has successfully convinced some Dubai buyers to regularly place orders for these fabrics. As such, Deepak has combined his strengths on both buyer-requested orders and fabrics of his own design in sustaining a rather regular demand from Dubai.

Although he doesn't sell fabrics in Mumbai, Deepak tries to visit his family and friends in Ulhasnagar and Mumbai every Chinese New Year: the only time when Keqiao's wholesale marketplace, as well as the Chinese factories supplying fabrics to this marketplace, is closed for a three-week holiday. But whenever Deepak is back in Ulhasnagar, he always feels the difficulty of readapting to the local way of life. For instance, Deepak said he would never drive his car or motorcycle for the first few days there. He was frustrated that the traffic infrastructure in Ulhasnagar and other parts in Mumbai is generally much worse than that in Keqiao. Deepak expressed amazement at how his hometown people see these hassles as inevitable:

When I see my cousins in India, I always wonder how they can handle it! Because they have many other problems daily which we don't have it here: there are water problems. There are electricity problems. So many problems. But we never see this kind of problem here [in Keqiao]! And they still manage to do other things along with all problems. I really admire them. How do they manage?!

One of his cousins came to visit Deepak in China and told him that Keqiao "is the best place" he had ever visited in the world; he was so impressed that anywhere in the city can be reached in ten minutes of driving, whereas "you need three hours" for the same travel distance in Mumbai. Deepak was convinced that even in a long-term future, Mumbai would not be able to catch up with Keqiao in terms of such level of infrastructural development. Mumbai (and Mumbaikars) would not change, Deepak felt, which made a Chinese-paced development impossible:

> If I'm there and I don't change myself, how are they going to develop it? It's we people. If I don't change myself, it's going to be the same. So that is a problem! Like I told you before, it's ourselves. If we don't decide we need to change, who is going to change for you? And why would they change for you? Because you are used to the same thing that what you're doing every day. You want to throw rubbish anywhere you want, you want to park the car the way you want, you want to drive the way you want . . . you can't change your city like this.

Such pessimism about the future of Mumbai stands in stark contrast with the satisfactions of his livelihoods in Keqiao. Even though Deepak still has a strong personal connection with Ulhasnagar and emotional attachment to Mumbai, he has since regarded Keqiao as "his Mumbai":

> I always have a great feeling that I want to go back [to Mumbai] maybe after one year or two years. But now when you have been in China for many years, you feel that it's already your country. This is my home . . . you know. OK, that [Ulhasnagar] is my homeland. I was born there. But Keqiao is the place where I should feel the same. It has been a long time, you know. [Ulhasnagar] is the mother who gave me birth, and [Keqiao] is the mother who has taken care of me for my whole life! In the future, nobody knows. But my choice? I won't never leave!

Notes

1. Ulhasnagar is a smallish city of around 600,000 people located within the Mumbai Metropolitan Region and connected to Mumbai by local train.

2. See Neha Vora, *Impossible Citizens: Dubai's Indian Diaspora* (Durham, NC: Duke University Press, 2013).

3. Many Sindhis who were believers in Hinduism and Sikhism fled their homelands in Pakistan after Partition. See Mark-Anthony Falzon, "'Bombay, Our

Cultural Heart': Rethinking the Relation between Homeland and Diaspora," *Ethnic and Racial Studies* 26, no. 4 (2003): 666–67.

4. For more information, see Mark-Anthony Falzon, *Cosmopolitan Connections: The Sindhi Diaspora, 1860–2000* (Leiden: Brill, 2004), 168.

5. For the collapse of Mumbai's textile industries, see Darryl D'Monte, *Ripping the Fabric: The Decline of Mumbai and Its Mills* (New Delhi: Oxford University Press, 2002).

15 **LUBAINA** FRAMING "DEVELOPMENT"

Lubaina Rangwala

TWO YEARS AGO, an American multinational corporation—one that produces more than 55,000 different products in myriad industries and employs more than 90,000 people across the world—approached the international non-governmental organization (INGO) where I was working at that time with a proposition: to develop a short two-week program for eight of the company's senior leaders, who would come to Mumbai to work with local Indian NGOs on issues related to "sustainable development." This encounter between the American multinational, which I'll call ABC, and the INGO, which I'll call the Centre for Sustainability Research (CSR), was orchestrated by a third party, a global consultancy that I'll call Global Exchanges. Global Exchanges' promotional literature explains that its mission is to facilitate "innovative partnerships" between global corporations and "local organizations"—everything from NGOs and social entrepreneurs to foreign governments—with the idea that the skills of the former might improve the "impacts and effectiveness" of the latter. The "exchanges" are set up as "experiential workshops" for senior leaders as part of their team-building trainings. The basic idea is to expose global corporate leaders to the complexities of emerging economies, to help them develop new skills and knowledge with an eye toward identifying new markets and creating new products.

Global Exchanges' lead manager—a woman named Gabi—sent the request for proposals to Mumbai-based CSR, asking us to draft two separate proposals to host two teams from ABC to work with us for two weeks. The projects were all to be located in Mumbai and were to have a "practical field component," involving discussions with "key stakeholders" and "influential decision makers" in the city. We exchanged several emails, ultimately homing in on the two sectors on which the two workshops would focus: water risk and air quality. Two groups of four senior executives from ABC would visit Mumbai for a two-week workshop, one on each theme. Responsibility for designing and facilitating the workshop on water risk was given to me.

My first task was to draft a project brief that articulated the complex context of water risk in Mumbai, with a detailed problem statement and a list of "stakeholder" meetings, activities, and expected "outputs." The team was interested in learning about possibilities for advancing "sustainable water solutions" in Mumbai, explaining that they were interested in potentially "solvable problems" that could be tackled using technological or managerial interventions: problems that might inspire product "innovation."

Now . . . I grew up in Bombay and have lived and worked in the city most of my life. I spent my childhood in the quaint cosmopolitan neighborhood of Byculla in South Bombay. Our apartment building was more than a hundred years old and had many structural and infrastructural challenges, among which water was primary. Water flowed out of our taps for two hours every evening, from 6:30 to 8:30, during which time each household opened the taps in their flats to fill their water-storage tanks. The water challenges we faced were the source of mild irritation and, occasionally, serious altercations that I overheard from my parents' bedroom window that overlooked the building's water tank and pump room.

Interspersed between the many apartment buildings in the neighborhood, which were largely occupied by middle-class and upper-middle-class families, about fifty poorer families lived in *baithi chawls*: single-story, brick, and tin-roofed homes of around a hundred square feet, with each home shared by anywhere between five and ten people. The fifty residences (home to more than four hundred people) shared a community toilet block and a single water tap. To meet their daily water requirements, the baithi chawl households each kept tall plastic tubs for water storage outside their homes. At 6:30 p.m., when the tap started gushing water, members from each family lined up and filled their buckets to transport water to the tubs outside their homes. Water was a unifying social factor that brought neighbors together to discuss the quality and quantity of water received that evening, and a point of conflict if the resource was being misused or restricted in any way. I spent hours looking outside the window, curiously and passively participating in the drama that played out every evening.

Growing up in this neighborhood, I developed a keen understanding that even with all the limitations in our own water-distribution system, our family still lived in relative water ease and abundance. For neighbors in the baithi chawls, by contrast, getting water meant considerable time and effort, and periodic dry taps led them also to forge—over time—political connections that enabled the prompt solution of water problems whenever they became acute. In this context I can recall more than one occasion when the taps in our own building failed to produce water or when the water was turbid or muddy, and we would walk over to our baithi chawl neighbors to ask their help and advice. It was they who knew who to call and what to say in order to get the water flowing again. I grew up with a keen sense of how the everyday rhythms and necessities of water access in the city brought people from different worlds together in awkward, politically infused relations of interdependence and exchange.

All of which is to say: ABC's request that I design a program that would present "solvable" water problems was perplexing, not least because large numbers of Bombay's residents have no officially documented connection to the city's water-distribution network to begin with. But also because the four-person delegation was visiting Mumbai for the first time and would stay only two weeks. What could we show them that could possibly be of any use, either to them or to us?

I began drafting a project brief to study "issues of access to safe and adequate water supply in slum areas of Mumbai." The idea was to explore what water risk looks like in various neighborhoods of the city. Gabi (the project lead from Global Exchanges) was excited about the "community focus" of the project, which she hoped would give the executives a chance to engage with "real problems" and "real people." But there remained for her a nagging question: what would be the final "output" for this project? I suggested this: given ABC's expertise in dealing with complex negotiations involving diverse stakeholders, perhaps it could help us develop a process for "decision making in complex urban scenarios" like this. Gabi liked the idea.

Next, we had to identify the "slum" community where this project could be sited; we selected Aslamnagar,[1] a slum settlement situated at the edge of the Deonar garbage dump in Mumbai's eastern suburb. Gabi suggested

FIGURE 15.1 Looking outside the window. A storyboard showing everyday rhythms of water access in my neighborhood. Drawn by and used courtesy of Chitra Venkataramani.

a local NGO called Apna Shaher ("Our City")[2]—which Global Exchanges had worked with in the past—and suggested that we have the NGO facilitate a meeting with the residents in Aslamnagar. Apna Shaher had been working on housing and infrastructure-related matters in Aslamnagar for over a decade. Given its history of collaborating with Global Exchanges, the lead contact in Apna Shaher was happy to oblige and also offered to take our American visitors on a guided walk through the neighborhood.

Aslamnagar is home to nearly 6,500 households, mostly Muslim families, many of whom work as "ragpickers" in the dump or else in other related businesses such as recycling. It is one of the most infrastructure-deficient areas of the city, where access to potable water, food, health care, sanitation, and education are notoriously undersupplied. Residents of Aslamnagar perennially battle waterborne diseases such as diarrhea, cholera, and typhoid, and they face myriad health risks posed by living close to toxic pollutants. I thought that encountering the material and institutional complexity of the neighborhood might prompt the team to expand its ideas of the scope and dimensions of Bombay's "water problem."

Determined to have them arrive in Mumbai with the goal of learning rather than solving the city's water problems, I recommended that the team have a look at recent research on issues of water supply in Mumbai. I mentioned a recently published ethnographic study of water in Mumbai[3] and even offered to arrange an informational "expert interview" with the author (who happened to be a close friend). I thought that perhaps hearing from an American scholar who was an expert in the field might help the American delegation to rethink their goals: less "solving" and more learning.

We had our Skype call on a Tuesday morning in April 2016. To my pleasant surprise, three of the four executives had actually read the book, so our conversation with the author of the study began with some pointed questions: "How do you think we can begin to investigate this problem of water risk in Mumbai? With whom should we be meeting? Tell us a bit about your research, your journey in Mumbai . . . did you feel *safe*?" The questions and comments poured in from the executives, excited, anxious, and intimidated. It was a stark change from their usual self-confidence.

"Mumbai is indeed complex," the author began, in an effort to address the most-basic misconceptions about water in Mumbai, "but that doesn't mean that it's incomprehensible." She explained to the American delegation how different areas of the city have their pipes pressurized at different levels. So, in practice, someone may have continuous water supply in the taps, but the water pipes supplying the storage tank will be pressurized for only a few hours per day. The important role played by municipal engineers and staff who work with the system every day and therefore know it best should be emphasized more often, as well as community groups, elected officials, global consultants, senior bureaucrats, and city planners, all of whom play critical roles in moving water through the city. After addressing their eager questions, the author ended the call with a word of advice: "Listen, watch, and learn. There is nothing you will be able to solve in this city in two weeks, but there is a lot you can learn from it."

Ten days later the executive team arrived in Mumbai. Our first meeting was with the former representative of the electoral district where Aslamnagar is located.[4] This politician's tenure in office had presided over significant extensions and improvements to the water infrastructure network in the area's slums. Generally speaking, arranging a private meeting with Mumbai politicians is extremely difficult, especially if the meeting is for the purposes of research and thus has little obvious or immediate utility to time-pressed officials. In this case, however, the request to meet with a team of senior executives from the United States was apparently interesting. In fact, all of our "stakeholders"—the ward engineer, the senior bureaucrat, the international water consultants, and the political leader—gave us generous thirty- to sixty-minute time slots. I was amazed; it normally takes me months of befriending the personal assistants to get meetings like these.

The politician invited us to his private office in the Fort neighborhood of South Bombay. His office was decorated with glossy prints of 3-D renderings of redevelopment projects in South Bombay. We gathered in a meeting room. He arrived in minutes, exactly on schedule. He was not only prompt but also forthcoming, sharing with our group the drawings of projects that he was hoping to execute in his district and plans for extending existing water pipelines to areas that are not currently serviced. It was a good meeting indeed (and for me the first encounter with an elected representative so apparently passionate about infrastructural upgrading). I left the meeting wondering: Was he so forthcoming because ABC is a leading brand in several industries? Did he think perhaps he could make a good case for some corporate social-responsibility funding? Or maybe he liked being in the "role" of a local politician, invested and committed to his social goals and his voters? Either way, the American contingents were impressed and were taken by the politician, someone who had the power to carry out projects. "*He* is our target audience," Phillip announced as we got into our vehicles to head north to Aslamnagar.

"Yes, he is important . . . but he's only one among many stakeholders," I added, urging them to stay open-minded about what we would learn from other interlocutors. As we drove closer to the Deonar dump, we could feel the air change even from inside an air-conditioned vehicle. As we left the highway and drove east, and then on a dirt road into Aslamnagar, I grew anxious and even regretful at having arranged this meeting. This will be a futile encounter for the residents of Aslamnagar, I thought to myself, many of whom may offer their time to share stories of struggle and courage to this group of Americans. But what was in it for them?

Two volunteers from Apna Shehar waited at the new water ATM that had been built in collaboration with two private investors in 2015. The water ATM sells clean drinking water to the residents of Aslamnagar using a prepaid card and is managed and operated by residents from the slum. The volunteers introduced us to Reshma and Kalpana, two resident managers of the ATM. As they explained the filtration system, residents came by, bought water, and carried it along to their homes. A crowd of residents and children gathered around us, curiously looking, laughing, snickering. The ABC executives were thrilled by the water ATM, which struck them as a "potential solution." As we walked out of the unit, Kim, who was from the Purification Department, was fascinated by the many filtration systems she had spotted in offices, homes, and institutions in Mumbai, and now this water ATM! It was a new market that ABC could explore.

This was my first time in Aslamnagar. We walked into the community through narrow streets lined with two- or three-story homes, many appended with ladders and external metal staircases dropping onto the street. Every home had one or more large plastic water drums at the doorway. The air was still thick from a still-smoldering fire in the Deonar dump that had officially been extinguished a week ago. We spoke to residents as we walked along. "How do you get your water? Is it a reliable service? Is it adequate for your family? How much do you pay per month?" Gillian enthusiastically documented every moment on her wide-lens camera. Children crowded her, requesting pictures of themselves, and she indulged them while she indulged herself.

We finally arrived at the *aganwadi*, the small community center and nursery created for women and children in the slum. This was a tiny, dimly lit room on the ground floor, about a hundred square feet in area with one street-facing window. As we entered the room, we saw a line of chairs placed along one side and a plastic woven mat placed along the opposite wall. We were asked to take the chairs, and women who came in just after us seated themselves on the mats. Gabi and I sat on the floor with the volunteers and local residents, and I played the role of translator. When they asked about water quality, residents shared stories of the unpredictable supply of water delivered at high prices through water tankers; furthermore, the water received is often murky, almost "black," so most household water-purification solutions would be futile. The complex nature of the problem became more apparent for the team, and they had clearly stepped out of their comfort zone to engage with the field. But in this attempt to complicate the problem for them, I suddenly found myself in the surreal position of a "slum tour guide," having packaged an experiential tour of "real-world problems" for international development executives to "solve" through product development.

As we walked back to our vehicles, the team members reflected on the encounter. They had enjoyed the meeting but were troubled as well. Phillip began: "But those people seemed so happy!" Gillian chimed in: "Yes, the children were smiling . . . they didn't look so poor." Phillip nodded: "Are you sure you haven't selected a rather *safe* slum for us to engage with?" The accusation caught me off guard, and I fumbled to respond. "We in Mumbai are not living in a war zone," I began haltingly, a bit defensively. "Maybe they're happy because they're better off than where they've come from. Maybe some of them have learned how to survive and thrive in scarcity. Or maybe our presence in their neighborhood was an entertaining diversion that made them smile. Who knows?"

A week later, the team presented its impressions on "decision making" in a complex, multi-stakeholder environment. One of my colleagues asked Gillian for her thoughts on localized water-quality solutions, and her response pleasantly surprised me. She thought for a moment and then explained that she had come to realize that the localized, technical solutions that they originally had in mind wouldn't really do much good in a context like Aslamnagar, where water supply is irregular, expensive, variable in quality, administratively complex, and politically fraught. "The problem is more complicated," she said. I thought this was a good takeaway: understanding the complexity of a problem should come *before* offering ready-made solutions. Kim (the quietest of the bunch) concluded: "I'm not sure if any of this [pointing to the presentation on the screen] will be as useful to you. But the experience has been invaluable for us. You have changed our ways of thinking about developing cities." I sighed with relief, but also with some ambivalence. On the one hand I had succeeded in packaging my city—and their experience of it—as a problem of "sustainable development" while also prompting them to rethink precisely what that might mean. Yet at the same time this feeling of "success" was qualified: the complexity of Mumbai's water problems is such that although I had achieved my goal of reframing the "problem," I hadn't managed to effectively redirect their boundless energy and resources in any clear way.

That evening I left for Dhaka, Bangladesh, for a conference on community-based climate change adaptation. As part of the conference's study trips, we visited slum areas in the outskirts of Dhaka city, where the primary livelihood was that of textile recycling. Local NGOs from Dhaka facilitated community engagements in similar small, dimly lit rooms in these communities, where we asked questions and local representatives translated them to community members. I had come full circle, from facilitator to consumer of development packaging.

Notes

1. The name of this neighborhood has been changed.
2. The name of the NGO has been changed.
3. Lisa Björkman, *Pipe Politics, Contested Waters: Embedded Infrastructures of Millennial Mumbai* (Durham, NC: Duke University Press, 2015).
4. Because of a change in gender and caste reservation of candidate's incumbent electoral district, the politician contested (and won) the 2017 race in another constituency.

16 **SHANKAR** DELIVERING AUTHENTICITY

Ken Kuroda

IT IS 9:30 A.M. on a hot October Monday in 2015, Bandra West station, Central Bombay. The station is jam-packed with southbound commuters making their daily commute toward the South Bombay central business district. I am standing in front of a group of men dressed in white *topi-kurta* uniforms rummaging through a sea of vertical metal cylinders splayed out on the ground. Shankar, my main informant and guide for the day, spots me and is extremely irritated: "You're late! Sorting starting! I have ten more. Come!" Shankar is a *dabbawala,* one of the 5,000 or so lunch-box deliverymen who deliver close to 200,000 *tiffins*—lunch boxes—on a daily basis to clients all around the city. The core of their business model, to deliver homemade food to laborers all over Bombay, has not changed over the past 125 years of their organizational history. The metal tiffins were being intensely scanned by the fifteen or so dabbawalas present, ranging from twenty-two-year-old Shankar to those who could be his grandfather, hurriedly sorting and loading these onto wooden crates to be carried onto the luggage compartment of the train. More dabbawalas are arriving with their batches of tiffin, hung beside their rusty bicycles or stacked on wooden pushcarts, while barking at pedestrians and auto-wallas (taxi drivers) coming in their way.

If space is squeezed in Bombay, so is time. Each dabbawala must deliver, on average, forty tiffins to diverse clients in different locations, all within the crucial time frame of lunchtime, between 12 p.m. and 1 p.m.; moreover, the 200,000 tiffins all come from different points, the individual domestic hearths of clients as well as small-scale catering businesses, rendering the entire logistical ordeal, upheld by a meticulous sorting system and painstakingly coordinated teamwork, an immensely complex one. Risk and uncertainty are endemic to their work. These range from everyday congestion, transportation delays, and road blockages to the frequent religious processions, political rallies, and devastating monsoon rains that temporarily destabilize the city. Because each tiffin goes through multiple hands, from pickup, sorting, to delivery, a single componential delay within this sixty-kilometer longitudinal supply chain will cause a catastrophic butterfly effect on the entire system.

Misdelivery of tiffin is a cardinal sin. In Bombay, and India at large, where diets and tastes are complexly informed by religious, caste, class, and community markers, ingesting the wrong type of food is more than an inconvenience, having the potential to induce utter moral and medical catastrophe and destabilize the bodily and mental humors from within. One crucial line that mustn't be crossed is the one between vegetarianism and meat eating, and in cosmopolitan Bombay one finds diverse communities observing their respected dietary habits based on a complex mixture of which gods they fast for and feast to, individual medical conditions, and their economic standing and aspirations. Shankar, who has among his clients both meat-eating Muslims and vegetarian Jains, warns me against such dangers: "What would happen if I deliver *sukha* [dry] mutton to a chaste Jain?" One man's meat is another's poison.

Not only misdelivery but also delivery time is a grave concern for customers, who require the tiffin while it is hot and fresh. Freshness of food is not only a matter of convenience but also of cosmology. Especially in Hindu and Jain South Asia, leftover foods, or *jutha*, are ritually and medically impure, as *leftover* implies loss of taste, nourishment, and vitality. Late tiffin is stale tiffin, which not only undermines the efforts of the home cook but also such religiously informed gastronomic ideals of cooked food as pure food. From an economic standpoint, being able to eat freshly cooked food every day is itself a marker of socio-material affluence in an environment where it is common practice among the working classes to eat leftover rice that has been left out in the open for a few days. What the predominantly middle-class dabbawala customers purchase at a thousand rupees per month[1] for their delivery services is a guarantee of swift delivery before the heat and chaos of Bombay putrefy their food. The dabbawalas have successfully tapped into such ingrained appetites for community-specific homemade lunches.

Back to the hot October Monday in 2015, my first tiffin delivery journey with the dabbawalas. I barely keep up with Shankar's pace as he weaves through an army of pedestrians coming at his way, into the serpentine alleyways of bazaars and *chawls* where he will pick up his designated eighteen tiffins from homes and brick-and-mortar catering companies. The first customer, whom Shankar says always brings him good luck, is Mrs. Sheikh, an elderly Muslim lady from Gujarat who has been sending tiffins to her two children for the past six years. The older one is a bachelor, a doctor in a prominent public hospital; the younger one is married, without children, but his wife works in a printing office and has no time to cook food for him. I ask whether she sees her sons often; Mrs. Sheikh, with a shy laugh, answers: "Absolutely not! They are very, very busy. But their tiffins always come back empty." An empty tiffin indexes a full stomach, and it is Shankar's job to connect mothers and sons, wives and husbands, across distances. The dabbawalas take their mission seriously. Shankar explained that as followers of the Varkari Sampradaya sect, a religious movement that broke off from Hinduism in the thirteenth century and puts supreme emphasis on unconditional *bhakti* (worship) of all beings in this world, the dabbawalas are performing bhakti through their work for their customers. They believe that their work is above mere manual labor because they are fulfilling the important task of feeding, which comes only out of intimacy. A homemade tiffin has weight and meaning, and many dabbawalas are not shy to express how they feel about their work. "Had we be delivering pizza for Dominos, we would not be doing as much bhakti!" Shankar jokingly told me once. We bid farewell to Mrs. Sheikh after drinking the *kokum-sharbat* (berry cooler) she had generously prepared. "Shankar is like my son; I see him every day. Kokum-sharbat is his favorite, so I prepare it every other day for him to enjoy."

As he gathers more and more tiffins around his shoulders, each tiffin weighing in at up to one kilo, his girth expands to almost double, making it difficult for him to maneuver through the narrow streets. A reckless motorcycle runs past us from behind in a near-miss collision, thanks to Shankar's quick reflexes and ability to hear its beeping amid the cacophony of the bazaar, tugging his left arm upward to avoid contact. Shankar is calm and confident; this is his turf. Each dabbawala is assigned a "delivery line" when they first join, which is the specific route from pickup to final delivery. A dabbawala's route will generally remain unchanged throughout his career, notwithstanding sudden injuries and changes in demand. In Shankar's case, his route involved pickups in two areas of Bandra East and deliveries to offices around Nariman Point in South Bombay.

After returning to Bandra station, I wait with a group of seven dabbawalas and many dozens of tiffins in front of the train's luggage compartment, which is reserved for commuters with large cargoes such as vendors and street hawkers carrying their products. The twelve or fifteen carriages of Bombay Local's Western Line are broken down into several categories, with first, second, women's-only, and disabled classes, each having different fares and etiquettes. But the two or three luggage compartments are, because of the limited space and the combined size of the passengers and their luggage, particularly difficult to maneuver during rush hour. As our 10:39 Borivali-Churchgate train approaches, the dabbawalas start taking their positions. The train stops for less than one minute, and within this short window many hundreds of commuters get on and off individual carriages. During peak hour, people start reshuffling inside the carriages minutes before arrival, calling out to people in front of them whether they will be getting off next; if one fails to advance toward the exit doors in time, the flood of incoming passengers will push the person seeking to alight straight back into the compartment. The sensation here is one of both floating and fighting.

As the numerous other vendors slowly crowd the area, Shankar, grabbing one end of his crate, warns me: "You get on when I say—quickly, *na*." The train comes into the platform, and I can already hear shouts coming from both the incoming train and the platform; commuters start jumping out of the open doors much before the train halts, carrying with them the velocity of the train, several of them almost running into me. I've seen passengers slip and fall (injuries are common), but today everyone is surefooted. Shouts become louder, and the dabbawalas form a group in an effort to protect their ground and ward off the dozen or so commuters with large bags full of clothes, gadgets, and vegetables who are also struggling to get a foothold. As the luggage compartment arrives ten seconds past 10:39—exactly at where the dabbawalas have camped—the shouting and screeching reach an almost-comic level, as if the passengers on the platform are conducting a military drill while others leap in a panic out of the train. Twenty seconds later, the alighting passengers safely off, the time to strike has arrived. The dabbawalas shout: "*Pudhe chala!* [Move forward!]" as they drive the two crates and batches of tiffin into the half-full compartment, swiftly sliding these onto the floor and neatly against the wall to make enough space for other passengers to load in their luggage. Some dabbawalas take up the much-coveted place next to the open doors, where the breeze can be fully felt, while others compactly place themselves on the ground. Shankar is nodding off amid this brief moment of rest. Once reaching Churchgate, he will carry his batch on his bicycle directly to the offices of his clients; then in the afternoon, he will repeat the journey, this time from office to home. Other dabbawalas have started singing *bhajans* (devotional songs) to celebrate their successful morning trip and to prepare for the afternoon. I also close my eyes, lulled by the humming of the train and the monotonous chants, reflecting upon my journey with the tiffin, engulfed in satisfaction that I am part of something important: the perpetual battle to feed Mumbai's hungry workforce.

What complicates these daily rhythms of the dabbawala work and network is the exceptional national and international fame their tribe has enjoyed since the late 1990s. Since 1998, when *Forbes* magazine wrote the earliest article on the dabbawalas for a mass audience, the Bombay dabbawala has become synonymous with hard work and mind-boggling organizational efficiency.[2] Conceptualized as "ingenious illiterates," the dabbawalas have been hailed with sensationalist accounts of "the common men of Bombay who logistically debunk the likes of Amazon and FedEx." Bombay's dabbawalas soon found themselves on international circuits of media moguls, management scientists, and business-school field trips. The dabbawalas have impressive résumés, including a case study by Harvard Business School, a BBC documentary, and an (all-expense-paid) invitation to Prince Charles's wedding in 2005, which was attended by four senior dabbawalas.

I was introduced to Shankar based on his reputation for both proficiency in English and his leading of "dabbawala tours" for tourists. I had not heard of the "dabbawala tour" but learned quickly after Shankar invited me for a *surmai* (kingfish) feast in his one-room chawl deep in Dharavi. While I was ruminating over how I might reciprocate the gesture, Shankar saved me the trouble, cutting right to the chase. "Let's talk business," Shankar said boisterously, laying out the details for the series of "full dabbawala day tours" that he had in mind for me. I would be invited to follow Shankar for a full working day, during which time I (i.e., the dabbawala tourist) would be permitted to "click all the pictures and videos" I desired. I flipped through his impressive portfolio binder, consisting of photo shoots with foreigners dressed in topi-kurta attire, dizzied by a full stomach and struggling to digest what he was proposing. Shankar scribbled a few numbers on his notebook and drew my attention toward it: "60,000. In one month you will know everything about the dabbawalas."[3]

My first feeling was of betrayal; the surmai was quite literally bait, and I felt embarrassed at having gobbled it down so naively. I explained that there had been a misunderstanding, that I was a student in Bombay to study culture and life, not a tourist or someone who makes documentaries. Shankar jumped up enthusiastically and smiled broadly. "Yes, I know!" He continued: "You are studying culture, right? That is very good. There is so much to our work that cannot be covered in one day. I will personally introduce you to my customers. One of my customers is a very big man working in Air India office. You will take interview and photo with him, and many more. But you cannot do this alone. You need me." He had a point. In the wake of the 2008 Bombay terrorist attacks, security for semipublic spaces such as offices, hotels, and malls had tightened, making it difficult for an outsider to just pop in. Shankar had access to spaces that I was keen to enter, and he was offering to share. He did not forget to instruct me not to tell any other dabbawala of our "contract" (as he put it) because this would be in violation of his team's rules. Moreover, he explained, others would be "jealous."

In retrospect, the proposal made me uncomfortable because it seemed to invalidate the sense of achievement for which I had been longing: the achievement of "access" and "insider status" that still sits at the heart of the discipline of anthropology. Proper ethnographic practice was supposed to entail the forging of *social* relations with informants, not cash-animated *contractual* connections like what Shankar was proposing! Interpretive ethnography is premised on the reflexive attention of the researcher to socio-relational processes of knowledge production by means of which the accounts come into being. If anyone with enough time and money can just come along and *buy* the accounts, then this would surely compromise the integrity and sincerity of the entire study, would it not? Yet for Shankar, it was clear that the premise of my "fieldwork ethics" was fundamentally flawed: in my principled insistence that I be granted access to his world *for free*—on the basis of, say, "friendship" or "trust"—I was being infinitely less fair than a tourist or documentarian who offered to pay a fair price for the information she sought. In expecting, or indeed fantasizing, our correspondence to be "real" and "authentic," as defined by being unmediated by money, I was paradoxically buying into a romanticized narrative of "anthropologist meets local" while looking away from Shankar's reality, where money was *always* productive of meaningful social relationships. The way he talked about his tours and how he showed me his photos convinced me of the fact that he wasn't *just* doing this for money (if there ever was such a one-dimensional position), but with as much pride and satisfaction as delivering tiffins.

For Shankar, his "official job" of delivering tiffins and his side business of giving tours complemented each other, in that the value of the tours inhered in the expertise animating the tiffin delivery business (his tours were conducted *while* he was delivering) even as the tours often embellished the scope and content of that expertise, thereby inflating its value (for example, Shankar's oft-repeated comments on the value of the dabbawala work in connecting loving mother and son, their religiosity as Varkaris, and so on). This cycle of value creation challenges naive conceptions of "authenticity" as something that is somehow prior to its discursive production as such, a conception that had been at the source of my initial repulsion toward Shankar's monetization of cultural insights. Here, the dabbawala tours join the "reality tours" of Dharavi slum tours and Dhobi Ghat tours, where it is similarly fallacious to separate any idea of "authentic expertise" from the performance and, indeed, the monetization of that expertise.

Moreover, Shankar himself was often inconsistent regarding his "business" ethic and in fact often reintroduced the discourse of "authentic friendship" when it served him better. Although he eventually convinced me to take on his proposition—paying a few hundred rupees and a cup of *chai* at the end of each day—he remained insistent that I not mention our arrangement to other dabbawalas. If his superiors were to come to know, he explained, they would most likely ask for a "cut" of the deal, which would certainly mean more expenses for me and less intake for Shankar. For this reason, he explained, I would do well not to speak to any of his colleagues, who might "snitch," although in retrospect it seems likely that this cautionary word also worked to protect his market share—to dissuade me, that is, from striking a deal with other dabbawalas. In this context, when introducing me to his team members Shankar always referred to me as simply his "friend," thereby evoking the very same conceptual distinction between authentic friendship and monetary transactions that I had with me on our first meeting. However, his colleagues knew better and would occasionally nudge me to disclose how much I had paid Shankar.

And Shankar forbade me as well from mentioning our arrangement to any of his customers because, as he put it, "Dabbawalas have a good image." Customers, he worried, might feel that his commercial tour guiding betrayed the ethic of bhakti and diligence that animated the low-paid work of the dabbawalas. Gaining quick "easy" money for tours could be read by longtime customers as a materialistic and selfish motive, a potential deal breaker for dabbawala customers who placed their own moral-gastronomic purity in Shankar's hands.

Shankar's ethical multilingualism shed new light on our initial encounter, which I initially formulated as a mismatch of moralities regarding what consisted of productive, authentic social relationships. Rather, this went beyond fieldworker and informant, and touched upon an important aspect of what it meant to live and work in contemporary Mumbai: the coexistence of multiple moralities and the perpetual need to command and manipulate these moralities in order to garner both monetary and sociocultural capital. The fieldwork encounter was but a particular node amid his many strategies to produce relationships, generate cash, and maintain his reputation and achieve a sense of entrepreneurship; for me, it was a particular node to gather meaningful information, to make sense of expert knowledge, and to enter a world with which I was unfamiliar, for my own pleasure and satisfaction.

Chapter 16: Shankar

1. A thousand rupees is approximately 15 USD (14.6 USD as of August 4, 2018). Customers, many of them working in government/clerical jobs, often earned a monthly salary of between 30,000 rupees and 50,000 rupees.

2. While *Forbes* is often credited with having "certified" the Bombay dabbawala network with "6-sigma" status, an international business standard used to assess the failure/defect rate of a production or supply-chain process, the original article merely estimates a possible misdelivery rate based on interviews. Nor have there been subsequent certifications, which owes to the lack of centralized mechanisms to track each delivery component. Yet the "6-sigma myth" continues on to this day as part of the dabbawala folklore. See N. Subrata Chakravarty, "Fast Food," *Forbes*, August 10, 1998.

3. At that time, Shankar's monthly salary as a dabbawala was anywhere between 10,000 and 15,000 rupees (150 to 220 USD), depending on high and low business seasons.

17 **MANAL-MUNA** COOKING UP VALUE

Tarini Bedi

THE FAMILIAR WHIFF OF SWEAT, salty sea breeze, and *bombil* snaked its way from the humid corners of the city through the air bridge to meet us right as the airline crew flung the heavy doors of the hardworking Boeing into a steamy Mumbai night. As I smacked my lips thinking longingly of all the fried bombil I would eat here, my phone began to beep. Solemn signs all over the air bridge warned the undisciplined, "protected area, no cell phone signal." However, my little Nokia, my hardy "Mumbai mobile," was recalcitrant, or perhaps all the airport security in the world could not keep out my caller, the inimitable Muna. I answered furtively, hoping nobody would notice as the familiar voice of Muna crackled over the line. *Muna* is shortened from *Manal*. However, in a post-1993 Mumbai, working-class Muslim women like Muna admit that they find it exceedingly difficult to find housing, employment, or social acceptance if they are clearly marked as Muslim. Therefore, she uses the more culturally ambiguous name Muna, which many around her confuse with the common Hindu name Mona. Muna happily banks on this ambiguity.

"Salaam, baby, and hello to Bumbai," said the cheerful voice on the other end of the phone. It has always been difficult to gauge how old Muna is.

Like many women of her generation, she marks her age through relational events and social and biological rites of passage rather than by the measures of calendrical days or years. Raised in Hyderabad by her widowed mother, all she knew of anything approximating a "birthday" was that she came into the world just ten days after her truck-driver father was killed somewhere between Hyderabad and Sholapur in a brutal automobile accident. She could be just ten years older than I or twenty, but she is a grandmother, so she calls all "English-speaking" younger women "baby." Even in my middle age, I am reconciled to this as are most of the other women she encounters. Muna never went to school and cannot read or write. However, she has taught herself to speak an impressive amount of English simply through the many lives she lives in the city. In this sense, her proclamation "Hello to Bumbai" is delightfully characteristic of the ways that those who acquire English in these messy and lived ways make themselves uniquely understood. "Baby, hello to Bumbai." How much more welcoming to this fiercely multilingual city where English breezes in and out of the lived vernacular than the sterile, standard, landing announcement from United Airlines: "Devio aur Sajjano, Mumbai mein aapka swagat hai!" (Ladies and gentlemen, welcome to Mumbai!)

I am losing my reception, but Muna's throaty voice continues to crackle into the phone: "I have sent my man, the same man as last time; you remember, his name is Sanjay. He is outside with a car to pick you up. Don't worry about waiting at the ATM for money. Modiji [the prime minister] has made sure that the ATMs are cleaned out of money. Tomorrow morning my other man, Dollar Dev, will come to your flat. You can give him all the dead thousand-rupee notes you have, and he will exchange for new notes. Dollar Dev is his code name, so don't mention his name to anyone else. Sanjay also has a *dabba* [box] of dinner that I have packed for you. Remember to take it. Phone me in the morning if you need anything else."

There was a sharp, piercing sound on the other end and then silence. My "Mumbai mobile" had accomplished the first of its jobs. I had a comfortable ride back to the place I was staying, some form of illicit access to cash even as the country was rife with chaos over Modi's demonetization, and, not least, food from Muna's kitchen. I could not help but hope that the dabba was packed with the characteristically eclectic mix of Muna's Hyderabadi roots and the adaptations to her Mumbai catering clientele: *tava* fried, masala *surmai*, *sabudane ki khichdi*, and *baghaare baigan*.

When I first met her, Muna ran a small catering business out of her one-room home in the Saat Rasta area of Central Mumbai. Here she prepared food for office workers, college students, and single men and women around Mumbai who found relish, economy, and, perhaps—like me—mostly the solace of home in her lovingly prepared and tasty meals. In Mumbai's working-class neighborhoods, a woman who conjures up large amounts of food to be transported by *dabbawallas*, drivers, and delivery boys to a range of eaters across the city becomes central to the ecology of the neighborhood, particularly to its early mornings, when the peeling, cooking, and washing up begins. Women like Muna live outside conventional economies of production and stake their claims not just through what they have to give but also through what they can demand from others.

The vegetable sellers in the Saat Rasta *bhaji* (vegetable) market counted on Muna's daily purchase of large quantities of the staples of onions, tomatoes, potatoes, and seasonal vegetables. Jadhav, the owner of the local *kirana* shop, automatically counted Muna's orders of rice, oil, and spices as part of his weekly accounts. She purchased supplies from him every three or four days but paid him only every month. This worked for both of them. Jadhav's regular delivery boys were given lunch by Muna whenever they delivered supplies to her, so he got away with paying them a little less than he otherwise would. When their boss was not watching, these young men would often help Muna with cleaning her house, filling and carrying buckets of water for her from the tap at the street corner, or doing other odd jobs for her around the neighborhood. This help allowed Muna a bit of time in the afternoons to watch her favorite television programs on the cooking channels, the recipes of which would often end up on the lunch menus the next day.

Two younger women, Asha and Malini, would arrive each morning to help Muna knead and roll the 150 *chapattis* (flatbreads) she packed each day. As Muna meticulously cut, sautéed, fried, and stirred, Asha and Malini listened to her deliberative instructions on each recipe. Both women admitted that Muna's inspiration was encouraging them to start catering businesses of their own. Muna's business, like almost all small businesses in Mumbai, ran entirely on cash. She delivered food daily; however, her clients paid her monthly in wads of cash. She did have a bank account with some savings at the nearby State Bank of India, but she was embarrassed to go to the bank alone because she could neither read nor write, which prevented her from knowing how to fill out a withdrawal slip, and the ATM machine, which made withdrawal much easier, rarely ever worked. This meant that she relied on a local moneylender to give her cash credit when she needed it. She paid this back at the end of each month with interest rates that she negotiated from month to month. The moneylender was Dollar Dev, as he had come to be known because he dealt with loans and exchanges of all kinds of currency, not just rupees. From what I gathered, Dev often traded interest for food from Muna. Muna also helped connect Dev to several other clients who needed easy currency exchanges or easy credit or who, like me during the recent demonetization, wanted to off-load dead notes for new ones long after the government's deadline to do so through banks was past. During the demonetization crisis in late 2016, most of Muna's clients off-loaded their "black" cash as payments to Muna for her food, knowing that she would find a way to give life to this dead cash through her connections. Further, given that many of Muna's clients lived and worked beyond the basti, she also had the capacity to connect many from the basti to employment opportunities across the city.

Food—that most intimate and corporal form of consumption—seemed to conjure a great deal of trust between the cook and the eater.

When her dabba clients across Mumbai wanted a driver, or domestic help, or an office peon, they would often give Muna a call. In Muna's life and those who she served, "currency" therefore took many forms; it was distributed, circulated, shared, and paid back as money, food, favors, interest, and opportunity, all duly delivered through care associated with the kitchen.

I met Muna many years ago quite accidentally as I was waiting at a shared taxi stand outside the Lower Parel station. She was with two husky young men whom I later learned were her sons, Altaf and Atif. They each carried two enormous aluminum tins, from the depths of which emanated delicious odors of garlic, chilies, and coconut. These were tins in which they delivered thick stews of dal fry, *ussal*, and *poha* to tailors at a workshop run by a woman who supplies cushion covers, curtains, and bedcovers to several American retailers. We all jumped into a taxi to Mahalaxmi, and when I discovered that Muna catered, I asked if she would be willing to send me cooked meals for the duration of my stay in Mumbai. She agreed to take me on as a *dabba* client, and the next morning a *tiffin* full of goodies arrived at my door delivered by Sanjay, general agent for everything Muna needed to get done. When putting in my food order for the next day via a neighbor's phone, I mentioned to Muna that I was having some difficulty getting a SIM card for Mumbai without a permanent address or a PAN (permanent account number) card. "Don't worry; I will fix it. Sanjay can get you a SIM card using my address and PAN. I do it for everyone here who does not have an address, so don't worry."

Sure enough, the next morning Sanjay arrived bearing a tiffin and an envelope with a SIM card. "Muna told me to get you this," he said. "Just pay me two thousand, five hundred rupees, and I will settle the accounts with her and with the man at the phone shop." I asked no questions or demanded no clarifications over the cost of the card. I simply passed on the cash to Sanjay and emerged into my fieldwork equipped with the much-needed mobile phone. A few weeks later, when I happened to pick up my food from Muna's house myself, I learned that this Muna-Sanjay-phone-man nexus had provided SIM cards first to two neighborhood women who helped Muna with making chapattis and then to several others who moved in and out of the basti bereft of permanent addresses. If the Mumbai authorities ever do an audit on cell phones in the city, Sanjay and Muna would probably emerge as "persons of interest" because of the sheer number of phone numbers attached to their names. Neither of them seemed to care about this, and each told me that they trusted the other enough to know that they would keep each other out of trouble if they ever had to. Sanjay and Muna are good examples of how ecologies of interdependence and connection in Mumbai's working-class neighborhoods function more generally; getting people connected by phone is a metaphor for the all other connections that these relations of trust and mutual dependence make possible.

Sanjay's sister Anita and his sister-in-law Sandhya were employed as cook's helpers in Muna's catering business. The additional household income helped Sanjay tide over the uncertainties of his own employment as a truck driver. It also made Sanjay feel more comfortable that the older, maternal Muna watched over the women in his household while he was away on the road. Sanjay is about twenty years younger than Muna; he is literate and has some experience with accounting. He often helped Muna with the accounting for her business. When her bigger clients did not pay up on time or tried to bargain over the contract, it was Sanjay who would show up to make the collection calls. Neither Sanjay nor Muna was quite clear on how much money her business actually made after all the expenses were paid off. While Muna was able to pay her rent and feed her family, the monetary value or profits of the catering business seemed less important to her than the value of the other kinds of capacities it helped her build and distribute. When Sanjay lost his job with the trucking company, Muna managed to get him a position as a contract driver to transport textiles from the factory to the tailoring workshop for her largest catering client. When Muna moved out of Saat Rasta in 2010, Sanjay's sister Anita, who had learned to cook under Muna, began her own catering business, which in turn employed several more women from the neighborhood. That section of Saat Rasta continues to churn with activity and smells from the steaming pots of stew. Anita credits

Muna with allowing them to dream of a business and then for showing them how to do it.

Muna first moved to this *kholi* in Saat Rasta when she gave up on her husband, Mansoor. Mansoor had remarried a few years ago and brought his new wife to live with them. When their children were young, Mansoor had held a string of different jobs but was unable to find long-term or stable employment in Mumbai. To make up for the uncertainty in the family income, Muna had worked as a cook and domestic help in the home of an upper-middle-class family. The job had paid enough for them to be able to rent a small space in a *chawl* in Mahalaxmi. Muna's older son, Altaf, was less interested in school than he was in working for the local event-management team that organized decorations for Hindu festivals in the neighborhood: Diwali, *dahi-handi*, and his very favorite, *Ganesh Chaturthi*. Muna told me that "Altaf was a true *Ganapati bhakht*." He was the most enthusiastic organizer of the neighborhood's Ganapati *pandal*, for which he would set up elaborate lighting, flowers, music, and disco balls. He would also sit at the pandal all night greeting worshippers and readjusting the fabric and dressing on the idol. He became so well known that many local politicians who used the pandal as a political platform would invoke Altaf's devotion as exemplary of Mumbai's pious youth. Muna encouraged this devotion because she felt that it would keep Altaf away from the "bad influences" of the underworld that young Muslim boys like Altaf who drop out of school are often believed to be attracted to. "It is better that he is a Ganaptai bhakht than a nonpious *musalman* don," she often said, only half-jokingly.[1]

Whereas Altaf had found his calling in Ganapati, Mansoor continued to flounder. Finally, the family that Muna worked with found Mansoor a job as an office helper for an Indian business family in Dubai. Mansoor wept profusely as he boarded his flight to Dubai, saying he did not want to leave home, but Muna insisted that it was best for the family that he earn some money abroad. Muna recalled that although he was treated quite well in Dubai, he was terribly homesick and could rarely talk through his tears over the phone. In a little over five months, much to Muna's anger, he came back to Mumbai and became increasingly distant and depressed. He would spend many days away from home visiting his brother and sister-in-law in nearby Vashi. His sister-in-law felt that he would be happier with another wife and fixed him up with her niece, whom he secretly married. Because Mansoor was still unemployed and unable to support his new wife, the newlyweds moved back to live with Muna and her boys. Muna visited many Sunni religious leaders across Mumbai to try to find a way to get divorced from Mansoor. However, everywhere she went she was told that since the *nikah* (marriage) had not been registered in the civil courts, a divorce without his consent was not possible. In frustration, Muna simply packed up and left the house with her sons. With the help of a local political leader who knew of Altaf's Ganapati pandals and who was associated with the *Akhil Bharatiya Sena* founded by the well-known gangster Arun Gawli, Muna found a kholi in Saat Rasta—the way (*rasta*) of seven (*saat*) roads. Saat Rasta was, and continues to be, a center of Arun Gawli's support. It is also a powerful spatial metaphor of urban connection; it the place where seven of Mumbai's roads converge and lead out.

Everyone in Saat Rasta knew that Muna was Muslim, but the ambiguity of her name made people less uncomfortable and made it easier for Hindu-Maharashtrian women in the neighborhood looking for paid employment close to home to convince their families that Muna's business was an appropriate one. News of Muna's successful business and the trust that she was building in the community that was the seat of Gawli's control traveled to the ears of the imprisoned don. Gawli and his brother are notorious protectors in this area and are referred to as "daddy" and "papa," respectively. Like Muna, Gawli's Muslim wife changed her name to Asha and embraced Hindu-Maharashtrian religious practices in the neighborhood. This could well be why Muna's biography got some attention from Gawli's men. Muna told me that Gawli's men had approached her twice asking her to join their party and to run for an election, but she had politely refused: "I don't want to get into politics; my business is food, not *sarkar*." When I pushed Muna further on this matter of politics, she admitted that those involved in politics in this area were actually doing quite a lot of good and that she would be fine joining them. However, she also felt that she would be putting herself and her family in danger if she actually joined a political party and had to face political rivals. She is afraid of how violent politics can become and therefore is more comfortable with keeping her influence rooted in food, a form of "politics" no doubt, but not of "sarkar." Indeed, Muna's connections to the city originated in this more intimate, feminized work of nourishment, but through this work I watched her become a critical circuit for so much else. I was the recipient of her largesse on many occasions and always felt the need to thank her profusely. I also always felt intensely obligated to her, as though I needed to offer her something more than I currently was. When I said this to her rather embarrassedly, she just laughed: "Don't worry about obligations, baby, you know like everyone else, I am mummy of Mumbai."

While Muna giggled at this declaration, it seems no accident that she presents the nature of her distributive labor through these logics of familial kinship. In a milieu where terms such as *daddy* and *papa* already dictate currencies of influence, *mummy of Mumbai* indeed seems the logical way for Muna to be seen as influential but also at the same time as domesticated and nurturing.

Note

1. See also Hardy (chapter 26) and Shivkumar (chapter 25) on the importance of "producers" and "production managers" in the entertainment and film industries.

18 **RAMJI** BUSINESS ENERGIZER

Lisa Björkman

RAMJI AND I SAT down for dinner at Govinda's restaurant at the ISKCON (International Society for Krishna Consciousness) temple at Juhu beach. He apologized for the lack of privacy; ordinarily, he would have invited me to the Borivali sanctuary where he generally receives people, but he was preparing to start a rather involved *tantric* ritual there tomorrow morning for a new client: a flagging industrialist whose two small factories (one in aluminum, another in plastics) had been underperforming. "Their technology is up to date even though the factories are not new," Ramji explained, but for some reason the little factories were having a hard time retaining market share. So the proprietor had asked Ramji for "help."

The proprietor, a Gujarati fellow who lives in the Mumbai suburb of Borivali (not far from Ramji's own home), had been given Ramji's contact information by a mutual acquaintance (also Gujarati) whom Ramji had helped in sorting out a family matter a few years back. "That man's son had become addicted to betting on cricket matches," Ramji explained. And worse yet, the boy had taken to drinking away his ill-gotten earnings. The boy was young, around eighteen or twenty, and no amount of sense-talking by his father had disabused him of his passion for sports betting. So the boy's father had reached out to Ramji for "help." The boy's father was the proprietor of a small Borivali shop dealing in antique coins; he had met Ramji when the latter had popped into the coin shop one afternoon in search of something very particular: a Victorian-era silver coin, something dating from around the time of the uprising of 1857.[1] The silver was needed for a *yantra* that Ramji was crafting for a client whose particular energetic imbalances were bound up with the vibrational resonance of that particular historical moment. A silver coin minted in that period would carry the vibration of the era, so he would melt down the coin and use the silver in forging the yantra.

But Ramji told none of this to the coin dealer that day; rather, he introduced himself—as he generally does—as a "medical doctor," which is indeed true. The trader promptly produced the very coin that Ramji sought and thus became Ramji's go-to period-metal guy: a nickel-brass coin from the 1980s? No problem. A bronze coin from the year of India's independence? Look no further. Over the following years Ramji became a regular at the coin shop, and the proprietor slowly developed an understanding of the unconventional uses to which his prized coins were being put. It was with this understanding that the coin trader approached Ramji in the shop one fine morning, asking whether there might be something Ramji could do for the man's wayward son . . . ?

Ramji agreed to take on the work. The coin trader prepaid for the yantra in cash (of the more contemporary paper-note variety), which Ramji then used to assemble the materials he would need to forge the yantra, to carry out the necessary consecrations, and to support the team of *pujaris* who would perform six months of continuous chanting, prayers, and ritual fires in the cave complex on the Gujarat-Rajasthan border, where much of Ramji's work takes place and where the yantra's "twin" would reside. Indeed, as Ramji explained, it's not enough to make a yantra and charge it with the correct vibration; the energy needs to be maintained at the right frequency and intensity for a specific duration. For this reason, Ramji makes an exact duplicate of each yantra, energetically pairing the twin with the one given to the client. Because the two yantras are materially and energetically identical, the vibration transferred by mantra to the yantra in Ramji's cave also reaches the one in the client's possession.

The yantra that Ramji gave to the coin dealer's son was in the form of a flat silver box, two-by-two inches or so. Inside the box was a silver plate, on which Ramji inscribed symbols and diacritics representing and instantiating the vibration of the *mantra* with which the yantra was energetically imbued. As Ramji explained, "The electromagnetic waves of the mantra charge the yantra to produce the requisite energy for the purpose of the mantra." The boy—who was told only that the yantra was "for his benefit" but not precisely what sort of "benefit" his father and the tantric had in mind—was tasked simply with opening the box once per week and staring ("for at least five minutes") at his own image reflected back to him in silver. Within a month, Ramji told me proudly, the boy had given up alcohol; within a year, he had completely lost interest in cricket. Shortly thereafter, he had launched a small enterprise manufacturing laminated posters. Wonderstruck at the miraculous turnaround of his wayward son, the coin trader had mentioned Ramji's talents to a close friend and neighbor—our industrialist of the flagging plastic and aluminum factories—who phoned up Ramji straightaway. It's this industrialist's work that would begin in the morning, Rajmi explained to me, which was why we had to meet here in Juhu instead of in Borivali.

RAMJI GREW UP IN the rajasthani city of Jodhpur, the youngest child in a largish, Gujarati-speaking extended-family household anchored by his father's father—Ramji's *dada*—who would become Ramji's guru. Ramji's dada was the official *purohit* for the *raja* (king) of Jodhpur, Ramji explained (hence their family name Purohit, which means "priest"), as well as for a handful of regional rajas, in an era when well-trained tantrics were in increasingly short supply. Ramji's dada was trained in the "oral tradition" by his own father until the latter's untimely death in Dada's adolescence, at which point the young purohit took over his father's official position in the royal court. In order to continue the training and sharpening of the young man's skills, Ramji explained, the raja summoned a famous tantric from Bengal who took up residence in Jodhpur and spent the remainder of his life passing on to Ramji's dada the mantras and rituals learned in his own childhood from his guru in Bengal. Ramji's grandfather's tradition is thus Bengali—his prayers and rituals are directed to "the Goddess," to whom Ramji refers as Kali Mata. All these gods and goddesses, Ramji explains, they're just orientations—perspectives even—on a single godhead of which we are all part: "Each of us may resonate with a different manifestation of this godhead; the decision of whom to worship is a personal matter." Ramji's dada chose the Goddess, taking up his Bengali mentor's tradition rather than that of his own father. Notwithstanding this language of individual choice, Ramji would also become a devotee of Kali Mata.

Ramji was trained by his dada—to whom Ramji refers as his "guru." Rajmi's dada had two sons of his own—of which Ramji's father was the younger—but neither of Dada's sons demonstrated aptitude or interest in their father's work.[2] Nor did any of the two brothers' four elder sons show a special flair. Two of Ramji's "cousin-brothers" (cousins raised in the same household as brothers) showed some interest in childhood but struggled to memorize the mantras, to sit still for so long and to endure the rigors of training. Ramji explained that the essence of tantric training is to learn "control of the senses," which requires the "practice of obedience" and the suspension of "logic-based" reasoning and questioning. This is was the hardest part for Ramji's elder brothers, for whom the curiosities and restlessness of childhood competed with the rigors of tantric training in "obedience." For Ramji, however, things were different. "It was easy for me," Ramji explained. "It came to me very naturally; it was never difficult." He recalled:

> My formal spiritual education began at the age of seven. I started to learn to chant mantras and was taught how to conduct Vedic fire rituals. At the age of eleven, I was taken to a room and directed to sit and chant—at the highest possible volume—until I was told to stop. I was never told how many days I would be spending in this room. For food, I was given only *dal* water—the broth from boiled lentils. Sleep was not permitted; if I fell asleep, I was awakened after one hour. Forty-one days later, my guru told me that I had qualified for tantric education.

The point wasn't to see whether he could do it, Ramji explained; rather, the continuous chanting effectively transformed his energetic makeup such that he would be able do the work of tantra. The initiation wasn't a *test* of already-cultivated expertise, in other words, but entailed the ritual production of the tantric expertise itself.

Ramji attended regular school alongside his brothers, spending any spare moment with his dada: early mornings, late evenings, holidays. Yes, his dada was strict, but that was because "tantra requires perfection." Dada relentlessly corrected Ramji's errors, but never with impatience or anger, always *pyar se*—with love. Ramji recalled the rigors of training with his grandfather with an air of wistful nostalgia. These days, when he's not engaged in some ritual or work for a client, Ramji spends his time poring over handwritten notes from his childhood training with his beloved grandfather. "There are many powerful mantras that I have not perfected," he explains. Perfecting a mantra—mastering the combination of sounds and intonations and volumes to produce the vibrational resonance by means of which the material world can be transformed—takes years. How does he know when he gets it right? "I hear it," Ramji explains. He explains that tantra is a "science of sound." He uses the English word *science*.[3] It is sound that allows Ramji to "intervene" in the world; his expertise consists in his ability to "hear" the "vibrational makeup" of the material world—of people and things—and to master the "technologies" (he uses the English word) that allow for alteration of the material world. I ask, "Can you hear *my* vibration?" He bobs his head: "Yes. If I focus, then I can hear."

AFTER COMPLETING UNIVERSITY, Ramji (on the insistence of his mother) went directly to medical school, where he excelled in his studies. And the very day he received his medical degree, having fulfilled his mother's wishes that her youngest boy "become a doctor," Ramji caught the train to Mount Abu to rejoin his grandfather. Ramji was in his mid-twenties when an offer of marriage for his younger sister arrived from a Bombay-based Gujarati family. Ramji's mother was raised in Bombay, and Ramji had spent a number of childhood holidays with his Nana and Nani—his maternal grandparents—who stayed in the Gujarati neighborhood of Borivali in Bombay's northwest suburbs. Ramji had traveled to Bombay on a few prior occasions, whenever his dada was summoned by this or that Borivali neighbor for some or another kind of "help." So it happened that on the occasion of Ramji's visit to Bombay to meet the family of the man who would become his sister's husband, Ramji's nana introduced the young tantric to a family acquaintance: a Bombay-based Gujarati who was keenly interested in Ramji's services. The fellow owned a small business and had recently taken to investing in land on the urban periphery. He made Ramji a proposal: move to Bombay and work for him. Thus, as his grandfather was to the rajas of Jodhpur, Ramji became the purohit for a man who would become one of Bombay's largest and most powerful real estate developers.

RAMJI OUTLINES THREE GENRES OF "help" requests with which people generally approach him. The most common relates to business and finance-related matters. A second kind of request is health related; a third is "spiritual." Requests for spiritual help are of two kinds, Ramji explains: the first kind comes from people seeking help with their own *evolvement* (he used the English word): relief from the suffering of this world and guidance on how to achieve earthly happiness and (ultimately) unity with god. A second kind of request, for "spiritual help," Ramji explains, tends to come from other spiritual "healers"—*sanyasis* (renunciates), for instance. Sanyasis may have renounced society, Ramji explains, but they remain in the material world—dependent on society for food and sustenance, which they accept in the form of gifts. But these gifts carry the energy and vibration of the giver, so a sanyasi may experience "energetic imbalances" as a result of these encounters. For this reason sanyasis sometimes come to him for "help with cleaning," Ramji explains, to help them maintain their energy and to process any karmic impurities. (Also among Ramji's "spiritual" clients are a handful of Hasidic Jewish healers, who approached Ramji at a new-age trade show in New York City seeking a very similar sort of "cleaning" help.) If Ramji is willing to "take on the work," then he tells the client how much money is to be paid—up front and in cash.

Ramji explains that these cash transfers accomplish two interrelated kinds of work: first (and most importantly), the money is a "medium for the energy" for which the client is seeking Ramji's help. The money conveys these energetic imbalances, and Ramji enlists his skills in mantra, prayer, and fire ritual to perform the work of energetic "cleaning." In what amounts to a sort of energetic "sliding scale" (my words, not his), the amount of money needed to correct an energetic imbalance will differ from person to person, according to his or her resources. The second, more conventional use of the money is that of exchange: Ramji uses the money to purchase the things he needs to prepare a yantra, which is why he needs the cash in advance. He searches out the right combination of metals to conduct the vibration of the mantras that will be sonically inscribed. He then forges the yantras by hand (he learned metalwork from his grandfather) and then "programs" the yantra with the precise vibrational energy needed. Each yantra is like a unique "prescription," Ramji explains, his vocabulary betraying his background as a medical doctor. "It is crafted for that person only."

RAMJI RECKONS that demand for his "help" is at least as much today as it was thirty years ago, when he moved to Bombay to work with the Gujarati land investor. Yet from among the many requests for his help, Ramji takes on a very small number of projects, the vast majority of which are for Bombay-based clients, and almost all are related to business. "Business is important work," Ramji explains, because business success leads to material "development" (he uses the English word) and, as a result, to a societal-level increase in "spiritual knowledge." Ramji explains the connection: "If someone was to try to sit and chant mantra while he was starving, it wouldn't be possible because he would be distracted and uncomfortable." In that way, "material sustenance is necessary before someone can devote energy to god." I ask: "But then why would you help a businessman who presumably already has enough to eat?" "Because business success creates employment," Ramji explains, "which is good for society." It is only when people are employed that they can meet their material needs and improve their lives in such a way that will allow them—"eventually"—to devote time to spiritual matters. I counter: "But what if some particular business success puts people *out* of work? If some business shuts down because of another's success or if technological innovation obviates human labor—then is this still 'development'?" Ramji explains: "Those people will find some other work. There may be some time lag, but the improvement is in the long run. They—or their children—will find better work in a new industry with better technology." I point out—citing the infamous closing of Bombay's textile mills since the 1980s—that historically this has not always been the case. He responds with an unworried shrug: "Those people must be doing *some* work; they survive *somehow, na?*" More important than any individual job, Ramji explains, is the "improvement" of the business environment as a whole and of the technological changes that drive "development" and increase "employment." While the various projects that he takes on are highly individualized, Ramji explains that the *maksad* (goal) of his tantra is aimed at the level of society. Indeed, Ramji's economic philosophy is a quirky combination of a Keynesian stimulus package and neoclassical trickle-down: on the one hand, tantric stimulation increases demand for some particular enterprise. This increased demand eventually leads to investment in labor-saving technological advances that will afford—at the societal level—greater aggregate leisure time for spiritual practice. Yet, unlike more traditional Keynesianism, Ramji's economic philosophy is absent any broader-level intervention to mitigate attendant recessions, depressions, and social dislocations (short term or otherwise) that might ensue. If people fall on hard times as a result of societal "improvement," Ramji explains, then it must be because of their karma. He smiles and adds, but then again, "Maybe it's also in their karma to meet me."

WITH RAMJI'S INDIVIDUAL PROJECTS invariably and admittedly having broad and variegated effects, I asked: "So . . . how do you decide which projects to take on and which to turn down?" He says: "I decide what work to do and not do; it's up to me. So many requests come, and I can only take on a few clients. I must decide; I listen to their vibration and then decide whose energy I want to work with." He explains that "some people come to me for ego-related reasons. They just want wealth and power." Ramji explains that he does not take on that sort of work.

I've been waiting for Ramji to mention these issues of wealth and power . . . and politics. After all, his Gujarati real estate developer had since become— by Ramji's own reckoning—"very politically connected." I asked: "Have you ever been approached by a potential client for some election-related work?" "No," Ramji shakes his head firmly. "Never. And if someone were to ask for that kind of work," Ramji added (unprompted), he would refuse. "Democracy is like *nature*," Ramji explained (using the English word), "so we must not interfere. If the *public* wants to elect some person, then that is *nature*; it must happen. If I were to interfere to make one person win the election, then how many other dynamics would I be affecting?" I demure: "But how is your business-related work any different? You make someone's business prosper, but then someone else's company may go bankrupt as a result." He shakes his head, repeating, "Business improvement leads to *development* for society as a whole. Politics is just about power. If it is someone's destiny to be in power, then we must not interfere." I press: "But you yourself said that business success is connected to politics—that your successful Gujarati builder is politically influential." It's an open secret, I point out, that electoral campaigns in Mumbai are financed largely by the real estate industry. Yes, Ramji answers, "but it was also that man's karma that I should come into his life." And in any case, he adds, money is neither necessary nor sufficient to produce political power. If a man has "good ideas" and "a strong voice," then he doesn't need money to win an election, Ramji explains, "because his power is the power of his voice." If someone is "eligible, no amount of money can prevent him from coming to power. Because when he speaks, people will *hear* that he is eligible." "Fair enough," I say, "but still, campaigns cost money. Let's say I have great ideas and I'm eligible and I have a strong voice and all . . . but I can't afford the campaign expenses involved in broadcasting my voice." Ramji is unfazed: "When you're eligible, you will be able to afford it because people will recognize your eligibility. And, just like that, the expenses will be paid for." He explains that there are two kinds of people in politics: the first kind of person is driven by ego, and the second is those who are eligible. "It's the job of the public to recognize who is who, and to support those who are eligible—those who will use their power and resources for the improvement of society . . . those who will create jobs and avert war."

Avert war? I ask Ramji: "Is tantra capable of averting wars and preventing violence? Would your tantra be able to resolve, say, the conflict in the Middle East?" "Yes, absolutely!" he says. "But it would be very expensive, all the rituals, and who's ready to pay for it?" I ask, "But if ending war is for the good of society, why don't you do it for free?" He explains, "See, it's not so much that the rituals themselves are expensive. Coconuts don't cost much. But the money is also *energy*—it is the *intention* of those who want to resolve the matter." Of course Ramji has his own intentions and commitments, and he "automatically" puts his skills to work toward these ends. He weathered the 1992–93 riots ensconced in his Borivali flat, praying and chanting throughout the duration of the violence ("It could have been so much worse . . ."). But in the case of international conflicts and military escalations, he explains, "the egos are so big that it would require an equal amount of commitment and intention"—money—to sort it out.

Notes

1. Beginning in May 1857 as a "mutiny" of Indian sepoys against the British East India Company, the year-long insurrection—ultimately unsuccessful—is sometimes referred to as India's first war of independence.

2. Ramji explains that Dada's daughters—as women—were not considered for tantric training. Times may be changing, however; Ramji maintains that he might consider training one of his daughters should either of them exhibit the necessary interest and aptitude.

3. Our conversations took place in Hindi.

PART IV DIFFERENCE

Anjali Arondekar

BOMBAY IS A CITY OF DREAMS, or so the story goes, a place of make-believe, where differences of gender, region, religion, class, and language (the list grows by the day) collide, mesh, and sometimes produce magical landscapes of possibility and futurity. As a "theatre of conflict," its actors are characters spun out of competing and often violent narratives of development, where survival and success go hand in hand with clashing stories of erasure and emergence.[1] If my opening comments are beginning to read like well-rehearsed filmic lines from Netflix's new series *Sacred Games* (an adaptation of Vikram Chandra's wonderful novel), a sprawling masterpiece about the messy underbelly of Bombay life, then I am on the right track. The characters in this section are all scrappy, complex, and often divided protagonists who speak to the everyday perils and pleasures of sustaining the "sacred" games of survival within an ever-expanding and often unforgiving cityscape. Their stories are familiar, ordinary even, and variously address a specific genealogy of difference as delineated through histories of sexuality, migration, religion, labor, caste, performance, and language. At the heart of each of these stories is a studied attention to how structures of differentiation accrue and/or cede value within the broader networks of a city where lives are constantly being made and undone by the machinations of power and location. We have here a wide array of liminal figures, each articulating a very distinct management of the politics of location and representation: Bhimsen Gaikwad, a self-taught Ambedkari *jalsa* performer, Laxmi, a *hijra* political strategist, Sultan, an Ismaili organizer, Raj, the street snack vendor, the multigenerational speakers of *Bambaiya* and Bombay Urdu, and Dharamsey, an archaeologist of knowledge and tradition.

For each of these characters, producing and sustaining individual and collective forms of belonging within the increasingly communalized urban landscape that is Bombay produce strategic gains and losses, compromises and heroics. Even as the short meditations assembled here emerge from a more or less contemporary engagement with Bombay, the questions they raise are of course deeply imbricated in longer histories of urban development. In fact, what these stories make abundantly clear is that the idea of difference itself has always been a spatialized, temporalized, and thus highly fraught site of constant contestation and emergence. Laxmi's gender identification as a hijra is as much of a shifting and affective historical form as are the many historical cadences of Bambaiya that inflect the speech of many city dwellers. Raj's Shiv Sena *vada pav raj* (street food kingdom) has much to offer and also to learn from Sultan's careful management of an Ismaili Muslim heritage, and vice versa. As such, it is equally fitting that the characters in this section do not cohere around a theme or genre; rather, their stories unmoor us from settled understandings of how identifications and representations of difference and belonging operate within a city like Bombay. There are no heroes or villains in these stories of situated difference, only a set of individuals and sensibilities that decode the demands of life in a megacity.

In "Bhimsen Gaikwad: Singer of Justice," Shailaja Paik travels to the home of Mr. Bhivaji, aka Bhimsen Gaikwad, a "famous octogenarian Ambedkari *shahir* (poet/singer)" as part of a larger project on *tamasha* (traveling folk theater) in the urban centers of Maharashtra and Pune. Paik, herself a *Dalit* feminist scholar/activist, is well tuned to the upheavals of caste, class, and gender, and she brings those sensibilities to her acquaintance with Gaikwad. They meet at his tiny working-class home in Dombivili, amid the traces of his expansive life as a performer and Ambedkar activist. We learn that Gaikwad is an autodidact, a Dalit migrant from rural Maharashtra who came to Bombay in search of a life and music, moving from one job to another (most significantly at Satguru's, a renowned arts store/gallery) until he earned the honorific "Bhimsen," a nod to his stature and influence within the local music circles he inhabits. Gaikwad recounts his early informal training as a singer and *kalavant* (artist), signaling continuously to the centrality of caste in the navigation of his *kala* (art) as a musician. What marks Gaikwad's story is his astute mobilization of music as the medium through which he can simultaneously both embrace and bypass the sign of caste. For instance, Gaikwad assembles a group of musicians, a *gayan* (singing) group equipped with the requisite harmonium, *dholak*, and banjo, who travel to many venues to perform. "Everybody invited us to perform," he tells us with great pride. "Muslims, Maratha, Koli . . . they called us 'Jaibhimvale' or 'Ambedkarvali Party'" and "respected our art and invited us to sing at their events." At the center of such popularity, we learn, is an ever-present reminder of the circulation of caste as marker of value and identification. Even as Gaikwad claims that there is no discrimination against his group as people from all castes and religions flock to hear their music, the group remains routinely marked as a "Dalit" and "Ambedkar" group. Here, music both expands and contracts the differences of caste.

Through Gaikwad, we also learn of how his Ambedkarite vision profoundly affects the variegated genres of music that he studies and emulates. As he speaks movingly of his political awakening at the *pret yatra* (death procession) of Babasaheb Ambedkar in his native Pune, he explains how his creative ambition is fueled by the risks and struggles at the heart of Ambedkar's anti-caste project. To do so, Gaikwad literally reinvents the songs and tunes he learns, smuggling in anti-caste content within settled genres such as popular Hindi songs. The difference of caste becomes the creative impetus for the distinction of his kala, a performative practice that breathes new life into the very aesthetic forms that sediment caste and labor hierarchies. Gone are the days of our bondage and slavery, his songs tells us, summoning instead a brave new world of social and political equality.

If caste, craft, and location set the stage for our first story, the second meditation by David J. Strohl moves us on to a very different milieu. "Sultan: Image Manager" invites us into the interior workings of the minority (albeit affluent) Ismaili Muslim community in Bombay. Sultan, a key figure and organizer in the community, plays the central character, providing the reader with precise details of the elaborate self-fashioning that goes into the success and growth of the Ismailis in Bombay. Unlike the cramped quarters of Bhimsen Gaikwad's *chawl* flat, we encounter Sultan either in plush air-conditioned offices in Santa Cruz or in the privileged enclaves of the South Bombay Radio Club. Servants and workers of all ilk flit in and out of the edges of this ethnography, marking the class status of the Ismaili community, making its struggles to stay relevant and nonpartisan within a divided urban landscape even more compelling.

Ismailis' problems, Sultan tells us at the very outset, is that their difference/belonging as religious and civil subjects is legible unevenly across communities in Bombay. For Hindus, they are mistaken as majority Muslims; for Muslims, they are perversely seen as not Muslim enough and as followers of an iconoclastic religious tradition. As Sultan succinctly puts it, "We're caught between the devil and the deep blue sea. When the riots come, the Hindus say we're Muslims, and the Muslims say we're Hindus." For Sultan, the Ismaili community's ability to be inclusive, expansive, and syncretic in its beliefs and practices can often lead to the community being cast as too flexible, incapable of marking its own differences and histories. Thus, the singular challenge, Sultan tells Strohl, is to fashion a representation of the Ismaili subject as one who is distinct yet inviting, progressive yet traditional, and, last but not least, a law-abiding and significant contributor to the city they inhabit. There is a certain self-referential irony in Sultan's laments around Ismaili misrepresentations; he interjects, "but we do not have it as bad as the Ahmadis do in Pakistan" and reminds Strohl that "when His Highness Aga Khan visits India, it's treated as a state visit." In many ways this ethnography echoes the structural ironies of the Ismaili agon of belonging and difference: it is both a record of the Ismaili success as a minority community and an account of the representational perils that undergird such success. One striking example of such an agon is the way the Ismailis handle the controversy around the placement of the photo of the Aga Khan in their central prayer hall. Wary of backlash from the mainstream Muslim community that would read such a placement as heresy against God, the Imam orders his followers to relocate the photo to the side walls, thereby continuing to honor the Aga Khan while keeping potential criticism at bay.

Maura Finkelstein's "Raj: Carting Cosmopolitanism" also engages with structures of self-fashioning in a rabidly divided Bombay, albeit in ways that both converge and diverge with Sultan's carefully scripted messages. This entry is food for thought, literally and metaphorically, as it walks us through the culinary empire that is the husband-wife duo Raj and Ketaki. But *vada pav*, that tasty morsel of Bombay's soul, is the true protagonist of this ethnography, its primacy as native Bombay fare narrated through a long history of divisive and violent communal and labor politics. Finkelstein's chief native informant, Raj, a different brand of *Marathi manoos*, moves us through this history, reminding us that vada pav began as a galvanizing instrument of *Shiv Sena*'s divisive politics. Shiva Vada Pav, during and after the ravaging labor strikes of the early 1980s, was meant to replace all "foreign" (read: non-Maharashtrian) foods and make hearty, Maharashtrian fare central again. Party supporters and striking laborers were invited to set up stalls selling vada pav in populous areas of the city, providing them part-time jobs while at the same time providing "street muscle" for the Sena. In turn, such workers were seen to be gathering electoral support for the Shiv Sena through the proliferation and popularity of such vada pav stalls. Finkelstein quotes Vikram Doctor's wry comment: "It's the only employment generation scheme that the Sena has ever been able to set up."

What makes Raj's (and connectedly that of his wife, Ketaki's) forays into vada pav entrepreneurship noteworthy is their rerouting of the founding regionalism and violence at the heart of the Shiv Sena's initiatives. Raj and Ketaki, we find out, broker vada pav into a menu of culinary diversity where the opening of a "Shiv Vada Pav" cart allows them to offer a range of South Indian and Western food options. As long as the cart says "Vada Pav," what is being sold under its auspices remains unexamined. And in case we read such diversification projects as progressive or secular, Raj quietly reminds us that his interests are not in the machinations of identity politics. It is at such counterintuitive moments that Finkelstein's ethnography provides its sharpest insights. There is no celebration of Raj as a dissident or radical voice; rather, Finkelstein turns our attention to the details of Raj's story where vada pav secures love, romance, and the security of family life. We learn that Raj and Ketaki meet and fall in love in a kitchen, work together as culinary entrepreneurs, and establish a life of upward mobility and eventual stability through their early forays into Shiv Vada Pav. Of note is the marked absence of any references to religion or region in their account of their success. As Finkelstein notes, "Raj never failed to remind me that his carts were about survival and not about politics: a deep-fried lifeboat in a sea of informal, insecure labor."

If vada pav is the overdetermined food of choice for the working-class Marathi manoos in Bombay, *hijras* (anywhere in South Asia) currently hold the same unenviable position when it comes to ethnographies engaging the difference of gender and sexuality. R. Swaminathan's "Laxmi: Dealer in Emotion" gives us a glimpse into the daily workings of a Bombay hijra known simply as Laxmi. In an ironic narrative twist, one of the key characters in the entry, a Shiv Sena leader, jokingly asks Swaminathan why he is writing about Laxmi and hijras in Bombay. "Write about us," he says, "there is no water, electricity, or jobs . . . their needs are nothing in comparison to ours." Laxmi is also aware of her value as a subject and repeatedly provokes Swaminathan by noting that he, like her, is also looking for a "good deal." More than any other entry in part IV, Laxmi's story weighs heavily on the exigencies of embodied difference and its instrumentalization within a monetized world.

For Swaminathan, Laxmi's story is key to understanding the shifting barometers of Bombay (Mumbai) as it moves from the distributive networks of Sena *shakhas* (neighborhood party offices) to the aggressively digitized branded communalism of an *Aadhar* (national biometric identification) age. Laxmi enters the scene at Elphinstone railway station and slowly moves through spaces and temporalities of the city, gaining access to and contact with a wide range of collectivities. Laxmi and her cadre of hijras are affective "banks," hoarding and distributing positive and negative sentiment to secure economic stability. They cajole monies from customers anxious about their masculinity, provide live entertainment at Shiv Sena and corporate parties, and engage a whole host of informants and factotums to augment the earnings of their community. Shame and humiliation, affective markers of segregation and difference, are astutely mobilized by Laxmi and her comrades to assist loan companies in recovering their debts. "We are either feared or shunned. We arouse shame," Laxmi tells Swaminathan, speaking directly to the emotive capital that hijras accumulate and distribute through their circulation. One of the most remarkable moments in the ethnography arrives when Laxmi directly addresses the challenges of representation and mediation facing stigmatized subjects. In so doing, she couples the misreadings of hijras with the misreadings of Narendra Modi, pointing out that if the Indian populace can conveniently forget his role in the Gujarat riots and "look at him differently," they can certainly extend the same courtesy to the hijra community. Such a damning analogy deftly calls up Modi's tarnished past and uses its political reframing to signal a different future for the "invisible" histories of hijras.

Edward Simpson's "Dharamsey: Assembler of Traditions" may seem far afield from the political and affective machinations of Laxmi and her collective of hijras. Yet Simpson's interests in systems of knowledge formation, in how and why we know our spaces and faces, echo many of the questions that Laxmi raises for her readers. If Laxmi calls on us to read "differently," to reexamine broader histories of political mobilization, Simpson's Dharamsey speaks to the complex sociology of religious and community identity in the city. In many ways this entry is less about an individual character, Dharamsey, than about epistemologies of knowledge formation and how they are informed and/or deterred by histories of migration and gentrification. Dharamsey is more an archival figure, a treasure trove of information, citation, and imagination, drawing his listeners, specifically Simpson, into new orders of meaning. It is thus no coincidence that Simpson encounters Virchand Dharamsey, aka Dharamseybhai, in the reading room of the Asiatic Society as he voyages to Bombay to learn more about the Kutch diaspora in western India. A well-known and respected figure in Bombay bibliophile and scholarly circles, Dharamsey introduces Simpson to historical figures such as Bhagwanlal Indraji (1839–1888) who, like Dharamsey, were decoders of the past and translated landscapes, inscriptions, and people as sources for understanding history. As such, Dharamsey becomes a sort of allegory for modes of reading belonging amid difference, specifically through the legacies of a past mired in histories of migration and the displacement of material texts and bodies. Simpson acknowledges a shift in focus even as he is composing his ethnography: "The more I thought about the encounter [with Dharamsey], the more I realized that it wasn't only about Dharamsey but about a broader history of scholarship and relations between the provinces and Bombay." As such, Simpson invites us to rework our orientations to knowledge production, exhorting his readers to think difference within and without our research methods and objects. To understand Dharamsey is to understand a broader network of signification, of translation, and of citation.

It is fitting that the section concludes with an entry on the vagaries of language and code switching, and the histories of difference they congeal in their manifold articulations. Simply put, how are communities of belonging and difference literally vernacularized? This is the central question animating Gautam Pemmaraju's rich and enlivening entry "Dalvi: Speaker of Cities." The characters here are spoken vernaculars, a set of linguistic and aesthetic formations, attached to the bodies of multigenerational speakers flung across the divided landscape of Bombay. Our protagonist is Bambaiya, a city dialect comprising a "wide word pool drawing from languages including Marathi, Gujurati, Konkani, Portuguese, and English" and mobilizing broad "types of slang, trade related and street registers, comedic use," invoking poetic and prose traditions from a range of historical and regional genres. Hovering over the entry is the shadow of Abdus Sattar Dalvi, a learned proponent of Bombay Urdu, who guides Pemmaraju through his tour of Bambaiya and its linguistic avatars and histories. Dalvi serves as a learned footnote throughout the entry, juxtaposing learned/archival wisdom alongside the interviews that Pemmaraju conducts along the way.

Pemmaraju introduces the reader to a cast of multigenerational speakers of Bambaiya who flag different registers of its impact and circulation. Even as such friendships have faltered, and religious divides hardened as communalism takes over the city of Bombay, Bambaiya, Pemmaraju writes, continues to take hold of the linguistic imaginations of the young people living within its confines. Mohammed Iqbal and Rafique Baghdadi are two young Bambaiya speakers who participate in such linguistic formations, touched more by their affiliations to film and gang culture. Throughout, Pemmaraju is keen to emphasize that Bambaiya embodies "the living languages of Bombay," that it is a palimpsest of and witness to enduring histories, traditions, and migrations of peoples and cultures. Even as literary fiction (give or take a few stories by Manto) eschews the charms of Bambaiya, its force as a proxy for Bombay toughness is best exemplified, Pemmaraju notes, in Sanjay Dutt's infamous onscreen and offscreen "angry young man" personalities. A scion of a famous Hindi film dynasty (his parents are Nargis and Sunil Dutt), he exemplifies the urban and urbane flavors of Bambaiya: Dutt is an ex-convict in real life, as he is the savior of disgruntled young men on the screen. His portrayal of gangster life (in *Munnabhai*, for example) is spliced with the incantations of Bambaiya, weaving us in and out of the jousts of urban struggle.

As we work our way through part IV's essays on difference and representation, it becomes abundantly clear that the scholars/authors behind these sketches are equally a part of the stories they tell, their political, intellectual, and affective ambitions and struggles writ large in the ethnographic canvases they paint for their readers. To speak to the challenges of scripting difference, as it were, is to speak directly to the mediations of politics, language, positionality, gender, and so much more in the stories each author tells. We see Shailaja Paik, for instance, foregrounding the burden of representation as she speaks directly to her difficulties with Bhimsen Gaikwad's Ambedkarite vision. How can we embrace Gaikwad, she asks sotto voce, if he celebrates Dalit patriarchy in his songs of transformation? Can his engagement with difference erase and escalate caste oppression all at once? What happens to the difference of gender within the kala of caste? David Strohl also underscores the strategic garrulity of his subject, who mostly provides him with scripted and authoritative answers to complex questions. As his entry concludes, we are left with a rich and fragmentary text whose ethnographic ambitions invite us to read and theorize further.

Maura Finkelstein's entry gives us a deft and often candid view of her main character, Raj. We are invited into his domesticity, his romance, and his economic future. Yet despite such ethnographic detail, Finkelstein learns little from Raj and Ketaki regarding any views on religion or regional divides.

Have their entrepreneurial voyages made them more aware (and even respectful) of religious difference? We know that Shiv Vada Pav bypasses the regional restraints imposed upon it at its formation, but Raj and Ketki appear remarkably reticent regarding how those restraints are affectively encountered and translated. These are questions that remain unanswered. Similarly, R. Swaminathan's own value as "Sweden's Mumbaikar" fashions the shape of his narrative. Laxmi becomes a valuable (and protected) commodity because of her relationship with him, a point made repeatedly by several characters in the sketch. However, we learn little of how such an attachment translates into Swaminathan's own deciphering of the substance of his ethnographic encounters. Questions of self, translation, voice, access, and mediation take center stage in Edward Simpson's and Gautam Pemmaraju's entries on knowledge formations and language circulation. Simpson speaks at length about his changed relationship to histories of migration after his meetings with Dharamsey, such that Dharamsey's "tradition" of learning becomes part of the broader canon of writers he studies. Similarly, Pemmaraju provides multiple exemplars of Bambaiya speakers and of the difficulties of navigating those vernaculars during the course of his interviews.

Together, these rich ethnographies present us with snapshots of the articulations and navigations of difference that are tantalizingly revelatory, even as they underscore the staged nature of their own exposure. The central challenge here is for readers to embrace these stories of urban living and learning as allegories for a larger meditation on the concatenations of difference in a complex historical landscape such as Bombay. After all, each of the characters we encounter here are shape-shifters, strategic actors in a city *tamasha* drama where differences settle and unsettle the workings of daily life. What is most illuminating about the ethnographies assembled here is that they refuse the liminality and/or exceptionality of difference. Rather, each essay engages sites of difference as spaces of efflorescent and plangent creativity, inviting us to participate in a special Bombay remix.

Note

1. See Mariam Dossal, *Theatre of Conflict, City of Hope: Bombay/Mumbai, 1660 to Present Times* (New Delhi: Oxford University Press, 2010).

19 BHIMSEN GAIKWAD SINGER OF JUSTICE

Shailaja Paik

ON JULY 11, 1997, the Maharashtra State Reserve police force opened fire on a protest march in the predominantly Ambedkarite *Dalit* (Dalit Buddhist) neighborhood of Ramabai Nagar in Mumbai's eastern suburbs, killing ten people. The marchers had taken to the streets in response to the desecration of a statue of the late Bhimrao Ramji *Ambedkar*—the revolutionary anti-caste activist and intellectual who is best known as the principal author of India's constitution. Images and icons of Ambedkar—affectionately known as "Babasaheb"—appear throughout Mumbai, particularly in the poorer neighborhoods and humble homes of areas like Ramabai Nagar, where a strong Ambedkarite Dalit community lives. The neighborhood is named after Ramabai, the wife of Ambedkar. The day before the Ramabai Nagar massacre, someone had draped a garland of shoes around an Ambedkar statue in the neighborhood. Six days after the killings, in the face of ample evidence that the police violence had been unprovoked, the officer who had ordered the shootings on the marchers was released from custody. Heartbroken by the officer's release—and the evidence it provided of the reactionary political climate that had overtaken the political movement to which he had devoted his life—Dalit activist/singer/poet and Ramabai Nagar resident Vilas Ghogre committed suicide.

The art and activism of Vilas Ghogre are the subject of Mumbai documentarian Anand Patwardhan's rather hopeful 1985 film *Bombay Our City*, which follows the tireless work of Bombay's Ambedkarite Dalit singer-activists to forge alliances with India's socialist movements, labor organizations, and leftist political parties—class-based movements that had often been silent on the violence of caste oppression. Ghogre had made it his life's work to build a left-wing alliance between Bombay's Dalits and Communists, and it was the failure of this caste-class political project—embodied in the poet's suicide in the wake of the Ramabai killings—with which Patwardhan opens his much darker 2012 sequel film, *Jai Bhim Comrade*.

I was not in Mumbai for the wave of free, open-air public screenings in Mumbai's Dalit-dominated neighborhoods (the inner-city *Bombay Development Department* [BDD] *chawls* in Lalbaug, Byculla, Worli, and Naigaon as well as suburban *vastis* such as Ramabai Nagar) that followed that film's 2012 release. But by all accounts, the *maidans* and squares that hosted the screenings were bursting at the seams, as Mumbaikars—Dalit and non-Dalit—silently watched Patwardhan's four-hour account of the decimation of left-wing Dalit politics and its supplanting with the right-wing identity politics and *Hindutva* (Hindu nationalist) agenda that has swept the country in recent decades.

The high-profile Mumbai screenings of *Jai Bhim Comrade* renewed my interest in performance in the context of my ongoing research about Ambedkari *jalsa* (Ambedkarite folk singing and drama) in Mumbai and Pune. The role of song, dance, drama, and poetry in the political and social life of Ambedkarites has received increasing attention in recent years: in literary sources, in documentary films such as Patwardhan's, and more recently with Chaitanya Tamhane's award-winning film *Court*. Yet for all their subtlety and power, such tidy framings of the relationship between Dalit poets and Dalit politics left me puzzled as well, sitting uneasily alongside what my research has found to be much more tenuous, complex, and contentious articulations. Over the course of my efforts to understand the changing character of uneasy alliances among poets, poetics, and politics, both inside and outside the Dalit community, I asked a friend to put me in touch with Bhimsen Gaikwad, a famous octogenarian Ambedkari *shahir* (poet-singer) from Mumbai, who retired from the stage some years ago. When I met Gaikwad in July 2017, he paid tribute to his icon, Babasaheb, singing for me one of his famous poems:

FIGURE 19.1 BBD *chawl* interior corridor with image of Babasaheb Ambedkar at the far end. Drawn by Anand Prahlad.

Awake, awake, working, working
Bhimrao [Ambedkar] worked for the people
He at times stumbled, but still he was tireless
He broke the chains of slavery
Many mighty had to bow to Bhimrao!

Most of Gaikwad's songs praised the efforts and life of Ambedkar to fight caste discrimination and violence, and to work for social justice in modern India. Yet Gaikwad's poetry also underscored a strict and highly gendered morality, eschewing any hint of sensuality and sexuality—especially, he explained, while performing in the presence of women. Gaikwad was critical of Dalit singers who violate these mores, accusing them of betraying the community by compromising on "propriety"; "nothing *phajil* [overly sexual] or *vait shabda* [sexually provocative words]" belonged in this art. Indeed, Gaikwad's anticaste poetry is strikingly heteronormative:

I am grinding grains
I pray that my husband lives long.
Babasaheb is my husband and God!
He has granted this mantra of social service
I clean and grind grains every morning
I am proud of my Bhim!

In Gaikwad's articulation of Dalit morality and identity, the imagination of the Dalit woman is restricted to that of homemaker; she is aware of Ambedkar and his politics, but she is without public voice of her own. Yet Gaikwad's portrayal of the rural Dalit woman grinding grains is an awkward fit in contemporary Mumbai neighborhoods, where the vast majority of Dalit women I know work outside the home and are certainly not shy with their public political voices.

My own identity as a Dalit woman with an active public life could not have been lost on Gaikwad and was on my mind when I joined him in his tiny one-room/kitchen home in Dombivili. During our conversation, Gaikwad noted my own caste background, referring to "our people" and to me in particular as a "Jaibhimvali-Mahar-Dalit-Buddhist."[1] This was a trend in my fieldwork more generally, as I found that Dalits welcomed me—"*aaplya* [our] madam"—embraced me, and spoke intimately with me as a member of "our" community. Gaikwad was very happy to know that I was studying the history and tradition of Ambedkarite song and drama. He was excited to discuss his work and enthusiastically narrated for me his life journey as a performer. Yet throughout our conversation, he remained notably silent on the uneasy way that my own life and work sat alongside the gendered moralities running through his poetry.

BHIMSEN GAIKWAD'S ORIGINAL NAME is Bhivaji Gaikwad. When he started singing for larger public programs and gaining attention, the shahir community recognized him for his voice and songs. His cousin Sambhaji detected this transformation and suggested that Bhivaji "change his name to Bhimsen," the poet recalled, "which would be more appropriate for a popular singer." As a result, the rural Bhivaji became modern and urbane, with the "kingly" and lofty name Bhimsen.[2]

Gaikwad's father, Barku, hailed from a family of farmers whose menfolk worked during the nonfarming season as traveling *tamasha* (folk theater) artists. Indeed, from the early decades of the twentieth century, *jalsa* (folk dramas) and tamasha were central to the formation of a vibrant Dalit public sphere, with traveling poets and activists using poetry and music to communicate with an audience that was largely illiterate. Ambedkari *shahiri* (poetry) performance acquired a particular political salience beginning in the 1930s, when artists began touring villages and cities to sing about social change.[3]

Barku Gaikwad had originally migrated from Shel-Pimpalgao (Pune District) to Pune city to join a tamasha *phad* (troupe) but left for Mumbai sometime around 1951 or 1952, after the phad broke up. In Mumbai he met famous theater owners, such as Dadu Indurikar and Madhukar Nerale of New Hanuman Theatre, Lower Parel, where he soon found work. Bhimsen Gaikwad thus grew up in Mumbai, surrounded with poetry, music, and dance. He recalled how almost every night there was some kind of performance:

> I was educated until class four in Pune. However, I was not very interested in studies. I had the opportunity to attend night school in Mumbai, but at the time nobody in the family paid attention to [my education]. Therefore, I did not pursue it. Anyway, I was more interested in singing and writing songs. I was not formally trained in singing. I simply watched, heard, and absorbed everything—*tal* [a musical measure], *sur* [tune], *antara* [interval], *kalpana* [idea], if the song was difficult or easy, and how the audience and actors interacted.

Gaikwad developed a passion for singing, training, and rehearsing on his own, learning *khatyal* (sensual and playful) *lavanis* (ballads), film songs, and devotional (Hindu) *bhajans*.

Mumbai embraced Gaikwad: "Pune was like a village," he recalled, "but Mumbai was a city. Shining marayachi—bhav khayacha phukat" [I liked to strut around, show off unnecessarily]. His family stayed with his paternal uncle Dasharath Gaikwad, who worked at a Muslim-owned mutton shop:

> My uncle's job was to collect the different meats: *mothyacha, bakricha* [cow or goat], and sell it. We all lived together in my uncle's room in BDD chawl number two. [People of different caste and religious communities]: Christians, *Apale* [our people: here Dalits], Halbe [Scheduled Tribe], Maratha [Other Backward Class], Phulvale [flower sellers], and so on. Even police lived in the six chawls. Everyone worked in their [caste] community circles. There was no intermingling as such. Of course, they attended our wedding and other ceremonies; however, they did not participate in Ambedkar or Buddha *Jayanti* (birth anniversary festivities).

Thus, Gaikwad emphasized the double movement in Mumbai of spatial proximity and social distancing among people of different religions and castes; people come together for certain activities, yet caste-specific events such as Ambedkar or Buddha Jayanti produce distinctions and differences.

Gaikwad himself began working when he was eighteen, finding his first job at the Satguru photo frame shop in the Fort area of South Mumbai:

> I started working [at the frame shop] with seven rupees in my pocket. I did all sundry jobs at the shop: checking on *chaha-pani* [tea, drinks, snacks] of guests, mopping and keeping the shop clean, and so on. Gradually, I also was promoted to higher-status jobs, like purchasing and delivery of items. [Working in the Fort] area of Mumbai surrounded by Muslims, Sindhis, Gujaratis—I learned Urdu, Punjabi, and Gujarati languages and sang in them too. After marriage, to make ends meet I worked multiple jobs. I lived at the Servant's Quarters in Colaba Dandi, and I used to clean cars for officers, wash the building floors, stairs, and so on. It was important to support my family.

Gaikwad worked during the day, but his nights were devoted to music and singing, not only Ambedkari music but film songs as well:

> I used to sing at different events in the city. Senior singers praised my singing and lyrics. They said I was careful in using *sope, sadhe shabda* [easy to pronounce, simple words]. I sang during Ganpati Utsav celebrations and worked with famous singers like Pralhad Shinde, Bhargav Chavan. [Most importantly,] I sang at Ambedkar and Buddha Jayanti and Babasaheb's [death anniversary] on December sixth. Activists associated with the Dalit movement—Shantabai Dani, Ghanshyamrao Talvatkar, Sumantrao Gaikwad—attended these events and praised me.

Gaikwad recalled that his life was a continuous effort to balance regular employment with his passion for singing, particularly in a political and social capacity. He participated in *jayantis* celebrations of community heroes such as Jotirao Phule, Ambedkar, and the Buddha, as well as at pan-Maharashtrian festivals celebrating Shivaji. Eventually, Gaikwad established his own Sanghmitra *Gayan* (Singing) Party at Chandanvadi-Girgao:

> In 1957 or 1958, I established my own gayan party. Earlier we earned only fifteen rupees, then later it was thirty rupees and gradually it increased. Muslims, Marathas, Kolis, and Agris invited us—whoever provided us some advance to cover our travel and also gave us food, tea, *paan-supari* [betel leaves and betel nut], and water. We also used to sing at *sarvajanik karyakram* [public events]. I set my songs to popular Hindi film tunes. For example, I sang "mukatyane jhukava maan, dyavi mulgi amchya mulala [lower your neck without a word, and give your daughter to our son]" to the famous tune of the song "pyar kiya to darna kya" [from the classic Hindi film *Mughal-e-Azam*].

Although Gaikwad's troupe performed for people of all religions, castes, and classes, his music always challenged caste discrimination, untouchability, and social injustice. For example, in the song just mentioned he instructs upper castes to keep quiet, to bow their heads, and to give their daughters in marriage to their Dalit sons—a reference to Ambedkar's famous strategy from the 1930s, when he began to advocate for intercaste marriage as a way to break caste distinctions and social hierarchies.[4] Setting his bold lyrics to Hindi song tunes increased the popularity of his music.

Once he acquired a harmonium, *dholak* (drum), and banjo, Gaikwad started his own low-budget show:

> Everybody invited us to perform. Muslims, Maratha, Koli . . . they called us "Jaibhimvale" or "Ambedkarvali Party." They respected our art and invited us to sing at their events. Experimenting with the gayan group, I also entertained the idea of starting a Tamasha phad, but it was too expensive.

Gaikwad recalls encountering little caste or religious discrimination, but he emphasized that non-Dalits invariably identified him and his party as a "Dalit" and an "Ambedkarite" group, caste-based recognition that did not appear to bother him; on the contrary, he was proud to be associated with Babasaheb's legacy.

Gaikwad enthusiastically remembers the days of Babasaheb Ambedkar's activism:

I saw Babasaheb in Pune and Mumbai. I was very young. I saw his *pret yatra* [death procession] also. I was very inspired by his work and diligent efforts. I tried to bring this into my songs. After Babasaheb's [work and movement, things were] different. I began to sing Ambedkari shahiri: "Jagale, bhagale, aare jati hita sathi Bhimrao kase vagale. Asave sagale, na rahave vegale, are jati hita sathi Bhimrao kase vagale" [He kept awake; he strove hard. Remember how Bhimrao Ambedkar fought relentlessly the problem of caste discrimination and untouchability. So that we have dignity, rights, and access to the public, so that we are not segregated due to caste, remember the way Ambedkar worked].

While audiences may not have been the source of caste discrimination, Gaikwad spoke of tensions inside the Dalit artist community, as well as between Dalit and non-Dalit artists, especially between Dalit Ambedkarite shahirs and Dalit and non-Dalit tamasha performers: "We learned new songs and tunes from tamasha, but they did not like us very much because we described their performances as vulgar. And for their part, they made fun of us if we did not sing well."

Although there were certain differences, the artists knew that they had to cooperate, learn, and bend certain rules to support one another. "Once, after we performed together in a village, *apale lok* [our people] asked them to organize another event in Buddhavada/Bauddhavada[5] [Mahar-Buddhist quarters]. They agreed, and then the tamasha kalavant requested us to [teach them] Babasaheb's songs because they felt they would otherwise lose popularity in the village." Gaikwad recalls how they mixed different tunes and easily navigated between different forms of folk singing, such as *kavvali* (sufi devotional music), *gavlan* (love songs of Hindu deities Radha-Krishna), and *pavada/povada* (panegyric), changing their contents.

This relatively easy arrangement shifted following Ambedkar's *diksha* (the conversion to Buddhism) on October 14, 1956:

[Following Babasaheb and] Buddhism, [we took] diksha [converted to Buddhism]. We changed the name from Maharvada to Baudhhavada. Others [non-Dalits] mocked us. Some Mahars did not take diksha, and clung to *baluta* [traditional portions of grain they received in exchange for their service to the village] and wanted to keep Mahar *vatan* [hereditary claims in a village, including claims to perform local services]. However, [Ambedkarite Dalits] rejected them. When those Mahars wanting to retain *vatandari* faced atrocities in the villages, they too wanted diksha. [In this social and political moment,] I sang a new song: "Why are you so stubborn about not leaving the past caste obligations? You will gain wisdom and understanding, respect and dignity, and so you will become a new person in Buddhism."

Gaikwad's life changed after his conversion to Ambedkarism and Ambedkarite Buddhism. He explained that although he did not formally convert to Buddhism, the new mentality and modern morality of diksha transformed him completely. Through his songs, he continued to challenge caste hierarchy, caste labor, and upper-caste domination of Dalits:

> We labored for you like slaves
> We ate the bread you gave us
> While keeping our pockets empty
> Gone are those days, *patil* [headman of the village] brother.

Gaikwad was committed to his political radicalism, but in contrast to other artistic traditions such as tamasha kalavant, he remained devoted to a gendered notion of "proper" morality that revolved around a conservative notion of Dalit womanhood. "Tamasha kalavant and our paths are different," Gaikwad explained. "Jalsa had *dholki, tuntune* [drum, one-stringed sitar-like instrument, just as we find in tamasha], but we did not have *nachya* [male dancers] or *nachee* [female dancers]." Gaikwad accused tamasha kalavant artists of undermining the community's morality, not only by having female dancers but for the content of the songs as well: "I could slap Pralhad Shinde [a famous shahir] [for what he has done with his singing]," Gaikwad raged. "It was shameful! When he performed, he sang one or two songs on Ambedkar and continued with all *altu phaltu* [loose morality] songs." By contrast, he emphasized that "singing justice" had a gendered character:

> When I present, women sit in the front row. Dharmala dharun gani [I sing songs that underscore morality, moral virtues]. [I write these songs in such a manner that] they are *dharmaupadesh* [instructions in morality] for women so that they are also able to sing these songs. For example, one song is about when they are at the *jata* [grinding stone] in the morning: "Aata kashala ga lajayacha, jaibhim bolayacha" [Why should we be ashamed now? Say Jaibhim and rise]. Today things have changed because everything is becoming business oriented. It is merely *karamnuk* [entertainment]!

Gaikwad sharply critiqued the popular karamnuk trend in the musical arts. He insisted that "Ambedkarite shahirs should not give in to the entertainment business. They should continue to focus on and dedicate themselves to their leader's agenda of deep social justice." Poets like him have a moral task to fulfill, Gaikwad maintains—not only artists but audience members as well—especially women, whose role in the struggle involves strict adherence to circumscribed codes of modesty and morality.

Gaikwad's gendered political vision is contradictory: his reactionary ideas and notions of "protecting" women would discipline and circumscribe the political voice of a new generation of (Ambedkarite) Dalit women: women like me. Yet sitting with him in his home, I realized as well that while I may not agree with Gaikwad's preferred answer to the question of how to respond to persistent and violent hierarchies of caste and gender in contemporary Mumbai (and in India more generally), to fixate on the contradictions would be to miss the tenuous and complex context within which Gaikwad formulates these particular ideas, and to overlook the *intentions* toward which they are directed. Indeed, while such contradictions may have set Gaikwad at odds with other articulations of radical Dalit politics, the lifelong work of Vilas Ghogre reminds us that Dalit poetry and song have also sought to bridge such rifts—by singing to life shared intentions.

Notes

1. Dalits and non-Dalits use different names to recognize "Dalits." Certainly, the naming of Dalits does not occur in a vacuum; it is socially, politically, and ideologically constructed in certain historical conjunctures, as I have analyzed in my writings on the history and politics of naming Dalits in Maharashtra. See Shailaja Paik, "Mahar-Dalit-Buddhist," *Contributions to Indian Sociology* 45, no. 2 (2011): 217–41.

2. Historically, *sen* and *sena* were suffixes used by kings. For example, the husband of the famous Rajput queen Padmavati was Ratansen.

3. For details, see Shailaja Paik, "Mangala Bansode and the Social Life of Tamasha: Caste, Sexuality, and Discrimination in Modern Maharashtra," *Biography* 40, no. 1 (winter 2017): 170–98.

4. For details, see Sharmila Rege, *Against the Madness of Manu* (New Delhi: Navayana, 2013); Shailaja Paik, *Dalit Women's Education in Modern India: Double Discrimination* (London: Routledge, 2014).

5. About half a million Mahars following Ambedkar converted to Buddhism on October 14, 1956. As a result of this political revolution, they changed the name of their residential quarters from Maharvada to Bauddhavada/Buddhavada. Gaikwad alternated between the words, but the meaning is the same.

20 **SULTAN** IMAGE MANAGER

David J. Strohl

IN EARLY APRIL 2007, I sat in the air-conditioned reception room of a law office in Santa Cruz while waiting for an appointment with Sultan,[1] a community leader and active volunteer in the Ismaili community. Mary, the office's receptionist, sat quietly working, occasionally stopping to take a call and, less often, buzzing into the main office to ask Sultan if he would like to speak with a caller. On the wall beside her desk was a human-sized picture of the Aga Khan, the Ismailis' spiritual guide, whom they consider the forty-ninth Shi'a Imam. I was eager to reconnect with Sultan, whom I had first interviewed several years earlier over fresh lime sodas at Radio Club in Colaba. Because Sultan had held nearly every important leadership position in the Ismaili community, I hoped to gain some insight into the work that officials do and their perspective on the issues facing their community. After Mary informed me that Sultan was ready to see me, I soon stepped through a door into an office stocked with contemporary furniture arranged for legal consultations. Sultan, a cheerful, middle-aged man wearing a neatly pressed suit and tie, greeted me from behind a large wooden desk.

After exchanging pleasantries and arranging for a servant to bring chai, Sultan took the initiative. He began speaking at length in English about the elaborate structure of community and development institutions established by the Aga Khan, the types of programs they run, and a little bit about the volunteer work he had done for them. I dutifully took notes, all the while struggling to think of a way that this abstract information about organizational structure would contribute to an ethnographic account of the community. As we got close to the end of our interview, I clumsily asked Sultan what I hoped was a more anthropological question: how have Ismailis fared in Mumbai's polarized communal politics? Without missing a beat, Sultan summed up their predicament in evocative language: "David, we're caught between the devil and the deep blue sea. When the riots come, the Hindus say we're Muslims, and the Muslims say we're Hindus. Why? Because when it's Christmas, we say 'Happy Christmas,' when it's Eid, we say 'Eid Mubarak,' and when it's Holi, we say 'Holi Mubarak.'" He paused for a moment, pushing himself back from the sturdy wooden desk decked out with awards for professional and community service, and added, "But we do not have it as bad as the Ahmadis do in Pakistan. They are not even considered to be Muslims. And when His Highness Aga Khan visits India, it's treated as a state visit."

I was surprised by Sultan's candor that day, perhaps because he initially steered our conversation to a somewhat technical—and safe—discussion of "organizational structures," "mandates," and "apex institutions." Or maybe it was because I had noticed that some Ismailis were reticent to speak about the difficulties of being a small minority within India's Muslim minority. But Sultan's statement encapsulated so much of what I suspected about the insecurity of being a double minority in contemporary India. Ismailis confront stereotypes about Islam and Muslims from Hindu friends, colleagues, and supervisors at work or school. Even before the election of Narendra Modi in 2014, Ismaili friends had shared their fears about violence orchestrated by Hindu nationalists. Yet as adherents of the Ismaili sect of Shi'a Islam, they also face criticism from some Muslims reformers, who point to differences between the ritual practices of Ismailis and those of the majority of the Muslim *ummah* (community).[2] For instance, Ismailis say a thrice-daily prayer, *dua*, which differs in form and content from the *namaz* (obligatory daily prayer) that Sunni and Ithna'ashari Shi'a recite five times and three times a day, respectively. Moreover, the Ismaili religious tradition has long incorporated a variety of "syncretic" elements, such as the "canonical religious hymns" (*ginan*) sung on auspicious occasions, spurring additional questions about their Muslimness.

Sultan suggests that Ismailis' problems stem, in part, from the ways others perceive them. He says that Hindus mistake them for Muslims, and vice versa, because they misunderstand the ways that Ismailis respectfully acknowledge other communities' religious traditions. Moreover, he alludes to how things might be worse for Ismailis if not for the recognition they receive from other Muslims and the Indian state. Ismailis do not face the same kinds of discrimination as Ahmadiyya do in India or, for that matter, in Pakistan.[3] And the Indian state acknowledges, albeit indirectly, Ismailis' contributions to the nation by treating their religious leader as a foreign emissary.

What Sultan leaves unsaid, however, is how Ismailis have actively sought to address these problems of perception. As I came to learn through my meetings with Sultan and other members of the community, volunteers do vital work to manage the community's image in a variety of India's publics. First, volunteers perform essential labor in Ismaili civic and religious organizations, work that bolsters the community's image as "responsible citizens"[4] and pious Muslims. Second, because institutional norms authorize them to speak officially on behalf of the community, and limit lay Ismailis' ability to do the same, volunteers play an important role in controlling the types of information about Ismailis that circulate in India's publics.

One reason that many Indians view Ismailis as responsible citizens, and the Aga Khan receives the privileges of a visiting head of state, is the "development" work done by the Aga Khan Development Network (AKDN). This is a transnational network of organizations working to provide economic and social development.[5] In Mumbai, AKDN runs Prince Aly Khan Hospital in Mazagaon, Diamond Jubilee High School for Girls in Umerkhadi, and Diamond Jubilee High School in Mazagaon. Other notable AKDN agencies include the Aga Khan Rural Support program, which works on issues such as sanitation and drought resilience in rural India, and the Aga Khan Trust for Culture, which renovated a public park near Humayan's Tomb in New Delhi.

Although all of these organizations employ professional staff to handle their day-to-day operations, they also make use of Ismaili volunteers to accomplish their various mandates. Sultan, like other volunteers, described this labor as *seva* (service). As in the broader Indic tradition of *guru-seva*, Ismailis characterize their volunteer service as a form of devotion to the Imam. Sultan, for instance, often described his volunteer work as "serving" or "working for" His Highness. He spoke glowingly of the opportunity that this work gave him to work closely with the Ismailis' spiritual leader at his home in France, while acknowledging the real strains that such travel put on his family life and career. But it was not just the Imam to whom Sultan directed his service. Sultan would sometimes talk about serving the *"jamat"* ("congregation," but used more generally to refer to the "Ismaili community") or "Indian society." Similar to the idea of social service emerging in Indian philanthropic organizations during the early twentieth century,[6] Ismaili seva is also directed at promoting the welfare of abstract collectives such as "society" and "community." In short, seva denotes work done for the benefit of others, whether that "other" is the Imam or a community.

While in the Ismaili community, service might consist of sweeping the floor of the Jamat-Khana or collecting the shoes of congregants prior to worship, Sultan belongs to a cadre of professionals who are called upon to provide their expertise to AKDN. Over nearly forty years of service work, Sultan has made use of his wide-ranging skills in myriad ways. He has used his extensive legal training and experience, for instance, to obtain the deeds for property that had long been in the Imam's family so that these assets could be liquidated and the proceeds put into a trust to fund development projects. In other instances, Sultan has made use of his fluency in English, Hindi, and Gujarati as well as his experience working with professionals. Sultan once served as the communications director for the Aga Khan's Council for India, a job that involves meeting with members of the press to increase public awareness about the community's many development projects. Speaking about that time, he said, "His Highness told me to give the people the information and build bridges. Let the jamat know what is happening . . . let the public know about the work the jamat is doing. So I did that because I believe in sharing knowledge."

This sharing of knowledge involves ongoing efforts by Ismailis in both Mumbai and the communities abroad to disseminate information about their philanthropic contributions to the local community in the English-language press. The articles that result from this work focus on the volunteer ethos of the community and highlight the fact that AKDN projects benefit everyone regardless of caste and creed.[7] On their own website (the .Ismaili), they associate such projects with the community's "responsible citizenship."[8] The careful use of publicity stands in marked contrast to practices that conceal certain parts of Ismaili social life. For instance, Ismailis forbid non-Ismailis from attending religious services in the Jamat-Khana, and all but the most general details about their religion are absent in newspaper stories or on their website. This selective use of publicity seems to serve a variety of purposes. On the one hand, many people, whether Hindu or

Muslim, know Ismailis based on the existence of these development institutions, which demonstrate the community's generosity and commitment to civic participation. However, the religious values and doctrines that inform much of this work remain largely in the background. On the other hand, these development projects create relationships between the Ismaili community and the state. One indication of these close relationships is the state visits that offer community leaders and the Aga Khan to meet with government officials; another is that in 2015 the Aga Khan received from Narendra Modi's government the Padma Vibhushan in recognition of his philanthropic work, signaling a close relationship between the Imam and the state administration.

Although Sultan is no longer in charge of communications, he seemed to continue some of this work during our meeting. He often highlighted the importance that the Imam's teachings and AKDN's work give to helping women. For instance, Sultan told me more than once about one of the Imam's "edicts" (*farman*), advising his followers to educate their daughters. In fact, should a family have a boy and girl and the means to educate only one, the Imam famously told his followers to educate the daughter.[9] In a similar vein, Sultan sometimes called attention to benefits that AKDN development projects brought to women in particular. While discussing the Aga Khan Rural Development Program's efforts to provide villagers with clean water in rural Gujarat, he said, "It is often women who have to go collect water. They have to walk for an hour sometimes with buckets of water. So the girls cannot go to school." These portrayals of the Imam and the community's work to educate women further the sense that Ismailis are "progressive" Muslims who, as loyal citizens, contribute to the public good. Even in our interviews, Sultan continues to do the work of a public relations professional, selectively providing information to manage the community's representation in academic work.

However, this strategy is a risky one, for even if it establishes Ismailis' citizenship, it reinforces negative stereotypes about Muslims. Whereas many Muslims admire the development work that Ismailis do—and it seems that the Dawoodi Bohras, who established Saifee Hospital on Charni Road in 2005, have even adopted elements of the Ismailis' developmentalist image-making strategy—it has the effect of establishing Ismailis as "model Muslims."[10] Like other discourses about model minorities, this one has the effect of claiming one minority's similarity to the majority while emphasizing the difference of another. If Ismailis are "model Muslims," it is because they do not partake of the putative antinational, backward, and violent behavior that some Hindus unfairly attribute to Muslims. That Ismaili NGOs engage in activities that are so closely associated with "responsible citizenship"—development and Western education—only serves to cast into sharper relief the imagined differences between Ismailis and other Muslims. Yet, unlike other discourses about model minorities, Ismailis, however exceptional some might consider them, are still linked to the Muslim community in Mumbai.

Indeed, Sultan's career as a volunteer has also included efforts to address some of the criticism that Ismailis face from other Muslims. Consider the following story he told me and his friend, Altaf, who happened to be visiting from Great Britain on the day of one of our interviews. In it, Sultan talks about being appointed chairman in 1993 of the Ismaili Religious Education and Tariqa Board (ITREB), which oversees Ismaili religious institutions:

> At this point there was a problem with the Tariqah Board. First, there was the new Talim curriculum developed by the Institute for Ismaili Studies. The Aga Khan wanted to put the Talim into practice, but the people were unhappy with the curriculum. Then there was also the issue with the pictures. Ismailis used to bow before the picture of the Aga Khan, but other Muslims think that is idol worship. That is forbidden by other Muslims, and they were upset. His Highness is very sensitive to these things, so he wanted us to move the picture to the side. He knew that Indians would be especially vulnerable to this kind of thing.
>
> So no one wanted to be in charge of ITREB. It was a real hot seat. So the Aga Khan appointed Sultan. He really put me on the hot seat. [*Turning to his friend*] You know, I had to go through a lot to get people to accept these changes.

Two things are notable in Sultan's story. First, he points to how changes in religious education and moving the location of photos in the prayer hall were a direct response to the criticism that Ismailis were receiving from other Muslims. Ismailis countered this criticism through a long-term program of religious education and, perhaps more immediately, through a relatively small change in their ritual space. Such changes might be considered a kind of "collective face work," in which communal religious praxis is altered to manage the Ismailis' image in the eyes of other Muslims.[11]

Second, Sultan reveals the ways that volunteers work as the Imam's "agents."[12] In other words, volunteers work on behalf of the Imam, furthering his, rather than their own, interests and intentions. As the Imam's agent, Sultan worked to ensure that Ismailis understood, and ultimately accepted, the purpose and intent behind the Imam's new religious education program and instructions concerning his photo. This relationship between the Imam and Sultan creates a sense of moral responsibility in which there is a separation between the "casually effective doer of a deed" and "its responsible author."[13] This separation is evident in the attitudes that Ismailis express toward changing the photo's location and the Talim curriculum. For some, the change was appropriate because it reflected the Imam's guidance and a more authentic understanding of Islam. However, others expressed doubts over these changes because they believed that they were the initiated by the leaders at ITREB acting independently of the Imam. Along these lines, lay Ismailis sometimes mock the way that leaders like Sultan play up their own close personal relationship with the Imam to inflate their reputations and to give authority to their utterances.

In addition to helping implement the Imam's religious reforms, Sultan also plays a role in representing Ismaili religiosity to others. Unlike some other volunteers I met, Sultan rarely talked explicitly about the Aga Khan's high-profile endorsements of religious pluralism. More often, he would allude to the practice of religious tolerance with more colloquial statements about how Ismailis respect others' religious traditions, such as when he told me that Ismailis acknowledge the holidays of other religious communities. At other times, he would explain the religious diversity of the Muslim world by describing different sects as being "cousins" or "siblings." In 2015, as we sat under the awning of a small Chinese restaurant on the Linking Road in Santa Cruz, Sultan lamented the rise of ISIL in Iraq and Syria. He wondered how there could be such violence between Sunnis and Shi'a, who were "like sister communities. They should live together in tolerance and let Shi'a do their own ceremonies and rituals." On the one hand, Sultan's allusions to religious pluralism endorse a view of religious inclusion that obviates many of the criticisms that Ismailis face from other Muslims. On the other hand, his statements have the effect of representing Ismailis as a progressive and tolerant community.

Sultan's position as a volunteer grants him an authority to speak openly about his community that few others can claim. The Ismaili Constitution, a document that in part describes the rights and the responsibilities of the Imam and his followers with respect to one another, prohibits Ismailis from making official statements on behalf of the community or the Ismaili tradition without the express permission of the Imam. As Sultan told me in his office in 2007, many Ismailis felt that they should speak about the community or religious tradition only if they have received permission from Aiglemont, the Aga Khan's secretariat in France. He added, "It's not true [that you need permission], but people feel this way. I have no problem talking with you because I know the rules."

In my own experience, lay Ismailis were often happy to speak with me, but with the caveat that they were offering their "personal" views that I should not mistake for the "official" statements made by the leaders of various Ismaili institutions. Although I have never heard Sultan use the term *official* to describe his own speech, most Ismailis would consider it such. In fact, I first received Sultan's contact information from an Ismaili who told me that Sultan's status in the community would ensure that I received "official information." In these ways, the authorizing discourses of the community's institutions imbue Sultan's speech with authority that others cannot claim.[14] Such authorizing discourses are reinforced by the honors and prestige bestowed on volunteers who have served the Imam for so long. In 2015 Sultan told me that he had recently received the honorary title of Wazir from the Imam in recognition of his years of service. When I congratulated him, he said with a laugh suggesting he was joking, "It's good. No one can tell me that I'm saying something wrong now!"

But authorizing discourses not only mark Sultan's speech as authoritative; they also specify the sort of information that circulates about the Ismaili community in the press and academic documents. Because volunteers like Sultan can speak with authority, and others cannot, their stories often make it into mass-mediated accounts of the community. Thus, paying close attention to the work of volunteers reveals not only the representational strategies used by Ismailis but also the culturally specific ideas about religious authority, hierarchy, and service that make this strategy possible.

Notes

1. All names in this profile are pseudonyms.
2. Ali Asani, "The Khojahs of South Asia: Defining a Space of Their Own," *Cultural Dynamics* 13, no. 2 (2001): 155–68.
3. See the glossary entry for *Ahmadi*.
4. The term *responsible citizens* is, as I discuss below, drawn from the Ismaili community's own official website (the.ismaili).
5. Paul Kaiser, *Culture, Transnationalism, and Civil Society: Aga Khan Social Service Initiatives in Tanzania* (Westport, CT: Praeger, 1996); Shafqat Hussain, "Multiple Sovereignties and Transnationalism in a Nation-State: Aga Khan Development Network in Hunza Pakistan," in *Democracy at Large: NGOs, Political Foundations, Think Tanks and International Organizations*, ed. Boris Petric, 190–204 (New York: Palgrave Macmillan, 2012).

6. Carey Watt, *Serving the Nation: Cultures of Service, Association, and Citizenship* (New Delhi: Oxford University Press, 2005).

7. Anupam Dasgupta, "The Aga Khan Is Back in City after 16 Yrs.," *Daily News and Analysis*, May 13, 2008; Press Trust of India, "Fighting Poverty Still to Be Primary Area of Focus: Aga Khan," *Daily News and Analysis*, July 13, 2017; Mohammad Wajihuddin, "Diamond Jubilee Year of Aga Khan Begins Today," *Times of India*, 2017.

8. "The Ismaili Community," Islamic Publications Limited, accessed May 28, 2019, https://the.ismaili/community-0.

9. A. K. Adatia and N. Q. King, "Some East African Firmans of HH Aga Khan III," *Journal of Religion in Africa* 2, no. 2 (1969): 179–91.

10. Ali Asani, "From Satpanthi to Ismaili Muslim: The Articulation of Ismaili Khoja Identity in South Asia," in *A Modern History of the Ismailis: Continuity and Change in a Muslim Community*, ed. Farhad Daftary, 77–92 (London: I. B. Tauris, 2011).

11. Erving Goffman, *Interaction Ritual: Essays on Face-to-Face Behavior* (New York: Pantheon, 1982).

12. James Laidlaw, *The Subject of Virtue: An Anthropology of Ethics and Freedom* (Cambridge: Cambridge University Press, 2014), 180.

13. Laidlaw, *The Subject of Virtue*, 187.

14. E. Summerson Carr, "Enactments of Expertise," *Annual Review of Anthropology* 39 (2010): 17–32.

21 **RAJ** CARTING COSMOPOLITANISM

Maura Finkelstein

IN NOVEMBER OF 2008 the right-wing political party *Shiv Sena* partnered with global giants McDonald's and Coca-Cola to launch their branded culinary vision: "Shiv Vada Pav." The "Vada Pav *Sammelan*" (festival or conference) was held in Shivaji Park in the central neighborhood of Dadar, down the street from the Sena headquarters. The Sammelan brought together twenty-seven *vada pav* vendors from Mumbai, Thane, and Pune for a tasting and quality competition: the winner's recipe would be branded "Shiv Vada Pav" and sold at a hundred dedicated stands throughout the city. McDonald's provided the *pav* (bread) for the competition, as well as a shining silver handcart to be presented to the winning chef.

Vada pav is the Mumbai equivalent of the American hamburger and just as ubiquitous. From the regulated rail platform carts to small family-run stands on the side of the road to large corporate chains, in Mumbai it seems that everyone is "loving it." The anthropologist Harris Solomon has argued that vada pav was "processed into the emblem of a political party,"[1] which transformed the Shiv Sena's relationship with vada pav into both evidence of party support for disenfranchised workers and a symbol of regional unity. Shiv Vada Pav initiatives were partially motivated in reaction to the prevalence of South Indian Udupi restaurants and stands making *idli* and *dosa* ubiquitous throughout the city. Shiv Vada Pav would replace South Indian street food and make Maharashtrian vada pav central again: a culinary metaphor of the Shiv Sena's hope to restore Maharashtra for Maharashtrians.

On that mild November evening I made my way from stall to stall, tasting as many of the free offerings as my body could handle. I carried a score sheet with me, but after the sixth sampling I gave up: I like vada pav a lot, but I can't call myself a discerning consumer. As we revelers slipped into a deep-fried coma, Sena party chief Uddhav Thackeray spoke on the importance of vada pav for Maharashtra's cultural identity. Above his head, party banners emblazoned with the faces of Sena leaders gazed out from under the McDonald's and Coca-Cola logos. This blatant globalism sat in quiet dissonance with the aggressive localism of saffron flags, adorned with the fierce tiger mascot of the Sena.

But the Sammelan was not only a celebration of Maharashtrian pride and an assertion of Sena politics; the history of vada pav also has links with economic desperation, as many stands were set up by the Sena for textile workers outside of closed mills during the strikes of the early 1980s. As the journalist and food writer Vikram Doctor reflected, "The Sena promoted vada-pav by allowing supporters to set up stalls selling it outside its *shakhas*. A colleague who tracks the Sena tells me it was a way to give part time jobs to party workers who also functioned as street muscle: 'It's the only employment generation scheme that the Sena has ever been able to set up,' he tells me dryly."[2] I found this employment scheme to have directly affected many of the Maharashtrian workers I met while conducting fieldwork in the textile mill neighborhoods of Central Mumbai. Although all of my Maharashtrian informants were Sena supporters, this relationship was far more embedded in vada pav than politics. This hot, fresh, and universally loved snack saved many mill workers when mill employment became impossible because of labor strikes and mill closings.

Throughout a decade of ethnographic fieldwork (2008–18) in one of the last functioning Mumbai-based textile mills (which I call Dhanraj Spinning and Weaving, Ltd.), I became close with a man I call "Raj." As a maintenance worker in the mill, Raj moved from department to department and seemed to make friends wherever he went. He was very cool: he wore gold chains around his neck, he sported a glossy mustache, and his wardrobe invoked a slick 1970s gangster aesthetic. In addition to enjoying his company, I discovered he was also the "answer man" at Dhanraj—my savviest guide through the rumor mill.

Raj and his wife, Ketaki, survived the instability of the 1980s and 1990s by benefiting from a scheme that their North Indian coworkers were barred from: selling vada pav in Central Mumbai. During the mill strikes of the early 1980s, vada pav saved the family from starvation, while many North Indian textile workers were forced to leave the city for their family homes in Uttar Pradesh and Bihar. While the couple closed down their cart when Raj rejoined the Dhanraj workforce after the strike, I discovered that his foray into the food cart economy was coming full circle: after retiring from Dhanraj in 2016, Raj intended to open up a Shiv Vada Pav cart.

Surviving the Unsurvivable

Raj and Ketaki were examples of survival in an unsurvivable city, a dying industry, and an unstable housing market. First, they continued to live in Central Mumbai, even as most of my informants were pushed into the suburbs. Second, they managed to be upwardly mobile within a community that was almost entirely downwardly mobile. And third, they figured out how to blend formal work and informal work in order to send both their children to college and purchase their own *chawl* unit in the heart of the city. The family emerged as an exception that proved the rule: most mill workers I met were holding on for dear life as their industry shrank and collapsed around them, often commuting up to four hours round-trip to work in the rapidly downsizing Central Mumbai mill at the center of my fieldwork.

Yet Raj and Ketaki were thriving. So how does one survive the unsurvivable?

In January 2016 I met Raj for tea and snacks at a restaurant down the street from Dhanraj. After retiring from the mill six months earlier, he told me he was now done enjoying his free time. After a brief catch-up he began to describe his new scheme: he had put in an application for a Shiv Vada Pav cart and was eagerly awaiting news of his permission. Any day now he expected to receive a permit for a new food cart in Kala Chowki.

However, when Raj told me about his new plan, we not only discussed it *in* an Udupi restaurant while eating dosa; he also told me of his hope to eventually make idli and dosa in *addition* to vada pav. He explained that while vada pav was popular, it wasn't popular enough to stand on its own. In fact, there was a huge demand for South Indian fare, and he planned to get in on the eclectic market. It seemed that the Sena's attempt to establish a hegemonic street food presence was actually opening up avenues for street food cosmopolitanism inside a Shiv Vada Pav cart. There may not be regional cosmopolitanism in Mumbai, but Raj was certainly invested in culinary diversity in the name of accessible capital.

A 2014 article in the *New York Times* quoted a street hawker, newly initiated into the "Shiv Vada Pav" empire, explaining that "the Shiv Sena is helping Maharashtrians like us. . . . So we should also help them by voting for them."[3] And, indeed, the Maharashtrian mill workers at Dhanraj—including Raj—all voted Sena and understood the party as representing their best interests, not just through its political platform but also through economic revitalization schemes like Shiv Vada Pav. However, just as the Shiv Vada Pav brand of regional unity through food processing (emerging from a history of localism and antiglobalism) established McDonald's and Coca-Cola as its engine, Raj understood Udupi fare as a necessary and lucrative avenue through which to expand his vada pav scheme. For Raj, this was not about identity, regionalism, or antimigrant sentiments. This was about profit and upward mobility in the wake of a transforming, capital-driven Mumbai. This was about surviving the unsurvivable.

Raj had plenty of experience with such a negotiation: this was not the first time he used vada pav and the Shiv Sena to save him economically. And this was not the first time he took a life raft and built a boat.

Love, Bollywood Style

In the early 1980s the Bombay textile industry was in chaos. Although the city had dominated global textile markets through the early twentieth century, the industry began to shift to South India and Southeast Asia beginning in the 1950s. This movement dramatically altered access to labor in the mill lands. Working conditions were dangerous, jobs were scarce, and pay was low. In late 1981 the union organizer Datta Samant was chosen by a large group of Bombay mill workers to lead them in a conflict between the Bombay Millowners Association and the union: the Rashtriya Mill Mazdoor Sangh (RMMS), which had represented the mill workers for decades. This led to a complete shutdown of the industry for over a year; financially, these job losses were devastating for mill workers.

On January 18, 1982—the first day of the strike—Raj decided to kill himself. Early in my fieldwork, in 2008, he asked me: "What kind of man can't support his wife, his future children? How does a man hold his head up after his livelihood disappears? A man is his work, and without that. . . ."

Raj explained that his marriage to Ketaki was far from simple; a love marriage rarely is. He remembered the first time he saw her enter the canteen where he worked, adjacent to Bharat Talkies (a cinema hall). She had come to see a film with her friends, and he couldn't stop staring at her. They were teenagers, and her laugh sucked the air from his lungs. He wanted to talk to her, to know what made her laugh so freely. He wanted to make her laugh like that, and he wanted her to look at him as her laugh settled into a smile that filled her face and crinkled her eyes into her forehead so deeply they only faintly flickered out from underneath her eyebrows.

Over the next few months he got to know the group of friends, and eventually Ketaki began to come to the cinema alone. Instead of heading into the film, the couple would sit together in the canteen: stolen dates on his work break. When Raj and Ketaki told me this story, they both told it together—alternating, interjecting, interrupting, laughing. They told me that he proposed and that her family disowned her, furious that their daughter would both take such initiative and with a lower-class (and caste) boy with no prospects, no less. But Raj's parents helped them out, and he found a mill job that promised him a great future. The *filmi* world of their dreams seemed to be coming true.

But then the textile mills went on strike. As Ketaki told me,

> When the mill shut down, my husband said he would commit suicide because it was a crisis, but I said, "No, No! How can you even think such a thing?" and I was very supportive. So at that time I started a vada pav and sandwich stall, so I was working. We couldn't wait for relatives to help us; we had to support ourselves. The stall we started was so near Bharat Talkies, so we knew we would have lots of crowds. We all know how to make vada pav, because we all make it at home. But I would also watch other people and see what they were doing. We hired someone to boil potatoes for us and make the filling, and I would make the balls and Raj would fry them.

Almost thirty years later I was told this as though the protagonists were narrating a script and not telling of the bleakest time in their lives together: they laughed and joked about a time when many men *did* kill themselves and Raj seriously considered such an act. However, in the present moment, in the comfort of their new flat, such desperation and despair seemed far away.

Although Ketaki had shown no culinary savvy before, she found herself to be a natural in the kitchen and also started making *tiffins* for the single men and students who lived in their neighborhood. She told me: "these days I make tiffins for the mill workers. And then there are the students, and also a teacher, a bachelor." One day—while Ketaki was at home preparing her tiffins—a woman from Procter and Gamble came by their chawl, selling sanitary napkins door to door. Inspired by the social element and mobility of the job, Ketaki asked the woman if they were hiring salespeople: "It was only thirty rupees a day, but it was something, so I decided to work. But I didn't stop the vada pav stall, so I would cook in the morning, go for work, come back by 3:30 p.m., my husband would take care of the children until then, and at 5 p.m. we would start the vada pav stall. Seventeen years later, and I am the [Procter and Gamble] manager!" Ketaki laughed gleefully as she told me this story, while Raj gazed at her lovingly. "She's traveled all over India with Procter and Gamble," he said. "She's seen so much of the country."

Eventually, the mills began to reopen, and Raj found employment at Dhanraj once again. But for years (and contrary to the hypermasculine message of the Sena), Ketaki was the main breadwinner in the family, and Raj told me of this with an air of pride and respect. "She is such a hardworking woman," he said. Of all the Dhanraj workers, Raj had done the best for himself, and he never failed to remind me that this success was due, in large part, to Ketaki's ability not only to work outside the house but to forge multiple successful paths for herself. While most workers did not experience such successes following the 1982 strike, the availability of vada pav stalls— a Shiv Sena initiative available only to Maharashtrians—allowed them not only to remain in Mumbai, downtown, and with access to income, but also to thrive economically during this bleak time.

Vada pav carts and poststrike mill employment furthered regional tensions in multiple ways. Not only did vada pav stall employment allow Maharashtrian workers to remain near closed mills while North Indian workers were forced to leave the state, but Datta Samant also put forward a reservation demand for Maharashtrian mill workers (80 percent of jobs to be reserved for Maharashtrian workers). North Indian workers understood this to be an extension of the Sena demand of "Mumbai for Maharashtrians." Vada pav carts and mill employment wove together informal and formal labor opportunities in a manner that dictated the demographics of the mill lands in favor of a Maharashtrian majority.

At least in theory.

Throughout the ten years I knew Raj he insisted that Maharashtrians and North Indians lived and worked in harmony. When I would ask him about tensions in the mill or the neighborhood, he would brush off my inquiries, citing mutual respect and affection that belied the messages emerging from Sena politics, mill land agitations, and the opinions of my North Indian informants. Similarly, he worked hard to reflect his optimism through the carts that he and Ketaki ran over several decades: by including South Indian idli-dosa in their Shiv Vada Pav cart offerings, the parochial regionalism of Sena politics sat uncomfortably alongside Raj's cosmopolitan culinary desires. The Shiv Vada Pav initiative to decenter South Indian Udupi restaurants through the proliferation of vada pav carts instead resulted in the failure of culinary nationalism through the further ubiquity of idli dosa as Mumbai street food, even if the people in question (South Indians) were not welcomed.

In many ways, it is vada pav that mediates this semisubversive tale. The Sena's Shiv Vada Pav initiative was fueled by politics: both through the homogenization of Maharashtrian street food culture and through the strengthening of a grateful voting block. By aiding struggling constituents in an insecure economic landscape, the party expected it would receive votes, ideological loyalty, and culinary nationalism. And there is no doubt that the Maharashtrian mill workers I met, including Raj, voted for the Sena. However, the culinary promiscuity of Raj and Ketaki's Shiv Vada Pav plan seemed disconnected from this drive for culinary nationalism, touted with such ferocity at the Vada Pav Sammelan in 2008.

And most interestingly, vada pav facilitated the fluidity of gender and family formation, as Ketaki was the breadwinner for much of her relationship with Raj in large part because of their food carts. This subverted the hypermasculinity of the *Marathi Manoos* ("sons of the soil"), a persona circulated by the Sena and enforced in part through the "muscle" of vendors outside the shakhas during the textile mills strikes of 1982.

Raj never failed to remind me that his carts were about survival and not about politics: a deep-fried lifeboat in a sea of informal, insecure labor. Raj and Ketaki did not intend for a radical social revolution through vada pav. However, as far as Raj was concerned, if their lifeboat managed to subvert exclusionary politics by providing a space where anyone (regardless of regional origin) could enjoy their street food of choice (regardless of culinary origin), well . . . there was good money in unity and diversity, especially on the busy thoroughfares of Central Mumbai. On the level of the street corner, Raj was serving up cosmopolitanism in a cart.

Notes

1. Harris Solomon, "The Taste No Chef Can Give: Processing Street Food in Mumbai," *Cultural Anthropology* 30, no. 1 (2015): 65–90.

2. Vikram Doctor, "An Attitude to Serve: Why Marathi Food Lost Out," *Economic Times*, May 17, 2008.

3. Choksi Mansi, "Before Elections, Mumbai Snack Turns into a Political Hot Potato," *New York Times India Ink*, March 12, 2014.

22 **LAXMI** DEALER IN EMOTION

R. Swaminathan

"IN THE CITY OF DEALS, we store all of God's good luck with us."[1]
Laxmi had asked me to come to the Elphinstone Road railway station[2] on a Monday morning at 8:30 a.m. sharp: "Come to the platform outside main ticket counter. I will be next to Naresh bhai's stall selling undergarments. Be on Parel side, not the Lower Parel side. Don't be late," she had instructed. I was late and found Laxmi and her group at "work" spearheading a rally called by the political party *Shiv Sena* in response to the Elphinstone Road station stampede of September 29, 2017, that killed twenty-two people.[3] Laxmi was standing in front of a man and shouting in his face: "Don't you have shame? Not even a month has passed since people died. You say how does it matter? You are impotent. Aren't you ashamed to call yourself a man?" The bespectacled man, in his early thirties, clean shaven, hair neatly combed, dressed in a crisp white shirt, dark-brown trousers, and tan leather shoes, seemed embarrassed. He avoided eye contact with Laxmi, who was draped in a shiny nylon red sari over a sleeveless navy-blue blouse. Her "sisters" were dressed similarly. One was holding the man's arm, another stroking his cheek and calling him "my dear," and the eldest one, Shaukat Ammi, guru of the group, was blessing him with long life saying, "I wish you my life too." Laxmi let him

go after he signed a petition that accused the chief minister of being an "impotent man." For the next hour, this was Laxmi and her group's modus operandi: surround men dressed in formal clothes,[4] call them "impotent," and embarrass them into signing the petition. Through this all, political leaders on stage gave speeches, pointing to Laxmi and her colleagues and saying, "This government is so impotent that even the *hijras* have come out." The word *hijra*, which translates roughly as "transgender" or "intersex," carries a somewhat derogatory valence in Mumbai. At 10 a.m. the rally wound up. An irritated Laxmi snapped at me: "I told you not to come late. The party people wanted to meet you. They don't trust anyone easily." Before I could explain, the local Shiv Sena leader asked her to join him for breakfast.

Laxmi followed the group, taking me along to "introduce Sweden's Mumbaikar" to the local leader. I corrected her: I am an Indian *in* Sweden. A more relaxed Laxmi joked, "No, you are *from* Sweden. My value has increased in front of them!" I realized later that she wasn't joking. At the office, Laxmi and her group were seated in red plastic chairs along a wall near the entrance. I was offered a chair with cushions inside the office. The local leader sat in a plush chair with a white towel covering its backrest behind a massive table. "How do you know Laxmi?" he asked, without looking at Laxmi or her group. I explained I met Laxmi a few years back for my research about the transgender community. "Why them? Everything is good for them. They earn from us and their old profession," he said smiling suggestively,[5] without looking at Laxmi and her group. *Old profession* was here clearly a euphemism for sex work. "Write about us. There is no water, electricity, or jobs," he said. "Their needs are nothing in comparison to ours." He stopped when the *poha* and chai arrived. Laxmi and her group were served on paper plates and plastic cups; I was served (like the local leader) on a porcelain plate and a bone china cup. After we had eaten, the leader gestured to one of his men. The man handed him an envelope with money. The leader counted some money and handed it to Laxmi, who in turn handed it to Shaukat Ammi. At that point, Laxmi's colleagues all stood up and touched Ammi's feet. Laxmi then took the money back from Ammi and counted it. "There is Rs. 15,000 as I asked," she said with a smile. The Shiv Sena leader smiled too: "I would have given you only 10,000. But you brought this writer from Sweden as promised. Happy?" Without waiting for an answer, the leader said to me: "You write about us." Laxmi was grinning. Walking to catch a taxi to go back to their room in Chembur, Laxmi said, "I told you my value has increased. You earned us Rs. 5,000. You are one of us now. We will treat you to *Samosa* and *vada pav*." Everyone burst out laughing.

We got into two taxis. Ammi, Laxmi, and Rehana traveled with me. I asked Laxmi how the money would be used. Ammi answered, "It's for the common pool." She paused, then added, "We use it for medicines and to pay off the police." Laxmi chimed in, "Ammi's mind works fast. She has invested in chit funds, given loans to shopkeepers and auto drivers." None of my further questions regarding money were entertained. Everyone lapsed into silence. My mind went back to conversations with Laxmi. One particular snippet stood out. "Impotence is an opportunity. We can demand our price," Laxmi had said during a conversation about her work and the city. To unpack it, one needs to hear Laxmi's story.

"IS IT TIME FOR ME TO DANCE?" Laxmi asked with a grin. I was meeting Laxmi after five years at the same spot on the rarely used platform 3 in Lower Parel station[6] where I first met her with Shaukat Ammi.[7] It's a private joke that she had cracked at me since she came to know that I don't have children. "Tell me it's time. I will dance for free," she continued. "I don't think you will get a chance," I respond. On cue she puts her hand on my head and "blesses" me. "You should come to Mookambika temple[8] with me. We can get any message across to God." Laxmi is an ethnographer's delight: frank and full of analogies. This joke is also Laxmi's way of reminding me of the first "proper" question I asked her: "How many times do you dance in a week?" Growing up in Delhi, I had seen transgenders turn up in every house where a baby was born and dance until the family gave them money. Laxmi had pointedly ignored my question. Ammi coaxed Laxmi to "educate" me. "Once or twice," she said, pausing for effect, "in a year." Everyone was laughing. "What do you think? We fill our stomachs by going to houses and dancing? What world do you live in?" asked Laxmi. "I didn't mean that," I said. Laxmi mellowed down and said something that captured her daily reality: "Every day we make ourselves useful to others. I do it, my guru does it, and so do you. We do it consciously. Maybe you don't do it consciously since you have a job. You might think you are naturally talented. But you too make yourself desirable—by acquiring degrees, for instance. You do it for a job and money. That's *your* deal.[9] I also have to look for opportunities every day because I also need money. This is a city of dealers. You are here because you want a deal with me."

There was a backstory to Laxmi's pointed words. I had met her a few years earlier as part of an ethnographic study that had been commissioned by a private company interested in how social taboos were used to achieve desired behaviors. While explaining to Laxmi what I intended to do as part of the study, I had described my conversation with her as an "informant interview." Laxmi later told me that the word *informant*, which she calls "informer," refers to a *khabri* (informer) in Mumbai. Khabris are people who pass on information to police for money, so she was afraid that I would report her to the police. I had explained to Laxmi that I was not being paid by the police but rather by the company that had hired me for the study. That was the "deal" that she was referring to again now. Laxmi and Shaukat Ammi used both English and Hindi words for *deal, dealing,* and *business* (*bijinej* or *dhanda* in Hindi) in their daily transactions.

LAXMI WAS BORN IN KARKALA, in Udupi, with both male and female sex organs. She came to Mumbai at age twelve, she explained, in the hope that the city might allow her to be a "woman." After meeting Shaukat Ammi, Laxmi underwent a ritualized "emasculation" procedure—performed by a senior member of the community—as well as an initiation ceremony similar to a Hindu marriage.

Laxmi describes her life as "neither here nor there," and describes the awkwardness of inhabiting a city that sees Laxmi but ignores her existence. To my question on how the city and its people make her invisible, she said, "Some are embarrassed and avert their eyes. They are surprised that we are still here in a modern Mumbai. The same people would come to us if there's a deal for them." After some moments of silence, Laxmi added, "The government says it wants Mumbai to be shiny like Singapore. Are there no people like us in Singapore? In Indian culture, we people used to be respected. I would go in the train every day. People spit and dirty the train or indulge in petting and kissing. *That's* fine. But if *we* board the train, everyone becomes strict." Shaukat Ammi said, "Some tolerate us if we do things expected of us. When I joined under my guru, I accompanied a group of four seniors in the Churchgate-to-Borivali train. We would travel up to Dadar and take the train back. I was naïve," she recalled. "I was only sixteen. During one trip, I blessed a young man. He asked me how much I charge for oral sex. He insisted we get down. We have three rules: no sex for money, no alcohol, no drugs. I was strong, and I beat him up. The railway police locked us up for the night. No one expects a hijra to hit back." This was the first time I had heard Ammi use the word *hijra*. Some groups use the word openly as a self-identifying term, but others consider it derogatory; Ammi's exaggerated emphasis clearly referenced the latter sense. A senior member of Ammi's group—Ruksana—nodded her agreement: "People dump their anger and frustration on us. We are like banks. We earn interest from others' emotions.

This is a city of deals. Some deal in diamonds, others in shares. We deal with emotions. We get angry only if it wins us a deal."

When I first met Laxmi five years ago, she was a rising member. But now Laxmi is the clear second in command to Ammi: "Today, parties call us for rallies and use WhatsApp to negotiate rates. They want to use our impotence to send their message. That's an opportunity for us. We can demand our price," adding that "our way of dealing with the city has changed." Laxmi disagreed with Ammi's view that they act from a position of weakness—doing only what "people like them" have to do. "We can be like [Prime Minister Narendra] Modi!" she said with a laugh. "He is still the same man who did those same deeds," she continued, referring to the prime minister's alleged connections to the 2001 Gujarat riots that killed a thousand people in his home state of Gujarat. "Only now everyone looks at him differently. He has become a *vikas purush*[10] [development man] with a fifty-six-inch chest in the last ten years." People need to look at us differently as well. We need to deal with people in a way that they'll see us differently. If we don't, we will always be invisible," she said. Laxmi is unwavering in her belief that everyone in Mumbai is a dealer:

> When I came to Ammi, I was thirteen and a man and a woman. I had both organs. I couldn't understand why. But later on I realized I am unique. It is believed among us that the one who is naturally born as man and woman can speak directly to God. I was given special treatment. When I started out 30-35 years back, we earned our livelihood giving blessings in society buildings and *chawls*. We were connected to building watchmen who were from Uttar Pradesh, Bihar, and Madhya Pradesh. These days everyone calls them *bhaiyyas* [younger brothers].[11] The watchmen were from villages where people like us were considered as harbingers of prosperity. They would give us information about births, deaths, marriages, and religious ceremonies so we would come to people's homes and receive money for our blessings. The watchmen never expected anything from us in return for this information because in their eyes this was just our job.

Mumbai has undergone major transformations since the 1990s, changes that Laxmi describes as having presented both challenges and opportunities. "A lot changed," Laxmi explained. "Political parties found a scapegoat in bhaiyyas for all the city's problems. The Shiv Sena forced society buildings to change their watchmen."[12] The earlier system in which a resident watchman and his family would work as maids, car cleaners, and gardeners crumbled. Resident associations gave contracts to private security firms, and cheap domestic help was recruited from nearby slums. "From buildings in Dadar, Chembur, King's Cross, Matunga, Shivaji Park, and Parel, many watchmen returned with their families to their villages," Laxmi recalled. "So we stopped getting the information. Not that *Marathi manoos* benefited. The buildings gave security duties to private companies, who got cheaper migrants from Orissa and Bengal as watchmen. In these states, people like us don't have the same status as in northern states. The new watchmen just didn't care."

The disappearance of North Indian watchmen was one blow. The changes to the chawls and textile mill areas of Parel, Lower Parel, Worli, Elphinstone Road, and Mahalaxmi were another. Laxmi describes the twin blows with a Hindi proverb: "Na ghar ke rahe na ghat ke," which translates into "We remained neither of home nor of the world." Many chawls were demolished and replaced with residential towers. Several textile mills were redeveloped into malls and offices. Laxmi was faced with a city that threatened to make her "invisibility permanent" by making it impossible for her to access spaces that at one point in time allowed her and her sisters to "ply their trade": "In chawls there were no watchmen, but people came to us on their own. Today, there are fancy buildings. We had to change, but our work remains the same. Anyone who approaches us with a pure heart will get desires fulfilled. We now bless small shopkeepers and cart owners."

Laxmi and her sisters[13] deal with the new modernity of Mumbai in other ways as well. Laxmi explains:

Companies want to work with us. Loan companies come to us since many customers don't pay. They send us to their homes or offices. We dance in front of them. Many repay out of shame. Officers now sit with us, have tea and talk about targets. Railway authorities also work with us. They want us to help in their Swacch Bharat[14] [Clean India] campaigns. We have gone to Churchgate station, where we have danced in front of people who were spitting. We tell them to respect India, which is their mother. Film people also come to us. There is a sister who has done films. It is being shown in theaters before movie shows.[15] It is a short film aimed at raising awareness of the discrimination that the transgender community faces every day. We are entering offices and attending meetings, something Ammi couldn't do ten years back. If old ways are disappearing, new doors are opening.

Asked why companies and governments are finding them "useful," Laxmi is blunt: "We are either feared or shunned. We arouse shame. Earlier, people found us useful because of our connection to prosperity. We were like positive banks for goodness. We are still banks, but deposited with fear. Companies and governments dip into us to shame others into 'good' behavior." I asked a final question: "If you had a magic wand,"[16] I began with a reference to Laxmi's favorite movie, "what would you wish?" She replied without hesitation: "I would wish that people wouldn't flinch when I touch them. We are humans too." She paused for a moment. "Which is why I will come to your house and dance for free!" She broke into a laugh. I wasn't sure whether it was still a joke or a longing for an older way of life.

WE INCHED OUR WAY through the congested back lanes of Chembur, and Laxmi, Ammi, and Rehana led me to their room. I had visited it several times. I saw new faces now, and I asked Laxmi about them. "We are still *born*, you know," she said, laughing. Ammi whispered something to one of the new girls, who disappeared. Just as I sat down, the girl, whose name I learned later was Padma, returned carrying a plastic bag filled with freshly made vada pavs and samosas and a steel jug filled with hot tea. "See? You are one of us now. For you, special vada pav, samosa pav, and tea!" said Laxmi dramatically. Everyone burst out laughing.

Notes

1. A quotation from a set of longer conversations with Laxmi conducted by the author in August 2017.

2. Elphinstone Road railway station (now renamed Prabhadevi) is one of the busiest stations in Central Mumbai.

3. See Jyotri Shelar, "Crushed: What Happened at Mumbai's Elphinstone Road Railway Station," *The Hindu*, September 29, 2017, www.thehindu.com/news/cities /mumbai/crushed-what-happened-at-mumbais-elphinstone-road-railway-station /article19775921.ece.

4. Laxmi explained that men dressed formally get quickly embarrassed and feel pressured.

5. Politicians often tactically use "transgenders." See R. Swaminathan, "When I Get Elected, I'll Dance in Your House," *Rediff*, February 18, 2002, www.rediff.com /election/2002/feb/18_upr_swam_spe_1.htm.

6. Lower Parel is in Central Mumbai. Trains rarely stop at platform 3.

7. Newer transgender groups are organized on religious lines. Older groups were often led by a Muslim guru and had Hindu transgenders. Ammi's group follows Hindu and Islamic traditions.

8. Mookambika Devi Temple is at Kollur in Karnataka.

9. Laxmi and Shaukat Ammi use both English and Hindi words. They use *deal, dealing,* and *business,* which they call *bijinej* and *dhanda,* interchangeably for informal daily transactions.

10. Prime Minister Narendra Modi has been given this sobriquet by several mainstream Indian newspapers, magazines, and television channels.

11. The term is often used in a derogatory manner to refer to a popular stereotype of an unsophisticated country bumpkin who has migrated from a North Indian village to Mumbai. See also glossary entry.

12. Several resident welfare associations (RWAs) gave contracts to private firms.

13. Laxmi uses *sisters* more than Ammi does.

14. The Clean India scheme seeks to reduce open defecation by giving subsidies to people to construct toilets.

15. See "Abuse Indian Transgender Go Through Everyday," Pocket Films, February 23, 2017, www.youtube.com/watch?v=TQWJyWKDAT8.

16. Laxmi's favorite movie is *Munnabhai MBBS*, where Sanjay Dutt refers to *Jhadoo ki Jhappi* (a magic kiss or a magic wand).

23 **DHARAMSEY** ASSEMBLER OF TRADITION

Edward Simpson

DHARAMSEY SUGGESTED a walking tour to enliven his thoughts. He explained that for the communities I was interested in—those settled in the city from the Kutch region of what is now Gujarat—there was a single key location, though now out of bounds, called Masjid Bunder (Mosque Port). It was to this part of Bombay that the Kutchi communities had been attracted in an elaborate form of chain migration during the latter half of the nineteenth century. The city expanded as new opportunities sucked people out of the impoverished and disease-ridden countryside. Dharamsey narrated this historical migration during our walks by pointing out road names, religious buildings, and the architectural reproduction of a provincial social order in the metropole. Regional merchants upped their game and opened offices in Bombay, but also often in other British-controlled parts of the Indian Ocean, with Zanzibar, the ports of the East African mainland, and the protectorate of Muscat being the most well known. In Bombay, much of the trade from Kutch in cotton and other commodities went through the Masjid Bunder.

Although the port was now a securitized area, the neighboring residential streets were accessible to us. Dharamsey was able to show me where the various Jain, Hindu, and Muslim areas had developed. There was a complex sociology to the explanation that opened my eyes to the depth of religious and community identity in the city, but also to the umbilical-like connection between the hinterlands of western India and the formation of one of the world's great maritime cities. The palimpsest of community, space, and time revealed during these walks mapped very accurately onto the communities in Kutch that I had spent the previous year trying to understand.

Upon arriving in the city, these communities established institutions necessary for proper civic and religious life (temples, communal halls, libraries). Dates in the foundations confirmed Dharamsey's chronology. Some of the civic institutions remained active, although much of the residential property had been rented out, even then. Tracing the migration of particular caste and religious groups from Kutch to Bombay was only part of the story. One could then see which communities were pioneers, which groups were integrated with the expectations of the colonial economy, and which communities preferred other communities as neighbors. Looking across South Bombay as a whole, to map the locations settled by the communities from Kutch, also suggested the subsequent fortunes and associations of these people as they grew and prospered with the city.

This time spent in the city during the 1990s was influential for me. Those months retain magical, if dusty, qualities. Partly because of these experiences, I have begun to think of fieldwork as a form of memory rut (of the kind made by hard wheels on soft farm tracks). From focused questions and emotional effort, field-note writing of live and chaotic experiences gradually takes shape and narrative form. Fieldwork features prominently in the biographies of anthropologists: scar tissue more noteworthy than the skin of normal life—the big year, so to speak, when memories are given exaggerated proportions by research design and analysis. That at least has been my experience (as I write about Bombay twenty years later with a clarity that the events of the last month have lost). Although I have never written explicitly about migration from Kutch to Bombay, the ways in which Dharamsey understood the ethno-sociology of community and connections strongly influenced my subsequent thinking on other matters.

One of the privileges of being able to look back on those times preserved as field notes is to wonder, no, marvel, about how I met the people I did. These encounters now beg questions: What kind of person comes forward to show hospitality to curious strangers? What kind of person becomes an informal spokesperson for cultural heritage or a city?

I believe that serendipity is only part of the story. There is also the magical realism of intermingling characters and a mutual understanding of the importance of questions and a way of valuing connections. The "field" has social shapes, contours of meaning, and established ways of conducting business. One aspect of routine business is to place watchmen at the gates to sound out who is coming to trade, proselytize, or ask questions. There is also the fact that in western India, as with many other parts of the word, there is a history of the go-between. The position is recognized and legitimate, though not altogether reputable or morally certain. In a city like Bombay, there are numerous categories of people who watch for the arrival of strangers of different kinds, pilgrims, the vulnerable, backpackers, migrant laborers, or travelers in need of a bed. So too are there those who keep a lookout for researchers, a disposition perhaps rather than a preoccupation.

How did I meet Dharamsey? Key in my over-practiced fieldwork memories are the days spent in the Asiatic Society in Bombay. I went there to turn the pages of the well-written Victoriana that then filled the shelves. I started to work in the reading room and began to see how the contents of that particular library had influenced the ways in which western India could know itself. The books on its shelves were those that had defined the ways in which we knew the history of western India and the ocean: the various editions of Periplus, accounts of the voyages of Alexander the Great, the monumental volumes that form the *Gazetteer of the Bombay Presidency*, and so forth. In that library, I gradually realized, the shelves of "history" hide a story of "go-betweens" as "native informants" collaborated with colonial officials in the production of imperial knowledge in the form of collections of proverbs, myths, legends, genealogies, and inscriptions. There emerged a category of translators and cultural and historical interpreters of India for foreign scholars. They may well have been present before the modern colonial period—perhaps there was someone to show Periplus around Cambay, for example; I simply do not know.

Gradually, I began to recognize faces in the reading room. They also began to see that I was a regular and was reading books that they themselves had read. Glances of recognition became "hello" and then conversations and cups of tea in the Parsi café in Horniman Circle. One of my new acquaintances was Dharamsey, who, as you already know, expressed a keen and knowledgeable interest in my research.

Virchand Dharamsey (born 1935)—more commonly known as Dharamseybhai—is a well-known and respected figure in Bombay as a scholar and bibliophile. He has contributed decades to the study of the city and culture, and of cinema and silent cinema in particular. He has written jointly with Amrit Gangar on Indian cinema and, as a lone voice, contributed to debates on soundscapes, film advertising, and the role of Gujarati culture in the earliest cinema.[1] An interest in archaeology, and the discovery of collections in the Asiatic Society, gradually matured into a full-length and entertainingly written biography of Bhagwanlal Indraji, a pioneer of modern archaeology in western India.

Bhagwanlal Indraji (1839–1888) was an interpreter of the past, a *bricoleur*. He read landscapes, inscriptions, and people as sources for understanding history. For Dharamsey, Bhagwanlal represented a new category of scholarship that combined traditional knowledge with modern critical methods.[2] He was not part of the English-speaking elite but was excellent at understanding the field and at interpreting historical documents. "In Bhagwanlal," Dharamsey writes, "we have that rare organic intellectual of colonial India whose erudition in the knowledge of 'tradition' was of a scale and quality that made him a scholar of peerless objectivity, which matched the requirements of modern empiricism, as well."[3] However, as an archaeologist in his own right, it has taken the work of Dharamsey to bring Bhagwanlal's contribution to the surface. Before, his efforts were buried in the scholarship of Bhau Daji, James Burgess, and others, names most associated with the making of archaeology and consequently modern understandings of the past in western India.

I have slowly learned that Dharamsey himself has been a generous and capable interlocutor for many other scholars. He appears prominently in the acknowledgments of all the recent handbooks and encyclopedias on Indian film and Bollywood. As the editors of one nicely acknowledge, "Virchand Dharamsey made available his encyclopaedic memory not only in his area of specialisation, but also to identify hundreds of film stills."[4] As Senake Bandaranayake, *the* late archaeologist of Sri Lanka, puts it in the foreword to Dharamsey's book on Bhagwanlal Indraji, "Dharamsey was always in great demand amongst scholars who knew him—or of him—and he enriched many a doctoral dissertation, perhaps sometimes without adequate acknowledgement,"[5] a claim Dharamsey also makes for the work of Bhagwanlal.

Dharamsey facilitated the research of the anthropologist Beatrix Pfleiderer, who names him in the frontispiece as collaborator and translator in her *The Red Thread*,[6] a notable study of the Mira Datar Dargah. In the 1980s he also helped to coordinate an archaeology expedition on behalf of the University of Pennsylvania.

I will return to that later. I am running ahead of myself. Back in the 1990s, I did not know any of the details of Dharamsey's life or of the significance of his contributions. Then I was confronted with a soft-spoken and sharp-minded man who seemed to know an uncanny amount about the topics and processes I was interested in. He made me feel excited about what I had been doing, a confirmation that helped me through some of the uncertainty of doctoral research.

Before arriving in Bombay, I had been in the port town of Mandvi in the Kutch District of Gujarat for more than a year. I was a student in anthropology and had been conducting fieldwork with seafarers and shipbuilders. As the months went on, Bombay became increasingly important for my fieldwork in Kutch. People were traveling back and forth all the time for business, to meet family and friends, and sometimes to pass an afternoon in a brothel. I would have arranged to meet someone for a chat and would frequently be told "Oh! He has gone to Bombay. Didn't he tell you?" The ease and regularity people with which would embark on what then seemed to me to be a significant journey was deeply irritating, as if they were just popping to the shops for milk and felt no need to share news of such a casual absence. Many hundreds of miles away from the city, you could be forgiven—based on a judgment of people's behavior and words—for thinking that Bombay was just down the road and we were in a suburb.

On the dockside in Mandvi, I would often sit with the late Naran Dhamji Kharwar. He had been a seafarer and, in his later years, had also become a custodian of local traditions and knowledge. He was respected as a community leader and an authority on the history of seafaring. As the years wore on, he lost his speech. Even then, he struggled with his voice and preferred to write out in an angular hand accounts of seafaring lore and miraculous tales of courage for me to take away.

All this became rather predictable as time wore on, as the local folklorists did not have a great range. However, there was a different story to be found in the landscape close to Naran's office that I never tired of listening to. Fifteen or twenty years earlier, an archaeologist had come from Bombay to Mandvi to survey the existent traditions of the sea. Instead of taking away sextants and navigation charts, as others had done, he worked to make the community proud of this heritage.

The archaeologist had labored in the heat of the sand dunes to uncover some rare and unusual hero stones, monuments to those who had died tragically at sea. Naran said that "the community knew they were there, but no one cared enough to care for them." Such artifacts are common in the region but generally display images of women who have sacrificed themselves on the funeral pyres of their husbands or images of male warriors on horseback who have been killed in battle. In contrast, these hero stones depicted ships and commemorated the sacrifice of sailors who were lost to the ocean. Over time, the stones had been scattered in the shifting sand.

The archaeologist and the local caste association collected them and installed them in a temple by the water's edge. The invention and assemblage of tradition in this story always seemed to me to be more valuable and sincere than it was flippant or kitsch. I did not make note of Naran telling me the name of the "archaeologist from Bombay," but I imagine he must have done so, considering how important the new temple was to him.

The numerous amateur historians I had met in Kutch also began to usher me toward Bombay: "There you will find the archives of our seafaring traditions." "You will not find that book here, but I have heard it is available in Bombay." Often, I would be told how expert historians and archaeologists had come on expeditions from the city and had taken away artifacts, records, and knowledge. There was a museum where these treasures had been catalogued and displayed. It was encouragements such as these that took me to Bombay and the Asiatic Society in particular, where I met Dharamsey.

With hindsight, there was something magical about the ways in which I met people during that period of fieldwork. I was naive and wide-eyed, which must have helped. In Bombay, in particular, it seemed easy, too easy almost, as if people wanted to communicate with me. There was an unexpected receptiveness to my questions, which probably played into an upswell of nostalgia and ideas about heritage. Looking back, I can also see that I and people like me were watched out for. At the time, my questions seemed to fit with the underlying logic of the place and the movement of people and ideas that had made the city. I had learned about India from my long stay in Mandvi, so it was gratifying to learn that the outlook I had gradually adopted was not quite as provincial as I had assumed.

Those early encounters with Dharamsey stayed with me over the years because he understood my own research so well. Talking to him was like balm. Gradually, over the course of conversations in the streets of eastern Bombay, it also emerged that he had once gone to Mandvi as part of a research team from the University of Pennsylvania. They had primarily been interested in field excavation of the ancient Harappan sites. However, in Mandvi they had been directed to an unusual collection of hero stones in the sand dunes near the seashore. Dharamsey himself had taken a keen interest in collecting and displaying the objects in a temple setting and remembered Naran fondly.

When I first set out to write about Dharamsey, I imagined confining my tale to our coincidental meeting in the Asiatic Society and his fantastic introduction to the social history of Bombay through his socio-architectural tours. However, the more I thought about the encounter, the more I realized that it wasn't only about Dharamsey but about a broader history of scholarship and the relations between the provinces and Bombay. Naran, who then sat for hours at a time on the derelict dockside reliving the historical comings and goings, had given me the crucial piece of the puzzle that enabled a chance encounter in Bombay to become deeply meaningful.

In all of this, the bricolage of Bhagwanlal's archaeology and his rare ability to read landscape, text, and people together has perhaps become Dharamsey's own methodology. Bhagwanlal supported the scholarship of those who made history in the nineteenth century, drawing together different forms of knowledge practice in ways that must have appeared simultaneously traditional and modern. Dharamsey has developed similar methodological practices in his own writing by producing, weaving together, circulating, and interpreting all sorts of signs and artifacts. Like Bhagwanlal, he is able to enlist bits and fragments from different languages, sources, and mediums in coherent meaning-making projects. Given the huge importance of filmic imaginaries in the contemporary city, it does not seem too much of a leap to see Dharamsey's interest in film as not only an object of empirical research and interest but also as an addition to his methodology, in which the cuts and juxtapositions of a skilled editor draw together a range of materials and conversations to make a narrative or for that matter a seafaring temple. In this, it would seem that Dharamsey's skills are shaped by the character and occupations of his city and those of the greater region.

In decades since Dharamsey and I walked the streets of Masjid Bunder, change has gathered pace. Most of the buildings that excited us have been demolished to make way for the new vertical Bombay. I no longer recognize the Kutch I knew in the city. Bombay has reached skyward; the eastern expressway has carved a path through the fabric of what was there before. The map he drew for me on one of our walks is a record of that time, a condensed expression of an aspect of a life of thought and a bringing together of people and things.

Notes

1. Virchand Dharamsey and Amrit Gangar, *Indian Cinema: A Visual Voyage* (New Delhi: Publications Division, 1998).

2. Virchand Dharamsey, *Bhagwanlal Indraju (1839–88). The First Indian Archaeologist: Multidisciplinary Approaches to the Study of the Past* (Vadodara, India: Darshak Itihas Nidhi, 2012), xx.

3. Dharamsey, *Bhagwanlal Indraju*, xx.

4. Ashish Rajadhyaksha and Paul Willemen, eds., *Encyclopaedia of Indian Cinema* (London: British Film Institute, 2012).

5. Senake Bandaranayake, "Foreword," in Virchand Dharamsey, *Bhagwanlal Indraju*, v.

6. Beatrix Pfleiderer, *The Red Thread: Healing Possession at a Muslim Shrine in North India* (Delhi: Aakar, 2006).

24 **DALVI** SPEAKER OF CITIES

Gautam Pemmaraju

Sali, bayat jodey ko baitha toh ek kilock key andar ek bayat
   jodney ko nai aata;
Pun tu jaanta, apun sar ka phirela juna shayar hai.

Usney mere ko ek mota sa chiroot haath mey diya aur bola key
   usko udata ja aur bayat bolta ja.
Bus, phir kya bolna; maine tabadtob ghajal bolkar vaisich tere
   paas aiyila hoon.

Damn it, sat to put together some couplets but even after an
   hour not even one;
But you know don't you, me, I'm a crazy old poet.

He put a thick cheroot in my hand and said smoke it up and
   keep the couplets coming.
And then, what more to say, I instantly made a *ghazal* [lyric
   poem] just like that, and now come to you.

THESE WORDS APPEAR in an unusual poem by Farookh Dehlvi a few years
prior to the close of the nineteenth century in a magazine that he published

in Bombay: *Abul Punch*. Hailing from Delhi (as his last name indicates), the journalist settled in Bombay, where he regularly published his magazine and wrote poetry. This poem has a character named Jakub Yusuf who is gallivanting across the city trying to write his *bayat* (couplets) to form an entire *ghazal*. From Haji Ali, Worli Gardens, to the *doonger* (hillock or mound) of Walkeshwar, the restless poet is seeking inspiration. With some struggle he completes a poem that he then gives to the narrator, Farookh, for publication, and when asked by the latter to stay on for chai, he declares that he is in a hurry, fearing he may miss the *hale* at the *godi*—his wages at the dockyard.

This poem was recited to me by an octogenarian scholar in a long conversation about the "social life" of Urdu in Bombay and what we may consider a city dialect: Bambaiya. Many paths of inquiry animated the conversation: variations across different neighborhoods; the wide word pool drawing from languages including Marathi, Gujarati, Konkani, Portuguese, and English; and broad types of slang, trade registers, comedic use, and other forms of street language. Bambaiya, a word derived from the name of the city, is also found beyond the streets in literary forms: poetry, prose, and dialogues and lyrics for the stage and for Hindi cinema. Additionally, the discussion also veered toward Urdu formal education, the creation of textbooks, and the establishment of institutions supporting and promoting Urdu education and literature.

Abdus Sattar Dalvi is arguably Bombay's preeminent figure of Urdu studies, linguistics, literature, and education. He has dual doctorates from Bombay University in Urdu literature and Urdu linguistics, the former on the work of the modern writer Mohammed Hussain Azad (best known for his canonical book *Aab e Hayat*) and the latter on Bombay Urdu. Following a stint at SOAS University of London, Dalvi became prominently entangled with Urdu in Bombay. Born in 1936, a native of Ratnagiri in the Konkan province of Maharashtra, Dalvi grew up speaking both Konkani and Urdu. Marathi and Hindi were also commonly spoken around him, so he became accustomed to several spoken forms quite early on. He moved to Bombay in the early 1940s, enrolling in a municipal school in Nagpada, where he developed a voracious appetite for books. He graduated from Ismail Yusuf College, where he studied Urdu, Arabic, Persian, and English before earning first a B.A. and then an M.A. in Urdu. He also learned Gujarati and studied Bengali as well. Dalvi professes a love of Indian languages and often says, "Mai Hindustan ki sabhi zabanon sey mohabbat karta hoon."[1]

Given his early association with Bombay and his predilection toward languages, Dalvi's proverbial "ear to the ground" is one of an immediate and intimate connection with the spoken forms in the city. Diverse linguistic, social, or labor groups operate in the city. Each of these groups has added to the sound and word pool, and regardless of persuasion, those who commonly speak Urdu/Hindi/Hindustani in the city draw from it freely. As Dalvi points out, *Mai jiine sey gir gayi* (I fell off the stairs) becomes *Mai dadar sey gir gayi*, interpolating the common Marathi/Gujarati word for *staircase*, instead of the conventional one used in standard Urdu/Hindi/Hindustani. *Soorat*, which Dalvi says is of Portuguese origin, was commonly used for gambling alongside *satta* and in lieu of the more common *jua*. In Bombay/Mumbai the local words *kanda, batata* (onion, potato) are used instead of the conventional Hindi/Urdu *alu, pyaas* used elsewhere. These common markers of a regional spoken Urdu/Hindi/Hindustani are at the surface of what is a deep pool of inter-intelligible and interoperable sets of words, idioms, catchphrases, and street/cinematic slang.

Dalvi's work calls attention to the way that many Bombay residents freely interpolate vernacular influences into a broader city-speak. People borrow not just from "their own" linguistic and regional backgrounds but also from languages common to their trades, which are also invariably influenced by caste and class. Some Bombay neighborhoods have long been home to distinctly Gujarati, Konkani, Marathi, Parsi, or Catholic communities and their trades. While Catholics and Parsis tend to use English dominantly, they have particular linguistic allegiances. The former may identify Marathi or Konkani (and sometimes Portuguese) as their mother tongue depending on where the families originate, while Parsis identify Gujarati as their mother tongue. Their distinctive manner of speaking English interpolated with words, phrases, and sounds influenced by their native tongues are immediate markers of their identity. Similarly, their native tongues influence how they speak Hindi/Hindustani and Bambaiya. While accents and word choices may vary across space, the dense exchange and interoperability make Bambaiya what it is—a *kichdi*[2] tongue, in Dalvi's words. Certain words used by the hand-loom workers and kite makers of Madanpura may not be understood by a Konkani Muslim trader in Byculla despite the geographical proximity of the two neighborhoods. But as Dalvi points out, Bambaiya is a "cover term" for the common tongue of the city wherein words originating in any of Bombay's myriad linguistic communities are freely borrowed by others.

FIGURE 24.1 Bambaiya Heartland: tongues of tradesmen and tough guys. Drawn by Ranjit Kandalgaonkar.

"Mera naam Mohammed Iqbal hai . . . urf bataun? Urf vastra."

"My name is Mohammed Iqbal . . . you want to know my nickname?
My nickname is vastra [blade]."—MOHAMMED IQBAL

MOHAMMED IQBAL OR IQBAL BHAI is a furniture maker in Jamli Muhalla, which is located on Bapu Khote Cross Lane, flanked on the north by Null Bazaar Police Chowki and on the south by Pydhonie Police station. He used to belong to the "Vastra Gang" in the 1980s. At that time he worked in his family trade as a blade sharpener (*dhaar lagana*). His nephew ran the gang he belonged to. "Hussein ney bahut wicket gira diyela hai," he claims, indicating that his nephew was a sharpshooter for the police, eliminating gangsters on contract. A typical Bambaiya phrasing, this would literally mean "Hussein has knocked down (or claimed) many wickets." The reference to wickets, a cricketing one, is typical street slang. Alongside this is also the verb form *gira diyela*, a Marathi hybrid for *gira diya*, its Hindi equivalent, literally meaning "dropped."

Following the murder of his nephew Hussein "Vastra" (Hussein Sheikh), allegedly by D-Company[3] gangsters, Iqbal bhai gave up his gang life. "Now I'm in white, no *bhai-giri*,"[4] Iqbal bhai says, explaining that there was more money to be made in furniture making than in sharpening knives. He is the youngest of fifteen siblings and consequently has nephews his own age and grandchildren the age of his children. Originally from Iraq, his family migrated to India around 1917 and settled in Bombay. The Jamli Muhalla neighborhood where he works and lives, flanked by the shrine of the Sufi saint Ismail Shah Qadri on one end and the Khatri Mosque on the other, is "safe," he claims, using the English word; no liquor or drugs are available there. Iqbal speaks a very distinct form of Bambaiya closely linked to gang culture. This form is what is popularly considered Bambaiya because of its appropriation by Hindi cinema. It is also referred to as *tapori* language. The use of certain words and cadences identifies an individual as a gang member or one who wishes to associate with gangs. Conversely, youngsters living in the area who wish to stay away from gangs choose not to use such words and phrases. *Peti* (literally box, but meaning a payoff), *khoka* (a crore of rupees—ten million), *supari* (literally betel nut, but denoting a contract killing), and *tapkana* (to get rid of or to kill) are common to gangs and are also an intrinsic part of film idiom.[5]

Consequently, Iqbal appears to be straight out of a Bollywood Bombay gangster film, but it is his natural way of speaking. He knows no other way.

This is a fascinating aspect of Bambaiya; it is inextricably linked to the language of cinema. The Hindi film screen in turn draws liberally from the sounds of Bombay street life.

The famous film writer Mohsin told a waiter at the Bombay Talkies canteen: "*Tum hum ko kal sey aap bolna*" (You address me with a respectful "You" from tomorrow). The waiter replied: "*Tum ko kal sey mai aap bolega*" (From tomorrow I'll address you with a respectful "You"). Bambaiya was made popular by Hindi cinema.—RAFIQUE BAGHDADI

I WALK AROUND DOCKYARD ROAD, Mazagoan, and Byculla with Rafique Baghdadi, a senior journalist and writer. He speaks of his life growing up in the area and his attraction to Hindi cinema, particularly to the writings of the celebrated modern Urdu screenwriter and short-story writer Sa'adat Hasan Manto,[6] who moved to Pakistan following Partition. Rafique's father worked as a technician in the famous film studio Bombay Talkies, which was established in 1934 by Himanshu Rai and Devika Rani, who were celebrated figures of early Hindi cinema. It was located in the then-distant suburb of Malad and produced forty films over a period of two decades. Rafique spoke Konkani at home with his mother and somewhat "polite," genteel Bombay Urdu with his father, but English and street Urdu/Hindi/Hindustani were the languages of the world outside of his home. Mazagaon had a prominent Portuguese-Catholic population and was broadly perceived as a Christian area. Rafique went to a local Catholic school, and his accent is very much a product of his neighborhood; alongside Hindi/Urdu/Marathi, a great deal of English and the odd Portuguese word were the languages of the streets around him, and switching between these languages was common. This mixed form of speech was replete with slang words, abuses, cinema dialogues, and other words that were never used at home. Mazagaon and Byculla have large settlements of Konkani Muslims, so their cadences and word choices differ quite a lot from what is spoken farther south in Nagpada, Dongri, and Pydhonie, where the influence of Muslim migrants from northern states of Uttar Pradesh and Bihar is strong alongside the dominant Gujarati Muslims communities such as Kutchi Memon, Dawoodi Bohra, and Ismaili Khoja.

Rafique's interest in Hindi cinema began very early on, in part because of his father's employment. He has written on Hindi cinema and has been particularly interested in Sa'adat Hasan Manto and his life in Bombay. He takes me on a walking tour that he has been conducting for years now, which includes the slum pockets in and around Nawa Nagar, the picturesque Catholic enclave of Mathar Pakadi, the popular Joseph Baptista Garden atop a water reservoir, and the main thoroughfares of the area flanked by Nesbitt Road to the north and Wadi Bunder to the south. We visit also Manto's erstwhile residences on Clare Road and Arab Gulli, not to mention the Jyoti Studio Compound below Kennedy Bridge, near Grant Road, where Manto was employed as a writer for the film producer Ardershir Irani's company Imperial Films. We end up at the old Irani restaurant Sarvi opposite Nagpada Police Station. Manto frequented the place and in fact set his short story "Siraj" (1951) on the street outside. It is a story of a conversation between the pimp Dhondu and the narrator Manto about a sullen, inscrutable, and melancholic prostitute named Siraj. Although Manto developed several characters of the underbelly, he rarely used the street vernacular. His characters speak a kind of artifice, somewhere between a cinematic, standard Hindustani with a few colloquial words for color and to distinguish the character:

> Saali ka mastak phirela hai . . . samajh mey nahi aata Manto sahab kaisi chokri hai . . . ghadi mey maasha, ghadi mey tola . . . kabhi aag kabhi paani. Has rahi hai, kehkeha laga rahe hai . . . lekin ekdum rona shuru kar degi . . . saali ki kisi sey bhi nahi banti.

> The bitch's head is screwed up . . . don't understand, Mr. Manto, what kind of girl she is . . . one moment a little, one moment a lot . . . sometimes fire, sometimes water. One moment she's smiling, laughing . . . and suddenly she starts crying . . . the bitch doesn't get along with anyone.

These words are spoken by Manto's character Dhondu to the narrator (also named Manto) on the street corner opposite Nagpada Police Station. Dhondu is often found there leaning against a lamppost and smoking a *bidi*. As can be seen here, the only clear indication that the character is from Bombay is the use of the word *phirela*, which is derived from the Hindi word *phira* (turned or screwed up) by appending it with the suffix *la*, as is the case in Marathi. Several Hindi words are similarly transformed into hybrid ones by the influence of Marathi on them.

Literary works have rarely seen main characters use Bambaiya. More often than not, characters from the city's underbelly are the ones who speak Bambaiya, while principal characters use a more polished Hindi/Hindustani/Urdu. It is perhaps in just three stories that Manto has employed Bambaiya words such as *vanda* ("fracas," Gujarati origin), *lafda* ("trouble," Gujarati origin), and *phirela* ("screwed up," Marathi origin). On that occasion he tellingly explicates in a footnote that an equivalent Urdu word does not exist. Bambaiya is also often used to convey humor on stage and film. Leading men in early Hindi cinema mostly spoke a standardized language belonging to an imagined realm that feeds simultaneously off of literature, real life, the stage, and cinema. It was mostly comic sidekicks who spoke street language. In recent decades, with a contemporary realism making its presence felt in Hindi cinema, there have been more and more characters speaking in a variety of speech forms. The lead and supporting actors of the *Munnabhai* films (a wildly popular triptych set in Bombay's storied under-world) are rare characters who exclusively speak Bambaiya—more precisely, the tapori variant of it.

Sanjay Dutt, the lead actor of the *Munnabhai* films, is an iconic Bombay personality whose life and manner demonstrate the recursivity in Bombay between the onscreen and offscreen worlds. Many of Dutt's screen dialogues (and those of his sidekick in the *Munnabhai* films) have become a part of everyday Bombay street slang. A successful Bollywood actor and the son of Sunil and Nargis Dutt, both screen idols of yesteryear, Sanjay Dutt was convicted in 1993 under a stringent antiterrorism law for possession of illegal weapons. He has portrayed a wide range of characters on screen in a career of nearly four decades, but he is especially remembered for his portrayal of gangsters—perhaps especially of Munnabhai, the "good-natured thug with a heart of gold." Dutt's onscreen street-speak is almost identical to his off-screen diction in his everyday life. More recently, given the rise of rap and hip-hop and the worldwide popularity of the Hindi film *Gully Boy* (2019), newer forms of street speech influenced by global hip-hop and American popular culture are making their presence known.

AT OUR LONG MEETING (one of many over the last few years), Dalvi spoke of what may well be the first example of Bambaiya or Bombay Urdu in writ-ten form. It is the autobiography of a man named Haji Bhai Miyan who was the patriarch of the renowned Tyabji[7] family from the Kathiawad region of Gujarat. Eschewing Gujarati as a means to express himself, Bhai Miyan chose to record his memories in a kind of patois, freely improvising and using ex-pressions and words that he had picked up in his adopted city. Earlier still, in the Marathi-language narrative chronicles *Mahimchi Bakhar* or *Mahikavatichi Bakhar* (fifteenth century to sixteenth century), Dalvi points to certain phrases in accounts of military campaigns as being Urdu. This is in relation to the settlement of the fourteenth-century saint Makhdoom Ali Mahimi in the area. The word *Bakhar* itself is possibly a metathesis of the Arabic *khabar* (news/information) or derived from the Persian *ba-khair* (literally: "all is well," a salutation). A few examples of writings from travelers, merchants, and Sufis also appear since the mid-eighteenth century, and Dalvi has been editing and annotating these for a volume on Urdu poetry of Bombay. From the *manzar-nigari* (scenic poetry) of a Rifa'i Sufi traveling from Surat, poetic descriptions of the great Bombay fire of February 1803, to the versified travelogue of Zareef Lucknowi around 1935, different "kinds" of Urdu have existed in Bombay alongside regional languages.

Given the Konkani Muslims of Mazagaon; the Ansaris and Memons of Nagpada and Madanpura; the Marathi mill workers of Central Bombay; the Gujarati merchants of Kalbadevi, Bhuleshwar, and Zaveri Bazaar; the Portuguese Catholic residents of Dhobi Talao Wadi and Bunder; the Parsis, whose enclaves are found across the city; and the Kolis, Pathare Prabhus, Kunbis, Bhandaris, and other communities considered native to the region, the varying influences upon the common spoken tongue of Bombay/Mumbai offer a great deal to consider. Abdus Sattar Dalvi and his late wife, Maimoona Dalvi, are probably the most important interlocutors in this area of study. Their published works and scholarly pursuits have not just mapped the life of Bambaiya (and Urdu) in the city but have also in doing so underscored the relevance and resilience of this kichdi language, whose sounds and rhythms continue to bring diverse people together and animate everyday life in Bombay/Mumbai.

Notes

1. This sentence translates as "I love all the languages of Hindustan." It indicates in part a certain postcolonial nationalistic ideal linked to Gandhian and Nehruvian values. In particular, it is strongly linked to Gandhi's ideas of a unifying Hindustani language for the nation, operating with both Devnagari and Urdu scripts. The various languages of the country are considered to be of great value to the nation at large, and the study of the languages has been viewed as a service to the nation as a part of nation building.

2. *Kichdi* (*kedgeree* in English) is translated as "hodgepodge," an unrefined mix of varying elements. It is a simple dish of rice and lentils cooked together for a quick and cheap meal, standard fare across the region. It is this sense of diverse influences freely intermingling into simple tasty fare that Dalvi draws our attention to through the use of the term to describe Bambaiya. Many of the interviewees I spoke to alternatively referred to Bambaiya as *bhel-puri*, a street snack with bold, spicy, tangy flavors to it. The analogy is quite keen to say the least; referring to the language of the city as something spicy and alluring that is ubiquitous and liked by all is a pretty accurate description of how Bambaiya is perceived by many.

3. *D-Company* refers to the transnational underworld operations run by Bombay-born gangster *Dawood Ibrahim* (see glossary).

4. This phrasing indicates that Iqbal cleaned up his act and transformed into a legitimate trader. "White" *dhandha* or trade is a common way of indicating a legal trade, whereas "black" is perceived as dubious or criminal.

5. *Petti* comes from either/both Tamil பெட்டி (*peṭṭi*, "chest, trunk, box, case") or Hindi पेटी (*peṭī*, "box, chest"); *khoka* is borrowed from Marathi खोका (*khokā*); *supari* appears to have Marathi origins: to give supari in Marathi is to employ someone for a purpose; *tapkana* is a verb connoting making something drop or fall through, thereby to kill or eliminate in slang.

6. Sa'adat Hasan Manto was an Urdu writer originally from Punjab who worked as a screenwriter in the Bombay film industry in the 1940s before moving to Pakistan in 1948. During his time he was considered a controversial figure because of his candid portrayals of prostitution and sexuality. He was tried for obscenity in court several times. He also wrote on the violence and inhumanity of Partition in a dark, satirical style. He is a celebrated figure now, and his unique voice and style remain a landmark in modern Urdu literature. In recent times there has been a revival of interest in his works, and two films have been made about his life.

7. Badruddin Tyabji was a prominent lawyer, an anticolonial leader, and the first Muslim president of the Indian National Congress.

PART V PUBLICS

Lisa Björkman & Michael Collins

IN A NOW-CLASSIC FORMULATION, social historian Benedict Anderson demonstrates how in nineteenth-century France, mass-mediating technologies (in Anderson's case, print capitalism) enabled people who would never actually meet in person—who may not have much to do with one another at all—to nonetheless conceptualize and represent themselves as a collective (in Anderson's case, as Frenchmen). That is, while theorists in the Habermasean tradition have called attention to how political subjectivity is constituted by means of public acts of communication (in a Kantian sense of the "public use of reason") as well as by the institutional contexts of the public sphere, Anderson's work emphasizes the communicative technologies by means of which mass political subjects—publics—come to know and represent themselves as such.[1] The profiles in part V are similarly concerned with the socio-material technologies and imaginaries enlisted in the production and representation of collective subjects: publics. The people profiled— self-described social workers, *karyakartas*, journalists, publicists, and production managers—are masters of publicity. Their stories call attention to some of the changing ways in which practices and technologies of mediation, social imagination, and self-making are animating new forms and formations of social collectivity and their representation.

Part V begins with Rohan Shivkumar's portrait of Shashi, a self-described "production manager" working in Mumbai's globally renowned Hindi ("Bollywood") film industry. "I had to do the production of my own wedding," Shashi remarks casually—his offhand use of the word *production* demonstrating the fluidity between Shashi's onscreen and offscreen lives. It is this recursivity between the material-practical city and the narratives, images, and spectacles that profess to represent it—recursivity between the world and the word, the *real* and the *reel*[2]—that the profiles in this chapter show to be characteristic of everyday life in Mumbai.

Shashi's story begins—"in classic Hindi film fashion"—with him and a friend running off from their village to Mumbai, to make a new life in the "city of dreams." Like other silver-screen runaways, Shashi's first encounter with Mumbai in the flesh is the iconic Victoria Terminus station, where he and his friend promptly "lose each other in the crowd." Hungry and alone, Shashi makes his way to the sea near the iconic Gateway of India, where he finds food, employment, and no dearth of "friends." "It is friendship that has sustained me in this city," Shashi explains, recalling how he spent the next two decades living and working on "the streets," meeting ends by making friends. And it is there on the Bombay streets as well that Shashi gets his first break, making his entry into the film world when a friendship that has developed over years of casual encounters on those very streets offers the stargazing street dweller a job on a film set. The rest is history.

There's an uncanny, déjà vu quality to Shashi's story, as if we've seen and heard this before. Which of course we have—in bits and parts and mythological tropes—in celluloid. However much of this account may or may not have actually have taken place onscreen,[3] the filmic quality of Shashi's autobiography seems to call into question the veracity of the account: how much of this story—which seems to be lifted straight from a Bollywood playbook—should we believe? Yet as Shivkumar's profile of Shashi makes evident, attempting to distinguish city life from its cinematic representations would miss the powerful insight that Shashi's narrative offers—i.e., the ways in which cinematic idioms and filmic representations provide a repertoire of concepts and possibilities that render Bombay life intelligible and navigable.

Shivkumar's portrait of Shashi establishes the central role of Bombay's cinematic imaginary as a "reading principle"[4] through which the city is perceived and sensed, deciphered, interpreted, and navigated, and whereby this variegated urban knowledge is enlisted in projects of self-making and city-making. We have already seen this reading principle at work: in Chandra's profile of Janu in part I, for instance, we observed how North Indian migrants are propelled to the "city of dreams" by "Hindi and Bhojpuri films made in the city." Similarly, in Pemmaraju's profile in part IV we saw the interconnection between Hindi film star Sanjay Dutt's onscreen and offscreen lives; famous as a silver-screen gangster, Dutt is also implicated in offscreen underworld plottings. These interconnections between lives is indexed by Dutt's use of Bambaiya Hindi, whose onscreen syntax traces the spaces and socialities with which offscreen lives are intertwined. In Shivkumar's portrait of Shashi—the production manager with a cinematic story—we see these dynamics come full circle: it is now Shashi who makes decisions (locational, sartorial) about what will appear on screen.

Removed from the glitz and glamour of the film set itself, Shashi's job is to "connect the dots" in film production. Shashi carries out his work by means of an ever-expanding database of personal contacts. But his efficacy derives not only from the reach of his social connectedness but also from his ability to quickly and creatively assemble people, places, and props, to improvise solutions to the ever-changing exigencies of making movies. As he moves around the city gathering whatever's needed for a film ("a helicopter or a needle"), his "repository of knowledge about people and places" expands, and images of locations and contacts are captured on Shashi's cell phone— the "primary tool of his profession." Indeed, Shivkumar notes that at the end of his first meeting with Shashi, the production manager "sizes me up and indexes me in his phone's address book as a possible contact."

With Kathryn Hardy's profile we move from commercial and corporate Hindi film production to the lower-budget Bhojpuri film industry, where, as Hardy tells us, "everyone, regardless of their status or role in the industry, is always looking for publicity." Although the Bhojpuri language is spoken primarily in North India, the Bhojpuri film industry is based in Bombay, where the infrastructure and expertise necessary to make movies are readily and cheaply available. Bhojpuri film is a low-budget business, Hardy explains, which means that unlike "studio-based systems" with regular in-house technical staff, Bhojpuri cinema is "project based": actors, dubbers, and production teams are continuously assembled, disbanded, and reassembled. Bhojpuri film production therefore demands "coordination between a tremendous number of highly skilled people."

Enter Anil Prakash, a self-styled "public relations officer" whose work sits at the intersection of "filmmaking and newsmaking" and thereby reveals the intertwining of—or rather false distinction between—the two. Like Shashi,

Prakash's work is liminal to the on-set activity of film production, but his news reporting and assiduous tab-keeping render him indispensable to Bombay's Bhojpuri film world. The public relations officer works tirelessly to draw people into his networks and to maintain his role as the industry's go-to source for reliable insider information on crucial things like actors' availability and production schedules.

Prakash's expertise consists on the one hand in pulling into fleeting alignment—just long enough for a film to get made—the scattered pieces and personalities of an industry that is constantly in motion, while simultaneously and on the other hand injecting the energy of publicity into the world of Bhojpuri film. The platform for his dual work—that of facilitating the production of Bhojpuri films and of producing Bhojpuri film-going publics—is *Hamara Mahanagar*, a Hindi-language newspaper that features Prakash's weekly full-page spread consisting of film announcements and industry gossip, as well as invitations to film launches and song-and-dance shoots—events that work like "press functions." Indeed, Hardy explains that Prakash is paid by filmmakers to publicize such events in advance of their happening, in the hope of attracting Mumbai's film-crazy news media. Prakash, in other words, assembles the people and things needed to produce a film, creates hype for glitzy launch events, turns up as the audience for such events (where he hobnobs and takes names), and then writes it all up in the full-color spread that he then circulates through Bhojpuri Bombay, thereby creating the "publicity" that coordinates the myriad in-motion bits and parts of the industry, while also providing "visibility" to struggling actors dependent on publicity for survival (their own and the industry's). His expertise consists in both the material production of Bhojpuri films and the communicative practices whereby Bombay's "Bhojpuri public" comes to know, represent, and reproduce itself.

The next three profiles explore these dynamics—the production and representation of publics—in the context of what is perhaps the city's most spectacular and highest-stakes iteration of theatricality, mass mediation, and publicity: electoral politics. Sarthak Bagchi's portrait of Gauravpant Mishra shows how the social collectivities animated at election time—manifesting as crowds at campaign rallies and performing their part at the polling booth— are produced and sustained longitudinally by Mishra's behind-the-scenes, off-season "social work." When we meet Mishra, he's sitting calmly at the edge of a large-scale election rally on Azad Maidan. Visibly pleased with himself, Mishra asserts that, as promised, he has contributed twenty people to this crowd. He adds proudly that his ward in South Mumbai was responsible for the largest turnout at an otherwise woefully underattended rally. Mishra's twenty people are all residents of the South Bombay constituency of Malabar Hill, where the self-described *karyakarta* also lives and works. And these income-earning activities are of the "social work" variety that we saw in profiles by Truelove and Banerji in part I: he facilitates access to government services (water pipes, school enrollments, death certificates) and helps area residents procure identity documents. Like Banerji's karyakarta Shazia, Mishra mostly (although not exclusively) performs such services on behalf of poor residents who reside in the unauthorized settlements that punctuate this otherwise plum address.

Bagchi's profile of Mishra not only provides insight into the relationship between the political work of producing publics that occurs during and beyond election season but demonstrates as well that attempting to disaggregate public-political from private-professional life in Mumbai is empirically untenable. Mishra's work as a Congress Party karyakarta is inextricably intertwined with his private-professional life as a Mumbai journalist: just like Prakash (Hardy's public relations officer), Bagchi's Mishra runs a weekly newspaper, *Nityanand Times*. And as with Prakash, we see how mass-media technologies are constitutive of that which this publicity professes to represent.

Mishra's newspaper has a limited circulation—only five thousand copies—around a third of which are distributed free of cost to the offices of various government employees. The newspaper functions as a sort of "visiting card," Mishra explains, delivered at regular intervals to important people at the Municipal Corporation and other public offices. Because of these weekly newspaper-cum-visiting-card distributions, Mishra's name is always already familiar to government officers. His reputation precedes him, Mishra explains, which facilitates his subsequent interactions with the various officials he engages in his karyakarta capacity. And it is this ready familiarity he enjoys with government officers by virtue of his professional reputation as a journalist that renders him in turn a reliable and effective go-to social worker. For most of the year, needless to say, Mishra's newspaper is not a terribly lucrative (or even sustainable) business. But during election season, Mishra recoups his losses: his strength as a "crowd maker" earns him respect from party higher-ups, who then make "donations" to Mishra's paper in exchange for publicity: Mishra writes laudatory candidate profiles, offers paid-news packages, and makes a tidy profit from overt political advertisement.

While Mishra's profile demonstrates the prosaic, off-season work required to produce, expand, and maintain networks of relations that are assembled and put on display during election season through high-profile publicity stunts—election rallies, mass meetings, "stage shows"—Simon Chauchard's profile of election "kingmaker" Srinivasan explores the expertise involved in producing and choreographing these sorts of spectacles. As the longtime confidant of a seasoned Congress Party politician named Ranganathan, Srinivasan's expertise consists in staging Ranganathan's campaign events: he choreographs rallies, facilitates door-to-door campaigns, and lubricates everything with cash to ensure its smooth operation. What's more, Srinivasan not only choreographs Ranganathan's campaigns but also supplies the senior politician with "access to an electorate from which he would otherwise be wholly disconnected." Whereas Ranganathan possesses what Chauchard terms "upward connectedness," which denotes access to money, to party leadership, and to key figures in the state bureaucracy, Srinivasan provides "downward connectedness," which links an exceedingly wealthy candidate to on-the-ground influencers (people like Bagchi's Mishra) whose intimate familiarity with neighborhood-level caste, class, linguistic, and material-infrastructural matters are critical for producing, performing, and publicizing strong and energetic support for the candidacy.

While Mumbai's cash-compensated election-season crowds are the subject of much moralizing hand-wringing about the so-called corruption of Indian democracy by practices routinely glossed as "vote buying,"[5] Mishra and Srinivasan demonstrate that these election-time, cash-lubricated public performances of political support must be understood in relation to the tireless off-season work of producing and maintaining the "connections" that are then activated at the time of election. Mishra's newspaper nurtures and maintains his connections with state bureaucrats, which (like Prakash's Bhojpuri paper) "amplifies" his message and extends the range and scope of his name recognition, and thereby his influence. This relational work links residents to government services, connects candidates with voters, and activates these carefully crafted connections in highly visible spectacles of public support.

While the profiles of Mishra and Srinivasan unsettle the boundary between the prosaic relational work of everyday life on the one hand and the spectacular, staged performance of those relations during an election campaign on the other hand, Bhushan Korgaonkar's profile of *lavani*-dancer-turned-event-organizer Madhu Shinde demonstrates the elusive character of the stage itself. When we meet Madhu, he is busily arranging a live dance performance at the fourteenth-birthday party for the eldest son of an up-and-coming Bombay politician named Doifode—"young and charming and flashy." As quickly becomes apparent, however, Madhu's dancers are not the only ones performing on this muggy afternoon. The dancers on stage draw a large crowd of partygoers, and in so doing the celebration as a whole works to broadcast the influence and affluence of their host, Doifode. "The birthday is a big public function," Madhu explains. "These days our work is mostly for people like Doifode—local leaders call us for birthdays or anniversaries, for anything really, any excuse to throw a party and entertain." Madhu's profile shows how political influence and its representations are inextricably intertwined in Mumbai, where reputation is always on display in the theater of everyday life. And Madhu's expertise born of a career as an onstage lavani dancer affords him a particular flair for how to go about putting on a show that will resonate.

Indeed, lavani is not just *any* dance; it is a form of dance theater that is dear to the Maharashtrian heart and finds its most avid and devoted fans among Mumbai's so-called *Marathi manoos* and Mumbai-based western Maharashtrians[6]—the bread-and-butter constituency of Bombay-based Marathi chauvinist political parties like the Shiv Sena and Maharashtra Navnirman Sena (MNS). Lavani is a staple of (non-election-season) neighborhood events organized by MNS—and Shiv Sena—affiliated social welfare agencies and NGOs in Mumbai's Maharashtrian-dominated strongholds, where regional dance, language, and edible delicacies are displayed and celebrated. In January 2018, at one such event in Andheri, a self-identifying "Punekar" explained that "Pune is our home," notwithstanding having lived in Mumbai for twenty years.[7] The man explained that he attends lavani shows anytime he can; sometimes he and his friends hop the train to Pune to attend *tamasha* festivals that feature lavani. Impressed by their passion, Björkman asked: "Don't you like any *other* kinds of dance theater here in Mumbai?" The man waved his hand dismissively: "In Mumbai there's just Bollywood dance." He gestures toward the stage, where a lavani dancer was winking and twirling on stage, adding "Inki style kooch aur hai" [Their style is something else].

Indeed, it is. Lavani is distinguished by its interactive, relational character. As Korgaonkar writes, "Lavani shows are outrageously and hilariously bawdy and suggestive, and meant to elicit response from the audience. . . . The distinctive feature of their art is in the eye contact that they maintain with members of the audience, drawing the audience into the show itself." Madhu is a seasoned lavani dancer, "a plump, middle-aged man," Korgaonkar writes, "who looked, danced, and behaved as a woman." In his late career, Madhu spends less of his time in a sari and more time (pants-clad) arranging dance-theater entertainment for local politicians and neighborhood leaders. But Madhu transposes the "style" mastered through his long onstage career in this newer work as an event organizer. "Offstage as on," Korgaonkar writes, "when Madhu unleashes his charm, the doors open—especially the doors of men." The style that Madhu has honed onstage and that he enlists in organizing his events is just what Doifode needs in order to broadcast his reputation and influence through "a big public function." In techniques of publicity, Madhu is indeed a master.

Like Korgaonkar's profile of Madhu, Ajay Gandhi's essay draws our attention to the elusive line between life and its representations. Gandhi introduces us to Poornima, an enterprising matron who administers a direct-sales business of plastic housewares, who assembles women in her neighborhood for political functions, and who intercedes in myriad quotidian neighborhood matters that will by now be familiar to the reader: making identity documents, getting kids registered for school, etc. And as with other characters profiled in part V, we see how the relational expertise that enables her to accomplish this "phatic labor"[8] is sought to be enlisted by others as a communicative technology. Gandhi describes how Poornima is approached by a Congress Party karyakarta—a man named Puduru who recalls Bagchi's profile of Mishra—seeking Poornima's help in organizing an *Aadhar* card (biometric identity card) registration drive. But we see how Poornima's Aadhar card services exceed their stated aims, becoming the site and pretext for staging a photographable event in conjunction with the appearance of a politician running for office in the upcoming municipal election. Needless to say, photographic evidence of the candidate's presence at the function would (like Mishra's coverage of Bhojpuri film launches) be "amplified" by means of the reproduction and circulation of these visual representations in the media and in campaign publicity.

Poornima seems willing enough to go along with Puduru's plan to parlay her social expertise into a publicity stunt. After all, Puduru's plan may well facilitate Poornima's own future work via shored-up relations with the candidate, should his bid for office prove successful. But as Gandhi intimates, the publicity photos are, for the social worker, just one representation among many; Poornima engages in her own practices of reflection and imaging in the *rangoli* (rice flour drawings) that she traces on her doorstop each morning. "Social relations depend on imaginative representation," Gandhi writes, "on aesthetic skills—of performing and projecting and connecting and dissimulating." Like her rangoli, Poornima's everyday social interactions involve not only "imagining" but also "actualizing" her relational world. Social relations are "given shape" (*rup dena*) through activities that navigate and reconcile social differences of language, region, caste, and especially gender by creatively enlisting her myriad skills in any and all aspects of neighborhood life. Poornima's relational work requires constant renewal and, like rangoli, is a performance designed to be observed and acknowledged by others. Her work is an aesthetic and generative process that "fashions something, connects entities, gives form to what had none."

WHAT ARE THE STAKES of the mass-mediated practices of publicity profiled in part V? Does the media saturation of social relations in Mumbai suggest that the city is under the "total administration" of the commercial-capitalist culture industry, as some critical social theorists might suggest? Or should we instead understand the activities of these liminal characters as sites of resistance and agency to capitalist hegemony—as the subversion of entrenched social hierarchies? The ethnographies profiled in this chapter seem to point us toward other questions, inviting instead to attend, as William Mazzarella has recently suggested we ought, to "the ambivalent ways in which the commodity images . . . may resonate."[9] Indeed, these stories from Mumbai suggest no dearth of ambivalence. Returning to Shashi's recounting of his filmic life, for example, we see that the production manager has cast himself as the hero of his own life story: a self-made man who emerges from the streets and realizes his dreams—of financial success, home ownership, romance, children, foreign travel. But of course, for all its Bollywood banality, Shashi's story (embellished though it may be) is exceptional: social mobility by definition presupposes hierarchy, and a great many of Mumbai's self-educated, cash-poor migrants do not achieve such dramatic, Shashi-style social mobility over a single lifetime. Shashi deftly transcends the brutal hierarchies that run through everyday life in the city: income poverty, lack of access to education, sometimes-violent ethnic and religious chauvinism. None of these—in Shahi's telling—pose an obstacle to the production manager's precipitous ascent: he marries a middle-class, educated girl of an elite social background; he parlays his street smarts into a respectable career in the technologically enabled knowledge economy.

In a similar vein, Korgaonkar's profile of Madhu reveals a variety of contradictory normative positionalities: on stage, Madhu dances (and charms) as a woman. And it is this capacity to charm that he parlays into his career as a political event organizer. Yet it is perhaps only as a "man" that this career is possible at all: the rough-and-tumble work of arranging mostly female dance entertainment for what are often (barring birthday parties) meant to be displays of heteronormative masculinity. Madhu's magic is that he is able to inhabit and *metabolize* these contradictions without needing to *resolve* them. Chauchard's and Baghchi's profiles, for their part, similarly show that the relational practices of social workers and party workers both reside in— while reinterpreting—the semiotic and socio-material geography of a highly unequal city in which political parties increasingly field wealthy candidates who are far removed from area voters. But in so doing, Srinivasan's profile suggests as well how, given the centrality of the expertise wielded by Srinivasan and Mishra, relatively cash-poor candidates might forge new futures. Perhaps like Poornima's rangoli, Srinivasan and Mishra are also "imagining and actualizing relations . . . bend[ing] into a desired silhouette." It is the changing and open-ended content of that desire and its representations to which these profiles call attention.

Notes

1. Although Anderson does not actually use the word *publics*, his work was an important touchstone for those who went on to theorize that term. For discussion, see Francis Cody, "Publics and Politics," *Annual Review of Anthropology* 40, no. 1 (2011): 37–52.

2. See Pandian's *Reel World* for a beautiful account of this recursivity with regard to Tamil cinema (Anand Pandian, *Reel World: an Anthropology of Creation* [Durham, NC: Duke University Press, 2015]).

3. Various components of Shashi's life story feel like an archetypal Bombay film, but it is a film that has perhaps never actually been made. Shashi may be an archetypal hero, Shivkumar quips, but he is "a copy without an original" (personal correspondence).

4. Vyjayanthi Rao, "A New Urban Type: Gangsters, Terrorists, Global Cities," *Critique of Anthropology* 31, no. 1 (2011): 3; see also T. Blom Hansen and O. Verkaaik, "Introduction—Urban Charisma: On Everyday Mythologies in the City," *Critique of Anthropology* 29, no. 1 (2011): 5–26; Jonathan Shapiro Anjaria and Ulka Anjaria, "Slumdog Millionaire and Epistemologies of the City," *Economic and Political Weekly* 45, no. 25 (June 12–18, 2010): 41–46.

5. Lisa Björkman, "'You Can't Buy a Vote': Meanings of Money in a Mumbai Election," *American Ethnologist*, 41, no. 4. (2014): 617–663.

6. Mumbaikars hailing from Pune, Satara, Sangli, Kolhapur, and Solapur, and Marathwada and Ahmednagar districts, all consider lavani as "theirs."

7. This conversation took place with Lisa Björkman.

8. Julia Elyachar, "Phatic Labor, Infrastructure, and the Question of Empowerment in Cairo," *American Ethnologist* 37, no. 3 (2010): 452–64.

9. As Mazzarella suggests, this very ambivalence may well be "the basis of whatever power and influence commercial culture is able to exert" (William Mazzarella, *The Mana of Mass Society* [Chicago: University of Chicago Press, 2017], 132).

25 **SHASHI** DOT CONNECTOR

Rohan Shivkumar

SHASHI MEHTA ALWAYS referred to himself as a "production manager" (he used the English term), which initially struck me as curious since he didn't seem at all an "industry" type—that is, someone who clearly worked in the heart of the Bombay film world. Rather, Shashi seemed to work at the outer edges of the industry, lubricating production processes and working out of his home, far from the glitz and glamour of the cinematic city. I met him through my friend Mukul, a cinematographer who had known Shashi from various shoots.

I brought Mukul along with me the first time I went to meet Shashi at his home—to interview him about his life and his work. He lived on the top floor of a Maharashtra Housing and Area Development Authority (MHADA) housing project, tucked behind a sprawling new residential complex along Grant Road, a bright white affair called Navjeevan, meaning "new life." By contrast, Shashi's modest MHADA building was Pepto pink, the color favored by the state housing authority for its low-income housing projects. The building had seven stories and no elevator. We trudged up the narrow staircase and turned into a dark corridor along which rooms lined up on both sides. We rang the bell.

The door opened, and we were suddenly in a sunlit world—a bright yellow room with a white ceiling with yellow trimming at the edge. The room was lined on both sides with gleaming white laminated furniture. The wall facing the outside was divided by a wall: in the space to the left, a kitchen counter abutted the only window; the other half housed the toilet. The living space, into which we stepped from the dark internal corridor, contained a long bed that served as the main seating space, opposite which a flat-screen TV floated above a small desk. Atop the desk sat a charging laptop. Knickknacks from around the world were carefully displayed throughout the flat: laughing Buddhas and ceramic horses decorated the glass shelves and the "showcase" shelves in the cupboards.

In the kitchen, Shashi's wife, Shireen, was busy preparing lunch, while his young teenage son lounged disinterestedly on the floor near the bed. Shashi was dressed in a loose blue T-shirt and track pants. He was a graying man in his early fifties with a slight playful smile on his face that did not seem to change across the entire conversation. This pleasantness, I was soon to learn, was his unique characteristic and essential to his work.

The conversation began easily enough. He asked me why I was interested in his life and work but then didn't seem to need much of an answer; it was as if he already understood that his story was somehow important. I was to learn later that narrating his life was something that he was quite used to. His story had been told before, and he knew how to tell it.

I started out by asking him about his work. Shashi explained that his job is to "connect the dots" in an industry that is notoriously fragmented. When a producer or a director needs a location for the climax, a cameraman with the right credentials, a prop, the travel arrangements, the hotel room assignments, a scriptwriter, a horse for the heroine, or an errand boy, Shashi is who they call. He says that his is the only name that everyone on the set knows. They yell, "Production! Shashi! Shashi! Shashi!" (in Surround Dolby, he quips, referring to how new cinema halls advertise their fancy sound systems), and it is his job to make sure that whatever they need is made available, however prosaic or idiosyncratic it may be: a helicopter or a needle. Once approached by a film's producer or a line producer, he performs any role that he is given to lubricate the process of production. There is no place for a big ego in this profession. While the others may indulge themselves in fancy ideas about who they are and what they are supposed to do, Shashi prides himself on doing everything, from sweeping the set to procuring the "right sandwiches for the Europeans," who Shashi tells me profess their relief, gratitude, and lifelong indebtedness.

Most of the producers don't like to get involved with the nitty-gritty of planning the shoot. They just give Shashi the basic information and the budget, and then Shashi connects the dots. Depending on the comfort levels of the producers and the pieces of the jigsaw that they have already fixed, he sets about filling in the gaps. Shashi has a "circle" of people with whom he is comfortable working. These are contacts that he has made through his work for many years within the industry. He trusts them, and they trust him. They know that they will get paid for their work in a notoriously fickle film industry. He curates from this circle a group of people, depending on the budget and whom he thinks will "gel" with the team. He presents these to the producer, who might make suggestions too. Shashi never forces "his people" into the team, as he knows that he is in this profession for the long run. He takes no commissions from anyone in the process, and he has no reason to push for the people within his circle. He says this has given him "repeat value": "Once somebody works with me, he will continue working with me. But no one will take me on unless they already know me because I have no degree, no credentials at all."

Shashi sees his work as matchmaking, finding the right mix of ingredients: "We have to see who will gel with the others. This chemistry has to be designed, as often one incompatible person can destroy the whole shoot." He describes himself as a sort of directory, a repository of knowledge about people and places in Mumbai. When an opportunity presents itself, specific circuits are completed, and the moviemaking machine comes alive. This requires him to have an extensive catalogue of people and places in his head. These ingredients are indexed by not only what they can offer but also in terms of their personalities: their ability to work with different kinds of people. He used to collect these in a little diary, but his diary has been replaced by his iPhone contact list with its more than three thousand entries, indexed according to profession, with notations.

To build this information store, every moment presents him with an opportunity. Every person he meets is a possible collaborator, every place a possible location. He keeps in his head a map of the city as a set of resources waiting to be tapped: "Every time I am moving across the city, I am actually scouting it for possibilities. Every location is being scoured for where I can get different kinds of shots. I always have a camera in my head. My eyes and ears are always open. Every time I meet a person for the first time, I gauge them in terms of how they can be useful. I get their number [*number dekha click kar diya*]."

The cell-phone revolution has transformed his work in many ways. His phone has become the primary tool of his profession. "These days people play 'mail-mail, WhatsApp-WhatsApp, message-message,'" Shashi tells me. "They send things back and forth, and things have become much easier. Nowadays they send me an image of a desired location saying, 'I want like this'; and I can send it off to my contacts saying, 'I want like this,' and soon I will have what they need. Google baba is like a godman that can answer many questions."

At the time we met, Shashi was working with Neha, a visual artist with whom he had worked on a previous project. This time she was working on an experimental video set in a Jain *dharamshala* (shelter) outside Mumbai. Shashi was in charge of location, food, and transportation, along with making sure that the workflow went smoothly. He was coordinating among the artist, the cinematographer, and the digital imaging technician. Our conversation is interrupted by a call from the assistant director, a young Indian American hoping to earn her filmmaking chops by helping out on this shoot. Shashi spells out instructions to her for an errand involving a trudge across town. He later admits that the matter could have very easily been resolved over the phone but that the errand will be "good for her," he claims. "She will learn." The pedagogic instinct is his own and has nothing to do with the requirements of the shoot.

As the conversation continues, Mukul and I ask Shashi how he got into this field. He responds with a tantalizing "Now *that's* a story you will not believe."

In 1972, at the age of thirteen, Shashi left home with a childhood friend to find a better life in Surat. Shashi was born in the North Indian city of Benares to a large family of sari weavers. Having the skill handed down to him from his family, he felt that he could build a better future in Surat, which had, at that time, many power mills. His father was a well-respected Ayurvedic doctor in the city, Shashi tells us, adding that his father wasn't very concerned when his son did not come home one day. Although the family looked for him in the streets of Benares for a week or so, they soon gave up, thinking that Shashi had drowned in the river, another casualty in that city of death. It was only four years later, after Shashi had made enough money to get back to Benares, that his family finally learned that he was still alive.

Meanwhile, Shashi and his friend had taken the train to Mumbai's Victoria Terminus and, in classic Hindi film fashion, lost each other in the crowd. With no money in hand, with nowhere to go, Shashi walked down the arcades of DN Road until the road ended and there was only the sea ahead at the

Gateway of India. Here, desperately hungry, he asked a man selling sugar-cane juice for work:

> The first man I asked chose to help me. He gave me a little bit of money and asked me to go get myself a *vada pav*. After that I worked as his apprentice and lived on those streets for twenty years. I found all kinds of work. I sold caps and souvenirs to tourists. I loaded and unloaded goods from boats, sometimes legal and sometimes illegal. I saw the city from the streets. I knew the local pimps and prostitutes, the gangs and the beggars. I stayed out of the crime on the streets as far as possible. I never smoked or drank. Those things didn't interest me, and thank god for that. What I sold on the streets changed regularly. My longest-selling single product was those spirographs that make colorful patterns on paper.
>
> Since that very first day, it is friendship that has sustained me in this city. Whenever I have been in trouble, it has been my friends who have helped me out. That's also how—while working on the streets—I got my first job in the film industry. The actor Tarun Dhanrajgir, he was a friend of mine. . . . He lived nearby, in Dhanraj Mahal.

For those who don't know, Dhanraj Mahal is an imposing red art deco apartment building stretching along the road that leads from the iconic Regal Cinema to the Gateway of India. It is the property and one of the many homes of the princely family of the Dhanrajgirs, who had migrated from Afghanistan to India in the fifteenth century. The family was part of Mumbai's wealthy and cultured elite. The female lead of the first Indian sound film, *Alam Ara*—released in 1931—was Zubeida Begum Dhanrajgir, a member of the family. Tarun himself grew up in Dhanraj Mahal and had a successful career as a model before turning to acting in the 1970s. As Shashi explains,

> Tarun Dhanrajgir and I were friends. We met regularly as I lived on the streets in front of Dhanraj Mahal. We got along well and would chat whenever we met, so he knew that I was always looking for work. Folks from the FTI [Film and Television Institute of India] were always around at his place. One day, one of them was making a corporate film for Larsen and Toubro, and they asked him whether he knew somebody who could help in organizing it. Tarun asked me if I would like to join the crew. I said yes. Since then I have been primarily working in the corporate films and the advertising films sector. I don't like the mainstream Bollywood system. I only work with a few mainstream producers whom I trust. The rest of them are thieves—they are always looking out for cuts and commissions. I

can't get along with that. I might get less money in this sector, but at least I am guaranteed payment. I have heard that the crew on *Sholay* has still not been paid.[1]

There was a time when there were many more corporate films. Now with the digital, PowerPoint seems to replace them. There used to be at least eighteen people on the crew: the sound guys with their Nagra, [portable audio recorders], the light guys, cameraman, his assistants. I had to coordinate with all of them. I gradually became known as the go-to guy for corporate film within L and T. I also shot in many of the steel plants around the country from Bhilai to Jamshedpur, and was soon called the "Steel Man Shashi" in our circle. I had made my first corporate film in 1988 at the age of twenty-nine. I only made my first feature film in 2003.

Being completely self-taught, I have had no godfather in the industry. I have managed everything I have only because of my friends. Every time I have needed anything—like this house that I live in—it has been friends that have stepped in with their generosity. I almost lost my hand in an accident, but my friends saved me, lending me money for the surgery. My friends gave money for my marriage and even helped me buy this house.

As we speak, his wife brings us tea and sandwiches with the crusts neatly cut off. Their son leans against the bathroom wall, playing with his phone and pretending not to listen to our conversation.

The story turns to romance. It begins with Shashi living on the streets of Colaba and watching the comings and goings of a Parsi (Indian Zoroastrian) girl named Shireen who works in a Chinese beauty parlor. Slowly they begin to develop a friendship that blossoms into love. This romance was never going to be easy. She was a middle-class Parsi girl who lived in one of the Parsi colonies on Grant Road;[2] he was a homeless drifter without a stable job. The courtship lasted for ten years. Her parents liked Shashi but were against the marriage. The only way he could convince them was to be able to get himself a house in the city. He had few expenses and would quickly spend whatever money he earned hanging out with his friends and watching films. But now he started saving money, and eventually he rented a flat in this very building. Three months later, he and Shireen were married in a Arya Samaj (Hindu) ceremony held in a Catholic hall on Princess Street. As Shashi recounts,

I had to do the production of my own wedding, the location, the decorations, were all done by me. I had the best Chinese food at the reception because all my friends were chefs at the Chinese restaurants in Colaba, and they did the catering. However, Shireen was excommunicated from the Parsi community for marrying an outsider and chose a new name. Shireen became Sheila.

After our marriage we moved into an apartment on the fourth floor. Our landlord had four houses in this building. After a few months, he told us to either vacate the apartment or buy it. Again, we had no money, and I had to approach my friends. Each of them offered what they could, from 10,000 rupees to 80,000 rupees. I was able to collect enough, and along with my savings we were able to buy this flat. We used some of the money that was left over to design the house the way we wanted it. Sheila is very particular about the way the house is kept, as you can see.

It was around the time that we bought this house that the new TV channels had started. A friend offered me a permanent job as a production manager in one of them, and I welcomed the opportunity to have a regular salary. They wanted to hire me for a permanent position, but I refused—I knew well that I could never grow in the organization as I did not have any officially recognized educational qualification. So instead I worked month to month. They paid me 3,000 rupees every month in addition to a 500-rupee per diem allowance to cover the daily expenses involved in the work. I began to save money, and over a period of eight or ten years I repaid my friends what I had borrowed, although very few of them expected it. From their perspective, they had given the money as a gift.

Today I have everything I need. I can afford food, biryani, even McDonald's. I still don't drink much but have started drinking because of my wife. She is a Parsi, after all, and they are *shaukeens*—they enjoy life. I have two sons, Ainesh, who is eighteen, and Jibinesh, who is twenty-four. Both of these names are very unusual and unique. We chose unique names. Jibinesh works in a calls center, while Ainesh is a dancer.

Ainesh, who until now was listening from his corner of the room, joins the conversation. We ask him what kind of dance he performs, and it turns out that he choreographs Bollywood-style dance, either for films or for "freestyle" dance performances at weddings and other events. He also works as a swimming instructor. He tells us that he wants to be a production manager like his father. He's already begun assisting on shoots. "I love [production] work because of my father," Ainesh says. "I want to be like him."

As we prepare to leave, Shashi pulls out his phone to show me a video from his recent trip to Amsterdam. The clip shows Shashi kissing the hand of the queen. He needs no prompting to tell the story: Troppenmuseum was curating an exhibition about Mumbai, and Shashi (of course) was one of the production people on the project—arranging for the *bhelpuri* (street snack) vendors, auto rickshaws, and even a compartment of a local train to be sent to Amsterdam as part of the show. During the exhibition one of the curators asked Shashi about his life. And after hearing his story—the very story he's just told Mukul and me—the Dutch curator decided to structure part of the museum exhibition around Shashi's life. It was during the opening of this exhibition that Shashi met the queen and kissed her hand. He keeps mementos of that day wrapped and organized in the loft over the wardrobe.

Shashi sizes me up and indexes me in his phone's address book as a possible contact. I am a profession and a location. In his mind I am most likely also a temperament, a predilection, a potential. From that day onward, almost every week I get Whatsapp forwards, wishing me a happy day.

Notes

1. The Bombay blockbuster *Sholay* was released in 1975.
2. See Vevaina's profile in chapter 11 for a discussion of Parsi housing.

26 **ANIL PRAKASH** AMPLIFIER OF CINEMA-INDUSTRIAL CONNECTIONS

Kathryn Hardy

WHEN I RETURNED TO BOMBAY in October 2016, the Bhojpuri film industry had changed dramatically from 2010, when I began fieldwork: film production had completely shifted from 35mm cameras to new digital formats, and the ascendant male stars were all new. I needed to interview several of these stars and was unsure how to get hold of them. I had one star's number, but he kept putting me off. I was debating how to proceed when I ran into Anil Prakash at a recording studio in suburban Andheri. He immediately set me straight: "Dinesh Lal can't meet you right now—he's in Hyderabad until Wednesday and going straight to Raipur after that. Khesari Lal is in Rajasthan on a shoot. Pawan Singh is in UP [Uttar Pradesh] and not coming back for two weeks. Manoj Tiwari? He's not doing this anymore; he's a politician in Delhi now!" He went on, rapid-fire naming the major and minor stars, their locations, future locations, schedules, and a rough hierarchy of their recent successes. Then he asked me when I'd returned and quickly took an interview with me for a new, unnamed website he was working for. Writing on an improvised slip of paper, he skipped over my own long-winded explanation of my research to note (with some geographic inaccuracy) that I had come from Wisconsin—I'm from Kentucky—to write a book about

Bhojpuri cinema. In his news story, my foreignness would be used to demonstrate Bhojpuri cinema's (actually quite limited) international reach, and thus of its growing prestige. For Prakash himself, I was another link in his dense chain of socially interrelated connections, many of which could also be mobilized for news stories. Both connections and stories were part of the work of public relations, and both could be monetized under the right circumstances.

In early January 2010, before I even formally began my research into the production practices of Bhojpuri cinema, I had been introduced to Prakash in the offices of *Hamara Mahanagar* (Our Metropolis), a Hindi-language newspaper published in Mumbai and aimed at the large population of North Indian labor migrants living in the city. Along with local Bombay news, the paper featured daily sections on news from Bihar and Uttar Pradesh, and a weekly full-page spread of Bhojpuri film announcements and gossip. Prakash had conceived of the page and continued to curate and write it, telling me it was the first dedicated Bhojpuri entertainment feature in a newspaper. Yet Anil Prakash did not exactly describe himself as a journalist. The editors at *Mahanagar* and the filmmakers with whom he cultivated relationships all knew him as a PRO, or public relations officer. His work intertwined filmmaking and news making: as a PRO, Prakash's job was to connect filmmakers and stars with press outlets for promoting their work and, at the same time, to provide newspapers with attractive entertainment content. By calling him a PRO, those in the newspaper business marked Prakash's profession as not quite journalism: even in a journalistic milieu where paid news and re-published press releases were common, Prakash's work was liminal. He was not part of the core reporting staff; he didn't have an assigned desk space like other journalists. The separate page for Bhojpuri film news meant that his written work was aesthetically distinguishable from the regular reporting, marked with a splashy logo in Devanagari across the top and never mixed in with news. Similarly, filmmakers also saw PROs like Prakash as separate from the core of the Bhojpuri film industry, which revolved around big-name actors and, to a lesser extent, directors, producers, and music directors—in other words, the "creatives" and the people with the checkbooks. The title PRO itself marked his space as a go-between tied to multiple stakeholders, a pivot point between film networks and news networks. Despite his liminal position—or perhaps because of it—when I met him in 2010, Prakash was one of the most well-connected people in the Bhojpuri cinema industry.

Although the Bhojpuri language is primarily associated with the relatively rural hinterlands of Uttar Pradesh and Bihar in the Gangetic plains of North India, the cinema industry that shares its name is based largely in Bombay. Filmmakers often purport to represent a preexisting rural public of Bhojpuri speakers, attending to their needs and interests. But in actuality, the industrial practices of Bhojpuri cinema produce new publics of self-consciously Bhojpuri-identified subjects in places like Mumbai.[1] The placement of the industry in Bombay has accelerated ideas of Bhojpuri's trans-regional border transgressions but is based on the practical, material considerations of filmmaking. All the necessary technical infrastructure of cinema production—camera rental agencies, professional lighting, processing labs, dressmakers—is concentrated there. Equally important is the well-established social infrastructure of cinema in Bombay.[2]

Making a film, even a low-budget, relatively low-prestige Bhojpuri film, requires coordination among a tremendous number of highly skilled people. Unlike studio-based systems, where the same group of artists and technicians works together consistently, contemporary low-budget Bombay cinema is project based. Electricians, art departments, camera crews, and other below-the-line workers are hired as teams, with younger, less experienced workers recruited as apprentices by senior technicians. Filmmakers—usually directors themselves, executive producers, or assistant directors—assemble new groups of people for one to three months of work, groups that then disband after the shoot is complete. Because of this, work schedules are inconsistent and unpredictable for all but the most elite actors in the industry, whose schedules might be planned up to two years in advance. Light men, cameramen, costumers ("dressmakers"), and low-level actors alike must constantly look for new work. Likewise, directors and producers are always on the hunt for skilled workers, as well as finance and distribution contacts. And everyone, regardless of their status or role in the industry, is always looking for publicity: not just being featured in the news but being known to others through reputation and continual face-to-face contact is essential to working in the film industry. For instance, a director looking for a last-minute voice-over artist didn't hold auditions, but merely asked other people hanging around at the sound studio for names of artists known to them. Forty-five minutes later, the second woman on the hastily assembled list—the first one who had answered her phone—was in the studio, dubbing for the film. Her qualifications were as follows: she had worked with one of the director's assistants before; she was thought to be from Bihar; she had a nice enough voice; she lived on Yari Road, within easy taxi distance from where we sat in Andheri; and, most importantly, she answered the phone and could be there immediately.

I once asked two young actors why they had come from Bihar to Bombay to try to break into an industry that was so centered on UP and Bihar. "You can't sit in UP," he said, if you want to meet anyone. You have to show up in Bombay and struggle. "Struggle se kaam hota hai, kaam se kaam," one actor explained. ("Struggle leads to work, and then work leads to more work.") Struggling means hustling to be seen, to meet as many people as possible, so that you might be the one they call in a pinch sometime down the line. Being present and being known are thus the two conditions of employment in the lower levels of the industry. Because of this, much of the labor indexed by *struggle* is showing up at functions, parties, film launches, film shoots: anything to meet more people with decision-making power. In this atmosphere the PRO's work is largely to activate the seething desire for connection in the industry.

The term *public relations* ordinarily describes the practice of maintaining a unidirectional channel through which information flows between an entity—for instance, a film or a celebrity—and an external public. But Anil Prakash's job seemed to point to a more broadly construed public, where anyone related to the industry might benefit from a general circulation of information. Prakash's work was to produce and generally amplify knowledge—about people, places, films, happenings. His twin assets were his network and his impressive recall of places, people, and events, and a nuanced sense of shifting social hierarchies. When I met Prakash for the first time, he spoke for half an hour almost without pausing, verbally sketching out the contours of the interrelated working relationships through which Bhojpuri cinema had been constituted and reconstituted as an industry over the past fifty years, accelerating in the previous decade. At first, I saw Prakash as he presented himself: a conduit through which anyone could be connected to anyone else in the industry, a sink of knowledge. At the time, I failed to see the ways that Prakash himself was a key social actor whose work defined the limits of the Bhojpuri cinema industry, recruiting historical events and loosely connected people into a tightly woven tangle of contemporary relevance. My notes from our first conversation are thus sketchy but telling:

> [Prakash] spoke exclusively in Hindi, very quickly, almost overlapping his words as he shot out name after name of directors, actors, producers, and so forth—more people than I could count, let alone write down. He assured us that he knew "*sab log*" [everybody] in the industry and would introduce me to everyone. . . . He mentioned a singer, Malini Awasthi, as one of the most important people in Bhojpuri music right now. Lata

Mangeshkar sang the title song for *Ganga Maiyya Tohe Piyari Chadhaibo* [*Mother Ganga, I Will Offer You a Yellow Sari*, the first Bhojpuri film ever made, released in 1962]. He just kept on telling me trivia, tidbits, names, places, connections between different people—I was a little overwhelmed.

It was not always clear who Prakash was working for, but it was immediately clear that he was always working: I ran into Prakash everywhere. He showed up in the distribution offices I visited. He came through the sound studio where I was studying the ubiquitous practice of dubbing. He would pop into the offices of stars as I interviewed them. He regularly sent me SMS invitations to *mahurats* (auspiciously timed film launches) as well as film shoots, particularly the song-and-dance shoots that, as the audiovisual highlights of film production, often doubled as press functions. Each function was an event that he could cover, but I quickly got the sense that he was also paid by filmmakers for publicizing press events. Writing his newspaper spread was clearly only a minimal part of his work. Through his reportage, he pulled directors, financiers, actors, distributors, and others into his networks. But then again, everyone else was preoccupied with networks as well. Actors, music directors, and even lower-level technicians displayed their social capital by inviting me to events and ostentatiously announcing their connections to others. When I casually mentioned a well-known music director, one character actor interrupted our conversation abruptly to say, "I know him well! We speak on the phone every day." To prove the point, he called the music director then and there, verbally clapping him on the back with studied informality: "How've you been, brother? Oh great, how're the kids?" These actors flaunted prestigious connections to underline their own high-level marketability and professional status. Prakash's mobilization of social capital was slightly different. Prakash actually monetized his connections, both by selling stories about well-known actors and exciting new films to newspapers and by selling access to the machinery of publicity to film producers and to actors themselves.

In person, the social infrastructure of Bhojpuri cinematic production was cultivated through a dizzying calendar of events, often *mahurats*, also called "launches," that hover between social engagements for those already working together and externally oriented marketing. I was told that mahurats happened only once the film's cast was finalized. To my surprise, the first mahurat I attended was also attended by a bevy of young men and women who couldn't exactly explain their connection to the film being launched. When I asked what part one young actress would play, she said "Heroine!"

and laughed. Later she admitted that she had not secured any particular role for that film but had attended the mahurat after being invited by her acting coach. She hoped to pick up a small role or at least have her face seen by directors and other actors. Events like these often doubled as informal employment fairs as struggling actors sought work as "junior artists" and filmmakers sought additional funding and personnel. These events were spatial hubs through which information about current and future projects, people, and money circulated. As people milled around, gossiping over samosas and fizzy drinks, the social ties that allow the industry to function were strengthened and reconstituted. News media did much of the other work behind the scenes: PROs like Prakash were likely to be paid by both news outlets and film personnel themselves to circulate articles about heroes, upcoming films, and recent releases. His informal sharing of information—the locations of the stars, the success of films—is likely even more valuable, although he is paid for this kind of information sharing largely in the currency of social access across the industry.

Toward the end of the year, when I revisited the offices of *Hamara Mahanagar*, Prakash was no longer in their employ. The editor explained that he was sure that Prakash was getting money from filmmakers to promote their projects. The problem with this was not so much that Prakash's editorial integrity was compromised but rather that he was not adequately passing these kickbacks along to the newspaper itself. The editor told me this as a matter of fact, not of particular moral judgment: these financial liaisons were expected. As I sat in the office, the editor called Prakash, asking, "Where have you gone off and died?" While the Saturday full-page spread was gone, Prakash seemed to stay well enough connected to the editor: he answered his phone and gave me instructions for attending yet another event that very night. For his part, Prakash was doing fine; he was simultaneously publishing articles in a Bhojpuri film magazine and two websites, and was working on starting a new trade magazine, all while he constantly drummed up enthusiasm and awareness for new films.

In Prakash's latest project, a blog with a splashy pink logo that reads "Anil News Network," he refers to himself not as a PRO but as a "film journalist and publicist." His blog is the online equivalent of the circulating talk at a film launch: with film-release details, shooting location schedules, reports about other film launches, and a sprinkling of political and romantic gossip, the blog is a clearinghouse for information about people and films. His source of income is possibly the filmmakers and actors about whom he writes, but this is not discussed on the blog. His value to the industry is partially as a kind of promoter; through his SMS blasts inviting everyone on his list to mahurats, shoots, and functions, he helps populate these events with Bhojpuri personnel eager to meet one another. He thus produces the social infrastructure of cinema so that directors can fill future last-minute roles and strugglers can get name and face recognition from people who might eventually hire them. Prakash makes sure that his own role in producing these networks is nearly invisible in the news reports that, at first glance, appear to be the final products of his labor. But his work demonstrates the productive capacity of publicity—not merely describing the goings-on of a preexisting industry but actively mediating social and economic relationships between filmmakers and news outlets, producing the contours of the industries themselves, and, eventually, showing a highly mediated glimpse of these industries to a broader public in Mumbai.

Notes

1. Kathryn C. Hardy, "Constituting a Diffuse Region: Cartographies of Mass-Mediated Bhojpuri Belonging," *BioScope* 6, no. 2 (July 2015): 145–64.

2. As Tejaswini Ganti explains, Bombay "has been synonymous with Indian filmmaking, identified as the 'birthplace' of cinema in India. . . . In addition to being the site of the first screenings of motion pictures in India, Bombay was also the site of the first film made in India—a wrestling match shot in the city's Hanging Gardens" (Tejaswini Ganti, *Producing Bollywood: Inside the Contemporary Hindi Film Industry* [Durham, NC: Duke University Press, 2012], 413). Bombay is still the center of the massive Hindi film industry, as well as for the smaller Marathi, Gujarati, and Bhojpuri industries, and continues to iconically stand for filmmaking in India, particularly North India.

27 **GAURAVPANT MISHRA** CROWD MAKER

Sarthak Bagchi

IT WAS AT A BIG ELECTION MEETING at Azad Maidan organized by the Mumbai Pradesh Congress Committee that I met Gauravpant Mishra. The meeting was big because it was supposed to be a grand launch of the election campaign in Mumbai for the forthcoming assembly elections in October 2014. The meeting, organized in August 2014, was arranged to declare the first list of twenty (or so) out of the thirty-six Mumbai candidates who had been awarded Congress Party "tickets" for the upcoming State Legislative Assembly polls. The meeting came at a moment of high uncertainty in Mumbai, with news in the media filled with high-profile defections and alliances across the political spectrum coming undone; almost every major political party ultimately contested the 2014 election independently.[1] It was in this fraught context that the organizers of that Congress Party meeting—in a show of strength—gathered no fewer than three former chief ministers—Narayan Rane, Sushil Kumar Shinde, and Ashok Chavan—to sit on the stage alongside the incumbent chief minister, Prithviraj Chavan. Notwithstanding this weighty and reassuring onstage presence, the faces of those milling about the corridors of the Mumbai Congress Party office adjacent to the Azad Maidan remained tense, and for good reason: the sea of chairs remained far from full; the audience hadn't turned up.

Some of the leaders at the event sought to blame the low turnout on the incessant monsoon rains, but others attributed the poor showing simply to the fading support for the Congress Party in Maharashtra. The party was already facing a huge anti-incumbency wave after three consecutive terms in power in the state, and the recent parliamentary election in May 2014 had handed Congress its lowest-ever tally of seats. But whoever or whatever might be to blame, the party leaders and candidates were worried about the message this low turnout would convey, the empty chairs calling into question the electoral viability of the Congress Party in the upcoming polls. Indeed, the dismal turnout was unlikely to go unnoticed by the city's news media, as the meeting was being held at Azad Maidan, just a stone's throw from the Mumbai Press Club and the Marathi Patrakar Sangh (Marathi Press Association). The media were not likely to be kind in reporting on the poor state of the Congress campaign in the city. From amid this stream of mostly anxious faces, one caught my attention for its calm unworried demeanor: Gauravpant Mishra was sitting leisurely in a corner near the entrance to the *maidan*, flanked by a motley group of party workers. I made my way toward him and introduced myself.

Mishra explained that he had just taken stock of the group of *samarthak* (supporters) that he had brought to the election meeting from his ward in South Mumbai's Malabar Hill constituency. Reassured after counting the twenty people whom he had promised to bring to the meeting, Mishra's face was showing the satisfaction and complacency of having delivered according to his responsibility. "I have done my part," he told me. "I have brought the people from my ward. If you check with all the people here, Malabar Hill constituency has the largest number in attendance here in the maidan today. Now it is up to the leaders." Thus said Mishra, putting the metaphorical ball in the party leaders' court—or in their maidan, in this case.

Over the following weeks of the campaign and its aftermath, I learned about Mishra and his work, both for the party and otherwise. Mishra's daily routines demonstrate the inextricably intertwined relationship between his political work and his professional life. "Politics is my passion, and journalism is my profession," Mishra explained to me, "but politics always comes first for me." This passion for politics is also reflected in his routine political engagements; every evening, without fail, he pays a visit to the Mumbai Congress office and participates in the daily congregations or gatherings that take place there: "I like to interact with people. Communication and connection are very important in politics. I meet many people every day and try to solve as many problems as I can, through the connections I have." On most days Mishra comes to the evening meetings at the party office armed with a list of grievances from the local residents of his assembly constituency that are then taken up with the respective authorities at the municipal corporation or other government functionaries.

While the Legislative Assembly constituency of Malabar Hill has one of the highest per capita incomes in India along with some of the costliest real estate in Mumbai (indeed in the world), the area is peppered as well with a scattering of unauthorized (or semi-regularized) *slum* or settlements. The low-income residents in these localities often need mediation to get government services such as water, electricity, and even an admission to a government hospital or school. Gauravpant Mishra is one of the number of people who do the work of negotiating with the government authorities almost on a daily basis for the survival of their constituents whose lives or livelihoods are criminalized, and who act as negotiators and intermediaries through their network of "known" people in the municipal corporation and also in *Mantralaya* (the state government headquarters), if need be. Mishra has in the past assisted many residents in the South Bombay neighborhood of Khetwadi with securing a hospital bed for a sick family member in the government-run hospitals in the locality. Mishra also points out that it is not only the slum dwellers and "illegal" settlers who require his help and benefit from his political connections, but his reach extends beyond these handful of nonelite settlements into the planned residential colonies and old residential localities of middle-class and lower-middle-class residents in the neighborhood of Khetwadi: "Earlier we had to spend a lot of time and effort [working for voters in] the slums, but now we have to spend a lot [money, time, and effort] in the middle-class and lower-middle-class localities too. They have become very demanding."

Mishra follows up on his various official requests with various government officers to see to it that problems are solved. It is during such follow-up exercises that Mishra's journalistic work comes in handy, his reputation preceding him: "Most of the officers at BMC know me because of the paper copy on their desk; it is like my visiting card," he says. Within the assembly constituency, Mishra's daily engagement with voters and face-to-face interactions are most prevalent among the voters in Khetwadi. Through a sustained political career and a public journalistic profile over a long period of time, Mishra is particularly useful for the Congress Party, reporting the grievances and civic issues faced by residents of his ward. Mishra credits his daily engagement and personal rapport with voters as a key to his mobilizing skills and the strength for garnering electoral support. He claims to have played a vital role in the victory of the Congress candidate in the 2012 and 2017 municipal elections in his district, where he actively supported (and positively reported on) the Congress campaigns.

Gauravpant Mishra's loyalty to the Congress Party is inherited from his family, and he insists that despite their poor showing, he is unlikely to jump ship anytime soon. Mishra was born in Bombay to North Indian parents who migrated to Bombay from Uttar Pradesh, where his family supported the Congress Party from "pre-Independence times." Mishra is a third-generation Congress Party worker, following in the footsteps of his father and grandfather. Mishra claims that his grandfather, who migrated from Uttar Pradesh along with his son (Mishra's father), was a prominent member of the Mumbai Congress Committee in its formative years, as early as the 1940s. Mishra's elder brother showed little interest in carrying forward the family's association with the party, so the mantle was passed on to Mishra, who performs his duties as a Congress supporter and party worker alongside his daytime job as a journalist.

His political and professional careers grew in tandem. His first writing job was for a Hindi daily, *Dainik Dabangg Duniya*, primarily covering stories in and around Mumbai (more specifically around the constituency of Malabar Hill), although the paper has several editions across different cities in India. Building on this experience in journalism and reportage, he subsequently launched his own newspaper, *Nityanand Times*, a small weekly newspaper with a circulation of only five thousand copies. In his paper, Mishra explains, he focuses on news items of local significance that are usually left out by large-scale and mainstream national dailies. Stories such as a protest march held by the local councillor or a small feud between local shopkeepers or the stricter and more vigilant stance of traffic police against drinking and driving in the locality usually dominate the pages of his newspaper. The focus on local issues allows the paper to highlight certain controversial issues from which other mainstream publications usually shy away, while also providing Mishra a platform from which to profile his preferred candidates—in the form of "paid news" and advertisement—which are important sources of revenue for the small newspaper.

Mishra uses his editorial discretion in a highly partisan way during election campaigns, when he prints out detailed profiles (almost always in a positive vein) of the Congress candidates in the constituency and also in nearby constituencies. During election season, his little newspaper becomes (unofficially, but with support from party leaders) something like a Congress Party mouthpiece. Unlike other parties in Maharashtra, Congress does not have an official newspaper for propagating its ideology and policies; Shiv Sena's official outlets, *Saamna* and *Sakaal*, allegedly supported by the Nationalist Congress Party, are both widely known and enjoy wide and energetic readerships in Mumbai. The Congress Party supports *National Herald* on a national level but lacks a genuine vernacular outlet that it can use to propagate its messages and political ideology. In 2012, however, Congress did start a monthly magazine titled *Congress Darshan*, which was later discontinued as an official party publication over some controversial articles.[2] The blurring of "real" news and "paid" news often becomes an important concern, especially before elections, and political parties use these publications for advertising themselves and often also for negative portrayals of the opposition. State patronage of such publications in terms of government advertisements by the party in power also plays a decisive role in keeping such newspapers close to the party line. However, while these other newspapers have a wider reach and a larger readership, Mishra's newspaper plays an important role because of its local focus.

Mishra and other "journalists" like him are very important parts of the Congress election campaign, as their small publications simultaneously give voice to highly localized concerns while carrying the party messages to the paper's readership, which Mishra carefully curates: from among the five-thousand-odd copies, Mishra marks nearly a third for direct and free distribution throughout the various departments of the Mumbai Municipal Corporation (BMC) as well as in several departments in the state government's administrative building, Mantralaya: "We send out weekly copies to several departments and to many officers with whom we have to interact almost regularly in view of our political work and to mediate on behalf of our people. So, through the newspaper, they already know me in advance when I contact them." In this manner Mishra uses his journalism to further his politics and uses his politics to broaden the circulation and visibility of his newspaper. Through his tireless political and media work in the constituency, Mishra maintains face-to-face interaction with voters all year round and not just at the time of the elections.

Of course, of the thousand or so people who eventually assembled in Azad Maidan for that not-so-big Congress election meeting, Mishra explained that perhaps only 30–40 percent of even *these* people would end up voting for Congress in the upcoming election. The participation of most of the people at the meeting had been arranged by people like him—activists and party workers—many of whom had encouraged people to turn up for the rally with promises of lunch or a few hundred rupees or perhaps even a bottle of liquor. Although the news media (particularly the English-language press) commonly characterized these gifts as efforts to "buy votes," Mishra pointed out that this idea was wrongheaded. The gifts had nothing to do with votes (Mishra made no secret of the fact that most of the people he had brought would not vote for the Congress candidate). Rather, such offerings were made in exchange for attending the meeting and being part of the crowd. Yet, notwithstanding Mishra's insistence that gifts and cash are not an attempt to "buy votes," he described the practice with concern and contempt, blaming both voters and leaders for making elections more "commercial" over the years: "Voters these days demand more and more from politicians, and politicians in turn have offered more and more money. This has made elections more commercial and more expensive than ever before." I asked if he too had offered anything—money perhaps?—to his twenty "supporters"? He shook his head. "If I could *pay*, then there would be many more people coming from my ward, and not just twenty!" This way, Mishra confirmed his solidarity among his group of supporters and his disdain for the "commercial" aspects of politics.

As mentioned earlier, the twenty supporters who came with Mishra to the Congress election meeting were all residents of Khetwadi area, and they all had come in contact with Mishra through his various activities in their ward, both his journalistic work and his interventions with government officers. Mishra reiterated that most of his group were not regular Congress supporters and many would not vote for Congress. Most of them were at the meeting as a personal favor to Mishra. Some had read his newspaper and wanted to attend and listen to senior Congress leaders. Some had nothing more interesting to do on that particular evening and hence decided to see the rally. "Bada meeting hai kaafi, dekhte hai kaisa hota hai" (This seems like a big meeting; we came to see how it unfolds), said one of the "supporters."

During the August 2014 meeting on Azad Maidan, Mishra introduced himself to me not as a Congress "party worker" (*karykarta*) but as a "crowd maker." But in light of the meeting's poor turnout, Mishra confessed to me a growing concern that the professionalization of the Bharatiya Janata Party (BJP) organization and command of the media was making the archaic Congress organization look increasingly inept and redundant. "The BJP MLA [member of Legislative Assembly] has made party work into a profession. He has salaried employees in his constituency offices in all the neighborhoods of the constituency. His party workers and karyakartas are not paid by the party or BJP but by his own [builder-backed] foundation. How can we ever compete with them? They work on salaries, while we just have our passion to strive forward," he said, while expressing his resentment about the nature of competition existing in his assembly constituency. For Mishra, given the current circumstances of what he calls the professionalization and corporatization of electoral politics, it seemed unlikely that Congress would defeat the incumbent BJP MLA in the Malabar Hill constituency. However, he insists that the contest is not yet over and that for him, whether or not they win this election, he has succeeded on his own terms. Indeed, Mishra sums up his career goals and political ambition by saying, "I am not insecure about my ability to do my work. It is better to be a kingmaker than deal with the insecurities and tension of being the king. I have long ago moved past the idea that political power only means winning elections."

Notes

1. Pre-poll alliances are a regular feature of Indian elections, in which political parties, usually sharing a common ideology, come together to contest the elections from a joint platform. In intensely competitive elections to the state assemblies, pre-poll alliances help political parties in sharing resources and gaining supporters from each other's fold. The Shiv-Sena and the BJP had been in a political alliance at both the state level and the center since the early 1990s. Similarly, Congress and the NCP, which arose out of a dissident faction of the Congress, have been in a pre-poll alliance since 1999. The Congress-NCP alliance had been in power at the state level since 1999 and was also part of the ruling United Progressive Alliance at the center from 2004 to 2014.

2. In 2015 *Congress Darshan* caused huge embarrassment to the party leaders when it published a controversial article with negative remarks on then-Party President Sonia Gandhi's Italian grandfather having fascist links and also allegedly blamed former Prime Minister Nehru for the ongoing "problems" in Kashmir. After a lot of hue and cry in the media, party spokespersons officially denied any links to the magazine, and the Mumbai Pradesh Congress Committee president, Sanjay Nirupam, sacked the editor in charge of content for the magazine. Incidentally, Nirupam used to be the editor of a Hindi version of the Shiv Sena house organ *Dopahar ka Saamna* when he was in the Shiv Sena.

28 SRINIVASAN KINGMAKER

Simon Chauchard

I FIRST MET SRINIVASAN in the lead-up to the 2014 Maharashtra Assembly elections at the office of Ranganathan, a well-known Congress Party politician who was battling to obtain a Congress ticket for these elections. A portly and groomed forty-four-year-old in a crisp white shirt, Srinivasan was sheepishly seated among other political workers and supporters, waiting for the person they hoped would soon become their candidate. A meeting had been called, and all were patiently waiting to pay their respects to Ranganathan. While he exuded more confidence than the average worker seated in the room, Srinivasan remained quiet and modestly presented himself as a *karyakarta* (political worker) the first time we spoke that afternoon. This is also how the others in the room that day, including Ranganathan, referred to him: a karyakarta, a simple worker.

From the moment Ranganathan arrived that day, however, it became clear that Srinivasan's domain of activity was more complex than the humble word *karyakarta* suggests. As Ranganathan sat behind his desk, facing several dozen men and women (also calling themselves karyakartas) who had pledged to canvass on his behalf, Srinivasan placed his chair slightly behind his, introducing to Ranganathan every one of the other people in the room before each was allowed to speak. Although Sanjay, one of Ranganathan's personal assistants (PAs), had been responsible for actually calling up these other workers on that morning, it was Srinivasan himself who had initially drafted the list of people to be invited. As became clear to me during the two campaigns that I subsequently followed in that part of Mumbai, Srinivasan plays a central role in Ranganathan's campaigns. A relatively invisible and silent figure himself, Srinivasan's work is producing highly visible (and often loud) spectacles of popular support for his *neta* (politician).

As the leading karyakarta of one of the neighborhood's foremost politicians, Srinivasan mainly operates as a social organizer. His main task ahead of elections is to recruit and organize a network of individuals who will subsequently take part in campaign activities and make Ranganathan's victory at the polls possible. These were the individuals who were present at Ranganathan's office that day and whom I would see time and again at meetings and processions during the following weeks. Also referred to as karyakartas, these individuals belonged to various communities and had a variety of day jobs, but each of them was engaged in some sort of "social work," most often, in this case, informal intermediation between citizens and local government.

Ali, a vocal supporter of Ranganathan and longtime ally of Srinivasan who is present that day in the office, is a good example of the kind of person Srinivasan seeks out. In 2014 Ali was widely known in the neighborhood for his connections to various government offices and community organizations. While I originally met him in his capacity of member of a local mosque association committee, he was mainly known for his work in "managing" the public toilet that the Mumbai Municipal Corporation had installed (and subsequently abandoned) in a nearby *slum-redevelopment* "transit camp." Ali's work consisted in hiring and paying crews of mostly down-and-out local men to clean and maintain the facilities, as well as collecting the fees that users paid in order to use them.[1] Ali vehemently professed not to make a profit on his toilet-related activities, but local residents insisted on the contrary. Yet while area residents were critical of Ali's toilet-related profiteering, their condemnations of him were measured and mitigated by his other areas of expertise, for which local residents regularly sought his help: families needing a good word put in to the local police department in order to get their relatives out of trouble would regularly call on Ali; those who might need help deciphering a bill or an application might also turn up at his toilet "office." Given the multiple hats that Ali wore, he was widely known across the constituency. And it was in light of this multivalent connectedness that Srinivasan sought out Ali's participation in Ranganathan's campaign.

Because of the impressive extent and range of their social and business contacts, people like Ali are crucial to political campaigns in Mumbai. Their specialized knowledge of one or several communities are highly valued by candidates eager to organize canvassing itineraries in the weeks leading to elections, and to more generally "manage" elections in these locations. They are able to point candidates toward individuals who may be able to sway relatively large numbers of votes at the local level and who as such require the attention of candidates, including their monetary attention. In the words of Srinivasan himself, recruiting the right set of karyakartas from among these self-professed social workers (*samaaj sevak*) was "the single most important factor" in a candidate's victory, adding that such support was "far more important than money."

As Ranganathan's lead karyakarta, Srinivasan made it his priority to convince the "best" (that is, the most connected) people among locally connected residents to work on Ranaganathan's campaigns. This is how in fact he spent the lion's share of his afternoons during the few weeks leading to the polls: in meetings with them or on one of his three cell phones, asking such individuals to participate or help organize a specific event near their place of residence. How he was able to convince these individuals to give their time to a political campaign (and in many cases, skip work) remains unclear. In a long discussion after the campaign, Srinivasan energetically downplayed the role played by short-term material gifts and cash payments to supporters and rally participants: "Of course we have to give tea and samosas, and these days chicken even. Otherwise people would go missing after three days! But most people end up joining us and working hard because they know that Ranganathan can do a lot for them and for the neighborhood once he is elected. They know that he will get their work done, as he did many times before. I remind them of that and pour their heart into the campaign."

Srinivasan's work during campaigns goes beyond this work of assembling a winning coalition of local influencers and political workers. In a stark departure from his non-election-season daily routine (according to Ali, in the offseason Srinivasan "never comes out of his home before 2 or 3 p.m."), Srinivasan was directly, indeed *physically* involved in day-to-day campaigning. He participated in most events, from early-morning meetings to late-night speeches, and personally handled myriad tasks up until the final hours leading up to polling day. Despite his almost comical lack of physical fitness, Srinivasan accompanied Ranganathan on most *pad yatras* (foot processions) and entered private homes and businesses alongside the candidate. He did not hesitate to carry the candidate's personal effects ("I have water for you and a towel"), to make room for him in a tight crowd ("Brother, please make room for Ranganathan Sir to access the exit"), or to scold youngsters who had lighted up garlands of firecrackers too early or too late ("Why did you not do what I said? I said 'When the jeep arrives, right before he steps out!'"). Srinivasan could also be seen on stages throughout these campaigns. While he never came close to approaching the microphone during these *chowk sab-has* (street-corner rallies)—he confessed to me his terror of public speaking—Srinivasan invariably sat on stage, in the second or third row behind his candidate. Insofar as he was often in charge of the arrangements and payments for such events, Srinivasan also often waited by the entrance to the venue for caterers or backstage to pay flag bearers or rally-goers. On more than one instance, I saw him leap off of stage in an effort to bring order to a room ("Please fill these seats on the front") and to distribute food packets and bottles of waters to attendees when the goods eventually arrived.

Taking direct control of so many aspects of the campaign suggests that Srinivasan either did not sufficiently trust any of his subordinate karyakartas to oversee minute details of campaign work or else was loath to share power. In any event, Ranganathan himself clearly gave utmost importance to Srinivasan's presence. On a day late in the campaign when a visibly exhausted Srinivasan was late for the departure of the day's planned pad yatra, Ranganathan considered simply canceling the event: "We are not leaving until Srinivasan comes around. Last time this happened there were too many problems, and we forgot to visit some people. . . ." Better not to go at all than to go without Srinivasan's guidance and run the risk of oversight, omission, or simply putting on a bad show.

In addition to playing a central role in the planning of campaign events, Srinivasan was also reportedly at the heart of the money-distribution systems that emerged during each of Ranganathan's successful bids for election. While I never observed the distribution of these sums first-hand, multiple sources in the neighborhood actually named *Srinivasan*, rather than *Ranganathan*, as the source of the money. ("This society was paid up by Srinivasan," I heard workers discuss on several occasions.) Such statements may suggest that Srinivasan was seen as the one who passed to them Ranganathan's money, but the lack of clarity and slippage here is telling: maybe the money was a gift from Ranganathan . . . but then again maybe it was from Srinivasan himself. The slippage suggests that Srinivasan is widely understood not as a simple intermediary. Indeed, as both Ali and a senior karyakarta named Wagdare later explained, it is Srinivasan who would identify targets and arrange meetings in the weeks leading to

FIGURE 28.1 Women leaving the campaign headquarters for a *pad yatra*, February 2017. Used courtesy of Simon Chauchard, photographer.

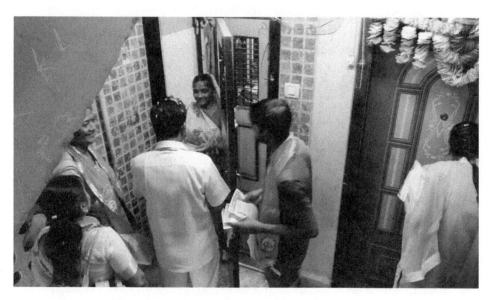

FIGURE 28.2 Candidate engaging in door-to-door campaigning, February 2017. Used courtesy of Simon Chauchard, photographer.

Election Day. These meetings included the candidate (or if he was unavailable, his son-in-law), locally influential citizens (typically, housing society presidents or temple or mosque association presidents) who professed to remain undecided, and seasoned karyakartas who were trusted enough to witness this type of exchange. Beyond these payments to locally influential figures, Srinivasan also ensured that payments were delivered to the various political workers he had assembled for various other events. In addition to the aforementioned karyakartas, these included the men and women who work "tables" on Election Day, providing voters approaching the polling station with information about their polling booth and voter number, but also, frequently, the Bombay Municipal Corporation (BMC) workers staffed inside the polling booth as election officials, whom he sometimes boasted to have "managed."[2]

Srinivasan's personal journey to the heart of so many political networks is less a story of predestination than of creative self-making. As did many others, Srinivasan landed in the northeastern part of Mumbai as a child in the late 1970s, after a long train ride from Vellore district (Tamil Nadu). His father (a landless peasant) had heard of opportunities in the manufacturing sector, opportunities that never fully materialized. Although Srinivasan's father had been a loyal and subdued Indira supporter in Tamil Nadu (a "calf of the Congress," according to Srinivasan), he initially struggled to penetrate Congress networks in Mumbai. This changed in 1992 as a dashing, educated Ranganathan managed to organize the local South Indian community and later managed to convince the local Congress leadership that their candidate needed to have a base there. Srinivasan, then twenty-two years old, joined the campaign at the request of his father, who quickly professed seeing in Ranganathan "a chance for South Indians." A manual worker with little education ("skipping classes I was good at," as he once told me) or political experience, Srinivasan "tirelessly campaigned" for Ranganathan that year. The campaign was a success—Ranganathan won with a seven-thousand-vote margin—with much of the success attributed to Srinivasan's newfound skills. Although his participation in the campaign had initially not been very enthusiastic, Srinivasan quickly found his neta during this work. His ability to connect with some voters and to pressure others through a variety of means was promptly recognized by Ranganathan, who increasingly gave him responsibilities ("Little by little, I gained his trust," Srinivasan recalled) and in turn prompted him to enter the leadership of local associational structures, soon ensuring both men's domination of the ward.

Insofar as the class and education differences between Ranganathan and Srinivasan are obvious (Ranganathan is highly educated, belongs to a rich mercantile family, and lives in a bungalow outside of the poor neighborhood he ran for office in), it is not hard to imagine what Srinivasan provides to Ranganathan: connectivity with and access to an electorate from which he would otherwise be entirely disconnected. While he is now a seasoned politician, the reasons that pushed Ranganathan to further associate himself with Srinivasan since 1992 are not mysterious: on his own, Ranganathan would presumably neither have been able to find the right local-level influencers nor even to find his way in the meandering lanes of the local *chawls* and slums. Although Srinivasan remains uneducated, his local knowledge and networks make him a necessary asset in order to win elections. Ranganathan has funds and contacts high up in the party (what may be termed upward connectedness), but Srinivasan provides him with supporters, influencers, and—through these—voters (what may be termed downward connectedness). This association in turn provides Srinivasan with privileged access to the higher spheres of Mumbai politics if and when Ranganathan wins, and with solutions to his neighbors' problems, which in turn provides him with status and some form of rent at the local level.

In light of the complementarity of the two men, and in spite of Srinivasan's dedication and demonstrative loyalty to Ranganathan for more than twenty-five years, their relationship may today have become more collaborative than hierarchical. All these years at the side of the neighborhood's foremost politician have provided Srinivasan with many perks and, maybe more importantly, status. Srinivasan is now at the center of multiple trades and exchanges in that part of Mumbai. As a chairman of his colony's housing society (the influential association that manages the relationship between dwellers of that colony and its builders) for more than twelve years, Srinivasan reportedly has enormous power over the allocation of apartments in the colony; repeated rumors heard at the local Nagori tea shop, and corroborated by Ali, had it that he also controls, and illegally rents out, more than ten apartments in the area. He also leads a team of more than forty "NGO workers," practically a for-profit contracting business that plays a daily role in the implementation of extremely heterogeneous BMC-funded public projects. As a member of the local South Indian temple committee, he collects funds and organizes festivals on behalf of a population of several thousands. Finally, as the owner of an internet/cable connection outfit now largely managed by his two elder sons, he provides many families with the opportunity to enjoy national news and internet, often by bending the law, extending cables, or hacking cable boxes.

In other words, Srinivasan's activities are hardly circumscribed to politics. Rather, connectivity and centrality in a social network are prior to his involvement in political campaigning, valued characteristics in a context where straightforward connections to the state authorities are complex but crucial. In this context, Srinivasan's multiple sorts of relationships and ongoing networks of exchanges in a variety of domains are the basis upon which political power is based—rather than the other way around.

Indeed, given Srinivasan's centrality to the neighborhood's social and associational life, it is hard to imagine how Ranganathan would win so consistently should Srinivasan decide to support another candidate or even to contest an election in his own name (the latter is highly unlikely, given Srinivasan's aversion to public speaking). Karyakartas such as Ali made this quite clear: "Without Srinivasan, Ranganathan would be finished. He may lose his deposit!"[3] Indeed, as many of my interlocutors have pointed out, when Congress denied Ranganathan the ticket (which happened on two occasions since 1992), Srinivasan refused to support the Congress candidates, each of whom then went on to lose the election. And by the same token, karykartas maintain that it is conceivable that even an unknown candidate could pull off a victory in a local election—provided that he or she enlisted the services of Srinivasan. While local residents and karykartas speak of Srinivasan with respect, deference, admiration, and fear—describing him as a "big man" or even as a "boss" (*maalik*)—perhaps Srinivasan's own English-educated son puts it best when he laughingly describes his father as a "kingmaker."

Notes

1. See Khanolkar's profile (chapter 4) for an extended discussion of the myriad mediations involved in community toilet construction and management.

2. I could never quite ascertain what this "management" implied.

3. In Indian elections a defeated candidate who fails to secure more than one-sixth of the valid votes polled in the constituency will lose his or her security deposit. Ali may have been exaggerating, but what's clear here is the importance and respect attributed to Srinivasan.

29 **MADHU** DOOR OPENER

Bhushan Korgaonkar

ON A SWEATY EVENING in June 2017, I went to meet Madhu Shinde in Naigaon, a neighborhood in Dadar East that has yet to see any signs of the redevelopment fever that has afflicted other areas of Mumbai. Exiting Dadar
station in the hazy twilight, I walked across a tiny playground before cutting
through a narrow alley between the *chawl* buildings that deposited me back
out into the heat of another playground. It's dusty, full of scattered rubbish
and sleeping dogs, and at first I hesitate, thinking perhaps I've gotten the
wrong address. But then I see a small structure that looks like it might well
be the party hall I'm looking for. Soon I hear the sounds of children playing
and then see the balloons tacked up on the main door. I've come for the
fourteenth-birthday party of the son of a neighborhood political leader, a
party for which Madhu has been hired to arrange the entertainment. And
then I see Madhu, smiling broadly and waving me over.

   We're meeting in person after an absence of nearly two years, Madhu and
I, and I'm shocked to see that his lovely long hair has been cropped short into
a military-style cut. Madhu reads my surprise: "What to do? Now my kids
have grown up, and we're looking for a groom for my daughter." He laughs

softly, adding, "And I have also aged. My old *nakhras* [coquetry] and craziness has to end, *hai na*?"

As the stage is being set up, the lights arranged, and the sound tested, a man approaches us. Madhu smiles broadly again: "Meet Mr. Doifode!" he says to me, gesturing toward the man. "It's his son's birthday today." Doifode is young and charming and flashy, dressed in a shimmering blue velvet shirt with matching trousers and jacket. Thick gold chains hang from his neck, some weighted down with heavy pendants. A thick gold bracelet burdens his wrist, and golden rings shine from each finger. "You'll have tea?" asks Doifode, clapping my shoulder and walking on without waiting for a response. "Don't be fooled," Madhu says in a whispered giggle. "He's a real miser! Watch, even the tea will never come!"

Madhu won't dance today; he's there only to manage the show. Madhu doesn't dance much these days but rather organizes dance shows. "People invite us to perform for all sorts of occasions," Madhu explains. "Weddings, [housing] society *pujas*, those things have always been common. But these days our work is mostly for people like Doifode—local leaders call us for birthdays or anniversaries, for anything really, any excuse to throw a party and entertain. This is a new trend among people like Doifode. Before, maybe his son would just have had party games and magic shows for his friends. But now the birthday is a big public function; see how many people have come for our dance and songs!" I ask whether the trend is a result of the rising fortunes of politicians like Doifode, and Madhu shakes his head: "No, no, we can do a show at any budget, for as little as Rs. 10,000. I never say no to anyone." Madhu explains that for people like Doifode, performances like these are similar to his flashy clothes and jewelry: no one is ever sure whether the wealth is real or if he's faking it. Part of Madhu's job is to put on a decadent-looking show at any budget. Given the constraints of a budget, Madhu works out the particulars, deciding "which artists to take along, whether to take a live band or use recorded tracks, how many costumes to carry, etc. I have a playlist of over one thousand songs—Marathi, Hindi, Gujrathi, Rajasthani, Bhojpuri, even some classical numbers—you name it, and I have it!" He explains that the dancers today will perform to recorded music. "The bugger doesn't have budget for live orchestra," he says, disappointedly. "Dance is no fun without live music." I laugh and tease Madhu: "If Mr. Doifode were as wealthy as he'd like his guests to believe, would you have tried your charms on him?" Madhu squeals in protest: "*No!* Eeeks! He's not my type at all." Madhu pauses and smiles slyly, nodding toward a young man just out of earshot, "but I quite like his younger brother; he's damn cute."

I DON'T REMEMBER the first time I actually *spoke* to Madhu, but I clearly recall the first time I *saw* him. It was late in the evening at Damodar Hall in Parel, sometime in 2001, and I had gone to watch an "all-male *lavani* show." I had recently become hooked on lavani, a form of dance theater that is currently experiencing something of a revival in cities and towns throughout Maharashtra, particularly in Bombay, where "banner show" lavani has been the most popular variety. In a banner show, professionally trained dancers perform three-hour shows in ticketed venues to the accompaniment of live music, punctuated by comedy sketches. Lavani dance is perhaps best known for its interactive quality; lavani shows are outrageously and hilariously bawdy and suggestive, and meant to elicit response from the audience. Dancers maintain that the distinctive feature of their art is in the eye contact that they maintain with members of the audience, drawing the audience into the show itself.

I had seen some stunning lavani shows featuring eminent dancers before, but *this* show—with men dancing as women—this was something else entirely. I had seen a couple of drag shows too, but still this was something different. There was neither the exaggerated femininity of the drag show nor the mockery that infuses the Hindi-Marathi comedy shows that I had seen on television. Here, in place of either idealization or mockery was a celebration and performance of femininity and womanhood in all its messy complexity, imperfection, pain, and beauty. A heavyset dancer crooned in a sweet falsetto as he stepped and swirled. I was so taken by the performance that I invited some friends to join me in watching the show a second time. After the show we sat around talking about the dancers, assessing which ones were most compelling in their femininity. We unanimously agreed that Madhusudan Shinde—or "Madhu," as he is fondly called—was the most captivating "woman."

Madhu was a plump, middle-aged man who looked, danced, and behaved as a woman. The *kambarpattas* (waist chains) he wrapped around his middle magically transformed his male-looking paunch into feminine-looking love handles. "We have to be very careful with our makeup and hairdo," Madhu told me, explaining that under the stage lights male facial skin can take on a greenish tinge despite daily shaving. "So we use an orange base to hide the roughness and disguise the green." But still, there was something else that set Madhu apart from the other dancers. Was it his voice? Yes, he sounded like a woman, his voice sweet and delicate. But then again . . . he never spoke or sang on stage! So there must be something else. I realized what was it only when a friend remarked, "It's his breasts—small and downward slanting.

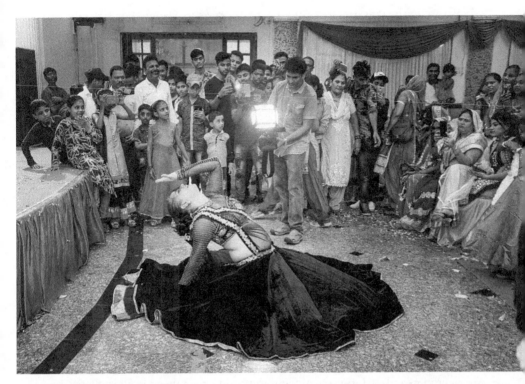

FIGURES 29.1 AND 29.2 A transgender dancer at a private wedding reception (*bida* function) in Mumbai. Event organized by Madhu Shinde. Used courtesy of Kunal Vijayakar, photographer.

FIGURE 29.3 Veteran lavani dancer Anil Hankare in performance. Used courtesy of Keya Arati, photographer.

FIGURE 29.4 Anil Hankare helps another dancer get dressed for a show. Used courtesy of Keya Arati, photographer.

That's what makes him a real woman." "Of course!" Madhu giggled when I told him this. "My figure has to be humble—just like me." It was on his advice that other dancers had reduced the size of their chest padding.

Madhu is known among the dancers for his unsolicited but well-intended advice. His expertise has won him influence not only among the dancers in his group but far beyond. Often arranging the details of contracts for lavani and Bollywood dance shows, and rentals of elaborate and expensive costumes like stitched nine-yard saris and ornamental jewelry, Madhu has parlayed his expertise in myriad ways. Offstage as on, when Madhu unleashes his charm, the doors open—especially the doors of men. I have seen government officials, political leaders, police officers, and shopkeepers—all manner of serious-faced, business-minded men—melting, laughing, and becoming eminently pliable and agreeable in the hands of Madhu's living lavani.

I PHONED MADHU THE WEEK following the Naigaon party to ask whether he might tell me a bit more about his life. He was happy to talk, so we met in a friend's apartment, a sea-facing flat in Versova. "My life is like an open book for all my friends," he began. "Don't you already know everything?" Madhu says it in his usual playful style, winking at me for emphasis. "I was born in 1970 in a lower-middle-class family. I am the second of the three sons born to my parents . . . a middle one! God made me a middle one—now why blame me for my middle behavior?" He winks again:

> I was never close to my father, but my mother always knew. She had a soft spot for me. Even when she caught me wearing a sari or jewelry, she would ignore it. To make things worse, I was fat, really fat. School kids were of two minds: "Should we tease him for his effeminate behavior or fat body?"
>
> As a child I had just one wish—to become a dancer. I passed my tenth-grade exams on the second try, and shortly after that my father passed away. My mother began working a menial job with monthly salary of only Rs. 350. Things were difficult. Then one day, my brother saw an advertisement in a newspaper for recruitment in a dance company, so I went for the audition. The person at the counter took one look at me and laughed: "Please don't break our stage!" I laughed too and went in. I must have performed well because I was selected. This was my real school, where I learnt all the skills and techniques which help me even today. My family was very happy. And I lost weight too.
>
> It was during these years that I became aware of my sexuality—I realized that I don't fancy women and that I'm attracted to men—to *real*

men. In those days there were no cell phones, no internet—but there were some cruising areas where I could meet men. Maheshwari Udyan was a mecca for *kothis*.[1] I met a guy there named Anant who suggested that I join his gang of *bida* dancers [wedding performers]. The payment was not great, but I was excited because finally I was getting to do what I really loved: dance as a woman. Generally, we managed to earn well through tips—there were nights when I earned more than a thousand rupees, which was a lot in those days. So that's when I learnt the tricks—how to dance and flirt in a way that would win tips. Because I was so good with makeup, people often took me for a woman—or at least maybe an *operation jhaleli bai* [a transgender woman who has undergone surgery]—unlike my colleagues, who looked like men dressed up as women. Even my name, Madhu, was ambiguous.

When I turned twenty-five, my mother and uncles insisted that a responsible, well-earning, well-behaved boy like me should get married. And I agreed, of course, because getting married is what I always expected I would do; it was just . . . normal.

Madhu has no regrets about marrying and is proud that he has a family of his own. He and his wife, Sushila, have two children, a girl and a boy, and they both look exactly like Madhu. While his family is well aware that the "man of the house" makes a living dancing as a woman, Madhu's personal life, he explains, is a "private matter":

Our first child was born in the first year of our marriage: a baby girl. My financial burdens grew with the birth of our daughter, and at the same time my younger brother fell terribly sick and we had to hospitalize him. He had a rare heart condition that required surgery. We pooled our savings, pawned jewelry, raised money in every way possible, but still we fell short. I borrowed from a private moneylender. At that time I was teaching Kathak and Bollywood dance at a local studio. Among my students was a pretty girl called Shama. She was fond of me and knew of my financial troubles. One day she confided in me that she works as a bar dancer in a bar called Night Queens in Andheri and the owner was looking for a male dancer who would dress and dance as a woman on Sundays. Having a kothi brings luck and prosperity, the bar owner believed. So I went to meet this bar owner, and he invited me to join immediately. I told my wife, we agreed, and so began my career as a bar girl.

On my first day at Night Queens the other bar girls renamed me "Honey." I liked my new name. "Madhu" means "honey," of course, but the English word *Honey* sounds more glamorous. The years I spent working as a bar girl were like a dream. We lived like queens! We were treated very well by customers and bar owners alike, and I never did a single thing against my will—none of us did. And I earned so much. We would dress up beautifully, wear nice jewelry, dance to all songs of all kinds—whatever was requested by the guests. We were rewarded with generous tips and were allowed to take home 40 percent. We would float out onto the floor, dance, flirt, and collect our tips. The guests treated us like film stars. We also looked and felt like film stars.

I learned to make false promises—to agree to a sex date but then never get around to fulfilling it. This was partly because most of my guests didn't realize I was a man. But it was also because the bar owner had given us strict instructions. "Never have sex with guests. Starve them sexually and keep them hopeful. Make them feel that you really love them. Make them long for you. Only then they will come here night after night and they will value you—financially and emotionally. Mind you, it's not just for my benefit but also yours," the boss explained to us, "because once you become their regular sex outlet then the love and the money will stop flowing." Our boss spoke the truth; it really worked. I never slept with *any* of my guests. Or hardly any—there were maybe two or three exceptions. The other girls from my bar didn't have sex with guests either. We weren't sexually conservative; it just made more sense professionally.

I learned so much during those years—so many new things, new places, new people. Our boss took on foreign tours—to Dubai, Sharjah, and Muscat. I had so many fans—handsome and wealthy men! I *minted* money abroad and returned to Mumbai flush with cash. But as they say, everything has an end. My life as a bar girl was over in less than five years. My brother had recovered completely, and my wife had found a job as a receptionist in a nearby polyclinic. And at the same time, dance bars had begun to get a lot of bad publicity. The news media published all sorts of nonsense about us, and my family began to protest my late nights and my unconventional work. My children were also growing up, and we didn't want them to be known as a bar dancer's kids. I felt sad leaving that life . . . but now I am glad that I got out when I did because soon after I left, this line of work became politically heated. In 2006 the government of Maharashthra banned bar dancing entirely.

But I've learned that whenever one thing ends, something else always opens up. It wasn't long before I met a choreographer who had come up with this idea of an all-male lavani show. I joined the troupe, thrilled to be on stage again. I had done a few lavani songs before, but this was the first time I learned the nuances of the art form from the stalwarts. We rehearsed for six months and opened our show in 2000. I owe so much to this show because it gave me public recognition, which I didn't have as a bar girl. It didn't give me nearly as much money as bar dancing, but it gave me a public persona, which opened all sorts of new doors.

I had always enjoyed male attention; seeing the desire in men's eyes gives me a thrill. But with the all-male lavani show I began for the first time to understand the power and significance of having female fans! I had always earned expensive gifts: jewelry, saris, TV sets, cell phones from my male fan club. But now it was women who were bringing me gifts: homemade delicacies and pickles, cosmetics, appliances. Surprisingly, it had the same effect!

We are interrupted by a phone call: "unknown number." He speaks into the phone:

"Namaskar. Who is speaking?"

" . . . "

"That date is free. We can surely work it out. What's your budget?"

" . . . "

"Yes, yes, it's possible with recorded music."

" . . . "

"Don't worry; I will give you the best dancers."

" . . . "

He hangs up and explains that the call was from a local political leader. "He's holding a rally and wants me to organize the entertainment." Madhu reads my surprise:

Yes, I do these things too . . . rallies. For any religious holiday or national festivals, or political campaign, these days everyone wants to have a big rally. They need girls and boys to dance, sing, play musical instruments, or just be there as a crowd. Someone has to dress them all. Same principle— tell me your budget, and I will give you the best service for the money.

Another round of chai appears. And once again the phone interrupts us. "*Ha beta*, yes, I am reaching by 7:30. Don't worry, I remember it . . . now let me call you back, I am in an interview." He finishes the call with his daughter and continues:

My daughter loves me a lot. But still, I miss my mother. She loved me unconditionally. She died few years back. I have just one regret—that she was once humiliated by a woman because of me. I was working in the bar then. A man from Nagpur was in love with me. Somehow his wife learned of our relationship and came to my home one quiet afternoon—all the way from Nagpur! My mother and my wife were home, but I wasn't. She said terrible things; she said "your daughter Madhu is a whore, she has destroyed my life. She will never be happy." Whoever had given her my address had neglected to tell her that I am not a woman. When I came home, my mother was ready with a stick; she started hitting me the moment I entered the house. My wife finally stopped her. And then all of us cried together. I can never forget that horrific night. My wife asked me to quit my job as a bar dancer the next day. Sometimes I wonder, why do I live this cursed dual life? I keep smiling, cracking jokes, and flirting around so everyone thinks I am very happy in life. But I always just wanted to be normal. I always wished that God had made me normal, heterosexual, like everyone else. Or most people anyway.

Madhu's phone rings again. He picks it up. He smiles. "No, darling, I am in an interview. Yes, *baba*, why should I lie to you? You want to speak to the journalist here? Now let me call you back. Promise I will. Bye. Love you. Muah." The wink returns: "That was one of my new fans."

We are almost done. Just a last formality: I ask Madhu if it's OK to use his real name. "Of course, why hide? I stopped using false names in 2000. No Honey, no Madhu, only Madhusudan Shinde." I explain that my essay has to include everything, including his life as a bar dancer, his affairs with men, and his romantic life. "No problem. It's going to be in English, *na*? Nobody from my circle will read it. It's OK." He gets up, then sits down again and says, "On second thought, change it. Why take a risk? I always play safe, you know; that's why I have survived, and I will continue to survive."

The wink, the smile, the playfulness return once again.

Note

1. *Kothi* is a common term used in Mumbai to refer to men who dress as and behave as women, and who are socially and sexually submissive.

30 **POORNIMA** DESIGNING RELATIONS

Ajay Gandhi

THE TRACING OF ornate drawings with rice powder would seem to have little to do with relating to others, with how to mediate dealings, buffer forces, and sustain ties. Often, transactional activities in the city are reduced to brute expediency: getting things done. Social action rests on imagining and representing. Practical exchange and tactical maneuverability have an aesthetics and an ethics. Yet these aspects are often peripheral to mechanics.

Spend time with Poornima; she will help you see differently. She is a canny entrepreneur, helpful neighbor, profiteering intermediary, and wry social observer. Poornima lives in a lane of squat houses in Matunga Labour Camp. As a lower-middle-class neighborhood, it bears countervailing traces: of aspiration and comfort, of the makeshift and fragile.

This crystallizes the geographic location, between the secure middle-class enclave of Mahim, directly west, adjoining the sea, and Dharavi, a vast hive of a *slum*, to its east. Labour Camp, as it is known, derives its name from a period, decades ago, when it served as a transit camp for people being resettled by the city. Typifying a wider urban logic in India, what was temporary became enduring. This momentary space for floating figures was gradually sedimented into the city itself. During the post-Independence period, the area had a concentration of Dalit migrants, often working for the municipality. Its constituents, rhythms, and loyalties, naturally, blend into adjoining Dharavi, a vast, complex patchwork of industries and migrants from south and north.

Like women-heads of adjacent households, Poornima sometimes draws *rangoli*—called *kolams* in South India—on her doorstep. Rangoli is a ritual painting tradition in western and southern India. Auspicious symbols, religious figures, and favored motifs are traced on floor surfaces and at thresholds. They are a means of warding off bad luck, welcoming visitors, and marking ritual or life-cycle events.

These visual representations can be austere. Commonly, they are drawn with white rice flour and amount to a few lines and dots. Rangoli can also be mesmerizing, especially at festival time, when households compete for eyeballs with designs of colored powder. Galaxies—stars, peacocks, hexagons, Ganeshes, flowers—arrest your vision while you are walking through the tight, workaday lanes.

I was introduced to Poornima and her husband, Madhavan, after I began my ethnographic project in the area in 2011. I was introduced to them by Raman, a mustachioed moneylender and neighbor. Poornima and Madhavan were in their early fifties, their children now married off. Madhavan worked in the Pest Control offices of the Bombay Municipal Corporation (BMC). He was also an active member of the Municipal Mazdoor (labor) Union. He was often away on union business. This meant tending battles regarding the municipality, jockeying with other city unions, and, quite often, squabbling within his own union. They lived with Poornima's niece—her mother had died giving birth to another sibling—whose intellectual disability renders her dependent on them.

My visits to Labour Camp initially involved Poornima. She was quick with advice and opinions on whom to meet. She also had an intermittently endearing—and intermittently suffocating—possessiveness. Not necessarily do only anthropologists swarm their interviewees; informants, too, domesticate their ethnographers. She would call people for me but then quiz me afterward. She nudged me away from other matronly competitors. She emphatically dismissed other neighborhood busybodies about whom I voiced curiosity. After some time, I realized, as one does in fieldwork, that she was well connected, gregarious, and kindly, yet her shadow loomed large, and I learned to step outside it.

But while clearing the initial fog and coming to some routine knowledge of Labour Camp, I am grateful to have her shielding. Poornima's sedate appearance suggests a respectable Tamil matron: black-and-white hair tied in a bun, sari starched and immaculate, a simple black pleather handbag hanging off her left shoulder. She is an alert, serious, well-respected, energetic, and powerful presence. If I meet her at her home in the evening, our discussions are constantly interrupted by business associates, political apprentices, and Labour Camp neighbors. In these dealings she moves easily among the many languages in which she is fluent: Tamil, Telugu, Marathi, and Hindi.

An evening in 2012 went like this: mid-afternoon, a courier named Raju who worked for Poornima's Amway-style direct-selling business arrived in his rattling Tempo. In the back, lashed with rope, sat several narrowly stacked boxes that Raju had brought from a warehouse. He quietly unloaded the boxes as Poornima, spectacles on, looked at the delivery manifest. Poornima's enterprise intertwines risk management, social assessment, and assiduous networking. She believes that brushed-steel kitchen containers and *tiffins*—a fixture in Indian kitchens—will soon go the way of the dinosaurs.

Poornima, you could say, is a believer in the desire for the disposable. In our interviews, she places emphasis on the relatively recent democratization, in India, of *bikta* (to sell) and *phenkna* (to throw away). She believes that young city people have a fickle mentality, a consume-and-dispose tic. More people getting more prosperous may not fetishize the inflexible and metallic as before (I note, in passing, that her rice and *dal* are in steel-lidded containers and that she has a copper vessel in a corner). Poornima fishes out, from one of the corrugated boxes, her contribution to species evolution: plastic sets of storage containers, nested like Russian dolls within one another. They still have a strong plasticky smell from the factory.

Poornima's business is largely tactical: she has an assembly of transporters, couriers, and saleswomen. Her labor is to direct them, say, toward new middle-class housing developments. There, aspiring housewives might be receptive to the idea of replacing steel lunch vessels with plastic ones. Poornima explained:

> My contacts tell me when there is a set of good, new towers ready for occupation, all at least two BHK [bedrooms, hall, kitchen] or three BHK. They can be in Navi Mumbai, Thane, anywhere. The families move in over some months. You cannot send men, strange men in a new place. You send nice girls, college-educated, from Monday to Saturday, when the men are at work. They say to the gate guards that they are visiting a relative on the fifth floor, nineteenth floor, whatever, and then they spend the day buzzing the doors, taking the elevators, talking to those

homemakers, convincing them that a new apartment also means they must have new kitchen things. When you have shifted houses, husbands will give their wives more freedom to buy. Then they fill in the papers with the girls, give a deposit. At the end of the day my girls give me the sales and inventory numbers. . . . I send Raju or someone else the next week with the order.

Poornima spoke with a certain matter-of-fact-ness (that doesn't preclude relish) about her moneymaking acumen. She sells other household things in similar ways: by connecting various dots in Mumbai's landscape that weren't connected before or at least not in the place, or at the time, that she is doing so.

Later that same evening in 2012, a relatively prosperous neighbor— a salaried Reliance Industries technician—came to seek out Poornima's help. She offered him some salty, spicy potato wafers, and they chatted for a bit. Poornima was an acquaintance of the man's wife, a quiet woman with two young children. The husband had come to inquire about getting their elder child admitted to a nursery. They'd had no luck with the area's "better" places, he explained: "The spaces for next year are full; even I offered to pay the year's tuition in full, and they are saying no."

Poornima listened quietly. After some time, she picked up her Nokia and dialed a number (a priest in Mahim, she tells us; she's known him for years). Putting on her outside *chappals* (sandals), she stepped out the doorway into the lane. The reason couldn't be for privacy, for her voice booms; Poornima was broadcasting her intervention to neighbors. The technician and I sat listening to Poornima, sadly eyeing the empty potato wafer package. Returning, she announced: "The church has a good nursery on the premises, not too far from Mahim station; they can perhaps put you on the wait list. I will talk to the deputy in charge." The man's face showed visible relief at having found an option for his child. Promising to update his wife, he slipped on the shiny black shoes he'd left at the entrance and left.

A few moments later, we're joined by another fellow, a Congress Party worker fishing for assistance with some work in his constituency, the G/North Ward. The man's name was Puduru (I'd met him on previous occasions in Poornima's home). He explained to Poornima that he would like her help with assembling neighborhood women for a function the following week. The official purpose of the function was an *Aadhar* card registration drive (at that time, people in Bombay's popular neighborhoods were getting identity cards converted to a much-heralded biometric system). But I knew from previous conversations that Puduru was less interested in actually registering Poornima's neighbors for the biometric cards. He wanted to corral the women at the Aadhar center—a makeshift table of laptops and technical staff at a secondary-school courtyard nearby—on the day when a Congress Party candidate for the BMC 2012 election would make an appearance. Hired photographers would snap shots of the man flanked by Puduru and the sea of women, which would then be used on party billboards.

Much of their conversation, in Tamil, was unintelligible to me, but after Puduru left, Poornima explained that she might be receptive to the request. She couched it not so much as a favor to him but as moral duty: "With Aadhar, the government will deposit money for children's medicine in the women's accounts. It will mean something to them."

Some months later, once I had settled into Labour Camp, my networks had expanded. Eager for a broader perspective, I evaded Poornima somewhat. It was then that I heard other interpretations of Poornima's motivation for helping Puduru: Poornima takes a commission from each woman who registers for Aadhar, one neighbor surmised. Given the ubiquity of such intermediary mercantilism in India, her theory might not be so far-fetched. What is "altruistic help" to one person is interpreted as self-interested "trade" (*dhandha*) to another. "Clean" (*saaf*) and "dirty" (*ganda*) work are differentiated not by any intrinsic quality but rather by a shift in perspective.

Poornima's life demonstrates how often this sort of gendered social activity is a kind of relational labor. Such work is often elided in male-centered analyses, yet it is critical to how urban sociality unfolds. Many studies and fictional representations of Bombay[1] focus primarily on the hustling of *men*—those whose charismatic and often violent potentialities are imagined to be at the center of how protean relations are produced and mediated. But as Poornima shows, male mediations are often bound up with a concurrent flow of women's relational work.[2] Indeed, in this sense, writing on social infrastructures in the global South repackages the relational labor that anthropologists have long described as kinship. But how are these intimate relations—ethically equivocal social engagements—imagined and represented? What aesthetics and ethics underwrite the forging of solidarities and relational possibilities in the contemporary city?

Many of Poornima's neighbors, like herself, trace their origins to some other place outside the city. Poornima is Tamil, and her parents migrated to Bombay at the prodding of her mother's uncle, who was in the leather trade. On the arterial roads that hug Dharavi and Labour Camp are innumerable small-scale shops displaying leather belts, bags, and jackets. These are manufactured within Dharavi. The area is a center for tanning and dyeing animal hides, a trade that has dwindled in recent years but remains a core industry. In her childhood memory, the entire household was oriented around the work. Her father worked at cacophonous drums that mixed industrial chemicals and newly skinned hides. Her mother and other women would afterward brush them and lay them out on rooftop terraces, where they would harden. She and her brother, before school homework, after household chores, would brush the hides after the sun had baked them, remove stray hairs and detritus, bring them in, and, if necessary, stack them next to their sleeping mat during monsoon downpours.

Now is a long way from then. Poornima has not been near an animal carcass in some time; she conducts "clean" and vastly more lucrative work. One thing remains: the smell from all those years handling hides: "Ugh, you don't want to know what kind of odor there was" [Eesh, poochna mat, aap ko nahin mante uska badboo kya tha]. But she has other, finer inheritances from that time, among them a fellowship, with other Tamil girls in the slum, in rangoli.

A YEAR OR SO LATER, sometime in December 2013, I turned up at Poornima's house after a long absence. I thought that I might find her busy, but instead I found her more relaxed than usual. It was a slow morning; a planned visit to Mulund to check with a distributor for her direct-selling operation had been postponed. Poornima invited me in, saying that she had to prepare for dinner. We chatted a bit as I munched on some tea biscuits while she worked in her kitchen.

In our earlier interactions, I expressed admiration for the rangoli in the lanes outside. Recalling my appreciation for her skills, on this morning, rifling through containers in her kitchen, she brought out one round tin with a screw-on lid. As she lifted it, a fine dust cloud rose from chalky rice powder within. We stepped outside into the noisy lane. Small children sat pants-less on the ground, while women on their haunches splashed water from large buckets of laundry. She swept the dirt from the area in front of her place and then bent down, remarkably agile and sturdy while pivoting into place.

Poornima cupped the powder in one hand and deftly drew intertwining, symmetrical lines, squeezing out the powder so that it fell precisely. Two young boys arrived, smiling and whispering and enjoying themselves. Rangoli are often drawn as geometric figures and may contain triangles, diamonds, as well as dots of different colors. A few other houses in the lane already had designs—they are usually done quite early in the morning. She laments, perhaps inevitably, of a decline in skill and ambition of the art: "The designs my aunt, my grandmother could do, girls today are simply ignorant."

She instructs me now: an unschooled surrogate. Her head is down, fingers pinching some flour, as I attempt the same. She sucks air in sharply as if I am about to make an error, saying "Tight, hold it tight. You must not let it leak, *rup dena* [give it a shape]." I'm hopeless at it—my rangoli turns into an undifferentiated white sandbox for ants. As I watch Poornima's hands, I am struck at her swiftness, the ways she squeezes a dollop of powder into a sphere, deftly turns it into the end of a line, and in this way fashions something, connects entities, gives form to what had none.

It is perhaps not so distant from what she does in life. In Margaret Trawick's classic ethnography of Tamil poetics and relationality, she notes that the way Tamil women draw their kolams (the Tamil version of rangoli) reflects their social worlds: their marriage choices and family patterns.[3] These are ephemeral miniatures of an intimate universe; friends, neighbors, and relatives become curvy lines and spaced dots.

Perhaps, in a looser way, Poornima, in her myriad relational projects—familial, neighborly, urban, entrepreneurial—is doing something like these powder designs. She is imagining and actualizing relations; she assembles them, links them, bends them into a desired silhouette. Social relations depend on imaginative representation, on aesthetic skills—of performing and projecting and connecting and dissimulating—that are often tersely viewed in rational-transactional or masculine-hierarchical terms. Urban sociality may be better understood as something like rangoli: as a universe, crafted and cut, an expression of skill and artistry.

Notes

1. See Thomas Blom Hansen, "Sovereigns beyond the State: On Legality and Authority in Urban India," in *Sovereign Bodies: Citizens, Migrants, and States in the Postcolonial World*, ed. Thomas Blom Hansen and Finn Stepputat (Princeton, NJ: Princeton University Press, 2005), 169–91; Vikram Chandra, *Sacred Games* (London: Faber and Faber, 2006).

2. See Veena Das, *Life and Words: Violence and the Descent into the Ordinary* (Berkeley: University of California Press, 2006); Claire Snell-Rood, *No One Will Let Her Live: Women's Struggles for Well-Being in a Delhi Slum* (Berkeley: University of California Press, 2015).

3. Margaret Trawick, *Notes on Love in a Tamil Family* (Berkeley: University of California Press, 1992).

PART VI TRUTH

Lisa Björkman

THE SIX PEOPLE WHOSE STORIES make up part VI deal in "truths." Their expertise consists in navigating the barrage of images, flows of information, and hall-of-mirrors–like appearances and absences that render the city (as indeed the world more generally) dangerously and deliciously unknowable and unpredictable.

The work that these people perform might be roughly divided into two domains of practice: the first involves the display of mastery in duplication and disguise; the other in investigation and truth telling. These seemingly opposing dimensions of knowledge-related practice are in fact two sides of the same coin that bring into focus a double-sided question: What domains of life are sought to be hidden—by whom, from whom, and to what end? And what domains of life call for investigation—by whom, for whom, and to what end? Asking these two questions together, and tracking both strands of knowledge-related practice through the profiles, bring into focus the anxieties that animate and gather around the practices of concealment and revelation that infuse everyday life in the city; one person's masquerades fuel another's drive to authenticate and verify. The accounts index societal-level changes that have brought these anxieties bubbling to the ethnographic sur-face of late in particularly demanding ways.

The ethnographies explore a range of contexts in which truth claims are multiple and conflicting, and where different versions of "reality" are—intentionally or otherwise—made available to different audiences. The profiles narrate situations that call simultaneously for investigation—that is, the sorting through and adjudicating of multiple truth claims—and for the con-cealing, dissimulating, or "turning a blind eye" to some or another bit of in-formation. These truth-making practices index society-level shifts that have called into question the knowability of the world, and the accounts reveal the anxieties, instabilities, and opportunities to which these shifts have given rise. The multiple and conflicting forms of "true knowledge" that circulate in various contexts raise important questions: What calls for investigation—when, by whom, and with what purpose? What forms of knowledge are pos-ited or deemed to be "true"—when, where, and by whom? With what stated intentions are truth claims posited, and to what end? What are the stakes—material, moral, practical—of this work of investigation and dissimulation? The accounts explore, on the one hand, the anxious work of producing and/or keeping out of circulation bits and fragments of information in contexts where accusations of duplicity or falsehood can pose great dangers: social, ethical, and material. We see as well, and on the other hand, the busywork of instantiating and authenticating desired versions of reality and the setting into circulation of these preferred "truths." The characters profiled in this section make it their business (sometimes quite literally) to produce, sort through, and adjudicate a cacophony of rivaling and irreconcilable truth claims, and to mediate the contradictions that they encounter in their efforts.

The accounts reveal how truth claims and practices of authentication and verification are enlisted in producing and enhancing different kinds of value: social, material, moral. And these valorization efforts are in turn bound up with the potential harm (or "damage," in the words of Udupa's "taximan," Afzal) that different versions of truth are poised to inflict. The profiles point to fraught questions concerning who has (or ought to have) access to what kinds of knowledge (and for what purpose), as well as from whom various forms of information are sought to be hidden. When is the making public of some previously hidden bit of knowledge contested, and what are the stakes of these contestations? When do the production and circulation of truth claims either shore up or work to unsettle entrenched hierarchies and forms of differentiation? And how might these churnings relate to the moralizing talk that gathers around these knowledge-production practices?

As I note in the introduction to this book, the people and practices profiled here are the subject of much moral-evaluative talk, both popular and scholarly, and we have argued that this evaluative talk maps the anxieties and contradictions of a rapidly changing city and society. The characters profiled in part VI are not only *subject* to such judgments, but we see as well that their busy investigations and mystifications are animated precisely by this sort of moralizing zeal. The business of truth making, far from value-neutral, is pursued with a fervor that articulates and acts on the fraught terrains of social upheaval that the previous parts of this book have explored and that such moralizing talk professes to describe and evaluate: the shoring up or unmaking of entrenched hierarchies; the reconfiguration of kinship and gender norms; the "development" and distribution of land and "property"; the (re)valorization of spaces, objects, bodies, and business; the territorialization of identity and "difference"; the conjuring of "publics." Ethnographic attention to the normative presumptions that animate such anxious inquiries and obfuscations in these fraught domains of activity reveals the multiple and sometimes contradictory moral and ethical commitments that underpin these truth-making practices.

In the first profile we meet Srimati Basu's "first lady detective" Rajani Pandit, the "self-appointed watchdog of profligate children, waste, and vice." Pandit is impelled into detective work at a young age by her unease at the "perceived transgressions" of a college friend ("tobacco and liquor and lying to the parents"). Her investigations are animated by anxieties born of a perception of widening and proliferating fissures between "wholesome middle-class narratives" and material-practical "secrets of kinship hidden in plain sight." At the same time, her own life choices are in tension with the heteronormative domesticity that she seeks to police and protect; Pandit personally foreswears marriage and children to pursue a detective career that has her running around the city at all hours of day and night, activities that draw the "disapproval and anxiety" of onlookers. She makes a living at policing the transgressions of others, violating entrenched social norms with an eye toward reinstantiating those same norms using the powers of knowledge and revelation: "Like the media who look for truth and want to bring the issues to people, I have the same work—I have to bring out the truth."

Whereas Pandit's investigations seek to "suture" multiple and conflicting "truths" into a single, desired version of reality, Atreyee Sen's profile of a "prison surrogate" named Pawan looks at the myriad audiences for multiple versions of truth, and at how the uneasy-but-necessary coexistence of conflicting versions of reality is made possible. Pawan makes a living serving jail time in the name of politically connected and better-off Mumbaikars who have been convicted of some or another crime—murder, rape, theft—but who are able and willing to part with some measure of cash in order to evade incarceration. Pawan makes no secret of his own moral compulsions; he expresses resentment toward rich kids who rape and murder but dodge prison. Yet we see as well how the compulsions of poverty impel Pawan to bracket these commitments and to enlist his own body in mediating the moral contradictions of a horrifically unequal and violent city and society. Pawan metabolizes these contradictions: on the one hand he takes pride in his status and virtuosity as "prison master" and in the small doses of respect that this status commands; he counts himself lucky for the opportunity to go on an all-expense-paid "holiday" to prison during the monsoon season, when his tiny slum home will be inundated anyway and when food will be hard to come by. Yet on the other hand, he expresses clear-eyed awareness of this dark irony and a keen awareness that life on the outside ought to be better than prison, even if—for him—it is often not.

Significantly, however, Pawan expresses these moralizing sentiments not in relation to his own surrogacy work but instead with regard to his late-career "business" venture, training a younger generation of surrogates. It is with increasing reluctance ("disillusionment") that Pawan sends "vulnerable boys—often arriving fresh from the village—into the ruthless prison world," into a life that they were poor and frantic enough to unwittingly embrace." And indeed after one of his trainees is sexually assaulted in prison, Pawan marches straight to the prison guards to express his outrage. It is the *surrogate*, Pawan insists, who makes possible the multiple and necessary coexistence of incompatible truths, reconciling the imperatives of equal-before-the-law proceduralism with the equally real existence of political power and authority to sidestep legal equality in the service of various forms of hierarchy: caste, class, and community. The surrogate metabolizes these contradictions with/in his own body: it is the surrogate's gut that processes the feces-contaminated milk and the surrogate's lighthearted humor and bawdy dance numbers that calm the nerves of guards and prisoners alike (and that win Pawan early release for "being a fun chap"); it is the surrogate's expertise in the arts of surviving prison life—expertise born at least in part of socio-economic compulsion—that buffers public servants and prison guards from the ever-present dangers that the contradictory imperatives of power and proceduralism pose. When a court-ordered "surprise prison check" reveals that some prisoner is not actually present in jail, it is not the political higher-ups who actually arranged the release who are held accountable, but rather the lower-level prison officers who simply carried out the release orders who are vulnerable to be targeted and sanctioned with allegations of "corruption." In this context, Pawan is outraged at the failure to protect his young trainees from violence on the part of the very guards who benefit from the surrogates' services. Yet the prison officers, in a particularly poignant exchange, offer no apology. And neither—more poignantly still—do the young surrogates abandon their perilous profession. Rather, they learn how to better navigate the dangers of prison life.

Pawan's profile reveals how moral commitments do not precede the acts of mediation in which they are enlisted but rather are always in formation—produced and transformed by the work itself. For instance, Pawan is initially agnostic regarding the violent and exclusionary ethno-nationalist political sentiments espoused by the political party that recruits him as "prison master." But over the years in prison, encountering and befriending religious and ethnic "others" behind bars (and recalling the theme of part IV), Pawan develops a distinct distaste for the Shiv Sena's brand of "hate-based party politics." He begins to avoid the party offices unless directly summoned for work. The limited options that Pawan faces for acting on his political and normative commitments—given the precarity of the aging prison master's life circumstances and his dependence on the beneficence of the party—are a powerful statement about the limits of electoral democracy under Mumbai's conditions of severe inequality.

Whereas Sen's profile shows how moral evaluations change and develop over time through material-practical encounters with difference, Sahana Udupa's profile of a taxi driver named Afzal demonstrates how such commitments can pull in both directions simultaneously. Reflecting on a bout of violence that had recently unfolded in Bombay, touched off by the viral circulation (over mobile phones) of a media clip (later revealed to be "false") that depicted horrific images of purported atrocities committed against Muslim communities in far-off places, Afzal speaks of the "damage" that mobile technology so readily unleashes. Afzal is clearly no fan of the rioting that ensued in response to the clip ("It was not our matter [*masla*] anyway. These attacks happened in faraway places"). Notably, however, Afzal's ambivalence toward technology and the "damage" it can prompt has less to do with any discussion of the "truthfulness" of the events that the images purport to represent than with the "excitement" of sentiments that the violent images cause. Whether and how the violence depicted in the clips might relate to matters involving his own community of Mumbai's Barelvi Muslims is unclear to Afzal. And yet the circulation of the images—whatever their provenance—amounted to a truth-telling call to action: "You should have seen the video, *medam*," Afzal tells Udupa. "Even you would have felt enraged. We saw children being dragged out, their throats slit, heads smashed." The images incited the unruly demonstrations that followed their circulation in Mumbai because the violence depicted in those clips resonated among Mumbai's ever-marginalized and riot-traumatized Muslim communities, for whom the bloody scenes represented in the images were a variety of truth, even if these *particular* events never actually happened. In this context of moral ambivalence, Udupa's account demonstrates, Afzal wields an "embodied form of expertise" that he uses to navigate this perilous terrain and "to ascertain the 'truthfulness' of the barrage of images and accounts that flow through the millions of Mumbai's tiny screens."

Afzal's navigation of the fraught moral terrain—between potential for damage and justification of rage—points to a second theme that runs through the profiles in this chapter: the way that the characters narrate the goals and *intentions* of their truth-seeking work often diverges dramatically from what the ethnographies then go on to demonstrate as the eventual outcomes or *effects* of truth-making practices. Set free into the city, truth claims are enlisted in a myriad of projects that may only be tenuously connected to any original designs of their utterers. Unruly truth claims are easily put to work in efforts to subvert the very efforts to (re)assert hierarchies and social orders in service of which such claims to verity had been authored. In Udupa's profile of Afzal we see how "in the midst of confusing allegations and refutations, . . . the Azad Maidan protest had soon slipped the grip of the organizers." The protest's coordinators had enlisted the affective potential of the "bloodbath" images to convene a crowd (echoing accounts from the discussion of "publics" in part V), but the virally circulating visual "evidence of Muslim massacres" generated "excitement" that exceeded the organizers' efforts to define, contain, and entextualize the meaning of the images.[1] While it is the recognizable and codified properties that lend the images their power and authority—their "iterability," in Derrida's terms—the innumerable contingencies of the myriad individual viewings introduce ambiguity into the meaning of speech events mediated by the millions of tiny screens, hence the ever-present possibility of "damage" that Afzal attributes to mobile phone technology—damage that in Udupa's profile resulted in a bout of unanticipated and undesired (on the part of the organizers) communal unrest.

The instabilities of linguistic mediations and the irreducible material-ity of signs more generally[2] are the domain that Annelies Kusters's profile of "master communicator" Sujit Sahasrabudhe deftly unpacks. The profile explores various contexts in which mutual understandings are sought out, as well as the many ways in which communication can go awry in polyglot Mumbai. A deaf activist, sign language instructor, and documentary film-maker, Sujit improvises tools and techniques (gestures, pens, lipreading, enlisting of bystanders) in pursuit of shared meanings in communication contexts where deaf signers and hearing nonsigners communicate. Sujit's communication practices are also a form of truth seeking, but what Kusters's profile so powerfully shows is that Sujit's mastery in the art of communica-tion inheres in his ready acceptance of this multiplicity and of the inher-ent instability of meanings; Sujit's life history affords him a keen awareness that attempting to pin down singular and stable truths—of where places are located, for instance, or of the value or price of apples—is not what will con-vince a taxi driver to deliver him to the hoped-for destination or prompt a fruit vendor to give him a good deal on produce.

Sujit recounts a formative experience from his childhood in which spoken communication went awry: after purchasing a train ticket for Vashi (mouth-ing the destination to the ticket seller) and boarding the train, Sujit found himself admonished when the ticket checker pointed out that the destina-tion printed on his ticket (written in the Marathi script, which English-educated Sujit could not decipher) had been issued not for Vashi but for Vasai. Kusters writes that after this experience, Sujit learned to remove speech from the repertoire that he uses in such contexts, employing instead a range of gesture-based techniques to specify place-names: when communicating with a rickshaw driver, he used gestures "to signify a landmark in the vicinity, such as boat (ferry), train (a nearby train station), shoe (referring to the statue of a shoe in Kamala Nehru park, to denote the park itself), or beach (a nearby beach), often in combination with pointing in the direction of the place." Kusters's profile shows Sujit searching out shared understandings of city space, proximity, and relative positioning of various destinations, surmising in each case which bits and fragments of the city that each of his interlocu-tors might use to orient himself: "over the flyover" or "on the other side of the tracks." When destinations are farther away, Sujit is seen using writing, in such cases often enlisting the help of English-reading and Marathi- or Hindi-speaking bystanders. In cases where no single shared point of reference can be arrived at using these signs and gestures, Sujit allows for a processual unfolding of the shared understanding of destination, indicating to a driver at the outset of a journey that "I'll give directions" along the way.

These intersubjective practices of searching for shared understandings are by no means limited to deaf-hearing communications in Mumbai, as Kusters's profile makes clear: "Because of his history of making his way through the city as a deaf signer, Sujit is a master communicator in Mumbai's markets and streets, where so many languages and language modalities are in play." Indeed, it is in Kusters's accounts of market exchanges and business transactions in Mumbai that the stakes of these multimodal communication skills can be seen most readily: "Sujit negotiated the price of a T-shirt at a clothes stall on Fashion Street, gesturing to reduce the price. The man nodded and said: 'How many pieces?' Sujit, thinking that he asked 'How much do you want to give?' gestured 'two' [₹200]." The eventually agreed-on price of the T-shirt—the "true value"—is seen in this account as inextricably bound up with the communicative practices enlisted in the *search* for an agreeable price. Neither the vendor nor Sujit can be sure of the interpretation of his own gesture or of the eventual use to which his own signifying practices will be put. On the contrary, we see in Kusters's ethnographies of Mumbai's multilingual markets how values emerge through the intersubjective practices of seeking them out.

Sujit's communicative expertise inheres in his awareness of the processual and emergent ontology of "truth," an awareness that is indeed exceptional. For other characters profiled in part VI, the unknowability of the world animates the restless work of investigation and meaning making by way of which the world is sought to be known. However, the insights offered by Kusters's "master communicator" raise important questions regarding the relationship between characters' self-narrations of the effects of their investigations and what the ethnographies actually show. To return to India's "first lady detective," Pandit's own normative commitments—to inherited caste, class, and gender norms—are at the front and center of her moralizing evaluations of "what needs to be investigated." As Basu writes, Pandit's goal is to unearth "evidence" that will "help people make informed decisions"—i.e., that will help certain people make precisely those decisions that are compatible with Pandit's *own* moral universe. Yet Basu's profile of Pandit goes on to demonstrate how the very same "truths" uncovered by her sleuthing—once unleashed into the world—exceed the designs of their author, becoming available to be enlisted in any number of projects, whether or not those projects are ones with which Pandit herself is in support. As Basu writes, Pandit's "revelations do not necessarily have predictable moralistic outcomes." We thus see how one of Pandit's clients whose fiancée turned out to be a bar dancer decided to marry her anyway, even though this may not have been the outcome that the conservative Pandit had in mind. Faced with this uncomfortable hijacking of her "truths" for normatively undesired ends, we see Pandit attempting to "domesticate" the unpredicted (unwanted) outcome within her own moral universe, reasoning that—bar dancer notwithstanding—it is on the basis of her investigations that a proper home and domestic life can be established (*ghar bassa sakte hai*).

"Truths," in other words—once crafted, uttered, and set into motion—are up for grabs and can be put to work in all sorts of ways, whether or not such projects were predicted or desired by the truth seekers who produced them. The profiles authored by Shetty and Gupte and by Bhide—read together—demonstrate the fraught nature and open-ended possibilities of such dynamics in the context of Mumbai's myriad, ongoing, and extremely high-stakes "development" (and redevelopment) projects and initiatives, projects in which the production of "survey data" and delivery of various kinds of reports loom large. Prasad Shetty and Rupali Gupte describe how a small-time stationer "became an overnight star" in the world of infrastructure consultancy following the 2005 Mithi River flooding, when his "good relations" with various government officers (relations born of his stationery "businesses") landed him a "report-making" gig with the Mumbai Metropolitan Authority Office. New to the world of government reports, ever-clever Chadda quickly discerns that the concerned authorities did not simply want "a document that explained the reason for flooding," but, more specifically, they needed a report that would demonstrate one *particular* explanation, an explanation that had been decided in *advance* of Chadda's inquiries into the matter. Chadda realized he needed to "prove" that the river had flooded because of the "illegitimate structures" along the banks.[3] Understanding the nature of the "truth" that his research and report making were supposed to uncover and report, Chadda assembled a team of surveyors to make drawings and "calculate" the number of "encroachments along the edges" of the river. After the resounding success ("skillful handling") of this first assignment and following the 2005 launch of the central government's Urban Renewal Mission—funds from which were released on delivery of this or that "project report"—Chadda found himself regularly recruited by state authorities "as a subcontractor in surveys of all kinds: head counts, house counts, family counts, traffic counts." This profile shows how the exigencies of expedience (Chadda's expertise was rooted not in "making good project reports, but rather in getting reports approved") often determine the content of the "truth" that surveys and other forms of "primary data" collection profess to discover through investigation and inquiry. Chadda's reports—like the surrogate body of Pawan the prison master—instantiate a version of reality upon which state authorities can act while allowing them to safely "turn a blind eye" to other, inconvenient truths.

Shetty and Gupte's profile of Chadda provides a gloves-off account of how legally and politically empowered categories such as "encroachment" or *slum* are enlisted in producing and shaping the very urban fabric of Mumbai that Chadda's research and reports profess to discover and represent (echoing our discussion of representation from part V). Chadda's profile is particularly powerful given the authors' direct experience with these dynamics in Mumbai; Shetty himself is a former state planner who worked for many years with the Mumbai Metropolitan Regional Development Authority. It is in the context of this stunning portrait of the social histories of government surveys' official practices of "data" production and reporting that Amita Bhide's profile of a "data entrepreneur" named Prakash takes on particular salience: Prakash is also in the business of report making and knowledge production but generally does so as a *sub*-subcontractor hired by consultants (that is, by people like Chadda) to carry out the actual work of door-to-door surveying and mapping. Chadda's profile suggests a watertight, top-down power-knowledge regime, but Prakash's story offers a very different picture, one in which those people who have the experience, skills, and knowledge required to access the "difficult" sociopolitical contexts and material environments of slums and *chawls* in order to produce knowledge in the first place—knowledge that will then be packaged as "data" into approvable reports—are able to advance *their* versions of "truth."

Prakash honed his skills growing up in a small Mumbai "slum" neighborhood and thus knows all too well the countless ways that the lived city exceeds the tidy categories of state reports. Drawing on the desires and ethical commitments born of his life experience, Prakash produces and wields knowledge toward ends quite different from the goals of those of, say, Chadda's patrons in government offices: where Chadda's reports would allow for the official ignoring of details that do not fall neatly within the empowered framings of institutionalized governance categories, Prakash seeks to document those same details, to render them legible, and to thereby reconfigure the boundaries of those same frames. We see, for instance, how Prakash draws on a fragment of information gleaned from a government survey gig to convince state authorities to grant compensatory housing to the residents of a swath of demolished homes under the auspices of an upcoming infrastructure initiative—as "project-affected persons." The power of Prakash's knowledge, in other words, inheres neither exclusively in his ready familiarity with the material and conceptual difficulties of slum life (difficulties with which most Mumbaikars are all too familiar) nor in his easy access to government offices, contracts, or to valorized founts of knowledge production such as the university. Rather, the power of Prakash's knowledge-production skills lies in the mutual interdependence of these often-antagonistic domains of truth making. Prakash maneuvers in this fraught terrain by deftly and carefully navigating between words and worlds, concepts and concrete, rules and realities in a city where everyday life routinely overspills empowered frames.

The people profiled in part VI demonstrate a keen awareness that the truths they produce and instantiate, once uttered, can be put to use in undesired ways. The dangers of this semiotic slippage—moral, ethical, material— are sought to be managed through the carefully curated work of self-narration. For our first lady detective Rajani Pandit, for instance, the work of self making—and by extension of self *marketing*—means stating her own moral commitments upfront, by repeatedly recounting (to customers and media correspondents) her "favorite cases"—that is, those that end up with the desired outcomes. But of course this means remaining silent about *other* cases and contexts in which the knowledge she uncovers may have been put to work in "wrong" ways. This careful curation and self narration means that the ethnographer (and by extension the reader) has no way of knowing about these instances of "knowledge used wrong," which is what makes Pandit's offhand mention of the bar dancer episode so telling. Pandit might hope that the work of exposing secrets sutures them over, "leaving the house (if not the roof) in place." But the ethnography in Pandit's profile reveals that it is precisely the instability and *unsutureability* of the knowledge-power regimes shaping family, gender, community, and class in contemporary Mumbai that capture Pandit's moralizing imagination and create demand for her services in the first place. Once "truths" are set free, they're just truths in a world of truths. This fraught relationship between the moral-evaluative presumptions of truth-seeking investigations on the one hand and the moralizing work of self narration/self making on the other can be tracked through each of the profiles in part VI. In an anxious effort to prove that certain truths are the most powerful and effective—indeed, the *real* truths—our truth seekers must keep their own secrets.

Notes

1. "Entextualized" language refers to language that has been objectified, in the sense that "chunks of discourse come to be extractable from particular contexts and thereby made portable" (Webb Keane, "Semiotics and the Social Analysis of Material Things," *Language and Communication* 23 [2003]: 14). See also Richard Bauman and Charles L. Briggs, "Poetics and Performances as Critical Perspectives on Language and Social Life," *Annual Review of Anthropology* 19, no. 1 (1990): 59–88; Michael Silverstein and Greg Urban, *Natural Histories of Discourse* (Chicago: University of Chicago Press, 1996).

2. Keane, "Semiotics."

3. Chadda's work recalls discussions in part II.

31 **RAJANI PANDIT** DETECTOR OF "TRUTHS"

Srimati Basu

"Detectives Are Born, Not Made"

One might imagine that invisibility is a private detective's most prized asset, that they want to blend in, assume generic identities, elicit seemingly innocuous information. The office of Rajani Pandit, who is often described as India's first woman detective (competing claims to this crown are beyond the purview of this essay), defies this presumption.[1] On a busy Dadar street of shops and residences close to the City Light market, minutes away from Sena Bhavan (the headquarters of the *Shiv Sena* and the locus of its influence) and the green space of Shivaji Park, a black-and-white unmarked door leads to a room indistinguishable from adjacent small apartments. But inside, among the usual office chair and desk and computer and phone and a couple of drawing-room chairs for guests, the rust-colored walls are ablaze with trophies and encomiums from civic organizations, political parties, and corporate and media commendations. Silver goddess figurines, elaborate clocks, and sculptures feature as prizes; the diamond "locket" pendant given to Rajani by Priya Diamonds, presented by then-Minister of Education Smriti Irani in a glamorous ceremony, is not in view. Photographs illustrating media stories depict what editors might imagine detective work to look like: Rajani talking on the phone, sitting at a desk, standing on the street corner, wearing shades, holding a magnifying glass to her eye. Among the pictures are one with *Bal Thackeray* with the Hindi caption "Hum Bhi Kisise Kum Nahin" (literally, "I'm no less than anyone either," echoing the title of a 1977 film, now a phrase in popular discourse), and a prominent image of *Amitabh Bachchan* gracing a JustDial.com award: the implicit approval of the two megastars of politics and film. News articles carry the monikers "Super Sleuth," "Ms Sherlock," "Lady Bond," "The Pundit of Detection," "Pahili Marathi Her" [The first Marathi spy/detective], "Mahila Jasoos" [a female detective/spy], and "Bharatatil Pahili Mahila Guptaher" [India's first woman detective].

This profusion of publicity says as much about its audience as its subject. The covertness of a detective's job becomes a proxy for mystique: the media imprinting Byomkesh and Bond and Holmes and Marple and Ramotswe onto Rajani exemplifies the impossibility of writing about her (including in this account) without the weighty romantic legacy of film and fiction. Scholars suggest that this association is no coincidence,[2] given that the figure of the private detective was created through a "symbiotic relationship" between the detective-agency business and the detective-story business in the "mutual pursuit of commercial ends."[3] Detective fiction highlighting mythical investigative acumen became increasingly popular just when professional detectives were being hired by large firms to undermine organized labor and monitor immigrant populations. Detectives have undertaken precious little "crime" solving on behalf of individual clients, although we can scarcely imagine them any other way.

However, the small private-detective firm is a rarity in all times and places. As an Indian private detective running her own business, Pandit stands out in comparison to police investigators or large corporate firms. Her gender adds to her exceptional status, a contrast both to the markedly homosocial male worlds of many fictional Indian detectives and to women detectives who were typically hired only on rare occasions to infiltrate select niches.[4] Media and civic publicity thus benefits her business.

Pandit's assignments typify routine private-detective work—primarily the business of sex and marriage and family (and thus the hierarchies of gender, sexuality, caste, and class) rather than homicide or forensics. But to see Pandit thereby merely as a mirror of family governance also falls short of its subject. Rajani describes herself as a "truth seeker": she highlights her curiosity, creativity, and nuanced moral judgment. Her fierce determination to grow up to be a detective, in lieu of the default of marriage, also challenges

FIGURE 31.1 A wall of newspaper clippings with the phrase *Lady Bond* in the center. Used courtesy of Srimati Basu, photographer.

normative futures. The daily work of suturing proper marriage alliances and monitoring women's respectability may mean shoring up ideologies of gender, caste, and class, yet Rajani depicts herself in these contexts as one who traverses realms and questions social assumptions.

AS THE CHILD OF A Crime Investigation Department (CID) detective, Rajani Pandit might have claimed hereditary expertise in investigative work. But seeing herself as being "born a detective" is critical to her narrative. Always a curious child, at age eight or nine she went up to a newly deceased woman on a bier in her building to check whether she had truly stopped breathing, what it meant to be dead. She describes observing schoolchildren making purchases she deemed to be misguided, then making them call their parents in her presence so she could report on how they had spent the money given to them for shoes. Rajani foregrounds an obsession with hunting "truth" beyond cases: "Like the media who look for truth and want to bring the issues to people, I have the same work—I have to bring out the truth" [Jaise media waale sach ki khoj karte hain, logon ko saamne baat laate hain, waise hi same humaara kaam hai, ki sachaai saamne la kar dena hai].

Being a detective was so far from the imagination of an occupational/life choice for a middle-class Marathi woman in the mid-1980s that it seems to have left people around Rajani searching for appropriate language to voice their disapproval and anxiety. Her father's refusal to accept her avocation was framed through his experience as a CID officer—that is, as a person who knew all too well why it was an inappropriate venue and choice for a respectable woman. Rajani narrates an all-round horror from neighbors: "Ladki aur ye business! Koi doosra business nahin mila?" [A woman and this business! Couldn't she find another profession?]. However, her mother demonstrated unwavering support, which Rajani attributes both to the higher social purpose she ascribes to her work as well as to a higher destiny: "Mummy said, 'It's good she's able to help people,' and now look how many people seek her blessing" (Mummy boli achha hai ki logon ke kaam aati hai; Aaj bade bade log aa kar pair bhi chhoote hain). An astrologer's forecast that Rajani was destined for fame favorably influenced her mother as well.

Other female detectives I have interviewed have been married, but Rajani claims that being single helps her professionally by freeing her of domestic distractions: "In the detective 'line,' if you marry then you can't solve others' problems. The home looms large; you have domestic responsibilities. The other work doesn't get done" [Lekin detective line mein shaadi kar ke na phir aap apne problem se logon ke nahin solve kar sakti hain kyonki ek ghar ka maahol hota hai, ek jimedaari rehti hai. Wo nahin ho paata hai]. Her single status might be a particular choice or a decision in line with that of other professional women. Unlike the fictional lone-wolf private eye, however, Rajani lives in an extended family with her mother, her brothers, and their families; they share both professional and domestic work. Rajani wakes early to finish numerous tasks around the house, gets her brothers' children ready for school, and then goes for a walk before beginning her detective work for the day.

Rajani's gender and unmarried status make her demographically atypical, but it is crucial to her work (and that of other women detectives) that she appear utterly unexceptional. She *has* to pass as forgettable everywoman in the park, the store, the schoolyard, even in undercover domestic work. A slight build, average height, medium skin tone, modest gold jewelry, a *bindi*, and *salwar-kameez*, all help make her look perfectly pleasant to the point of anonymity.

THE FIRST "CASE" that set Rajani off was unpaid and unsolicited, demonstrating the gut-feeling nosiness that best characterizes the legends of her profession. As a second-year college student, she decided to begin "checking the background" of a woman from her college based on suspicion of her activities: "I had some doubts about her behavior. I thought, it looks like she lies to her mummy and daddy. Come on, let's get to the truth about her" [Mujhe doubt aaya ki us ka behavior theek nahin hai. . . . Maine socha, mujhe lagta hai ye mummy, daddy se jhooth bolti hai na, to is ka sab sachhai nikalwaati hai]. Her first step was to get a home address by going to the college office: telling the clerk that she needed the address in order to send a birthday gift produced prompt results.

The college-mate's parents were startled and defensive at her unsubstantiated allegations when she showed up at their home. "Her mother said, 'You must have some sort of enmity with her; my daughter's not like that,' and cited her daughter's excellent exam results and accomplishments. But her father said, 'It's a college atmosphere; anything can happen; why don't we check?' He came with me—I took him around by paying for taxis out of my own pocket, showing him what the girl does, the schemes she has got involved with" [kin logon ke chakkar me hain]. The schemes in question: "She did everything—smoking, drinking. Other things went on besides her studies. And the thing is, people take advantage [of one] when one is known to have been out of control with drinking. . . . So after encountering the truth, he said, 'You're a "spy!"' I laughed. 'I have no idea what a spy is.'"

While this was not a client, given that *she* paid for *him*, Rajani narrates that these little jobs got word out there (*phail gayi*), eventually culminating in an interview in the prominent Marathi paper *Loksatta*. Along the way, as she worked a series of office jobs, primarily at pharmaceutical and medical supply companies, she would often offer to solve small domestic problems for coworkers. A colleague entrusted her with the delicate job of looking into theft at her home, where a new daughter-in-law and a domestic worker were the inevitable prime suspects. Rajani figured out that a younger son was the thief and was attempting to frame his new sister-in-law, who had caught him at something nefarious. Her reputation got another substantial boost following a reporter's profile: she met him when he saw a small story on her in a Tamil paper. He hired her to look into his sister's husband's background, resulting in Rajani traveling to this husband's rural home to discover that he had another wife and family there.

All these shameful, furtive double lives that Rajani exposes are no coincidence. Kate Summerscale traces the word *detective* etymologically to the Italian *de-tegere* (unroof): "The original figure of the detective was the lame devil Asmodeus, 'the prince of demons,' who took the roofs off houses to spy on the people inside."[5] Unroofing, being laid bare to the outside, transmits a history of queasiness with the idea of the detective as a person who knows too much about those very secrets that people would most protect, a discomfort with a person who can get too close. The potential for exposure makes matters delicate and fraught, even if secrets remain difficult to act upon.

I learned in my interviews with Indian detectives that the bulk of their clients come by with cases about family matters, even though background checks for corporate clients bring in the most money. Noncorporate business has spiked in the last few years: the three biggest categories are surveillance of children (around drugs or sex), "pre-mat" (background checks for prospective matrimonial matches), and "post-mat" (investigating spouses). This preponderance of family cases indexes the anxieties around kinship, sexuality, caste, and class. Detective work targets the nodes that preserve class and gender regimes: for example, the thriving business of following high school and college students to sniff out drugs or sex aims to uphold class-caste-religion-appropriate endogamous marriages, to ensure the pursuit of men's careers and women's marriages with an eye toward optimum upward mobility. It mediates the political economy of marriage *and* divorce, drawing out embarrassing information that contemporary kin networks are unable to access and delivering scoops potentially fungible in courts. But such ideologies of caste/class-based heteropatriarchy are normative and invisible, serving to maintain the illusion of meritocratic culture, so they must necessarily be covered over, with the ever-present danger that "the detective hero might at any moment turn to reveal his grinning double, the voyeur."[6]

Rajani Pandit's nose led her to such secrets of kinship hidden in plain sight within wholesome middle-class narratives of family life. The account of uncovering a thriving college-mate's "other" life hints that Rajani found this success galling. In her moral universe, Rajani conflated the perceived transgressions of tobacco and liquor and lying to the parents, and sought to convince them of the dangers of a slippery slope. The other two cases described above similarly highlight her penchant for looking within normative family discourses: in one, Rajani doggedly tracked down the rural family of the perfect urban husband, and in the other, she ferreted out a thieving son who sought to pin his crime on his sister-in-law, a new bride who could be easily maligned in an unfamiliar affinal household.

Rajani foregrounds her moral opprobrium, her role as a self-appointed watchdog of profligate children, waste, and vice. In the cases above, she represents her skills as being exercised to vindicate a duped wife or an accused daughter-in-law, respectively. But notably, her exposés thereby reinforce patriarchal control of mobility, sexuality, and resources. The "wild" college-goer is made ready for a "decent" woman's life; the daughter-in-law is restored to a potential happy life among affines; the cheating husband is prevented from doing further damage so that his second/urban wife may move on. The "truths" she unveils are, in other words, behaviors that violate patriarchal (and class and caste) norms. Her vigilance is directed toward preventing norm transgressions, with the "rescue" of the wronged second wife justifying the overreaching surveillance of a college student having a seemingly good time.

But if the detective's métier is to look trouble in the eye, she is also in the position of being able to view family relations more unflinchingly, even to recalibrate scripts of respectability. In counterpoint to the case where the husband led a double life, Rajani recounts being asked to track down cases of women who were serially involved in seeking partners through matrimonial advertisements while still mid-divorce (and financial settlement). She thereby reminded me that she represents wronged husbands as well as wronged wives. She makes a point of emphasizing that her revelations do not necessarily have predictable moralistic outcomes: when she found out for a male client that his putative bride, part of a family in dire economic straits, was a bar dancer, he seemed sympathetic to his fiancée's plight and did not immediately reconsider marriage. Such an account helps shore up detective work as a productive process, challenging representations of the detective as a marriage wrecker wallowing in murky secrets. Rajani's view of her work is rehabilitative: "social service, work for people—you can set up a home based on such information" [social role yaane logon ka kaam . . . aap ghar bassa sakte hai na information ke baad]. But findings may also have unpredictable outcomes: unmasked secrets might launch alternate conjugal possibilities or catalyze more complex reckonings.

THE DETECTION OF FAMILY PROBLEMS seems genealogically akin to other jobs of managing conjugal systems. A private detective such as Rajani Pandit inhabits information networks within economies of marriage that might previously have been occupied by mediating figures within contained community circuits: the *ghatak* (marriage broker), male and female barbers, small traders, even visiting kin and neighbors. These figures circulated bits of knowledge vital to establishing the traffic of marriage, knowledge invisible in formal negotiations. Detective work in family matters similarly purports to help people make informed decisions, now even ranging across states or countries and involving financial forensics or social media.

Perhaps the biggest difference between the contemporary detective and the ghatak of yore is their role in mediating the legalities of marriage. In civil courts, secrets can be important for seeking divorce and determining the quantum of financial settlement or housing (based on notions of "fault"). These same secrets can be invoked in criminal contexts such as kidnapping, unnatural sex, or rape as a failure of promise to marry, sometimes helping to leverage more advantageous civil settlements.[7] Detectives' information about prospective or existent partners helps bind these spaces of law.

The murky official standing of detectives is best exemplified by the ways in which they are both visible and invisible to the police. Most often faceless, they hand over evidence that clients may choose to share with police or lawyers; such evidence may have to be reinvestigated to officially count. Rajani narrates being laughed at when trying to get a private investigator's license, meaning that there is no way to *be* official. Yet, she recounts, the police themselves hire private detectives for family matters or for off-the-books investigations such as election alliances.

Business thrives through these contradictions: Pandit has drawn on her reputation to diversify into various entrepreneurial activities. For example, she has developed courses in detective work. I interviewed one of her former (unpaid) interns (in fact, it was she who led me to Rajani), who was told at the end of her internship term that she was being given the option to pay a

FIGURE 31.2 Rajani Pandit posed with some of her awards. Used courtesy of Srimati Basu, photographer.

hefty sum[8] for a training course and thereby be professionally though unofficially certified. Some of these interns get hired as operatives.

Rajani's two brothers help run the logistics of the business and do occasional investigative work; she meets all clients and stays involved, especially with less-than-simple cases. She is the face of the company, and its success relies on her mystique, established through her account of cases demonstrating her instincts and fast thinking or her knowledge of hidden social practices. Her favorite case foments the legend: working undercover as a maid for six months, she helped catch a killer when he returned to visit the woman who had hired him. Rajani narrates with relish that she dropped a knife on her own foot in order to have an excuse to run to the doctor so that she could promptly call the police. My sense is that the case is a favorite because it showcases her instinct and ingenuity, the rare occasions a detective gets to do "criminal" work, featuring an undercover disguise reminiscent of film and fiction. It highlights the liminal class and occupational spaces the detective is imagined to traverse, while being tantalizingly silent about any code switching of linguistic or bodily habitus required to inhabit the role. Repeated in many media accounts, the case works to satisfactorily validate the loop between image and experience.

MYSTERIOUS DETECTIVES who cut through baffling puzzles may be more satisfying to our imaginations than the reality of routine surveillance of youth and marriage, but are detectives nonetheless critical sources of privileged covert knowledge as the unroofers of the myths of family life? Rajani Pandit's guiding logic and investigative tactics demonstrate the ways that detective work may reinforce patriarchal, heteronormative, class, and caste morality rather than unsettling its norms. Secrets are exposed only to be sutured over, leaving the house (if not the roof) in place. The detective herself must necessarily be a shadowy figure, delivering the traces that facilitate the state's governance of family.

Yet Rajani's account reveals the possibilities of unroofing secrets: she can urge clients to look beyond the narrowest of moral criteria, and the evidence she delivers may have its own unpredictable outcomes. Her persona also signals that the detective is no mere compliant deliverer of evidence for others' needs: the contradictions and exceptions marking her life narrative (the resolutely single female detective, her intrepid curiosity, and her keen entrepreneurial sense) challenge scripts of gendered possibility. Courting media visibility to emphasize the invisibility of detective work, Pandit crafts an irrepressible presence in dogged pursuit of her truths.

Notes

1. The data in this paper draw on an ongoing project on female private detectives, law, and family in India, based primarily on extended interviews. The interview with Rajani Pandit took place in December 2015.

2. John Walton, *The Legendary Detective: The Private Eye in Fact and Fiction* (Chicago: University of Chicago Press, 2015); Kate Summerscale, *The Suspicions of Mr. Whicher* (New York: Walker, 2018); Erica Janik, *Pistols and Petticoats: 175 Years of Lady Detectives in Fact and Fiction* (Boston: Beacon, 2016).

3. Walton, *The Legendary Detective*, 152.

4. Janik, *Pistols and Petticoats*; Walton, *The Legendary Detective*.

5. Summerscale, *The Suspicions*, 156–57.

6. Summerscale, *The Suspicions*, 158.

7. Srimati Basu, *The Trouble with Marriage: Feminists Confront Law and Violence in India*, ed. Claire Renzetti, Gender and Justice (Oakland: University of California Press, 2015).

8. The amount was Rs. 60,000 or 70,000 by her recall, about $1,000 USD at current exchange rates, quite a large sum of money, not much less than other vocational or professional degrees in some fields at the time. For comparison, the intern was paid Rs. 150 per day for (minimal) transportation expenses, and clients paid a few thousand rupees as a daily fee.

32 **AFZAL TAXIMAN** RUMOR NAVIGATOR

Sahana Udupa

AFZAL DROVE the *kaali-peeli*, the iconic black-and-yellow taxi of Bombay, on the breezy main road along the sea in Colaba, into the lanes and corners of Andheri East on a warm afternoon in 2013. I had just finished interviewing cyber police officials at the police commissioner's office and was on my way to another interview destination in Andheri. In his early twenties, Afzal was a thinly built man; from the backseat, I could see his petite figure occupying just a portion of the oversized driver's seat. As he steered our way through the busy roads, his body curved and swayed to the moving wheels, giving me a glimpse of his long white kurta, *topi* (white skull cap), and sparse beard. He turned back occasionally to answer my questions and rose with an air of theatricality each time he launched into a long commentary: on mobile phones, on the wealthy people of Bombay, on the world at large. In retrospect, I wonder how this ceaseless easy conversation would now be interrupted by the tablet screens popping up in the backseat of taxis worldwide and in Olas and Ubers in India, providing private and on-demand music and video entertainment that comes at the cost of the ready sociality of the tech-free taxis (unless, of course, the passenger or the taxi driver chooses to ignore the gadget, which is not unlikely).

"Only those with money [*paisevale*] earn the respect in Bambai," Afzal remarked almost plaintively, gesturing for more conversation. I was keen to listen to Afzal's narratives; they moved from remorse and reflection to humor and jibe, in a mild show of flirtatious candor. I was then in the midst of untangling a concatenation of events around a public protest that had tragically turned violent in August 2012 on the Azad Maidan, a large public ground in the heart of the city. Raza Academy, a Sunni Barelvi organization based in Bombay, had organized a rally to protest violent attacks by the ethnic Bodo groups on Bangladeshi Muslim migrants in Assam and by Buddhist monks against Rohingya Muslims in Myanmar. Initially planned as a peaceful rally, the Azad Maidan protest had soon slipped the grip of the organizers. With torched vans, burned tires, and police action, the *maidan* had descended to a state of disarray and violence. The protestors expressed their anger against the police and mainstream commercial media—both seen as part of "the establishment"—by burning down outdoor broadcasting vans of television channels and injuring journalists and the police. The police later charged more than fifty protestors for various crimes under the Indian Penal Code, including murder, rioting, and molestation.

Several conspiracy theories surrounded the unfortunate event. Some suspected that the "mischief makers" were planted by Mumbai's political parties to sabotage the rally. This appeared as a convincing argument for many media commentators, who tallied the efforts of various political parties—Maharashtra Navanirmana Sena (MNS), Indian National Congress, Samajwadi Party, and All India Majlis-e-Ittehadul Muslimeen—to capture the votes of the Muslim residents, who constituted 2.2 million people, or 18 percent of the city's population. Others suspected transnational Wahabi connections and still others the hand of the underworld.

In the midst of confusing allegations and refutations, what remained consistent was the reference to a "video clip" loaded with images of bloodbath and a running text inscribed on the graphic visuals. The clip had circulated on smartphones through WhatsApp and Facebook days before the protest rally, presenting the images as evidence for the Muslim massacres in Myanmar and Assam. The multimedia message was said to have reached every Muslim household in Bombay, causing a stir through the community. Engaged in an anthropological reflection on the intersections between political and digital life, I was intrigued by the work of the "viral" multimedia message (MMS) in the tragic episode.

I listened to Afzal intently because he had started to talk about the rapid spread of smartphones in the city. Afzal's family had come to Mumbai from

Uttar Pradesh, and his brothers and uncles worked at small car-repair jobs in and around the city. Afzal had worked for a *seth* as a driver for some years, but was asked to leave two years ago. I suspected that something could have gone wrong at the job with the seth. Sensing that the reasons could be delicate, I didn't push him on the details. "Now I run the taxi," he said, but "I don't own the car."

His taxi was a Premier Padmini, the locally manufactured car synonymous with Bombay's postcolonial urban mobility.[1] But the self-employed taxi trade epitomized by Premier Padminis was under acute threat in Mumbai following the city administration's decision to launch a "taxi modernization" policy in 2006. Citing Singapore as a model, the policy promoted corporate-owned fleets boasting "modern" cars fitted with global positioning systems.[2] Owner-operated Premier Padmini kaali-peelis of the pre-liberalization era were described as "outdated" and targeted for phasing out. The decision to "modernize" Mumbai's taxi system had disrupted the delicate networks and relations of mutual obligations that had grown around the taxi trade. Drivers would lose their autonomy over when and where they run the taxis, while cooperative sharing of resources in close-knit kin and ethnic groups would be forced to contend with corporate fleets and investments.[3]

Afzal was aware of these threats facing kaali-peelis. But he didn't speak in despair of any of these changes. Not even about the rifts and coalitions of caste, religion, and nativism that shape labor in the taxi trade and other businesses.[4] Rather, he spoke enthusiastically about mobile phones and their riveting modernity. The reference to smartphones was so spontaneous that I didn't have to expend effort to steer his musings on the city toward the research topic high on my mind. Afzal was thrilled about smartphones and all the wonders they could do. "I have not invested in a smartphone yet," he revealed, "but most of my family members have." He said his aging father had just purchased a smartphone. "Kharidliya medam, abhi parishan he, kya karna usko maloom nahi" [He has purchased the smartphone already, Madam. Now he is worried because he is clueless on what to do with it], he said, laughing out loud at his father's predicament. The tiny gadget seemed to have a mesmerizing presence in Afzal's life and of those he knew closely. I was curious to know why Afzal didn't want a smartphone for himself. "It can do a lot of damage," he remarked, again in a tone of theatrical emphasis, not expecting that the word *damage* would trigger a string of questions from me; by then, Afzal had gathered enough about my research focus on the digital circulations that had animated the Azad Maidan events.

That morning I had been listening to a long police narrative about how smartphones were responsible for the "riots" on Azad Maidan: how the technology itself was responsible for the havoc. The bloody images that had circulated before the rally were "false," the police report asserted; none of those photos or videos featured actual Muslims in either Myanmar or Assam. The word *damage* in Afzal's spontaneous response had caught my attention, resonating more powerfully than he had anticipated. "What damage do you mean?" I asked. I prompted him further to see if he was aware of the Azad Maidan rally. "Are you a Barelvi Muslim?" I asked. *"Medam,* you seem to know quite a lot about us," he remarked instantly. But he didn't sound alarmed. He was eager to tell me all about the rally. "It was not our matter [*masla*] anyway. These attacks happened in faraway places. But people are "taken by excitement" [*josh mein aagaye*], he said, appearing to distance himself from the events of the rally. The next second, however, he was less sure about this distancing. "You should have seen the video, *medam*; even you would have felt enraged. We saw children being dragged out, their throats slit, heads smashed. You would have been totally convinced. I am sure," he said, explaining how after seeing the WhatsApp images it was hard to *not* to be moved by the images, be convinced of the video's truthfulness, and participate in the protest.

Afzal's impassioned description of the video and its "truthfulness" gave me the first glimpse of how the protestors experienced the much-rumored role of the mobile video. Afzal's narratives also reflected his work as a taxiwala: moving people from place to place, along with the objects, stories, and rumors that they carry. His experience of navigating the city offered a vantage point from which to assess and comment upon the "truthfulness" that smartphone technology affords. Just as ethnographers like me relied on Afzal to lead us through the city—to connect the dots and provide the links and comment upon the conjectures—taxi drivers in Bombay (as in cities worldwide) have always worked as key sources of knowledge. Afzal's capacity to corroborate and correct the flows of information came from his daily movements in and around the city, weaving a web of knowledge with the stories he gathered and carried in the taxi.

Afzal's accounts convinced me to seek out interviews with people who had actually been present at the protest. And Afzal, in the cordiality of the taxi space, readily offered to take me to people whom he knew had participated. He seemed thrilled by the prospect of extending help to a stranger who had taken an interest and was keen to know more. He had guessed (correctly) early in our conversation that I was "Hindu," and my accented Hindi was evidence of my South Indian origins. In a "culture of suspicion" that

entrenches everyday encounters between Hindus and Muslims in Mumbai—
a culture that, as anthropologist Radhika Subramaniam writes, is "neither the solid
antagonistic stance of hostility nor . . . an apprehensive response to danger . . .
[but] an unthinking, habitual, cultural interaction . . . that snags the stray
observation"—my knowledge of Barelvi Muslims came as a surprise to Afzal,
earning his admiration.[5] That I was keenly following an episode involving his
community intrigued Afzal even more. On my part, I was tuning up my pos-
ture, language, and hints that I would give out as a female stranger in the
city to see if I would be trusted and offered an unencumbered narrative. I
would speculate on what they might think of me and my research, continuously composing a shifting set of as-if propositions. Such interactional dynamics are a common feature of ethnography, where ethnographers and
interlocutors confront and resolve confusions, anticipate action, as well as
contend with complete failure at gaining trust and audience. Afzal seemed
to be excited by the prospect of helping me navigate the trails of the Azad
Maidan episode. He was ready to drive me around the city and introduce me
to his family and friends, to help a stranger who had taken interest in the
matters close to his heart. He promised to bring his taxi in the mornings
and park it in front of the multistory residential complex where I was staying with friends in Wadala to check if I needed the ride and introductions.
But not to worry, he assured me. If I didn't turn up and another customer
appeared, then he would just go ahead without me; he was driving a rented
taxi after all, and his daily income hinged on the number of rides he made.

The spontaneous sociality of the taxi space, layered with religious and
regional markers and laced with an exciting exchange on smartphones, provided my initial entrance into the complex episode of the Azad Maidan rally.
While listening to the accounts of Afzal's friends and family, I began to make
sense of how the rumored realities of far-off places had been pulled into
the intimate embodied worlds of the Azad Maidan protestors through the
myriad tiny screens of the smartphone. The narratives signaled the growing
importance of viral mobile media messaging for religious politics in India, a
point that I have discussed at length elsewhere.[6]

However, the interactions with Afzal also revealed the unique position
of the taxi drivers as mediators of knowledge in the city. Afzal's knowledge
made him an indispensable actor in the city's knowledge infrastructures. He
corrected, corroborated, and added his own affective energies to the flows of
information that circulated through media channels.

The ready sociality of the taxi space inside Afzal's kaali-peeli opens up important methodological questions regarding ethnographic knowledge creation

(discussed in the part VI introduction), but it also speaks to the intimate and protean spaces of communication instantiated by the taxi travel. These moments of sociality temper the flows of online messaging that tweak or fabricate contexts—of circulations that can potentially set the city ablaze in indignant response and ill winds of animosity. The light cheeriness of Afzal and the taxiwalas modulates the viral "testimony" of the virtual world. In spite of social media bringing all manner of images and narratives that can tear asunder the delicate fabric of trust between religious communities in Mumbai, Afzal, like many taxi drivers I met in Mumbai, enlists an embodied form of expertise to ascertain the "truthfulness" of the barrage of images and accounts that flow through the millions of Mumbai's tiny screens. It is now well established that the hybrid spatialities of the city, characterized by dynamic flows of mobile and locative media, "not only dissolve the fixity of traditional modes of spatial enclosure, but problematize the unified presence of the subject traversing their contours."[7] The virality of digital media flows disrupts the spatial fixity of structures composing the urban space, injecting a new velocity and momentum to relational ties. Such flows sometimes give a legitimate space to voice collective concerns; other times they can be brutal in infusing targeted rumormongering. Afzal mediates such digital leaps and flows—the ability to move from point to point in a networked space—with a sober temporality that can moderate the restlessness of digital virality. With social media and new technologies rapidly unleashing violent images and rumors of intrigue, the slower spaces of stranger sociality like those inside Afzal's tiny taxi allow for navigation, reflection, and safe passage.

Notes

1. Tarini Bedi, "Mimicry, Friction and Trans-urban Imaginaries: Mumbai Taxis/Singapore Style," *Environment and Planning* 48, no. 6 (2016): 1012–29.

2. Bedi, "Mimicry."

3. Bedi, "Mimicry," 1013.

4. Barbara Harriss-White, *India Working: Essays on Society and Economy* (Cambridge: Cambridge University Press, 2003).

5. Radhika Subramaniam, "Culture of Suspicion: Riots and Rumor in Bombay, 1992–1993," *Transforming Anthropology* 8, nos. 1–2 (1999): 101.

6. Sahana Udupa, "Viral Video: Mobile Media, Riot and Religious Politics," in *Media as Politics in South Asia*, ed. S. Udupa and S. McDowell (London: Routledge, 2017), 190–205.

7. Scott McQuire, *The Media City* (London: SAGE, 2008).

33 **PAWAN** PRISON MASTER

Atreyee Sen

MIGRATION ANTHROPOLOGIST Karen Fog Olwig once told me that people migrate for strange reasons and that it's unfortunate that academics promptly box these stories into categories of suffering. However, Pawan claimed that he did suffer when he came to Mumbai from Gadchiroli, a small town in Maharashtra, after his transistor radio broke. He loved singing to Bollywood music. He had been learning dancing moves and could easily mimic both male and female Bollywood dance stars. But when his radio broke, he realized he didn't have enough money to buy another one. He hung around tea shops listening to songs being played on the radio. Pawan was upset that his low-caste parents, who were both cooks in a small housing colony, could not afford a new radio. Frustrated, he decided to run away to Mumbai. He thought he could find work in the big city, get himself a radio, and never be without his "request romantic songs hour" again. He was barely twenty when I met him for the first time in 1999. Tall, dark, with thick curls on his head, he was yet another singing slum dweller I had encountered while conducting ethnographic research among the urban poor in Mumbai.

Once in the big city, Pawan realized that finding work was not easy. He ended up sharing a room with three laborers at the edge of a suburban rail line. His first experience being locked up in a neighborhood police station came after he tried to steal a radio from a local shop. "Of course," I thought. Pawan entertained everyone in the police station with his songs and dancing. He was so good at gyrating to Bollywood music that the police constable eventually passed him a long strip of cloth through the prison bars. Pawan wrapped the cloth around his waist and danced like Madhuri Dixit, a famous Bollywood actress, and did some exciting twirling, which made both the prisoners and the policemen applaud with laughter. Two days later, Pawan was released for being a fun chap, and while saluting goodbye to the inhabitants of this small police-prison world, he realized it was also his first experience of *masti* (fun) in Mumbai.

Pawan was arrested again, several times, sometimes for grievous offenses, such as aggravated assault, and sometimes for intoxicated misdemeanors in public places. He ended up in many institutions, even in the infamous Arthur Road Jail and the Taloja prison, which often hosted highly criminalized populations. In every prison that Pawan encountered, music went with him. He would sing and crack jokes, and kept the prisoners, his cellmates, the jailer, and the wardens entertained. "It was not perfect, mind you," he said. He didn't like the fact that he had to sleep on urine after prisoners pissed on the floor when wardens refused to let them out at night. He did catch deadly infections, his body was covered with insect bites, and pieces of shit would pop up in the milk because the wardens stole the pure milk and topped up the cans with water from the toilet. Pawan learned over time to churn the milk to see if the shit floated to the top. If it remained at the bottom of the cans, the milk would be infected enough to lead to an outbreak of diarrhea. If it floated to the top, Pawan and other prisoners would quickly scoop it out to limit the spread of disease. He also learned to seal open wounds with white candle wax and alcohol sneaked into prison by jailers. Sometimes the prisoners would break into fights, and the guards would give the inmates a thrashing. Through music, dances, mimicry, jokes, and keeping the wardens in good humor—sometimes by singing, sometimes by giving the jailers a good back massage, sometimes by mediating between an aggravated prison population and the wardens—Pawan managed to gain enough knowledge about the moods and maps of prison management to keep both the prisoners and the wardens "in his pocket." A lot of characters were huddled together in this enclosed and deadly space, so Pawan could study people quickly. He knew exactly what song to sing and what joke to crack to cheer up, manipulate, and get information from people around him. "A true ethnographer," I once laughed to him. "*Kya?*" he asked ("What's that?").

Pawan's reputation as a smart prisoner spread far and wide. Many former prisoners told stories about how Pawan used his magical powers to stop a fight and save lives. Or how he managed to get an extra banana for a sick prisoner by gently persuading one of the wardens. Or how he sweetly blackmailed a married warden who was sleeping with a young girl in his slum, often to get a lesser workload.

One morning (out of prison) as Pawan lay in his shanty smoking a joint, one of his mates said the local *Shiv Sena* party leader, Anant, had asked Pawan to visit him in the *shakha* (local branch of the party office). Pawan was confused at first. He was aware of the local nationalist party politics, but he didn't understand most of it. When Pawan walked into Anant's office, Anant looked up at his visitor and said, "Welcome, welcome, prison master." Pawan didn't know whether he was in trouble or whether his reputation (of being an excellent prison navigator) was being acknowledged by Anant. The Shiv Sena leader asked Pawan whether he would be willing to be a prison surrogate. "We will ensure that you are looked after in prison," said Anant. Pawan was even more confused. "Think about it," said Anant, and Pawan walked out of the shakha. "Prison master," thought Pawan; it was an interesting title in English.

Pawan sat in a snack shop and spotted a local Shiv Sena party worker (*karyakarta*) sipping tea. Pawan thought this was a good moment to ask the fellow what exactly was required of the prison master. "You are good with prisons," the man told Pawan. All Pawan had to do was go to prison instead of criminals affiliated with the Shiv Sena who didn't want to serve prison sentences. Pawan was still perplexed. He asked whether it was possible to pass off as multiple men in prison; there were prison records tucked away in the dusty shelves he had encountered in his own criminalized life. The party worker explained that the Shiv Sena had enough clout to doctor prison records by swapping photos and fingerprints between offenders and surrogates, but they still needed a human body to carry out the prison sentence. Most prisons were understaffed and held far greater numbers of prisoners than they were designed for. Despite the laxity of the court system in Mumbai, one of the ways to keep the fragile prison system in check was apparently to "fill it with surprises": surprise prison checks by central police officials, random lineups and counting of heads by senior officers, and the unpredictable desire of a random judge to produce a prisoner in court. This required that a prisoner be present to serve at least a part of the sentence. Pawan did not offer me any stories of surprise checks, but he explained that a bail and parole system in which bureaucrats, judges, and policemen were regularly bribed allowed many prisoners with political affiliations to get released early. He often referred to these payoffs as "*system mein tel dalna parta hain*" [keeping the system well oiled] so that the practice of prison surrogacy ran smoothly. But this process of appealing convictions and getting surrogates released took time. "In the meanwhile, someone has to go to jail. What if before the bail application, there was a random check?" asked Pawan. The party worker was surprised that Anant had not taken the time to explain to Pawan that he would get a lot of money for every "exchange" of offenders.

Over the next few days, Pawan was given party paraphernalia: wall clocks, calendars, and photographs of the late *Bal Thackeray*, the much-revered founding leader of the Shiv Sena. Pawan was branded as a party guy and held in high esteem for his service to the political group. In reality, however, Pawan was not sure whether he cared much for the party. He was satisfied that he had some knowledge, which did not involve formal education, that he could deploy in the world to make an income. "It's a dangerous game," he said, "but you have to be a good player to keep all the cards on your side of the table." I didn't understand his card metaphor. But I agreed that it was dangerous to have a finger in many pies: criminal activity, prison, the slum environment, the party. . . . But Pawan felt protected by the Shiv Sena, for his services were indispensable in Mumbai's burgeoning crime districts. He was aware that the offenders he replaced in prison might later want to kill him and remove all evidence of a crime. But Anant would not allow that, as there were many crime lords and rich kids all over Mumbai who needed to be free in the city while Pawan took their place in jail. "I am going on a holiday" is what he used to tell his shanty mates when on a prison assignment. At that time, Pawan did not yet see himself as just another disposable body bobbing around in Mumbai's enormous floating population, one that could be unscrupulously thrown in prison by party leaders. He was not searching for middle-class "respectability" but rather an acknowledgment that his skills were marketable in the crime/politics–based economy in the city.

And so Pawan became truly renowned as the "prison master." He performed his first surrogacy in prison when he was about twenty years old, and until at least the time of this writing he remained a prominent prison expert under the banner of the Shiv Sena. He went to prison for rape, torture, domestic battery, drunk driving ("I didn't even know how to drive!"), vandalism, and many other offenses that he didn't commit. He had so many prison identities that he barely remembers all of them. He did resent going to prison for spoiled boys accused of rape or murder who had paid the Shiv Sena a large sum of money to stay out of jail. Pawan said many of these sentences were often longer than a year, but the party would secure Pawan's freedom after a few months through legal loopholes. The jailers would say, "Pawan, back again? Who are you this time?" and everyone would laugh together. "Did you do rape or murder?" Pawan would often say, "I am not sure. Shall we look at the records together?" and there would be more peals of laughter.

Pawan was most grateful to be in prison during the rainy season, when his shanty in the slum would be flooded. At least he got food and shelter in prison, and despite the damp walls and leaky roofs, he didn't have to be shivering wet. Sometimes, during these rainy-season "holidays," Pawan sang monsoon songs from Bollywood films, which made other inmates lovelorn. He smoked only an occasional joint and didn't chew tobacco, just to ensure that he never lost his singing voice. Sometimes late at night when everyone was fast asleep, Pawan would sing softly to the rats hiding in the prison walls. Once he sang his favorite monsoon prison song to me in his mellifluous voice:

> Lagi aaj sawan ki phir woh jhadi hai
> wohi aag seene mein phir jal padhi hai
> lagi aaj sawan ki phir woh jhadi hai
> Kuch aise hi din teh woh jab hum miley teh
> chaman mein nahin phool dil mein khiley teh
> wohi toh hai mausam magar ruth nahin woh
> mere sath barsat bhi roh padhi hai
> lagi aaj sawan ki phir woh jhadi hai.

> It's once again those monsoon rains
> that has set fire to my heart
> it was on such a rainy day that we met
> away from the gardens, the flowers bloomed in my heart
> it's the same weather, but it's not that season
> the showers are crying to share in my tears
> it's once again those monsoon rains.

Pawan grew older, and he was getting less work. The rate of sundry crimes grew steadily but were mostly committed by younger party members or by affluent youths with connections in the Shiv Sena. Pawan's hair had grayed quickly. He was irritated that people named their children Tiger or Rocky, which were names he couldn't identify with. A series of terrorist attacks and bomb blasts in the city meant that police practices became stricter in prison; Pawan could not pass off as a young Tiger anymore. Pawan became worried as his income waned. He didn't marry because of his erratic visits to prisons, and he felt lonely because he was no longer regularly visiting a range of jails where he had earlier been treated as a king. Shiv Sena leaders began to worry: while crime rates in Mumbai held steady, Pawan was becoming too old to be a surrogate. The surrogate needed a surrogate.

There were times I speculated about Pawan's sexuality. He passionately sang songs about love and broken hearts but didn't seem to crave a steady relationship. In our conversations he described how much he enjoyed wearing long skirts and dancing like Bollywood heroines, and he loved to barter flirtatious exchanges for prison privileges with male guards. He was evidently thrilled that he received flattery from both inmates and jailers. But with me, he didn't entertain conversations pertaining to the myriad sexual innuendoes that ran through his stories. He only underlined his success as a specialist who could plot a course in and out of prison sentences with ease. "People would say 'come back soon,'" he laughed. "Who says that to inmates leaving prison premises?" Pawan took pains to tell me that he went to *female* prostitutes when he came out of prison, "just for a treat," using a chunk of money he received for his services.

One day Pawan spotted two boys in his slum; they had just arrived from their village. Pawan followed them about for a few days. They were lean, didn't have enough to eat. They waited for a long time at the *nakas* looking for work as daily laborers. Someone had told Pawan that they were brothers: the boys had hoped that an uncle would look after them for a while, but this man was nowhere to be found. Pawan called the boys to his shanty. He said, "I am Pawan, the prison master." The boys were perplexed by this introduction. Pawan felt his stomach churning because he was going to introduce these boys to a life that they were poor and frantic enough to unwittingly embrace. Pawan explained his "line of work" to the two boys, who were initially reluctant to join him. He would take a cut from the money made by the boys, and in exchange he would teach the boys how to negotiate prison life without being hurt or killed. Eventually, the boys accepted the offer of employment, and Pawan felt excited that he had started his own "prison business." He introduced the youngsters to Anant, who was evidently pleased with Pawan's entrepreneurial abilities. Pawan taught the brothers how to talk to prison wardens, how to laugh with prisoners, how to stay out of certain fights, and how to mediate in some clashes. The boys became his greatest followers.

When one of the brothers eventually went for his first prison assignment, he was promptly gang-raped by other prisoners. Or so Pawan thinks.

"Something very bad happened to him there; neither of the brothers would talk about it," he said. When the boy came out, he was a changed fellow. He struggled with walking, eating, and smiling. He was inconsolable. Pawan was angry. He went to the prison and asked a guard why his employee was mistreated in prison. The guard said, "Pawan, you are one of our men; everyone knows you well. You send a beautiful young boy to prison—what did you think will happen?" I do not know whether Pawan himself escaped being raped in prison. Perhaps he did so by either offering himself voluntarily to men or by flaunting his party credentials. Pawan was not open to this line of questioning. Nor were his neighbors, who described Pawan simply as an expert in an unusual field of service.

In more recent years, Pawan was not a happy man. He felt that he was not tough enough to send vulnerable boys—often arriving fresh from the village—into the ruthless prison world. Despite everything, the brothers stuck with Pawan as his apprentices. Without any children of his own, Pawan felt distressed to see the boys changing into hardened men with criminal records. Pawan wondered whether it was his music that had kept him "soft" through all those years of dipping in and out of prison life. But now he was tired. Even his favorite prostitute mocked him for failing to have sex like a "charged horse" as he used to. While I never probed the matter, I supposed that Pawan might also be nostalgic for his former "prison master" days as the sexual, sensual, young dancing man, soothing tempers and softening hearts in a harsh, homosocial carceral cosmos. He still doesn't engage with hate-based party politics. I always sensed that his distancing from virulent nationalism was related to his proximate (if not intimate) understanding of ordinary people from different religious and regional backgrounds, while journeying through various cultures of confinement.

When I last met Pawan, he spoke of his parents. They had probably died, he thought. He had never discussed his work with the occasional relative who passed through Mumbai and found a way to contact him. Anyway, those family encounters evaporated as he spent more time in prison. Pawan did not send any money home. He felt that the money was not clean enough for his parents to appreciate as a gift. He was content to spend it on drink and prostitutes. Pawan, now in his forties, worried about his future. He felt stuck in his life in the slum. Spending long periods of time in prison had kept him from investing in a family life of his own and having any real friends. He didn't have to go to prison as often as he did before, so his skills had little value. For the aging prison master, freedom was his new prison.

34 **SUJIT** MASTER COMMUNICATOR

Annelies Kusters

When I was growing up, I used sign language with my deaf family and gestures with hearing people. But in my school, many teachers said that when we grow up, we must be able to speak. . . . They said that if we can't speak, it's difficult to travel. Now I'm grown up, I've traveled the world and have visited many different places in India. . . . Because I can speak? No, I use gestures. These teachers thus made incorrect assumptions.—SUJIT SAHASRABUDHE

I FIRST SAW SUJIT SAHASRABUDHE during the International RYLA—The Deaf Way conference, with "RYLA" standing for "Rotary Youth Leadership Awards." It was held in Ichalkaranji, West India, in November 2006. I was one of a few foreigners, and he was standing on the stage: a twenty-eight-year-old deaf man giving a presentation in Indian Sign Language (ISL) about ISL courses. I was impressed by his confidence and the clarity of his signing. During a break, he approached me, and we started to sign to each other, my signing an awkward mix of British Sign Language and International Sign, but we managed to communicate somehow. After this conference, I joined him and several other deaf Mumbaikars and foreigners in an overnight bus headed to the metropolis. He led us around his city, taking us on the Mumbai local trains and showing us the Necklace, the Gateway of India, and other landmarks. He took us to street markets, introducing us to Indian snacks and haggling with sellers when we wanted to buy souvenirs. I was immediately fascinated by the ease and confidence with which he navigated Mumbai, this bustling city, and in particular by his frequent and successful communication with hearing people using gestures. Those days in Mumbai were the beginning of an ongoing personal and professional relationship: a few months later, he was a key participant in a small research project on the Mumbai trains; still later, he became my husband.

Sujit comes from a lower-middle-class Marathi Brahmin family. He does not speak. He is a native ISL signer who can understand different variants of ISL, which he learned as much from his parents' various friends and their respective signing variants as from having spent his youth in a residential deaf school in Chennai. For ten years he taught ISL courses to prospective interpreters and ISL teacher-training courses to deaf community members. He has also been involved in several deaf organizations in Mumbai, including being general secretary of the Yuva Association of the Deaf and vice president of the India Deaf Society. In short, he has a strong network in the Mumbai deaf community and a good metalinguistic awareness of ISL.

Sujit's recollections of his childhood schoolteachers' admonitions that he must learn to speak sat uneasily next to my own research findings on deaf people's everyday communication strategies and language choice in Surinam and Ghana.[1] That work—which had observed deaf people signing and gesturing with hearing people—had discovered that when people from different linguistic backgrounds meet, they typically don't get stuck in the sort of communicative void that Sujit's Bombay teachers forewarned. Rather, people will use gestures to communicate, often combined with mouthing (mouth patterns which can be partially derived from a spoken language), speaking, and/or writing in different languages.

I am a deaf Belgian woman from a mostly hearing family (I have one deaf younger sister), and I found the way of communicating across language divides to be striking, a dramatic contrast to my experiences and observations in European cities and towns, where hearing people are generally much less able to respond when they are approached in gestures by deaf people. Throughout my relationship with Sujit, I witnessed the mastery and ease with which he communicates using gesture in myriad contexts—in Mumbai, in India, in Europe, and now in the UK—and thus came to understand that he is a communication virtuoso. This realization inspired a research project focusing on deaf-hearing gesture-based communication, in which Sujit and I carried out linguistic ethnography in public and parochial spaces such as markets, shops, food joints, and public transport in Mumbai. It is commonly said that India's southern states and rural areas feature a wider repertoire and/or more frequent use of conventionalized gestures than do northern states and cities. Nonetheless, we chose to carry out our study in Mumbai—the most culturally and linguistically heterogeneous city of India—because of its legendary diversity. The project culminated in the production of a full-length ethnographic documentary called *Ishaare: Gestures and Signs in Mumbai.*[2]

ONE AFTERNOON IN EARLY 2014, Sujit and I decided to head to the Taj Hotel in the suburb of Bandra to meet some friends who had traveled from Belgium. We took the train to Bandra station, where we sought an auto rickshaw to take us to the Taj. The driver, noticing our signing, asked: "Hospital?" Because we are deaf, the driver had guessed we wanted to go to AYJNIHH, the much-attended Indian national institute for deaf people where Sujit had previously worked (providing audiological testing, ISL courses, hearing aids, and so on), which is close to Lilavati hospital. Sujit responded "Taj" (mouthing without voicing) and gestured "tall" (with two hands moving upward to indicate a tall building) and pointed in the direction of its location. The driver nodded, motioned with his head for us to sit, and took us to the correct place.

Sujit and the driver had mouthed/spoke key words ("hospital," "Taj") to replace or specify a gesture ("tall building") that would be too general otherwise. Similarly, when Sujit ordered *sev puri* at street stalls, he would refer to how these Bombay street-food treats are eaten, enacting how puri are held in the hand and then shoved in the mouth. The enactment in itself would be too general because it would fit several different puris sold at the stalls, such as *pani puri* and *dahi puri*. Thus, Sujit would either specify the gesture by mouthing "sev puri" or by pointing to the sev puri crackers, which differentiate sev puri from other kinds of puris. Other examples are enacting holding a mango in an outstretched hand and then mouthing "*amba*" or making the general gesture for "document" and mouthing the English word *passport* or *certificate*. In the example above, both deaf and hearing people lip-read each other's strategically chosen words and names in combination with gestures.

On one occasion, Sujit and I wanted to visit a research participant in Tilak Nagar, a neighborhood in the suburb of Chembur, by auto rickshaw. I had written down "Chembur Tilak Nagar" (in Roman script) on a piece of paper and showed it to the driver. He shook his head to indicate that he could not read it. Sujit mouthed "Chembur," which the man immediately understood. He asked (in speaking): "Chembur?" which Sujit lip-read and then nodded confirmation. The driver nodded that we could get in. At that moment, a passerby in office clothes who had been observing us approached us. I showed the paper to this man, who spoke to the driver. Now the driver had an extra confirmation and a more specific location: Tilak Nagar. Later, when I asked him to sign a receipt, he did so in the Devanagari script.

When we wanted to return from Chembur to Mulund by another auto rickshaw, Sujit mouthed "Mulund" to the driver and pointed in the direction of its location. The driver did not understand. I took a pen and gave it to Sujit, who wrote "Mulund" on the palm on his hand and showed it to the woman who was just getting out of the same rickshaw. In gestures, the woman asked him for a more specific location in Mulund. Sujit mouthed "east" and did an eastward movement with his hand. The woman communicated it to the driver, who asked for an even more exact location. The woman relayed to Sujit by speaking and gestures. Sujit, expecting this question, gestured that he would give directions to the driver along the way. In the two examples above, mouthing immediately works in one instance but not in the other, as is the case for writing. Gesture-based communication often consists of such combinations of gestures with writing, reading, mouthing, speaking, and lipreading, among which people move smoothly. And sometimes, people other than the original interlocutors contribute to this mix, without Sujit allowing himself to lose control or oversight over the situation.

People not only write and mouth/speak in combination with gestures; they also use their hands to involve objects. People show objects by tapping them, pointing at them, or holding them: calculators to indicate prices, pointing at pictures and menus to order food, showing samples to customers, or showing weights at vegetable stalls. Our ethnographic film *Ishaare* shows Sujit using a saltshaker when communicating to a waiter that the food was too salty, but also to indicate that the lime soda should be salted (00:08:42) or should not be salted (00:09:16).

Pointing to documents is another important strategy: once when Sujit wanted to order a vegetable sandwich topped with cheese, which was not present in the menu, he pointed in the menu at "vegetable sandwich" and then at the word *cheese* in "cheese sandwich," and then indicating in gestures that the cheese should be on top of the vegetable sandwich.

Gesture is a central part of everyday transaction and communication in the city and is by no means peculiar to deaf people. In Fashion Street, at a road stall that sells clothes, Sujit asked for the price of a shirt by first calling over the vendor by waving his hand, then touching the shirt and gesturing "cost." The vendor responded by speaking "Five fifty. *Paanch sau pachaas* [five hundred and fifty]. Five fifty." Sujit rose his hand as if to ask "five?" and then the vendor and his colleague (standing on his left side, behind the clothes rack) simultaneously gestured and spoke. The vendor on the right gestured "five five zero," simultaneously saying "five five zero," and his colleague gestured "five half," simultaneously saying "five fifty."[3]

In this transaction the price of a shirt is initially offered in two different languages, English and Hindi; the vendor probably assumed that one of those would surely be understood. When Sujit did not respond verbally and rose his hand as if to ask "five?" (to check if he had understood correctly), the vendor and his colleague quickly changed their approach and gestured the information while also speaking. In so doing, they simultaneously offered four different tracks of the same information: both communicated simultaneously in two different modalities (speech and gesture), and both communicated the same information in different ways. In another example, Sujit ordered face cream in a medical shop, and the shopkeeper, understanding that Sujit had asked for something to smear on his face, took out face wash and face cream, expecting that "certainly one product of the two will be the right one" (*Ishaare* 00:06:59). These vendors' quick reformulation of the price in four different simultaneous tracks, or the strategy to offer multiple objects at once, and their ease in doing so suggests that gesturing is not merely a linguistic strategy they use with deaf people.

Communicating effectively in Mumbai is something that people learn through everyday interactions in the city. For instance, while living in Mulund-East during the first three years of our marriage, my daily grocery shopping on the street markets involved much trial and error, especially in the beginning. I had to learn gesturing conventions and marketing scripts. I had to learn the usual price for fruits and vegetables and how to communicate about them. I had to learn to understand the various ways in which hearing people express themselves. Numbers were expressed in multiple ways, such as "ten ten ten ten ten" (with both hands), "five zero," or just "five" to communicate the number fifty. The meaning of number gestures depends on context: in a vegetable stall, "fifteen" is likely to mean ₹15 or ₹150, in a clothes shop ₹150 or ₹1,500, in a mobile phone shop ₹15,000. I also had to learn to interpret whether a number gesture refers to size, weight, amount, price, time, and/or combinations of these. When buying tomatoes, for example, pointing at the tomatoes and gesturing "one" means you want "one kilo of tomatoes" (rather than "one tomato"). A vendor gesturing "one three" could mean "this is ₹13," "you get three of these lemons for ₹10," or "one kilo for ₹300."

FIGURE 34.1 Sujit pointing toward a saltshaker and motioning to grab it, to indicate that the lime sodas should be salted. Screenshot from the film *Ishaare*. Used courtesy of Annelies Kusters, filmmaker.

FIGURE 34.2 Sujit shakes some salt on his palm to indicate that the lime sodas should be salted. Screenshot from the film *Ishaare*. Used courtesy of Annelies Kusters, filmmaker.

FIGURE 34.3 Sujit points at the saltshaker and then shakes his hand to communicate that there should be no salt in one of the lime sodas. Screenshot from the film *Ishaare*. Used courtesy of Annelies Kusters, filmmaker.

Sujit began learning to communicate in Mumbai street gestures in childhood—for instance, while accompanying his mother on shopping trips. Sujit faced communication barriers with hearing people but then often found another way to understand and to make himself understood. He told me stories about how he explored Mumbai on his own during his school holidays. Once as a teenager, he went to Vashi by local train. He had communicated the location via speech to the ticket officer. When the conductor asked him for his ticket to check, Sujit was admonished for having a ticket for Vasai instead. Sujit presented this as a revelatory experience, after which he built up a repertoire of strategies to communicate place names. When booking an auto rickshaw, Sujit would often be understood when he gestured to signify a landmark in the vicinity, such as boat (ferry), train (a nearby train station), shoe (referring to the statue of a shoe in Kamala Nehru Park, to denote the park itself), or beach (a nearby beach), often in combination with pointing in the direction of the place. He would more frequently mouth or write down faraway destinations than near ones (as in the examples above), in combination with pointing and specifications in gestures such as "I'll give directions," "over the flyover," or "on the other side of the tracks."

The learning process can also involve learning to lip-read, mouth, and write unfamiliar words. Sujit went to English-medium schools and had no formal instruction in Marathi in his childhood. Upon the insistence of his

FIGURE 34.4 Sujit raising his hand to ask "five?" Screenshot from the film *Making of Ishaare.* Used courtesy of Annelies Kusters, filmmaker.

father, he learned the Devnagari alphabet so he could decipher bus numbers, shop names, and place names in Mumbai. His extended family speaks Marathi, but his parents and brother have always signed to him. Sujit explains: "I know some Marathi because many vegetable vendors speak Marathi. At first I didn't understand and asked again and again. . . . I practiced the mouth movements in Marathi such as *pau* [250 grams], but I don't know how to spell this word. I just remember mouth movements such as *pau* as a series of pictures in the mind."

Actually, lipreading is mostly educated guesswork for both deaf and hearing people, so it is important to carefully choose the words that are mouthed or spoken and to combine them in helpful ways with gestures. When the vocal tract cannot be accessed and gestures are minimal, Sujit has to do a fair amount of educated guesswork. He is rather good at it. In the example of the rickshaw in Chembur, he understood the woman's question not because he could lipread her but because he could guess what she asked. However, while guessing what a person says often works, it can also lead to misunderstandings when unaccompanied by additional clarifying gestures. For example, Sujit negotiated the price of a T-shirt at a clothes stall on Fashion Street, gesturing to reduce the price. The man nodded and said: "How many pieces?" Sujit, thinking that he asked "How much do you want to give?" gestured "two" [₹200]. The man pointed at the T-shirt he held in his hand and at another one while saying "Two piece? This and this?" Sujit then remedied the misunderstanding.

FIGURES 34.5 AND 34.6 The vendor and his colleague (standing on his left side, behind the clothes rack) simultaneously gesture and speak. The vendor gestures "five five zero," simultaneously saying "five five zero," and his colleague gestures "five half," simultaneously saying "five fifty." Simultaneously, Sujit mirrors "five." Screenshots from the film *Making of Ishaare*. Used courtesy of Annelies Kusters, filmmaker.

While many hearing Mumbai street sellers, shopkeepers, and rickshaw drivers are adept in communicating with a wide range of people of different cultural and linguistic backgrounds, including deaf people, because of Sujit's history of making his way through the city as a deaf signer, he is a master communicator in Mumbai's markets and streets, where so many languages and language modalities are in play. Navigating the city in often trial-and-error ways and making use of his visual skills made him particularly adept at producing and understanding gesture-based communication. Understanding and producing gestures is something Sujit does better, more skillfully, and in more diverse ways than many hearing people do because he is so experienced in it. Being a fluent signer who is also smart and resourceful, who loves his city, and who loves navigating it makes Sujit a master multimodal communicator in Mumbai's multilinguistic domain.

Notes

1. Annelies Kusters, *Deaf Space in Adamorobe: An Ethnographic Study of a Village in Ghana* (Washington, DC: Gallaudet University Press, 2015).

2. Annelies Kusters, *Ishaare: Gestures and Signs in Mumbai*, edited by Visual Box, produced by mpg-mmg, 2015, https://vimeo.com/142245339.

3. Annelies Kusters, *The Making of Ishaare: Gestures and Signs in Mumbai*, edited by Visual Box, produced by mpg-mmg, 2015, https://vimeo.com/142241532.

35 **CHADDA** REPORT MAKER

Prasad Shetty & Rupali Gupte

THERE WAS ALWAYS A NEED FOR small supplies at the Metropolitan Authority Office (MAO)— diaries, small stationery, books, quick exhibition products, models, etc. But the elaborate tendering process for procurements takes time while stationery needs are often urgent. For this reason, another route is available for such "petty purchases": the MAO could officially invite three quotes and then procure the goods and services from the bidder with the lowest one.

At the MAO, whenever there was such a requirement, everyone called Chadda. He had some five companies all doing various kinds of things: printing, retailing of stationery and hardware, event management. Whenever anyone called from the MAO, Chadda would be ready with three quotes from three of his companies, each signed by a different person on different letterheads. He also ensured—by regularly meeting officers, sending gifts for Diwali (Hindu festival of lights), chatting with them about life, and generally maintaining an *accha* (good) relationship—that he and no one else would offer the three quotes.

Chadda's precipitous journey from stationery supplier to infrastructure consultant started when he was called to get some quick surveys done of the Mithi River, which flooded in 2005. The floods had caused havoc in Mumbai and outrage against the government for loss of life and property. The chief minister asked the MAO to provide a report on the river within a fortnight. Chadda was busy putting up stalls for an interior design exhibition when he was summoned to the MAO office. The officers there asked Chadda to quickly get some surveys done of the Mithi River. He had never done anything like this before but quickly figured out that the MAO wanted a document that explained the reason for flooding: a "report." He spoke to some MAO planners who speculated that the river must have flooded because of "illegitimate structures" along its edges that reduced the width of the river, causing constraints on the movement of water and subsequently flooding the area. He realized that he had to prove that the water movement was hampered because the width of the river was reduced by encroachments along the edges. He hired some surveyors and a couple of planners to do a survey of the edges of the river. A drawing was made, and the number of encroachments was calculated. An argument was developed about why the river had flooded, and Chadda became an overnight star.

Word of Chadda's skillful handling of the Mithi River survey spread quickly, and soon the stationer found himself recruited as a subcontractor in surveys of all kinds: head counts, house counts, family counts, traffic counts. Chadda was quick at delivering results, and everyone at the MAO wanted that. Along with sensing the value of primary data, he also figured out that it was quite simple to organize such data. All he needed was some social worker or planner to make questionnaires and some literate people to go out and fill them up.

The 2005 launch of the Urban Renewal Mission by the national government changed everything for Chadda. This initiative aimed to upgrade infrastructure in more than sixty cities with a population of more than one million people. The government's rather straightforward strategy was to simply pump money into these cities. But in order to *get* the money, cities needed to have a clear plan— a set of priority projects and detailed reports on each one. The government's kitty was finite, and cities were to compete for the money; whichever city could make the best project reports and get them approved by the national scrutiny agencies would get the money first. The idea was that this kind of competition would push the cities to plan better, to plan faster, and to build implementation capacities. But that's not what happened; instead, cities turned to consultants. Beginning in 2005, the number of consultants floating around the country increased dramatically. And Chadda joined the bandwagon. Within a few months, he had hired a few engineers and a planner, and had registered his own consultancy company.

Because he had already done a large number of surveys in the metropolitan region of Mumbai, he had an advantage over other consultants in the region.

Chadda's company's first project involved making a detailed project report to develop a solid-waste system for a city near Mumbai. There were already formats for making such reports on the Urban Renewal Mission website. Moreover, he was able to get copies of reports from other consultants. He understood that the required reports were in a standard form and could be easily made with available data. The real challenge was to get the reports approved through the various stages: first by the local municipal representatives, then by the state-level nodal agency, then by the parliamentary and state legislature representatives, then by the evaluation and scrutiny agencies set up by the national government, and finally by the national-level committee of senior bureaucrats. He had to navigate through a series of political, technocratic, and bureaucratic systems.

Aware of these challenges, Chadda decided to build his niche in this field. He found it rather straightforward to get approvals from political representatives, who saw these projects as large contracts from which kickbacks might be earned. Bureaucratic approvals were even more straightforward. With lower-level officials, petty gifts such as iPhones, silverware (usually a small silver idol of Ganesh), gold coins, and winter wear for children did the trick. In the case of mid-level officials, a foreign-study tour or expensive gadgets for children worked wonders. Higher-level officials were trickier because they had to be paid in cash—work that Chadda generally subcontracted to another sort of specialist. The most difficult of all was to get approvals from the technocrats: the people Chadda referred to as the "sincere types." Generally, a good engineering or planning argument worked with technocrats, but sometimes political or bureaucratic pressure had to be used. But Chadda was always a step ahead; he met constantly with all the officers and politicians involved, chatting with them, giving them gifts, and maintaining his "accha relationship." Chadda explained that this made them feel a little indebted toward him, which was always helpful later on. Chadda's expertise, in other words, was not in making good project reports but rather in getting reports approved. And that was precisely what was required by the Urban Renewal Mission.

The mission involved many approval processes: getting the plans and projects accepted, getting funds, getting approvals for implementation, getting good reports from monitoring agencies, etc. Chadda was most useful in lubricating difficult processes. Different governments would use him to get their work approved. Although there were always officers demanding various kinds of bribes, there were equal numbers of people who were adamant about not paying or receiving any bribes and insistent about going through the "right" procedures. Chadda was useful, for he could manage both groups. Also, there were always times when petty requirements had to be fulfilled. A flight ticket to Delhi was the most annoying one because it would require special permission and in the context of hurried processes, there was never time to get approval for such flight tickets, which were exorbitantly priced if purchased at the last moment. At these times, Chadda would not only arrange for flight tickets but also make pick-up and drop-off arrangements. This was his way of maintaining "accha relationships." Moreover, there were always awkward times when officers from Delhi and their family members had to be entertained when they visited. Here again, Chadda would arrange for everything: visits to temples and malls, cars with drivers, hotel arrangements, bar visits, and many more things desired by the officers. During times when officers came for inspections, Chadda would set up special teams for hospitality. For city and state government agencies, Chadda was a boon: he was able to handle all these demanding situations.

Over the years, Chadda has produced reports of all kinds: water supply, sanitation, drainage, housing, transportation, and even e-governance. Today, Chadda Associates is one of the twelve consulting firms approved by the national government to advise it and take up projects across the country in the e-governance sector. Chadda even competes with international consultants for projects. Not infrequently, he even manages to get them.

36 **PRAKASH** DATA ENTREPRENEUR

Amita Bhide

IN 2018 THE SETTLEMENT of Bhim Nagar in Govandi was demolished without warning by the *Mumbai Municipal Corporation* (BMC). Because the neighborhood (which is situated on state government land) had come into existence on the wrong side of the 2001 *cutoff date*[1] Bhim Nagar's 1,500 families had been evicted from their homes without any provision for alternate housing. A team from the Tata Institute of Social Sciences (TISS), where I work, has been engaged in improving the human development situation in Bhim Nagar and neighboring localities since 2011, so leaders from the settlement called us up to discuss what could be done. We were scrambling for some way forward when I received a call from Prakash. He not only knew of the neighborhood, he knew something else as well: the plot of land on which Bhim Nagar's now-crushed homes were situated fell within the scope of an upcoming infrastructure upgrading initiative—the Mumbai Metro project, for which his small consultancy firm was conducting a basic socioeconomic survey (BSES) of households to be resettled. Wielding this crucial piece of knowledge, Prakash obtained permission from the "principal contractor" (that is, the one that had been contracted by the Mumbai Metropolitan Regional Development Authority [MMRDA] for the survey project and that had chosen Prakash's own small company as a subcontractor) to survey the demolished structures, which fell inside the project zone but which until that point had not been scheduled for inclusion in the survey. By surveying the residents of the now-demolished structures, Prakash was able to demonstrate the structures' earlier existence and thus their former residents' eligibility for compensation as "project-affected persons" in conjunction with the upcoming project. Prakash's initiative succeeded in convincing the state authorities to agree in principle to include these re-created structures and residents in the rehabilitation component of the project.

The ingenious and creative ways that Prakash uses his knowledge have impressed me ever since I first met him sometime in 1992, when he was young and boyish, ever enthusiastic, an earnest expression always animating his round, pimply face. He was short, bespectacled, and about twenty years old. It was the start of India's Adult Literacy campaign, a nationwide initiative that had a particularly strong presence in the slums of Chembur, Mankhurd, and Govandi: the backyard of the Tata Institute of Social Sciences, which I had recently joined as a professor of social work. My students and I were keen to become involved in the literacy campaign and had sought some help in figuring out what it might mean to "do literacy work in informal settlements." Prakash had grown up in a nearby settlement called Sunderbaug, which means "Beautiful Garden": a cluster of two hundred or so humble huts (some of bamboo and tin, others of brick and mortar) tucked between the Deonar Bus Depot and an industrial estate. He had recently passed his high school exams and had just enrolled in a college degree program (no small feat in a neighborhood where regular power cuts meant he was often unable to study after sunset), all while holding down a full-time job as a housecleaner. It was from this already-packed schedule that Prakash carved endless hours to devote to the literacy campaign, becoming one of the area's most active volunteers. It was in this context—of the literacy campaign—that I met the young man, who would go on to introduce me and my students to community leaders throughout the eastern suburbs, teaching us how to enroll learners and start classes. Prakash was an inspiration and a role model who taught me about the agency, the fighting spirit, and the aspirations of Mumbaikars, who are often imagined flatly as "the poor" or else vilified as "encroachers." Instead, Prakash seemed the embodiment of aspiration and change, and he encouraged others to follow.

Years later, in 2006, Prakash registered an organization called the Team of Research Investigators and Process Services (TRIPS) that consolidated the expertise he had gained during nearly two decades of piecemeal work, and he officially made knowledge his business. His work encompasses the diverse worlds of knowledge production inhabited by academics, researchers, non-governmental organizations, private-sector consultants, and various state authorities. Prakash does not call himself a researcher. Rather, he explains, he works *for* researchers: collecting information about the city (especially its poorer neighborhoods), processing it as "data," and then providing these data to people and institutions who want or need them but lack either the time or desire to navigate the messy entanglements of producing knowledge, especially in difficult places like "slums." Prakash's data services thus connect diverse scales and circuits of knowledge from the micro-local to the transnational. His presence in these circuits is largely invisible and is rarely reflected in authorships, acknowledged by primary consultancies, or given credit in the acknowledgments sections of academic works. Yet he is also indispensable to several of the actors who represent the visible parts of the knowledge economy, helping them decipher and peek into the life worlds of the poor and the unmapped in villages and informal settlements. In the process he has managed to establish a business, eking out a comfortable life for himself while employing a few others as well. Knowledge is power, as Prakash well knows, and he thus conducts his work according to his own code of provisional and practical ethics. He deftly and carefully navigates between words and worlds, concepts and concrete, rules and realities in a city where distances between empowered categories and everyday life on ground are great.

PRAKASH WAS BORN IN A SMALL VILLAGE in western Maharashtra. When he was still a small child, his parents moved to Bombay, leaving Prakash and his two brothers in the care of relatives to complete primary education in the village school. When Prakash was around ten, the three brothers came to Bombay to join their parents, who had by then bought a house in Sunderbaug. In Bombay, Prakash struggled to balance his studies with a series of odd jobs: as a domestic worker, waiting tables at a bar, working in a small-scale factory, and sweeping floors at TISS, which is where I first met him. The adult literacy campaign ignited an activist flame in the young Prakash, who had already been exposed to "development work" by his association with former TISS faculty member Dr. Madhav Chavan,[2] a key organizer of the literacy campaign, in whose home Prakash was employed as domestic worker. As a teenager, Prakash had been inspired by Professor Chavan to organize a literacy class in Sunderbaug, aided by two petromax lamps donated by the main campaign organizer. Prakash was gradually pulled into this work on a full-time basis, moving from literacy to social awareness and mobilization, and finally joining Dr. Chavan on a full-time basis when the professor founded the NGO Pratham, a mission for enhancing primary education in the city. Prakash showed aptitude for such work: the ability to collaborate with people of widely different backgrounds and orientations, convert ideas into practical programs on the ground, innovate with strategies, and communicate the significance of the work in terms that resonated with multiple audiences. His career was on an upward path in close parallel with the growth of Pratham. Prakash was given opportunities to oversee educational work in two administrative wards in Mumbai, participate in international conferences, and extend Pratham's work in the Raigad district and in Pune.

The year 1997 brought a series of crises in Prakash's life: Sunderbaug was demolished, and his home was constantly under threat. Dr. Chavan shifted to Delhi, and Pratham's work in Mumbai and Maharashtra was becoming more professionalized. In this context, as a person with high levels of skill and passion but no formal training or credentials, Prakash found himself without a clear path. "NGOs provide work to an enormous number of people," Prakash reflected, "but they offer little opportunities for real advancement or self-development." That same year, Prakash's choice of a life partner from a lower caste unleashed family conflict.

After the Sunderbaug demolition spree calmed down and his life resumed a measure of normality, Prakash began work independently on a series of data-collection projects. Then, in 2001, Prakash joined one of my own projects: a study of the use of slum-rehabilitation schemes in Mumbai that had been commissioned by the Maharashtra's Slum Rehabilitation Authority. In the course of the project, Prakash developed an intense interest in issues pertaining to land and housing. He went on to work with a developer that was formulating a project around redevelopment of Dharavi.[3] He also worked briefly with a globally connected Mumbai-based NGO called the Society for Promotion of Area Resource Centres (SPARC), which uses "self-surveys" as a claims-making strategy. As SPARC's website explains, "Self-conducted enumerations and surveys allow communities to speak from a position of knowledge, and give the poor ownership over information that is critical for understanding collective conditions, legitimizing claims to land and benefits, identifying real solutions, and negotiating with authorities. Recognizing the accuracy of community-led surveys, authorities have increasingly partnered with us on slum surveys, ranging from citywide slum counting and profiling to detailed socioeconomic baseline surveys for upgrading or resettlement projects, often used for eligibility determination."[4] Prakash recalled how his experience with SPARC "gave me an insight into the mechanics, power, and politics of censuses, surveys. I learnt that primary data was an important resource."

Prakash launched TRIPS as a family firm, run out of a small space above his home in Sunderbaug, out of which he, his wife, and a handful of employees conduct studies and process data. It was through his earlier work with me and other organizations regarding "surveys" that Prakash discovered an untapped market: Mumbai was full of researchers, many having considerable understanding of "the field" but with little time to carry out the ever-fresh rounds of empirical data collection so essential for academic degrees and scholarly publications. Some of these studies are linked to development plan reservations and land ownership, and others are large-scale population surveys on subjects ranging from education to occupational health and political participation. There are surveys of socioeconomic conditions among particular "groups": Scheduled Castes and Tribes residing in Mumbai, for instance. Prakash estimates that he and his team of researchers have so far contributed to the research underpinning more than sixty doctoral dissertations. A handful of these were projects for researchers from outside India who are unfamiliar with local languages, but most of the studies were carried out to help India-based scholars. TRIPS fits neatly into the emerging "business" of Indian academia, where a doctorate often has an instrumental value. He shares his observations frankly: "While many foreign researchers act as co-investigators, Indian researchers mostly just outsource their entire studies to us." Perhaps especially in such cases, the presence of TRIPS is rarely acknowledged.

A second major source of clientele for Prakash is the booming Mumbai industry of "slum" surveys and studies. Over the last decade and a half, informal settlements have emerged as a frontier of contestation in Indian cities: they are bound up with the high-stakes markets of urban land and housing. Surveying households and their land assets is the base on which entitlements and subsequent policies are determined. Although NGOs previously occupied this space, private-sector players have more recently entered it. Prakash's firm has developed an expertise in conducting such studies and collecting ground-level data, linking this knowledge base to land records and GIS tools, often as a subcontractor or even a sub-subcontractor. Some of the surveys in which Prakash has played a role are in Dharavi (one of the most contested redevelopments in Mumbai in the recent past), in BDD Chawls (also a highly contested redevelopment project), and among households affected by upcoming infrastructure projects in the city (the Mumbai Metro, for instance). TRIPS does not feature as a primary contractor or the consultant in these studies and thus is not visible as a key player in a field dominated by consultants, academic, or research organizations and NGOs. On the other hand, he has clients across all these institutions.

A third group of Prakash's clients is in the world of "social-impact assessment" (SIA). These assessments comprise studies of socioeconomic baselines of people in proposed project areas and are aimed at assessing the vulnerabilities, the project's impacts on people, and possible mitigation measures and compensations. This is a field that has been opened up through new legislation for land acquisition, which has made environmental- and social-impact analysis mandatory for infrastructure projects. Both project proponents and state actors are committed to the cause of attracting investment, and "sustainable development" can seem more of a fad than anything else. In this context, SIAs and environmental-impact assessments (EIAs) are bothersome rituals rather than meaningful processes that might inform or moderate project-related decisions. Thus emerges a space that academics have abdicated and is inhabited by consultants. As Prakash points out, it is politically sensitive work as well: the people who are being studied often have little information about the projects in conjunction with which they are being assessed. The high-stakes nature of such projects means as well that information about research findings—real or rumored—is easily put into circulation for political purposes. "What happens to project-affected people doesn't really matter too much for most agencies," he observes, drawing on his first-hand experience. He has learned that "the results of a social-impact assessment can usually be foretold" and that "authors or creators of reports often lack expertise and are frequently even unable to make sense of data that we give them."[5] Prakash has undertaken SIAs for various kinds of projects: freight corridors, airports, base profiles for "financial inclusion" schemes, skill-development programs, and surveys of corporate social responsibility project impacts. He has developed a regular business in this stream, and his services generally command about 5–10 percent of the total project cost.[6]

This is a space with few standards or ethical guidelines and much methodological confusion. Experiences like these have propelled Prakash to develop his own system of ethics in his practices. He believes that primary data—that is, data generated through direct interaction with people—are of critical importance at the current juncture, where land, resources, and their management are at a transitional point in India. Ethical challenges faced at this tail end of research are linked to an imperative to engage with local communities whose cooperation is essential for such a task. It is partly also linked to Prakash's own background as a person who has struggled through adverse socioeconomic circumstances and who stays in an informal settlement. Prakash believes that many firms are unable to generate primary data because they are unable to explain the purpose behind studies to the research subjects, and so are denied access. In his own practice, therefore, the principles that he has adopted are to give sufficient time to explain the purpose of a particular study and the potential power of knowledge that will be produced. He also ensures that data are returned to the communities where they were generated. He makes a point of following up with communities in which he has carried out research. He is especially proud of the role played by his team in difficult field sites such as the Dharavi Redevelopment Project and the BDD Chawls, localities where investigators were initially refused entry and where sentiments were stacked against the projects.

His role as an on-the-ground investigator, needless to say, provides Prakash with access to information of multiple kinds. This itself is a source of power. Prakash has access to sensitive and key information in advance of many projects in Mumbai as well as in other regions throughout Maharashtra. He has access to detailed records of landholdings, development plan reservations (and changes), and information regarding actual land occupancy in Mumbai. He applies this knowledge in creative (and sometimes subversive) ways, according to his own system of practical ethics. Back home in Sunderbaug, for instance, his own home remains vulnerable. Through his regular contact with development projects, plans, and city planners, Prakash recently learned that plans had been approved for a road that would slice the Beautiful Garden in two. The original position of the road passed next to the bus depot, but he learned through a contact at the municipal planning office that the plan was changed in order to protect a building, one that Prakash knew to have been illegally constructed (with political backing) on public lands. Armed with this information, Prakash created a strong case for the restoration of alignment and removal of road reservations in Sunderbaug, using documentary evidence, GIS, and plan maps. His practice thus interweaves personal, communitarian, and business agendas.

Although Prakash's work sits at the tail end of the research and knowledge economy, he strives to expand the capacities and scales at which TRIPS operates. From a sole proprietorship he has moved to form a company that now employs five people (in addition to himself and his wife). He has developed his technical capacities and now complements socioeconomic studies with those linked to GIS, the capacities of data processing, and now the use of tablets, and he has transitioned from a proprietorship to a registered company: JD Group of Social Research and Processing Services. In 2017, in an effort to expand the range of services he can provide—and in light of his growing awareness of the importance of land laws—Prakash began to study for a degree in law.

EVERY TIME I MEET WITH PRAKASH, his stories fill me with questions and curiosity, discomfort and wonder at Mumbai's knowledge economy—at its operations and the speed at which it has grown. There is no doubt that "knowledge economy" is today a global field that engages several entities: international organizations, governments, bilaterals, corporates, funders, academic organizations, think tanks, consultants, and civil society organizations. Several of these circuits existed for a long time as unlinked, parallel circuits that did not even acknowledge one another's existence.

Prakash's experience demonstrates how circuits of knowledge at multiple scales have begun to intersect in multiple ways and how distinctions between knowledges have become diffuse. He is located at the cusp of these intersecting circuits and is a part of the practices described above. The "opportunities" that are his "business" raise extremely uncomfortable questions about the state of knowledge and the process of producing and disseminating the same. Prakash has found a niche business located in the labyrinthine complexity of the city—material, legal-institutional, linguistic. He moves easily through the complex social and spatial layers of the city, the product of his expertise imperceptibly shaping things from the ground up, enabling the entitlements and inclusion of several parties who are otherwise unable to advocate policy at the top rungs and transform the obsession with real estate development by inserting some pragmatism within it, in some instances.

A key issue that the narrative highlights is the importance of "primary data" and the relative inaccessibility of the "ground" to the institutions and actors who are active, key players in the myriad urban development projects underway in the city. This is what makes Prakash's skills so indispensable . . . and powerful. His personal growth trajectory has made him develop forms of practice and ethics that lead him to develop more accountable relationships with the communities from which data are extracted and engage in attempts to reverse some of this "extractive" relationship. However, such personalization is highly vulnerable because of its position at the tail end of knowledge. Yet the importance of primary data, their invisibility, and Prakash's own practices, such as in the Bhim Nagar situation, problematize the notion that knowledge production is a top-down, one-way process. Knowledge is always in formation, vulnerable to subversion by the porosities and possibilities inhering in its production.

Notes

1. See also the discussion in the part VI introduction.

2. Dr. Madhav Chavan taught at the university Department of Chemical Technology and initiated a mission approach to literacy in 1990 wherein he invoked a plethora of governmental and nongovernmental institutions and volunteers to achieve total literacy in a defined time period.

3. Dharavi is often described as Asia's largest slum.

4. Society for the Promotion of Area Resource Centers (SPARC), "Enumerations, Mappings and Surveys," www.sparcindia.org/enumerations.php.

5. See the profile by Shetty and Gupte (chapter 35).

6. SIAS themselves represent roughly 1–2 percent of overall project costs.

CONCLUSION OTHER PLACES, OTHER TIMES
Lisa Mitchell

IN JULY 1792, Avadhanam Paupiah, a *dubash* in the South Indian city of Madras, was convicted of conspiracy for forging evidence against his employer's chief rival in one of the most famous trials of that era.[1] As combined translator, cultural intermediary, agent, and economic middleman, the dubash in eighteenth-century southern India mediated not only commercial exchanges but also linguistic and cultural differences. Admired, feared, relied upon, and reviled (not always by the same people), dubashes—like many of the people portrayed in this book—operated within often invisible interstices, facilitating action and sometimes wielding great power but also attracting deep ambivalence, critique, and accusations of corruption. Paupiah's three-day trial, which included more than twenty-seven hours of testimony, resulted in his sentence of imprisonment for three years, a fine of two thousand pounds, and one hour in the pillory (the last remitted in response to the jury's recommendation of leniency).[2] However, his employers at the time—John Holland, acting governor of Madras and his brother, Edward Holland, third member of Council and president of the Board of Revenue—retired with their vastly larger fortunes to England, escaping prosecution.[3]

As a touchstone for the rapidly changing values of the time, the life and fortunes of Avadhanam Paupiah can be seen as a window into the shifting dominance of competing structures of power and meaning. And, in conversation with the profiles presented in this book, his life can prompt us to consider how the methodological innovations of this volume can use the close attention to brokerage to productively intervene within conversations elsewhere. Recalling Björkman's opening definition of *brokerage* as "the morally fraught but socially necessary work of transgression, translation, and transborder navigation," we can use Paupiah to demonstrate that rather than being about Bombay per se, or even about the present moment, this volume seeks to use the various attentions, ambivalences, and accusations that intermediary figures attract as indices that point to broader, multi-scalar, historical-political shifts. To mobilize the interventions of the preceding portraits of Bombay brokers for the consideration of other times and places, then, I offer a conclusion to this volume that illustrates and reinforces three key arguments.

First, the role of brokers is never static but is always changing—indeed, the effectiveness of brokerage depends on its ability to negotiate change—whether in the form of growth (often of different things at different speeds: populations, resources, commodities, demand), rapid confrontations of difference, new goals or desires, or the appearance of new poles of power or prestige. We can therefore use attention to intermediaries as effective pointers to help us better understand exactly *what* is changing within wider circuits of knowledge, practice, and meaning. Putting the practices of eighteenth-century *dubashes* into conversation with those of the people profiled in this book, we can see more clearly that particular types of brokerage work often emerge at times of transition, transformation, or confrontation of multiple intersecting systems of meaning.

An illustration of this point can be seen in the shifting significance of the category of the dubash over the course of the eighteenth century. The historian A. V. Venkatarama Ayyar, writing in 1929, offers us the following definition:

The Dubashes are a class peculiar to South India and in the early days of the East India Company they played a prominent part in its affairs. The word *Dubash* (Hindustani *Dubhāshia, Dobāshi* literally a man of two languages) means an interpreter. They were first employed as interpreters between foreign European traders on the one side and the sons of the soil on the other. In the course of time they combined the post of broker with that of an interpreter. The post became lucrative and they were held in high esteem.[4]

Avadhanam Paupiah, described as belonging to "a poor but learned Brahmin family in Nellore District," began his career as a humble *gumasta* (clerk) in the East India Company's Sea Customs office, with many from his community network already employed by the British in Madras.[5] His eventual employment by the Holland brothers helped make him one of the most powerful dubashes in the city and an object of both admiration and fear. He was described as "one of the most talented but notorious of that class who flourished in the latter half of the 18th and the beginning of the 19th century."[6] Historian Susan Neild-Basu writes that it was their "dual identity with the dominant agrarian castes of the region and with former local bureaucracies which made these dubashes such effective and valued associates of the Company at a time when its political and administrative interests were beginning to overshadow its commercial involvements," suggesting that they were valued for their unique knowledge and connections at a time when these attributes were indispensable.[7]

Yet dubashes were also figures around which great ambivalence collected by the end of the eighteenth century. Lionel Place, collector of what the British referred to as the Jaghir (later the Chengalpattu District) from 1794 to 1799, called them "a debased creation," "ignorant to an extreme," and a "diabolical race of men," commenting that "these sorts of knowledge which should seem necessary to their vocation are supplied by cunning and the art of circumvention." He argued that their influence had grown disproportionately in recent years and that the local population needed to be liberated from "the shackles of Dubash Domination."[8] By the early nineteenth century, their influence had come to be characterized as "evil" and the term had become a derogatory label, with the verb *dubashed* used to indicate that one had been swindled or outsmarted.[9] So notorious did Paupiah become among Europeans that he was portrayed as a villain in Sir Walter Scott's 1827 novel, *The Surgeon's Daughter*, in which he is presented as lacking in honor and consumed by schemes and machinations. One of the characters finds the "artful Hindoo" Paupiah by approaching "that necessary appurtenance of every government, a back stair, which, in its turn, conducted him to the office of the Bramin Paupiah, the Dubash, or steward of the great man [the president of the Council at Madras], and by whose means chiefly he communicated with the native courts, and carried on many mysterious intrigues, which he did not communicate to his brethren at the council-board."[10] Of the man himself, he writes, "the thin dusky form . . . wrapped in robes of muslin embroidered with gold, was that of Paupiah, known as a master-counsellor of dark projects, an Oriental Machiavel, whose premature wrinkles were the result of many an intrigue in which the existence of the poor, the happiness of the rich, the honour of men, and the chastity of women had been sacrificed without scruple to attain political or private advantage."[11]

Still others blamed the corruption of dubashes on the influence of East India Company officials, portraying dubashes more as victims than as victimizers. "Paupiah was a typical Dubash of the lower type," writes C. S. Srinivasachari, "but his corruption was largely a consequence of the corruption in which even some of the Europeans themselves indulged."[12] Venkatarama Ayyar concurs, observing that "in fairness however, to Paupiah it must be said that he is more sinned against than sinning and that he was not the sole offender but rather an unscrupulous but effective instrument in the hands of others whose high station rendered the acts with which they had been charged, infinitely more criminal in them than in Paupiah," describing the Holland brothers as his "political but evil-minded superior[s]."[13] And Neild-Basu writes that "the notoriety ascribed to the late eighteenth-century Madras dubashes arose largely from their active participation in the freewheeling political intrigues and financial dealings of the era. In this they were only following the lead, and often the explicit directions, of their English patrons. . . . Charges of oppression and extortion of merchants were commonly laid against them, but only after their patrons had departed and their cloak of invulnerability removed."[14] Eugene Irschick similarly sees dubashes as standing "simply as a symbol of British bewilderment and powerlessness in the face of an apparently inscrutable local system," recognizing that they "provided a site important in the production of knowledge," connecting "an extensive network reaching the area outside Madras town."[15]

Few of these condemnatory portrayals, however, seek to understand how dubashes and their expertise were understood by those who enlisted their services. Kanakalatha Mukund suggests that, in fact, the respect commanded by dubashes among local people in the villages of the presidency offered competition to the East India Company's government at Madras and threatened to undermine its authority. With the decline of the demand for Indian textiles in England, brought about by the industrializing cloth industry in Britain, the East India Company increasingly turned its attention to administration and revenue collection. After 1783, the East India Company sought to increase local revenue assessments, a move that met with fierce local resentment and opposition. Needless to say, this opposition was often led by dubashes, who sought "to gain the loyalty of the inhabitants" by accepting "all the claims of the latter about the shares of the crops between the cultivator and revenue officers, and the various customary claims on the produce by the agricultural laborers."[16] Dubashes often attempted to set themselves up as patrons in their own right: endowing temples; supporting poets, dancers, and musicians; funding festivals; and hosting feasts.[17] Rather than preceding colonial interventions, new manifestations of practices such as perjury, deception, and forgery among native actors can be seen as having been produced by the expanded attestation procedures, discretionary authority, and surveillance powers that were extended to upper-level British administrators during this period.[18]

Ultimately, however, dubashes were actors whose historical role was short-lived.[19] We see a range of evidence for the declining significance of the figure of the dubash. Neild-Basu suggests that "by the early 1800s the term *dubash* had nearly disappeared from official nomenclature (except in some private businesses and households), owing as much perhaps to its negative associations as to its unspecified meaning in an age of greater administrative complexity." Part of the reason for this, she explains, is that "many of the jobs which had been performed . . . by a single dubash in the more loosely structured eighteenth-century Company government were now more precisely labeled as 'interpreter,' 'accountant,' 'secretary,' or 'manager.'"[20] We can also see the waning import of the dubash mirrored in the words of Walter Scott's narrator, Chrystal Croftangry: "It is scarce necessary to say that such things could only be acted in the earlier period of our Indian settlements, when the check of the Directors was imperfect, and that of the crown did not exist. My friend Mr. Fairscribe is of opinion, that there is an anachronism in the introduction of Paupiah, the Bramin Dubash of the English governor."[21] By the publication of Scott's novel in 1827, the figure of the dubash had already become anachronistic. British authority had largely succeeded in displacing the value of local forms of knowledge and expertise, and dubashes were no longer able to offer significant challenges to the authority of the East India Company. English education was increasingly replacing earlier markers of scholarship, and employment in the company administration had come to be seen as the most coveted path to social mobility.[22]

Second, this volume is interested in how the labors of particular individuals in a specific place and time embody larger translocal processes. Brokerage work—sometimes visible labor but also labor that is not transparent and can take place almost entirely behind the scenes—mediates contradictions and lubricates frictions (often new or novel frictions), and close attention to brokers can therefore offer unique methodological entry points into understanding both local and more-global processes of transformation. The profiles in this book not only offer insights into the preexisting conditions and ongoing labors that produce the skills, networks, and knowledge bases that make intermediaries able to carry out particular acts of brokerage but also reveal the discursive and material labor (carried out both by brokers and by those who seek to disenfranchise or usurp them) that goes into creating, challenging, maintaining, and defending the boundaries of institutional forms of authority and that makes the policies, laws, certification procedures, and identities associated with them appear unproblematic and self-evident, particularly at moments of upheaval or transition. The profiles thus draw attention to the fact that distinctions between licit and illicit activity, or between "expert" and "nonexpert" forms of knowledge, are often discursive rather than empirical. These profiles together offer a methodological intervention that seeks to reveal the framing mechanisms that produce and legitimate the categories and meanings within which each actor operates, and that influence who gets to be identified as an "expert" or why some activities are regarded as legitimate while others are not.

Avadhanam Paupiah was not the only dubash to be convicted of crimes in late eighteenth-century India.[23] Although the British expressed anxiety about dubashes as a class and by the early nineteenth century sought means of altering the broader structure of dependence upon them, they were subjected to trial and found guilty of misdoings as individuals, while their British employers largely escaped without censure (most with vastly larger fortunes than those ever accumulated by dubashes). Those labeled as dubashes were often penalized for possessing the very skills for which they were originally hired. And yet dubashes, like many brokers who excel at what they do, benefited from hereditary caste and familial connections, as well as from early immersion in a culture of literacy and multilingualism and a well-developed system of apprenticeships, all of which offered strategic advantages and positioned Brahmin dubashes to take advantage of the new economic opportunities offered by the presence of Europeans, first as traders with their links to foreign markets and later as administrators who intensified revenue collections.[24] But their power largely depended on their relationship with their employers, and as the East India Company gained a monopoly over trade and strengthened its authority in the subcontinent by the end of the eighteenth century, the labor of intermediaries increasingly began to be seen as eating away at the middle of the value chain. This became even more evident as the company's interests shifted from trade to revenue collection, and any decrease in the bottom line became suspect.

Finally, attending to brokers and their practices of brokerage enables us to bring into focus the ways in which this work—in conjunction with the "legal-institutional [and] discursive mechanisms" referred to by Björkman in the introduction—serves to produce, define, and alter definitions of the legal and the illegal, the criminal and the political, the public and the private, individual interests versus those of collectives, the formal and the informal, and expert knowledge versus nonexpert knowledge. An example of this can be seen in the dramatic changes that occurred over the eighteenth century in relation to one specific practice with which dubashes were frequently associated: that of giving and receiving gifts.

P. J. Marshall reminds us that in the earliest days of the East India Company, "Company servants were paid small salaries and were permitted to provide for themselves out of the profit of private trade."[25] In addition, there was not just a tolerance of gift exchanges as a means of lubricating channels of economic exchange, but such exchanges were often represented as essential for establishing diplomatic relations and the political legitimacy that enabled the assumption of state-like administrative functions.[26] But as the company's authority expanded, such practices began to be redefined: they were no longer essential features of diplomacy but increasingly seen as corruption and as evidence of the "venality" and inferiority of local Indians employed by the company. In 1765 a covenant was introduced that required East India Company officers to agree not to accept gifts valued at more than four thousand rupees and to seek approval for gifts worth more than one thousand rupees. The covenant was expanded in 1770 to prohibit the acceptance of "any Gift, Reward, Gratuity, Allowance, Compensation" from any trading partner, but even this was slow to affect the exchange of gifts in practice.[27] These introductions were aimed primarily at eliminating corruption among the company's European employees. However, in a speech to the House of Commons in 1772, Robert Clive sought to defend the actions of the company's servants and displace blame for their "corrupt" practices onto local employees:

> Indostan was always an absolute despotic Government. The inhabitants, especially of Bengal, in inferior stations, are servile, mean, submissive, and humble. In superior stations, they are luxurious, effeminate, tyrannical, treacherous, venal, cruel. . . .

From time immemorial it has been the custom of that Country, for an inferior never to come into the presence of a superior without a Present. It begins at the Nabob, and ends at the lowest man that has an inferior. . . . The Company's servants have ever been accustomed to receive Presents. Even before we took part in the country troubles, when our possessions were very confined and limited, the Governor and others used to receive Presents; and I will take upon me to assert, that there has not been an Officer commanding his Majesty's Fleet; nor an officer commanding his Majesty's Army; not a Governor, not a Member of Council, not any other Person, civil or military, in such a station as to have connection with the Country Government, who has not received Presents. With regard to Bengal, there they flow in abundance indeed. . . . The Company's servants, however, have not been the authors of those acts of violence and oppression, of which it is the fashion to accuse them. Such crimes are committed by the natives of the Country acting as their Agents and for the most part without their knowledge.[28]

Comparing local brokers and intermediaries upon whom the British were dependent to the seductions of a beautiful women, Clive continues:

Now the Banyan [broker, intermediary] is the fair lady to the Company's servant. He lays his bags of silver before him to-day; Gold to-morrow; Jewels the next day; and, if these fail, he then tempts him in the way of his profession, which is Trade. He assures him that Goods may be had cheap, and sold to great advantage up the Country. In this manner is the attack carried on; and the Company's servant has no resource, for he cannot fly. In short, flesh and blood cannot bear it.[29]

The following year, Parliament passed the Regulating Act of 1773, further constraining the behavior of East India Company servants and marking the entrance of the British government into the administration of India.[30] By 1829, however, Sir Edward Colebrooke was still arguing that "the proscription of such social practices undermined the ties between the British and the Indians, for whom gift-giving also held important social functions."[31]

Dubashes were not just vilified from above, however. In a 1790 petition presented to the East India Company, the "shopkeepers of Beetle [Betel] and Tobacca against Suncoo Chinna Kistnama Chetty" related their longstanding battle against Chetty for "selling inferior product at higher prices" and failing to follow the "established Rule or Custom among former Renters to burn or otherwise destroy all damaged and immerchantable Tobacco as unfit for use," but instead "mix[ing] it with other Tobacco and sell[ing] it at the above Extravagant prices as good and merchantable in full Breach and Contempt of the Conditions of the said Cowle [1787 agreement with the East India Company]." They accused Avadhanam Paupiah of reneging on a promise he had made to them to "give Severe Justice" to Chetty, arguing that this was because Chetty had "sent for the Governor's said Dubash [Paupiah] to his House and gave or presented him a Ear Jewels set with Emeralds worth of about 6 or 700 Pagoda which the whole People of Madras kew [sic] well."[32]

Mattison Mines has argued that up until the end of the eighteenth century, Madras and its surroundings represented "a kind of frontier society, where zamindari rule and a rough, merchant's sense of common law combined." The weak administration during this period, which we might characterize as an earlier era of interregnum, meant that "society was highly personalized, antagonisms were rife, and relationships constantly in flux, a product of personal competition and opportunistic alliances between individuals rather than of Company hegemony or even of local social hierarchy."[33] However, this "plasticity" did not continue into the nineteenth century. As the institutional power of the East India Company solidified and new values and categories were empowered—these new meanings achieving hegemony across the economic and social spectrum—the import and social salience of brokerage faded. But the life of Paupiah—like the lives of all of the people profiled in this book—makes visible both the boundaries of the frames through which we understand action, as well as the materials, objects, people, and practices that simultaneously conjure as well as exceed, challenge, and disturb those boundaries.

Notes

1. He was later accused of forging bonds in a second case but died before the case was tried.

2. A. V. Venkatarama Ayyar, "Dubash Avadhanum Paupiah and a Famous Madras Trial," paper read at the Twelfth Public Meeting of the Indian Historical Records Commission, Guntur, 1929 (Calcutta: Government of India Press, 1930), 34.

3. Venkatarama Ayyar, "Dubash Avadhanum Paupiah," 29.

4. Venkatarama Ayyar, "Dubash Avadhanum Paupiah," 29.

5. Venkatarama Ayyar, "Dubash Avadhanum Paupiah," 28.

6. Venkatarama Ayyar, "Dubash Avadhanum Paupiah," 1.

7. Susan Neild-Basu, "The Dubashes of Madras," Modern Asian Studies 18, no. 1 (1984): 14.

8. Lionel Place, "Report on the Jaghir," Madras Board of Revenue, Misc., vol. 45, Tamil Nadu Archives, July 1, 1799.

9. Neild-Basu, "The Dubashes," 3.

10. Sir Walter Scott, *Chronicles of the Canongate*, vol. II, *The Surgeon's Daughter* (Paris: A. and W. Galignani, 1927), 253, 247.

11. Scott, *Chronicles*, 248.

12. C. S. Srinivasachari, *History of the City of Madras* (Madras: P. Varadachary & Co., 1939), 197.

13. Venkatarama Ayyar, "Dubash Avadhanum Paupiah," 36.

14. Neild-Basu, "The Dubashes," 8.

15. Eugene Irschick, *Dialogue and History: Constructing South India, 1795-1895* (Berkeley: University of California Press, 1994), 73.

16. Kanakalatha Mukund, *The View from Below: Indigenous Society, Temples and the Early Colonial State in Tamilnadu, 1700-1835* (New Delhi: Orient Longman, 2005), 154.

17. Kanakalatha Mukund, "New Social Elites and the Early Colonial State: Construction of Identity and Patronage in Madras," *Economic and Political Weekly* 38, no. 27 (2003): 2860-61.

18. Bhavani Raman, "The Duplicity of Paper: Counterfeit, Discretion, and Bureaucratic Authority in Early Colonial Madras," *Comparative Studies in Society and History* 54, no. 2 (2012): 229-50. See also the discussion of the British "information panic" of the early nineteenth century: "the feeling of the fledgling colonial administration that it knew nothing of local society and that the locals were combining to deny it information" (C. A. Bayly, *Empire and Information: Intelligence Gathering and Social Communication in India, 1780-1870* [Cambridge: Cambridge University Press, 1999], 174).

19. Raman, "The Duplicity of Paper," 16.

20. Neild-Basu, "The Dubashes," 4-5.

21. Scott, *Chronicles*, 252. See also later editions in which this comment is converted into a footnote—e.g., Walter Scott, *The Novels of Sir Walter Scott, with All His Introductions and Notes*, vol. V, *The Surgeon's Daughter* (Edinburgh: Robert Cadell, 1847), 737. The new Edinburgh edition of the Waverley Novels republished the *Chronicles of Canongate* in 2001. In the editors' synopsis of the work, they observed that "each of the stories and Croftangry's narrative may be read independently, but together they constitute a themed work in which the narrator treats of the cultural conflicts in the new Britain and its growing empire in the thirty years from 1756," reinforcing the idea that the work sought to capture a period of rapid transformation and that the dubash figure reached its pinnacle during these years.

22. By 1835, the English Education Act had formalized the privileging by the British administration in India of English education over that in Sanskrit, Persian, or vernacular languages of the subcontinent. See also Thomas Babington Macaulay, "Minute by the Honorable T. B. Macaulay, 2nd February, 1835," in H. Sharp, ed., *Selections from Educational Records*, part I (1781-1839) (Calcutta: Government Printing, 1920), 107-17.

23. Paupiah's brother Avadhanam Ramaswamy, along with Sankarapuram Venkatachella Chetty and Appayyangar Bramin, were tried along with him in 1792, and all were convicted (Venkatarama Ayyar, "Dubash Avadhanum Paupiah," 32–33). Another dubash, Pachaiyappa Mudaliar, was charged with "usury and extortion," and his relative, Manali Chinnia Mudaliar, was charged with "misuse of power." Yet another, Venkataranga Pillai, was charged with "embezzlement and collusion in bribery," which resulted not only in a large fine but also in the loss of his *shrotrium* (government-granted tax-free estate) and title (Neild-Basu, "The Dubashes," 17–18, including fn 49).

24. Neild-Basu, 5–6.

25. P. J. Marshall, "The Personal Fortune of Warren Hastings," *Economic History Review*, new series, 17, no. 2 (1964): 299.

26. Frank Birkenholz, "Merchant-Kings and Lords of the World: Diplomatic Gift-Exchange between the Dutch East India Company and the Safavid and Mughal Empires in the Seventeenth Century," in *Practices of Diplomacy in the Early Modern World c. 1410-1800*, ed. Tracey A. Sowerby and Jan Hennings (London: Routledge, 2017), 219–36.

27. Mark Knights, "The History of Corruption and the Benefits of a Historical Approach," in *Corruption, Social Sciences and the Law: Exploration across the Disciplines*, ed. Jane Ellis (London: Routledge, 2019), 38.

28. Robert Clive, "Lord Clive's Speech in the House of Commons, on the Motion Made for an Inquiry into the Nature, State, and Condition, of the East India Company, and of the British Affairs in the East Indies, in the Fifth Session of the Present Parliament, 1772," 42–43.

29. Clive, "Lord Clive's Speech," 44.

30. Danby Pickering, ed., "An Act for Establishing Certain Regulations for the Better Management of the Affairs of the East India Company, as Well in India as in Europe," in *The Statutes at Large, from Magna Charta to the End of the Thirteenth Parliament of Great Britain, Anno 1773*, vol. XXX (London: John Archdeacon, 1773), 124–43.

31. Knights, "The History of Corruption," 38.

32. "Petition of Shopkeepers of Beetle [Betel] and Tobacca against Suncoo Chinna Kistnama Chetty," Revenue Department Sundries, no. 10, Betel renters petitions, Tamil Nadu Archives, May 1, 1790, 12, 26.

33. Mattison Mines, "Courts of Law and Styles of Self in Eighteenth-Century Madras: From Hybrid to Colonial Self," *Modern Asian Studies* 35, no. 1 (2001): 37–38.

Aadhar national biometric identity system linked to state entitlements.

Advanced Locality Managements (ALMs) neighborhood voluntary organizations in Mumbai entrusted with the management of solid waste, sanitation, and environmental protection. The advanced locality managements are similar in function, orientation, and scope to the RWAs (residents welfare associations) active in Delhi and other Indian cities.

Ahmadi adherents of the Ahmadiyya movement. Pakistani law designates Ahmadis as non-Muslims because they allegedly profess the belief that the movement's founder, Mirza Ghulam Ahmad, was a prophet, contradicting the idea that Muhammad was Allah's final prophet.

Akhil Bharatiya Sena Literally "All India Army," the Akhil Bharatiya Sena is a Mumbai-based political party founded in 2007 by underworld personality Arun Gawli.

ALM See Advanced Locality Managements.

Ambedkar Bhimrao Ramji Ambedkar, a revolutionary anti-caste activist and intellectual who is best known as the principal author of India's constitution.

arangetram first public performance of a bharatnatyam dancer.

Arthur Road Jail the oldest, largest, and most infamous of Mumbai's prisons.

Azad Maidan vast open stretch of ground in South Mumbai, next to the Mumbai Municipal Corporation (BMC) headquarters. Azad Maidan is a designated site for public protests, demonstrations, and various public meetings.

Bachchan, Amitabh one of the most enduring megastars of Indian cinema since the 1970s, now prominent also in film production and other media.

baghaare baigan slow-cooked, intensely flavored eggplant curry that is a specialty of the Hyderabad region.

baithi chawl single-storied *chawl*.

Bangali/Bengali term used to describe people from the Indian state of West Bengal and from the country of Bangladesh.

bania caste designation that refers to Hindu traders and merchants.

basti literally, "settlement." *Basti* is often used interchangeably with *slum*.

BDD chawl *chawl* constructed by the Bombay Development Department.

benami literally, "anonymous." In the context of property transactions, it refers to a situation where transactions are conducted in others' names, often to avoid taxation and to enable money laundering.

bhai literally, "brother." Colloquially used to indicate gangster, mafioso, or strongman.

bhaiyya literally, "younger brother." In Mumbai it is used in a sometimes-endearing and sometimes-pejorative sense to refer to migrants from the North Indian states of Bihar and Uttar Pradesh.

bhajan literally, "sharing." Refers to devotional songs often sung as a lyrical and melodic expression of bhakti.

bhakti worship and devotion for a deity. A concept popularized in the Hindu text *Bhagavad Gita*, it became widespread among Hindus throughout history because of numerous Bhakti religious movements.

bharatnatyam classical dance form that originated in South India.

Bhojpur a region encompassing parts of eastern Uttar Pradesh and Bihar where the Bhojpuri language is spoken.

bhoomipujan ceremony held at the initiation of a new project related to land. The guest of honor is invited to strike the first blow to the land, to break open a devotional coconut, and to distribute sweets.

bida dancers female, *hijra*, or transgender dancers who are commissioned to perform at weddings.

bidi hand-rolled cigarette, filled with tobacco and wrapped in a tendu leaf.

bindi dot on the forehead worn by some women, especially Hindu women.

BMC Brihanmumbai Municipal Corporation, also known as Bombay Municipal Corporation. Used interchangeably with Municipal Corporation of Greater Mumbai (MCGM).

Bombay Development Department (BDD) Established in 1920 by the British government, the BDD was tasked with developing land and housing for the city's growing industrial labor force, which at that time largely comprised Dalit migrants from rural Maharashtra. The BDD built approximately 50,000 tenement rooms in 195 *chawl*-style buildings, situated on 87 acres of land in central areas of Mumbai. In both colonial and postcolonial Mumbai, BDD chawls—especially those in Delisle Road, Byculla, Worli, and Naigaon—were important sites of Communist and Ambedkarite political activism. At the time of writing, redevelopment of the BDD chawls is under discussion by the government of Maharashtra.

bombil local variety of lizard fish, also referred to as Bombay Duck.

Budh Vihar temple devoted to Gautama Buddha.

chajja the projecting eave above a window functioning as a sun and rain shade. In Mumbai's popular neighborhoods, this window framing is often the most decorative feature on the façade.

chawl working-class residential housing in Mumbai, originally built for factory workers in industrial areas and mill lands. In contemporary Mumbai, *chawl* is used in reference to a variety of architectural forms and contexts but generally refers to blocks of relatively modest housing where apartments share amenities such as toilets and courtyards, although it is increasingly common for working-class *chawls* to have individual toilets.

Chhath Puja winter festival dedicated to the worship of the Sun God, mainly celebrated in Bihar and eastern Uttar Pradesh.

chowk sabha street-corner meeting or political rally.

corporator used interchangeably with the Hindi/Marathi *nagarsevak* to refer to the 227 elected municipal councillors who make up the executive branch of the Brihanmumbai Municipal Corporation (BMC).

cutoff date see *slum*.

dabba/dabbawalla literally, a box. However, in Mumbai it usually refers specifically to a box of food that is prepared at home but intended for consumption in the workplace; the dabba contains a full meal as it would be eaten at home. Dabbas often travel long distances and are carried by professional food carriers called *dabbawallas*. Although dabbas are often prepared by someone in the family, as people have less time to cook for themselves or live away from family, professional home cooks increasingly provide catered meals to office workers all over the city.

Dahi-handi Dahi-handi gets its name from a legend of baby Krishna, who loved milk and yogurt so much that he would try to steal it from people who would hang their supplies high, out of his reach. Young Krishna, the story goes, would reach the pot by building a human pyramid with his friends. In Mumbai this plays out as a community tradition in the Hindu festival of Janmashtami, when teams of young people compete to form human pyramids that try to break pots of yogurt. Builders and politicians regularly sponsor the prize money for these Dahi-handi teams.

dal lentil-based stew that comes in a myriad of varieties.

dalal See the discussion in the introduction.

dalit castes formerly known as "untouchable."

dargah Muslim shrine honoring revered religious figures.

Dawood Bhai Dawood Ibrahim Kaskar (commonly known as Dawood Bhai) is Bombay-born underworld personality, perhaps best known for his role in orchestrating a series of bomb blasts in 1993 that killed 257 people in Bombay. As the kingpin of a global crime syndicate, it is popularly rumored that Dawood Bhai lives in Karachi under the protection of the Pakistani intelligence agency. His name is on several terrorist wanted lists, including those of the US Federal Bureau of Investigation. Hailing from a Konkani Muslim family, he grew up in the South Bombay neighborhood of Dongri and is a native speaker of Bambaiya.

dhandha trade, profession, business, or work. In certain contexts it can connote morally dubious forms of income generation, especially commercial sex work.

dua prayer, often used in contradistinction to the obligatory, five-times-daily Islamic prayer known as *salat* or *namaz*. Ismaili Muslims use the term *dua* to refer to a liturgical prayer they say thrice each day.

farman religious edict issued by the Ismaili Imam. Although the word means "command," Ismailis often describe these edicts as "guidance" (*hidayat*), emphasizing that complying with these edicts is considered voluntary rather than compulsory.

floor space index (FSI) According to Mumbai's Development Control Rules, the ratio of buildable area to plot size is known as Floor Space Index (FSI). An FSI of 1, for instance, would allow a plot of land of 100 square meters to accommodate a building with 100 square meters of floor space. Ever since the sanctioning of Bombay's first set of development control rules (DCRs) in 1967, the amount of permissible development in various parts of the city has been regulated by an FSI-based limitation of the buildable area on a given plot. Although these official limits on floor space changed only slightly with Bombay's second and third development plans in 1991 and 2014, the revised development control rules are peppered with officially sanctioned loopholes that, in practice, have enabled builders to construct—plot-wise—at much greater heights and densities. There are a few policy tools by means of which these plot-wise loopholes work. Under the provision for "Reservation FSI," for instance, an owner of a piece of land that has been zoned in the development plan for some "public purpose" (a library, school, or hospital, for example) can construct the planned public facility themselves and then hand it over to the municipality in exchange for which they can use forfeited development rights on the remaining plot for commercial construction—with a now-greater FSI. The development control rules provide for a variety of ways that incentive FSI can be generated, but some ways generate significantly more incentive FSI than others—for instance, the redevelopment of substandard buildings and *slums*. The incentive FSI allowed for slum-redevelopment projects is the highest in the city. See also *Transferable Development Right* (TDR).

ganda literally "dirty," but also has figurative-moral meaning as "disreputable."

Ganesh Chaturthi ten-day Hindu festival that celebrates the god Ganesh.

gavlan love song about Hindu deities Radha-Krishna.

Gawli, Arun well-known gangster turned politician in Mumbai. He rose to power and notoriety in the Central Mumbai area of Byculla. He began his career in the underworld with the gang known as the Byculla Company and finally took charge of his own gang in a working-class neighborhood called Dagdi Chawl. He has been arrested several times and has contested and won elections from jail to the Maharashtra State Assembly. He is currently serving a life sentence for the murder of a political opponent.

ghungroo bells worn around a dancer's ankles to create sounds while dancing.

ginan Ismaili devotional hymn.

Gokulashtami the birth of the god Krishna, celebrated with the festival of Dahi-handi.

hafta money collected on a weekly or monthly basis.

hijra minority community that is often described as either transgender or third gender and that inhabits complex grids of gender and sexuality.

Holi Hindu festival of colors, usually celebrated in February–March to mark the end of winter and the beginning of spring.

ISL (Indian Sign Language) sign language used by deaf people in India that has emerged in its schools for deaf children and exists in multiple variants across India.

idli and dosa popular South Indian snack and breakfast foods that are ubiquitous in Bombay. Idlis are steamed fermented rice cakes; dosas are a sort of crepe made of a mix of rice and lentil flour. Both are generally served with chutneys and sambar, which is a lentil-based stew.

Jai Bhim literally, "Victory to Bhim," the phrase references Bhimrao (Babasaheb) Ambedkar and is a rallying cry among certain Dalit groups.

Jain/Jainism world religion originating in the fourth century BCE, widely considered the first cousin of Buddhism, with which it shares its central doctrines of salvation from Karmic reincarnation through worldly renunciation and ahimsa (nonviolence). One central Jain attribute is to observe strict lacto-vegetarianism, which is connected to the commitment to ahimsa. There are approximately 4.5 million followers in the world, mostly in India.

jamat congregation, gathering. Ismaili Muslims often use this word to refer to the Ismaili community.

Janmashtami annual Hindu festival that celebrates the birth of Krishna. On the day after Janmashtami, Dahi-handi is celebrated.

jayanti festival celebrating a birth anniversary.

jhopadpatti literally, a cluster of huts (jhopad). Used in Mumbai interchangeably with *bustee, vasti,* and *slum.*

junior artist category of low-status actor who plays a bit part, cheers in a crowd, or serves as a paid audience member on television shows.

kabadiwalas an important scrap business in the management of solid waste in India. Kabadiwalas collect scrap material door to door and then sell the materials onward for a small profit to people engaged in the disposal of waste also for a small profit.

kamina person who commits fraud (*labar*) as well as one who is vile (*tuch*). Defying the good-versus-evil binary that characterizes the commonsense concepts of morality, *kamina* conveys a sense of trickster and scoundrel.

karyakarta doer or worker. In Mumbai, *karyakarta* is often used interchangeably with the English term *social worker* or with another term referring to the trade or field of specialization: "party worker" "plumber," "contractor," "paniwala" (water supplier). The work of karyakartas is at the heart of local electoral politics, so during election season a person maintaining a longtime affiliation with a particular party might be referred to as either a "Congress Party karyakarta" or a "Shiv Sena karyakarta." In practice, however, the partisanship even of party-affiliated karyakartas is quite fluid at the local level.

kathakali dance form originating from Kerala, where traditionally men dance as men and women and perform tales from the *Ramayan* and *Mahabharata.*

khabri police informant, often used in a pejorative sense of "spy" or "tattletale."

Khetwadi locality within the Malabar Hill constituency of South Mumbai, famous for its middle-class residences and some of the oldest temples in Mumbai. The area is also known as a hub of the diamond trade and has a substantial Gujarati population.

kholi "inner" room or chamber. The term is popularly used to refer to a one-room living space in a multifamily building or *chawl.*

kirana small neighborhood shop that sells basic nonperishable food supplies.

kokum sharbat sweet fruit drink popular in Maharashtra.

kothas residences of female dancers or tawaifs.

kothi a common term used in Mumbai to refer to men who dress as and behave as women, and who are socially and sexually submissive.

lavani art form from Maharashtra where the woman dancer sings and dances for an often all-male audience.

lungi garment worn wrapped around the waist like a skirt, generally used by men.

Mahaparinirvan Diwas Babasaheb Ambedkar's death anniversary, on December 6.

Maharashtra Samjukta Movement the movement and organization started in 1956 that led to the creation of the independent state of Maharashtra in 1960.

Mahashivaratri "great night of Shiva," a large Hindu festival for those who worship the Hindu god Shiva. There are many legends behind why Shivaratri is celebrated, including it being the birthday of Shiva and the day he saved the world from destruction.

mahurat literally, any designated auspicious time for something to happen. In the film industry this refers to the auspicious and often fully ceremonial "launch" of a film, which is also a major intra-industry publicity event. In the Bhojpuri film industry the mahurat is often conducted at a music studio or meeting hall and includes at least a ritual breaking of a coconut along with press events, possibly along with some gestures toward recording the film's songs.

maidan large, open public space.

Malabar Hill plush and rich neighborhood in South Mumbai, located at the southernmost edge of the city. Apart from housing the magisterial governor's residence, the neighborhood is famous for its wealthy residents, with some of the highest-net-worth individuals in India calling the hill their home.

mantra word or a phrase that, when repeated, is held to produce atmospheric vibrations that can effect material changes in the cellular makeup of the body or atmosphere.

Mantralaya official secretariat for the Maharashtra State Government, located in South Mumbai.

Marathi Manoos Marathi-speaking people of Maharashtra and some of its border regions in Goa and Karnataka. This is also a colloquial term that Marathi-speaking inhabitants of the city were given by the Marathi-nativist ("sons of the soil") movement, started and spearheaded by the political party Shiv Sena.

Maulvi Muslim religious scholars.

MCGM Municipal Corporation of Greater Mumbai, also known as Brihanmumbai Municipal Corporation (BMC).

media-goondas fly-by-night journalists who are often in the business of extortion, using their investigations about "illegal" activities (especially construction-related activities) to blackmail landowners and builders.

MLA member of Legislative Assembly, here of the state of Maharashtra.

MMRDA Mumbai Metropolitan Regional Development Authority.

MP member of Parliament.

mujra performance involving dance and songs, usually performed by courtesans, attended by men.

Musalman a faithful believer in Islam; a Muslim.

naka/naka market road juncture or crossing (Marathi); naka market refers to the place where local day laborers gather each morning in search of work.

Nakshatra Shanti puja ceremonial ritual that is performed for those born under the influence of an inauspicious Nakshatra (star or group of stars); the ritual is intended to reduce the ill effects of the Nakshatra under whose influence one is born.

nalla stream carrying rain and wastewater.

Navratri nine (nav) nights (ratri) of Hindu holy days celebrated in the fall of each year.

NCP Nationalist Congress Party.

nikah the marriage contract made according to Koranic beliefs and officiated by a religious rather than a civil authority.

Other Backward Castes (OBC) government of India designation for caste group-ings entitled to caste-based affirmative action ("reservations") in public-sector jobs, education (public and private), and political office.

pad yatra religious or political procession on foot.

pandal temporary stage or elevated structure erected for the display of idols during Hindu religious festivals.

Pani Haq Samiti people's campaign working in Mumbai's jhopadpattis that has been actively working toward improving water access for the urban poor.

pav bhaji Maharashtrian street food snack.

pavada/povada alliterative poetry recounting the achievements of a warrior, the tal-ents and attainments of a scholar, or the powers, virtues, and excellences of a person.

poha popular Indian snack of pressed or beaten rice stir-fried with potatoes, curry leaves, peanuts, and spices.

potli personal belongings tied up with a cloth.

puja ritual worship or prayer.

Ramjanambhoomi said to be the birthplace of Lord Rama in Ayodhya. Hindu nationalists claiming that the Babri Masjid had subsequently been built on this site demolished the mosque on December 6, 1992, leading to riots in Mumbai and other Indian cities.

saaf clean; also has literal as well as figurative-moral meaning as "proper."

Saamna newspaper run by the political party Shiv Sena, known as the Shiv Sena's "mouthpiece."

sabudane ki khichdi savory tapioca stir-fry that is a common breakfast or teatime snack in Maharashtra.

Sakaal Marathi word meaning "morning," but also the title of a local newspaper with ties to the Nationalist Congress Party.

salwar-kameez and dupatta traditional North Indian wear comprising a long top, loose bottoms, and a long scarf.

samaaj sevak social worker. Sometimes used interchangeably with *karyakarta*.

samosa savory fried snack usually made with a filling of spiced potatoes.

sarkar ruling authority or government. Also used as a term of address meaning *master* or *lord*. Historically used to refer to the court of a king.

Scheduled Castes and Scheduled Tribes (SC/ST) historically stigmatized and marginalized caste groupings (formerly "untouchables") that are officially entitled to affirmative action ("reservations") in public-sector jobs, education (public and private), and political office.

seth a respectful term that refers to a merchant, banker, moneylender or otherwise prosperous person; commonly used in Bombay in reference to bosses, or employers, or chiefs.

seva voluntary service.

shakha Literally "branch" in Marathi, this term describes political party offices located in various localities and constituencies.

Shiv Sena Maharashtrian nativist and Hindu nationalist political party. The Shiv Sena launched itself as a pro-Maharashtrian political group that demanded employment and other preferential treatment for local workers over migrants, especially in Mumbai. The party was involved in bouts of communal violence in Mumbai in the 1970s, 1980s, and 1990s, and it has presided over the Mumbai Municipal Corporation continuously since 1985. After its participation in the 1992–93 communal riots in Mumbai, sparked by the destruction of the contested Babri Mosque in the North Indian temple town of Ayodhya (see entry for Ramjanambhoomi), the Shiv Sena turned toward a stringent Hindu nationalist rhetoric in order to gain acceptance within the Sangh Parivaar (the assemblage of pan-Indian Hindu nationalist cultural and political organizations). In 2019 the Shiv Sena entered into an strange-bedfellows alliance with the National Congress Party and Congress Party to form the government of Maharashtra.

Shiva ling phallic symbol that is considered an abstract representation of the Hindu god Shiva. It is used for worship in Shiva temples.

sindoor vermillion, worn on the parting of the hair by married Hindu women.

sirdar leader of a labor gang.

slum Although the word *slum* is frequently used in Mumbai interchangeably with terms such as *encroachment* and *illegal area*, there is nothing in the Maharashtra Slum Act's official definition that associates this category of settlement in contemporary Mumbai with formality or informality of tenure claims, or with planning or lack thereof. Legally speaking, the 1971 Maharashtra Slum Areas (Improvement, Clearance and Redevelopment) Act allows to be "declared" a slum "any area [that] is or may be a source of danger to the health, safety or convenience of the public of that area or of its neighborhood, by reason of the area having inadequate or no basic amenities, or being insanitary, squalid, overcrowded or otherwise." The declaration of a neighborhood as a "slum" does not adjudicate "legal" from "illegal" land; rather, it renders a neighborhood eligible for various "improvement" schemes and facilitates public investment in underserved neighborhoods.

Slum Rehabilitation Authority (SRA) Established in 1995 by the newly elected Shiv Sena government, the Slum Rehabilitation Authority is a planning authority under Maharashtra's Department of Housing. The mandate of the SRA is to serve as planning authority for "slum areas" within the jurisdictional boundaries of the Municipal Corporation of Greater Mumbai.

Slum Rehabilitation Scheme (SRS) In conjunction with country-level liberalizing reforms, in March 1991 the government of Maharashtra launched a new set of development control rules (DCRs) granting private-sector developers of tenement-style slum-redevelopment housing incentive-development rights as a kind of housing cross-subsidy; by compensating builders of slum-rehabilitation tenements with development rights, it was imagined, the urban poor could be rehoused at little or no cost to the state government. The basic idea behind the 1995 Slum Rehabilitation Scheme (an amped-up, more market-reliant version of the nonstarter 1991 Slum Redevelopment Scheme) was to use exclusively market incentives to demolish all of the city's slums and to rehouse eligible residents in mid-rise tenement buildings—now as title-holding property owners. Political leaders in Mumbai sought to legitimize this highly peculiar policy framework (which anti-migrant detractors denounced as "rewarding squatters" and encouraging migration) through a two-part strategy: first by excluding from Slum Rehabilitation Scheme eligibility any household that could not provide documentary proof of residence in a structure as of a January 1, 1995, cutoff date and, second, through a government circular passed in 1996 on the heels of the new Slum Rehabilitation Scheme, which disallowed even the provision of civic amenities and other permissions to houses and households whose structures (and whose residence in those structures) could not be proven to meet the cutoff date of eligibility for some hypothetical slum-rehabilitation scheme.

surmai South Asian variety of mackerel also known as kingfish.

survey pauti (slip) issued as evidence for having been enumerated by the various governmental agencies in Mumbai such as the collector, the BMC, and the census authority.

Taloja Prison situated in Navi Mumbai's Khargar region, this prison, currently housing 850 inmates, also has a juvenile home for young offenders.

tamasha traveling folk theater and dance theater.

tantric performer of tantric rituals.

tapori stereotypically violent, street-smart, gangster-type fellow (generally male) who makes a living from illicit means, also known as a hustler or a rowdy. The figure of the tapori looms large in the Bollywood film industry (not unlike the figure of the American "gangster") and is often a sympathetic character having a distinctive style of speech and aesthetic.

tawaifs In the sixteenth-century North Indian Mughal era, the term *tawaif* referred to sophisticated courtesans who were extremely knowledgeable in dancing, singing, and the arts, and who were responsible for teaching these skills to young noblemen.

tava a flat or concave frying pan.

TDR Transferable Development Right.

teen patta variety of poker popular throughout India.

Thackeray, Bal charismatic leader and nationalist philosopher who founded the Shiv Sena in 1966. He was the most influential and controversial figure in Mumbai's political landscape and remained loyal to an anti-migrant, anti-Muslim agenda until his death in 2012.

tiffin both homemade lunch and a lunch box.

tikali used interchangeably with *bindi*.

topi-kurta cap and garment for men.

Transferable Development Right (TDR) When incentive development rights (see *floor space index*) from the construction of roads, reservations, or slum redevelopment cannot all be used on-site (even with a much-higher FSI), then a property developer is issued a Certificate of Transferable Development Right. These development rights can either be loaded onto properties in higher-value suburban areas or else sold on the free market. Through the instrument of TDR, development rights (FSI) became not only transferable from one location to another but also from one holder to another. Since the approval of a revised set of development control rules in 1991, the market in TDR has become integral to financing both new construction and redevelopment projects throughout the city.

ussal a popular Maharashtrian dish made of sprouted pulses.

vada pav popular snack in Mumbai and Maharashtra consisting of fried balls of spicy potatoes and chickpea flour placed between two buns (pavs).

Varkari Sampradaya religious sect with thirteen-century anti-Brahminical origins.

vasti Marathi equivalent of Hindi word *basti*. See also *slum* and *jopadpatti*.

Vithoba deity worshipped by Varkaris; avatar of the god Vishnu.

voter ID election identification card.

world-class city The decades following India's liberalization-era policy shifts since the 1980s have witnessed distinct efforts at all levels of government (central, state, municipal) to remake Mumbai as a so-called "world-class city," often citing the model of Shanghai, Hong Kong, or Singapore. This project has involved a vision of a transformed city marked by a dense multinational business and finance sector, luxury housing, and a sanitized experience of the street, oriented toward sensory enjoyment and consumption by a cosmopolitan elite. The vision has also been taken up by many of the city's new middle class, who have developed civic associations aimed at often anti-poor "urban beautification" initiatives, such as slum removal and clearing footpaths of hawkers.

yantra often translated as "instrument" or "machine." In tantric practice, a yantra is a metal object inscribed with markings that represent a mantra in a graphic form.

zaari lace work.

CONTRIBUTORS

Anjali Arondekar is an associate professor of feminist studies at the University of California, Santa Cruz. Her work engages the politics and poetics of sexuality, caste, and historiography within South Asian and Indian Ocean studies.

Sarthak Bagchi is an assistant professor at the School of Arts and Sciences, Ahmedabad University. He is interested in questions of informal politics, processes of democratization, networks of patronage politics, and issues of citizenship and their impact on state-society interactions.

Tobias Baitsch is an architect and urban researcher. He holds a PhD in urban sociology from EPF Lausanne and is a scientific collaborator at Bern University of Applied Sciences.

Sangeeta Banerji is a PhD candidate in the Department of Geography at Rutgers University. Her doctoral research focuses on practices of fixing within one of the world's largest urban bureaucracies, the Municipal Corporation of Greater Mumbai.

Srimati Basu is a professor of gender and women's studies and anthropology at the University of Kentucky and author of *The Trouble with Marriage: Feminists Confront Law and Violence in India* (2015) and *She Comes to Take Her Rights: Indian Women, Property, and Propriety* (1999).

Tarini Bedi is an associate professor of anthropology at the University of Illinois at Chicago and the author of two monographs: *The Dashing Ladies of Shiv Sena: Political Matronage in Urbanizing India* (2016) and *(Auto)Biographies and (Auto)Mobilities: Roads, Labor and Kinship in Mumbai's Taxi Trade* (forthcoming).

Amita Bhide is professor and dean at the School of Habitat Studies, Tata Institute of Social Sciences, Mumbai, and researches urban informality and social movements.

Lisa Björkman is on the faculty of urban and public affairs at the University of Louisville and a research fellow at the Max Planck Institute for Social Anthropology in Halle. She makes excellent lemon pickles.

Uday Chandra teaches politics and history at Georgetown University, Qatar, and is author of the forthcoming book *Resistance as Negotiation*.

Simon Chauchard is an assistant professor of political science at Leiden University and author of *Why Representation Matters: The Meaning of Ethnic Quotas in Rural India* (2017).

Ka-Kin Cheuk is an Annette and Hugh Gragg Postdoctoral Fellow in transnational Asian studies at Rice University.

Michael Collins is a postdoctoral research fellow at the Centre for Modern Indian Studies at the University of Göttingen.

Daisy Deomampo is an associate professor of anthropology at Fordham University and author of *Transnational Reproduction: Race, Kinship, and Commercial Surrogacy in India* (2016).

Maura Finkelstein is an assistant professor of anthropology at Muhlenberg College and the author of *The Archive of Loss: Lively Ruination in Mill Land Mumbai* (Duke University Press, 2019).

Ajay Gandhi is an assistant professor at Leiden University's Faculty of Governance and Global Affairs, with research interests in urban, political, and economic anthropology, and a geographical focus on South Asia.

Rupali Gupte is an urbanist and architect based in Mumbai and is cofounder of the Collective Research Initiative Trust, School of Environment and Architecture (SEA) and BardStudio.

Kathryn C. Hardy is an assistant professor in the Department of Sociology and Anthropology at Ashoka University. Her current research interests include language and communication, mass mediation, and water buffalo. She lives in New Delhi.

Lalitha Kamath is a trained urban planner and an associate professor at the School of Habitat Studies, Tata Institute of Social Sciences, Mumbai. Her research interests focus on everyday urbanisms, local governance and planning, urban state transformations, urban infrastructure, and public participation.

Prasad Khanolkar is an urbanist based in India and is currently teaching as an assistant professor of geography at the Department of Humanities and Social Sciences, Indian Institute of Technology–Guwahati, Assam.

Bhushan Korgaonkar published a book titled *Sangeet Bari* in 2014 chronicling traditional *lavani* artists' lives. He also writes short stories.

Ratoola Kundu teaches at the Center for Urban Policy and Governance. Her research revolves around multiple forms of socio-spatial exclusion in cities of the global South and the role that urban planning and policy play in negotiating urban inequalities.

Ken Kuroda works in marketing for a Tokyo-based firm called Mitsui & Co., where he sometimes catches himself attending to the distinctive work culture at the historical firm with a distinctly ethnographic sensibility.

Annelies Kusters is associate professor in sign language and intercultural research at Heriot-Watt University.

Lisa Mitchell is an associate professor of anthropology and history in the Department of South Asia Studies at the University of Pennsylvania, and author of *Language, Emotion, and Politics in South India: The Making of a Mother Tongue* (2009) and *Hailing the State: Collective Assembly, Space, and the Politics of Representation in the History of Indian Democracy* (forthcoming).

Shailaja Paik is an associate professor of South Asian history and author of *Dalit Women's Education in Modern India: Double Discrimination* (2014).

Gautam Pemmaraju is a Mumbai-based writer and filmmaker focusing on history, literature, sound aesthetics and production, and art. He has a special interest in the cultural history of Hyderabad and the Deccan, and has made a documentary film on Dakhani, the vernacular Urdu of the region.

Lubaina Rangwala is an urban planner from Mumbai, currently holding the position of senior manager, urban development and resilience, at the World Resources Institute in India.

Llerena Guiu Searle is an assistant professor of anthropology at the University of Rochester who studies urbanization, finance, and domesticity, and she is the author of *Landscapes of Accumulation: Real Estate and the Neoliberal Imagination in Contemporary India* (2016).

Atreyee Sen is an associate professor in the Department of Anthropology at the University of Copenhagen, Denmark, and the author of *Shiv Sena Women: Violence and Communalism in a Bombay Slum* (2007).

Prasad Shetty is an urbanist and architect based in Mumbai and is cofounder of the Collective Research Initiative Trust, School of Environment and Architecture (SEA) and BardStudio.

Rohan Shivkumar is an architect, urban designer, and filmmaker practicing in Mumbai, and the dean of research and academic development at the Kamla Raheja Vidyanidhi Institute for Architecture and Environmental Studies. His work ranges from architecture, interior design, urban research, and consultancy projects to works in film and visual art.

Edward Simpson is a professor of social anthropology and director of the SOAS South Asia Institute. His current research is interested in the relationship among infrastructure, automobility, and the global-sustainability agenda.

David J. Strohl is an assistant professor of anthropology at Colby College. His work has appeared in *Contemporary South Asia* and *Religions of South Asia*.

Rachel Sturman is an associate professor of history and Asian studies at Bowdoin College. She is currently writing a book on the history and current operation of Bombay's building industry.

R. Swaminathan is a visiting research fellow at Uppsala University's Department of Cultural Anthropology and Ethnology, as well as author and editor of five books and several papers, including the forthcoming book *"It's Worthless for You, but It's Gold for Us": Narratives of Waste from Mumbai's Ragpickers.*

Aneri Taskar is a PhD student in the Department of Urban Affairs at the University of Louisville.

Yaffa Truelove is an assistant professor of geography at the University of Colorado with research focusing on urban and feminist political ecologies of water, southern and comparative urbanism, and infrastructure in Indian cities.

Sahana Udupa is a professor of media anthropology at Ludwig-Maximilians-Universität München, where she leads a research project on online nationalism and extreme speech funded by the European Research Council.

Lalit Vachani is a documentary filmmaker and researcher at CeMIS (the Centre for Modern Indian Studies) at the University of Göttingen.

Leilah Vevaina is an assistant professor of anthropology at the Chinese University Hong Kong, and her research focuses on religious endowments and urban space in India and the Indian diaspora.

Page numbers followed by f indicate figures.

Bambaiya: description and speakers of, 234, 239-41, 287-88, 289f, 294n2; in Hindi cinema, 291-93, 299; link to gang culture, 290; in written form, 293
Bandaranayake, Senake, 281
Banerji, Sangeeta, 30, 113, 117, 301
bar dancers, 343-44, 346, 363, 365, 373; ban on, 152n4; quarters of "underground," 147f
barter system, 30, 116-17, 124
basti, 219, 220
Basu, Srimati, 357, 362-63
Baviskar, Amita, 136n6
Bedi, Tarini, 30, 166, 167, 172
belonging, 34, 234, 236, 239
Bengalis, 131, 148, 226
bhai, 124, 126, 127n1
bhaiyyas, 274, 277n11
Bharatiya Janata Party (BJP), 327-28, 328n1
Bhide, Amita, 363, 364
Bhim Nagar neighborhood, 119n5; basic socioeconomic survey (BSES), 405-6; demolition of, 113-16, 137-41, 139f, 405; proof of tenure and resettlement, 143-44
Bhojpuri film industry, 102, 299-300, 315-21
biased/unbiased advice, 25, 28-29
Bihar state, 106, 316-18
bindi, 146, 371
Björkman, Lisa, 52, 54, 115, 166-67, 169-72, 303, 415, 420
blackmail, 64, 386
Bollywood, 12, 27, 249, 281, 298, 303, 321n2; Bambaiya usage in, 240, 287, 290-93; depiction of gangsters, 54, 65, 240; music, 384-85; total films produced (2012), 41n55
Bombay Municipal Corporation (BMC), 60, 78, 130, 326, 334, 335; hydraulic engineering department, 45n103; illegal construction and, 112, 131; maintenance department, 81, 83; political connections with, 48, 52, 84, 86, 110, 121-22, 126, 324; sanitation workers, 134

Bombay Our City (1985), 244
Bombay Parsi Punchayet (BPP), 118-19, 154-60, 161nn4-5
Bombay Sewerage Disposal Project (BSDP), 88
Borivali neighborhood, 224-25, 228, 232
British administration, 418-19, 421, 423n18, 423n22
brokerage, 3, 14, 25-26, 415, 418-19, 422; ambivalence toward, 39n34; political and economic, 6-8, 23; practices glossed as, 5, 15; theory of action and, 16
brokers: changing roles of, 415; corrupt mediations of, 19; fees, 24, 25; as key figures, 14, 42n71; local knowledge of, 28, 98, 419; scholarly debates about, 7; terms for, 39n30. See also *dubashes*
brothels. See *kothas*
Buddhism, 250-51, 252n5
building construction: of *chawls*, 60, 61f; illegal, 131-32, 411; labor, 53, 75, 101-6; masculinity and, 65; occupation certificate (OC), 78-79, 80; permissions and approvals, 52, 62, 78, 83-84, 112; political connections and, 63-64, 123; regulations, 48-49, 52-53, 62, 74-75; remodeling, 68, 76n3; sharing of profits, 141; "symbolic wall," 51, 75, 76f
business: direct-selling, 349; family, 130, 193; of Indian academia, 409; profits, 172, 178-79, 188-89, 220; registration, 188; *tapori/dhandha* distinction, 34, 163-64, 171; of truth making, 357. *See also* entrepreneurialism; trade
Byculla neighborhood, 89, 168, 200, 244, 288, 291

Callon, Michel, 15-16
capital, 99, 117, 193, 265; accumulation, 97; circulation or flows, 9, 14, 55, 96; emotive, 238; social and cultural, 98, 215, 319
capitalism, 14, 26, 49, 55; global, 8, 11, 48
cash payments, 52, 85, 229; catering business and, 218-19; currency of, 170-72; election campaigns and, 327,

331, 332, 334; engineers and, 81, 84–85; ethnographic practice and, 213–14; in exchange for publicity, 301, 316, 319–20, 325–26; housing costs and, 75, 77n8; prison sentences and, 358, 387; social relationships and, 22–23, 117, 149; social worker services and, 30, 116–17, 125, 144, 149

caste, 240, 248, 266, 272, 408, 416; higher, 6, 37n12, 55, 134; language and, 288; music and, 235, 249–51

catering business, 30, 166–67, 169, 172, 217–20; preparing *tiffins*, 209, 210

cell phones. *See* mobile phones

census classifications, 45n103

Chandra, Uday, 53, 299

charitable trusts, 158. *See also* Bombay Parsi Punchayet (BPP)

Chauchard, Simon, 302, 306

Chavan, Madhav, 407–8, 413n2

chawls, 1, 275; *baithi*, 200–201; Bombay Development Department (BDD), 244, 245f, 248, 409, 411; building of, 54, 60, 61f; definition, 161n2; "widow," 118, 155

Chembur suburb, 81, 271, 276, 393–94, 406

Cheuk, Ka-Kin, 167, 170, 172

CitiSpace, 132, 135n3, 136n7

citizenship, 7, 34, 127, 257; responsible, 256, 258

claims making, 34, 109–10, 111, 115–16, 408; against the BPP, 119, 155–56

Clean India campaign, 275, 277n14

Clive, Robert, 420–21

Coca-Cola, 262–63, 265

coin traders, 225–26

Colaba neighborhood, 124, 312, 378

collectives/collectivities, 172, 238, 256, 297–98, 300, 420

commercial licenses, 2, 22

common property, 158

communalism, 234, 238, 240, 254, 258; Parsi, 155, 158, 160

community-based organizations (CBOs), 50, 56, 88, 89–90, 91

community connections, 279–80

community service, 255–57

Congress Party: *Congress Darshan* publication, 326, 328n2; election campaigns and *karyakartas*, 301–2, 304, 323–28, 329–32, 333f, 334–36; NCP alliance, 328n1; publicity stunts, 350–51

consultants, 25, 364, 405, 409–10; global, 164, 167, 204; infrastructure, 401–4

contractors, 82, 113, 405; Shivajinagar housing, 51–52, 68–69, 71–76; workers and, 102–3, 104

corporate films, 311–12

corporations, 158, 262

corporators, 79, 111, 130, 132

corruption, 8, 16, 22, 23, 302; cash-fueled, 30, 116, 125; definitions and discourse, 18–20; *dubashes* and, 414, 417; East India Company and, 420; prison and, 359; urban development and, 111

cosmopolitanism, 265, 268–69

crime, 358, 387–89, 421; arrests for, 385, 419; detective work on, 368, 374, 375–76

Crime Investigation Department (CID), 370

crisis, 11–13, 40n48

currency, forms of, 30–31, 164, 167, 169–72, 219. *See also* cash payments; money

customs agents, 27

dabba, 217, 219

dabbawala, 166–68, 171, 208–15, 215nn2–3

Dadar neighborhood, 1, 105, 128, 136n8, 337, 367

dalal, 2, 14, 139–40, 144; term usage, 26–28, 44n98, 45n103

Dalits, 39n35, 252n1, 348; Mahaparinir-van Diwas, 134–35, 136n8; poets and singers, 244, 246–52; Rambai Nagar community, 243–44

Dalvi, Abdus Sattar, 239, 287–88, 293–94, 294n2

dancers, 251, 313; *bida*, 340f, 343; for birthday celebrations, 337–38; *lavani*, 302–3, 339, 341f, 342, 344–45. *See also* bar dancers

data collection, 364, 402, 407, 408–12

deaf-hearing communication: Indian Sign Language (ISL), 391–92; ordering at restaurants, 394, 396f, 397f; shopping and vendors, 394–95, 398f, 399f; travel and navigating, 361–62, 393–94, 397–400

dealers, 272–74, 276n9

debts, 103, 238

Dehlvi, Farookh, 286–87

democracy, 7, 11, 19, 302, 359

dengue fever, 105

Deomampo, Daisy, 165, 167, 169, 172

detective fiction, 368

detective work: clients and cases, 371–76, 377n8; gender norms, 370–71; recognition and publicity, 367–68, 369f, 375f; truths and moralizing discourses, 357, 362–63, 376

development, 33, 47–56, 233; community, 54, 62, 138, 255–57; "doing," 59–60, 62; global corporate solutions, 164, 199–201, 203–6; impact assessments, 410; infrastructure upgrades, 402–3, 405; "no development" zone, 61f, 62; planning, 5, 52, 110–12, 122, 411; rights, 52, 80; survey data for, 363–64. *See also* property developers; urban development

development control rules (DCRs), 111, 130, 133

dhandha, 148, 163–64, 171, 273, 276n9, 294n4, 351. *See also* business

Dhanrajgir, Tarun, 311

Dhanraj Mahal (building), 311

Dharamsey, Virchand (Dharamseybhai), 234, 238–39, 241, 278–84

Dharavi neighborhood, 20, 49, 212, 214, 347–48, 351–52; redevelopment project, 408, 409, 411

didi, 53, 101, 102, 104–6, 147

dietary habits, 209

difference/differentiation, 34, 172, 233–41, 274, 305, 357, 359

displacement, 54, 60, 110, 137, 143, 239

divorce, 221–22, 373, 374

Doctor, Vikram, 263

dosa, 263, 264, 268

Dubai, 192, 194–96

dubashes: decline, 418; definition and roles, 14, 415–16, 423n21; gift exchanges, 420–22; notoriety and corruption, 414, 416–18, 424n23; strategic advantages, 419

Dutt, Sanjay, 240, 277n16, 293, 299

East India Company, 13, 26, 232n1, 415–22

economic growth, 8, 96–97

economic liberalization, 47, 52

elections, 231, 336n3; BPP, 159–60; campaigns and *karyakartas*, 301–2, 322–28, 329–32, 333f, 334–36; cash gifts and, 30–31; pre-poll alliances, 328n1; role of *dalals*, 139; voters, 327, 334, 379

electronic waste. *See* e-waste recycling

elites, 6, 12, 37n12, 47, 52; Parsi, 118–19

encroachment: along the Mithi River, 363, 402; on public spaces, 130–34, 135n4; removal in Bhim Nagar, 139, 143; slum dwellings and, 60

energy (vibrations), 170, 172, 225–26, 228–29, 230; money and, 171, 229, 231

engineers, 45n103, 52, 78–86, 204, 402

English Education Act, 423n22

entrepreneurialism, 5, 8–9, 39n35, 49, 56, 140, 374; food cart vendors, 237, 241; trust and, 10

ethics, 171, 181, 213–15, 347, 351, 410–11

ethnographic practice, 4–5, 15–16, 33–35, 348, 365; field-note writing, 279; forging of social relations, 32, 213; interactional dynamics, 382; key figures and, 42n71; monetary transactions and, 213–15

e-waste recycling, 165, 167–70, 182–84, 185f, 186–89

exchange, relations of, 30–31, 45n106, 116, 125, 163–64, 420

fabric traders, 167, 169, 191–97

family, 53, 179–80; business, 130, 193; detective investigations and, 371–76; prison time and, 390. *See also* kinship festivals, 60, 91, 106, 249, 418; Holi, 254; Mahashivaratri, 66; *pandals*, 221–22; *tamasha*, 303

film production: Bhojpuri, 299–300, 315–21; managers, 298–299, 305, 307–314

Finkelstein, Maura, 236–37, 240

floor space index (FSI), 79–80

flour business, 163

folk singing, 250

food cart operators, 236–37, 263–69

food couriers. See *dabbawala*

framing theory, 15–16

frictions, 4, 37n9

Gaikwad, Barku, 247

Gaikwad, Bhimsen (Bhivaji), 234–35, 240, 244, 246–52, 252n5

Gandhi, Ajay, 304

Gandhi, Mahatma, 144n5, 294n1

Gandhi, Sonia, 328n2

Gangar, Amrit, 281

gangsters, 222; Bollywood depictions, 54, 65, 240, 293; D-Company, 290, 294n3

Ganti, Tejaswini, 321n2

gardens, 132–33

Gateway of India, 298, 311, 391

Gawli, Arun, 222

Geeta Nagar neighborhood, 124

gender norms, 106, 268, 350, 351, 357, 362; detective work and, 368, 370–71, 376; home ownership and, 181; public and private spaces and, 64–65; tantric training and, 232n2. See also women

gesture-based communication, 361–62, 392–95, 397–400; images, 396f, 397f, 398f, 399f; Indian Sign Language (ISL), 391–92

ghatak, 374

Ghogre, Vilas, 244, 252

gifts: for bureaucratic approvals, 403; for Diwali, 401; for election rally-goers, 327, 331; exchanges of East India Company, 420–22; land, 17; *lavani* dancers and, 345; money as, 30–31, 116, 313

globalization, 7, 12, 37n9

gods/goddesses, 66, 131, 226

goondagardi, 64, 65

Goswami, Manu, 42n72

governmentality, 56, 177

Gramsci, Antonio, 11, 13, 40n48, 41nn62–63

Gujarati language, 287–88, 292, 293

Gujarat state, 16n1, 238, 257, 274, 278, 282. See also Kutch region

Gupte, Rupali, 363–64

Hamara Mahanagar (Our Metropolis), 300, 316, 320

Hankare, Anil, 341f

Hansen, Thomas Blom, 15, 43n74

Hardy, Kathryn, 299–301

hegemony, 13, 41n63, 305, 422

hierarchy, 34, 35, 235, 357, 360; caste, 251, 252; of smartness, 95, 99; social, 249, 305, 318, 422

hijras, 234, 237–38, 270–76, 276n76; *bida* dancers, 340f, 343

Hindi cinema. See Bollywood

Hindi/Hindustani language, 36n4, 44n98, 287–88, 292, 294n1

Hindus, 210, 236, 254–55, 258, 381–82

historiography, 6, 13, 37n12, 41n63

HIV/AIDS, 148, 150, 151

housing: BPP management of, 156; *chajja* design, 70f, 71f, 71–72; contractors, 50–51, 68–69, 71–76; MHADA, 307; middle-class, 349; private development of, 52; resettlement, 60, 79–80, 115, 143, 364; society, 121–22, 335, 338; temporary, 20. See also *chawls*

humanitarian grounds (HG) policy, 79–80, 115

hustling. See *tapori*

identity card. See Aadhar card

idli, 263, 264, 268

idols. See gods/goddesses

illegality, 20, 420; building construction, 48–49, 54, 59, 62–63, 131–32; e-waste industry and, 183, 184, 187; reputation and, 64; social work and, 110, 115, 122; temple construction and, 111–12. See also corruption; informal sector

Indraji, Bhagwanlal, 239, 281
informal sector, 183–84, 187–89, 192
informants, 213, 238, 268, 280, 348;
    police, 150, 273
internships, 374–75, 377n8
interregnum: Gramsci's notion of, 11, 13;
    scholarly usages of, 40n45, 40n48, 422
interrelated connections, 167, 299, 302,
    318–21, 353
investigations, 35, 355–56, 362–63, 365;
    primary data collection and, 364, 411.
    See also detective work
invisibility, 167, 273–75, 367, 374, 376, 407
Iqbal, Mohammed, 240, 288, 290,
    294n4
Irschick, Eugene, 417
Ishaare: Gestures and Signs in Mumbai
    (2015), 393, 394–95, 396f, 397f, 398f, 399f
Ismaili community, 235–36, 253–60
Ismaili Religious Education and Tariqa
    Board (ITREB), 258–59

Jai Bhim Comrade (2012), 244
Jains, 209
jalsa, 234, 244, 247
jamat, 256
jhopadpattis, 123, 124, 127

kaali-peeli, 378, 380, 382
kabadiwalas, 186
Kali Mata Mandir (temple), 112, 131
Kamath, Lalitha, 54–55
Kamathipura (red-light district): build-
    ings, 153n5; redevelopment plans,
    151–52, 152n3; sex workers, 117–18,
    145–51, 152n1
Kapoor, Pankaj, 24–29, 44n97
karma, 167, 170, 230–31
karyakartas, 23, 54, 60, 64; barter *vs.* cash
    payments for, 30, 116–17, 125, 144; BJP,
    327–28; Congress Party, 301, 304, 322–
    28, 329–32, 334–36; everyday actions
    of middle-class, 121–27; illegal work
    and, 110–11, 115, 122; procuring identity
    documents, 113, 115, 140–44, 301, 304;
    sex industry and, 117–18, 145–52

Kaskar, Dawood Ibrahim (Dawood
    Bhai), 294n3
Keqiao (China), 167, 191–92, 194–97
khabri, 4, 150, 273
Khanna, Tarun, 10, 11
Khanolkar, Prasad, 50–51
Kharwar, Naran Dhamji, 282–84
Khetwadi locality, 324, 327
kichdi, 288, 294n2
Kini, Nagesh, 132
kinship, 167, 172, 179, 223, 351; fictive, 53,
    103–6; food-mediated, 166; networks,
    60, 106, 372; secrets of, 357, 373
knowledge production, 32, 213, 364–65,
    412, 417; data collection and, 407, 411;
    methodological practices and, 238–39,
    284; public relations work and, 318–21;
    truth claims and, 356
Konkani language, 287–88, 291
Korgaonkar, Bhushan, 302–5
kothas, 146–52
kothi, 343, 346n1
Kundu, Ratoola, 23, 117–18
Kuroda, Ken, 166–68, 171–72
Kusters, Annelies, 361–62
Kutch region, 239, 278–79, 282–83, 284

labor: brokerage, 418–19; construction,
    48, 69, 71, 74–75; distributive, 222;
    e-waste sector, 183–84, 185f; forms
    of, 172; mill workers and strikes, 237,
    263–68; moralizing, 29; recruiters,
    53, 101–7; relational, 351, 353; value of,
    25–26, 168, 172
land: access, 109–12, 115; agglomeration,
    55, 97–98, 99; agricultural, 60, 62;
    claims, 19, 109, 112, 113, 119, 143, 408;
    gifts, 17; holdings, 41, 188; produc-
    tive, 164; regulations, 133. *See also*
    encroachment
landowners, 60, 63–64, 98
languages, 36, 239–40, 287–88, 290–94,
    294nn1–2, 316. *See also* deaf-hearing
    communication
lavani shows, 302–3, 339, 341f, 342, 344–45
left-wing politics, 244

legal frameworks, 23, 49, 51, 52–53, 111; e-waste sector, 186–89

Liases Foras, 24–25, 28–29

liberalism, 25–26

literacy campaign, 406, 407, 413n2

loan companies, 238, 275

local expertise, 10, 34, 50, 55–56, 166, 418; film production and, 299, 309; of political workers, 355; real estate investment and, 98–100; of surrogate agents, 176–81; value of, 28–29, 169–70

locality, constructing, 50, 55–56

Locke, John, 25–26, 109

Lower Parel suburb, 247, 270, 275, 276n6

Madras, 416–17, 422

Mahalaxmi neighborhood, 92, 221, 275

Maharashtra government, 17, 36n2, 88, 152n4, 344; pollution-control board, 183, 186, 187

Maharashtra Housing and Area Development Authority (MHADA), 20, 24, 307

Maharashtra Navnirman Sena (MNS), 134, 303, 379

Maharashtra Samjukta movement, 128

Mahimchi Bakhar, 293

Mahim neighborhood, 132, 347, 350

mahurats, 319–20, 321

maidans, 128–30, 132, 155, 244; Azad, 300, 322–23, 326–27, 360, 379, 381–82. *See also* public space; Shivaji Park

Malabar Hill neighborhood, 323–24, 328

Malad suburb, 124, 126, 163, 291

Mandvi port town, 282–83

Manto, Sa'adat Hasan, 94n1, 240, 291–92, 295n6

Mantralaya, 324, 326

mantras, 225–27, 229, 246

Marathi language, 163, 287–88, 290, 292, 295n5, 397–98

Marathi manoos, 128, 141, 236, 237, 268, 275, 303

mardangi, 64–65. *See also* masculinity/hypermasculinity

markets: developed *vs.* emerging, 10; exchanges, 164, 170, 172, 362; externality,

15–16; fabric, 192, 195–96; food-related, 166; formal/informal, 170; global, 8, 169; making, 164, 171; property, 28–29; real estate, 55, 140; value and, 167–68, 170

marriage, 141, 222, 266, 343; detective investigations and, 372–74; gender norms and, 357, 368, 370–71; intercaste, 159, 161n4, 249, 312; legalities of, 374

Marshall, P. J., 420

Marxism, 6–7, 36n5

masculinity/hypermasculinity, 64–65, 238, 268, 305; impotence and, 270–71

Masjid Bunder (Mosque Port), 278, 284

materiality, 15, 31, 33, 37n9, 169–71; mediation and, 164, 167, 169; of signs, 361

Mathew, Johan, 27

Matunga Labour Camp, 347–49, 351

maulvis, 93

Mazagaon neighborhood, 255, 291, 294

Mazzarella, William, 305, 306n9

McDonald's Corp., 262–63, 265, 313

media-goondas, 64

medical care, 105, 124, 149, 177

Mehrotra, Palash Krishna, 12

Mehta, Shashi, 298–99, 305, 306n3, 307–14

members of the Legislative Assembly (MLAs), 114–15, 124, 126; Bhim Nagar demolition and, 114–15, 139, 141, 143; Malabar Hill, 323–24, 327–28

methodological strategy, 4–5, 284

Metropolitan Authority Office (MAO), 401–2

migrant workers, 53, 101–7, 149

migration, histories of, 238–39, 241, 278–79, 348, 384

Mill, John Stuart, 26

Mines, Mattison, 422

Mishra, Gauravpant, 300–302, 304, 306, 322–28

Mithi River flooding, 363, 401–2

Miyan, Haji Bhai, 293

mobile phones, 104, 216, 331, 382–83; circulation of violent images, 359–60, 379, 381; film production work and, 299, 309–10, 314; potential damage of, 380; SIM cards, 219–20

Paupiah, Avadhanam, 414–19, 422, 422n1, 424n23

Pemmaraju, Gautam, 239–40, 241, 299

Pfleiderer, Beatrix, 281

pimps, 27–28

plastic housewares, 304, 349

poets and poetry, 244, 246–47, 252; Bombay Urdu, 286–87, 293–94

police, 19, 138, 374, 379; *hafta* payments, 22, 150, 272; housing contractors and, 51–52, 75; *khabri*, 150, 273; sex work industry and, 149, 150; stations, 292, 385; violence, 243

policy making, 8, 181, 186–87

"political connections," 28, 98, 201, 324; within the BMC, 84, 86, 110, 121, 126; Bunty Singh's, 63–64; election campaigns and, 301–2, 324, 330–31, 336; of housing contractors, 69, 74; maintaining good relationships, 403–4; real estate industry and, 231; of social workers, 110, 113, 116, 122–27, 138; SSP toilet project and, 91, 92

political workers. See *karyakartas*

power: authority and, 35, 65, 112–14, 116, 141, 358, 360; class and education and, 117; colonial, 13, 41n63, 42n70; contingency and, 19; *dubashes* and, 414, 416, 418; East India Company, 419, 422; information and, 411; politics and, 231, 332, 336; relations of, 32; sovereign, 7, 11; surrogate care and, 177; violence and, 54

practices, concepts, 4, 36n5, 355–56

Prakash, Anil, 299–301, 315–21

Pratham, 408

Premier Padmini, 380

printed circuit board (PCB), 182, 184, 186, 188

prison surrogates, 357–59, 384–60

Procter and Gamble, 267

project-affected persons (PAPs), 79, 115, 116, 143, 365, 406, 410

proof of residence, 2, 21, 49, 90, 119n4, 126–27; eligibility for resettlement and, 113, 115, 140–41, 143–44; for SIM cards, 219–20

propane cylinder deliveries, 2–3, 22, 35–36

property, idiom, 34

property developers: Kamathipura, 118, 151–52, 152n3; land agglomeration, 55, 97–98, 99; land transfers and, 17, 43n84; private, 52

property market, 28–29

property rights, 34, 48, 49, 52, 80, 109–10; Parsi claims, 119

prostitution. *See* sex workers

protests, 243–44, 360, 379, 381–82

public interest litigation (PIL), 129, 130, 132, 133

publicity, 17, 34, 156; bad, 344; for detective work, 367–68, 369f; film industry and, 299–300, 317, 319–21; Ismaili, 256–57; for *lavani* shows, 345; for politicians and election campaigns, 300–304, 351

public relations work, 257, 299–301, 315–16, 318–21

publics, concept, 34, 255, 297, 300–301, 317, 357

public space, 65, 111, 130–34, 135n4, 136n6

purohit, 226, 228

Purti, Sonam (Janu), 53–54, 101–7

Raheja Constructions, 123

Rambai Nagar neighborhood, 243–44

rangoli, 304–5, 306, 347–48, 352–53

Rangwala, Lubaina, 166, 167, 169–72

rape, 358, 388, 389–90

Ravat, Ashok, 111–12, 128–35; photos, 129f, 131f, 135f

real estate: barons, 52; Bhim Nagar, 140; brokering/nonbrokering, 24–25, 28–29; developers, 78, 96, 123, 130, 146, 151, 228, 230–31; development idiom and, 48; investors, 28, 55, 95–100

reality, versions of, 356, 357, 364

reflexivity, 32

religious conversion, 250–51, 252n5

report making, 363–64, 401–4

representations, 34–35; cinematic, 12, 298; of difference, 234, 238, 240; gendered, 351; of Ismaili community, 236, 255, 257, 260; political influence and,

representations (continued)
303; of publics, 297-98, 300; social
relations and imaginative, 304-5, 353;
of urban India, 11

reputation, 69, 142, 155, 179, 301, 303, 324;
enhancing one's, 54, 64-65, 121, 215, 259

resettlement, 76n2, 80, 408; building
construction, 54, 60, 61f; proof of
eligibility, 67n1, 113, 115, 140-41, 143-44

rice flour drawings. See *rangoli*

rickshaw, 361, 393-94, 397, 398

Right to Information Act (RTI), 130, 132, 133

riots, 13, 232, 236, 254, 381; Gujarat, 238,
274. *See also* protests

risk: management, 2-3, 349; new kinds
of, 11; real estate, 97, 98; taking, 8-9;
water, 166, 200, 201, 203

ritual practice. *See* spiritual and religious
practice

Saat Rasta neighborhood, 217-18, 220-22

Sahasrabudhe, Sujit, 361-62, 391-95,
396f, 397-400; photos of, 396f

Sanjay Gandhi National Park, 60, 67n1

Sanjaynagar neighborhood, 54, 59-60,
62-67

sanyasis, 228-29

sarkar, 222

Sarkar, Sumit, 37n12

Sartori, Andrew, 26

Scott, Sir Walter, 416-17, 418, 423n21

seafaring, 282-84

Seal, Anil, 37n12

Searle, Llerena Guiu, 28, 55

secrets, 357, 365, 372-73, 374, 376

self-making, 8, 35, 298, 316, 334, 365.
See also entrepreneurialism

Sen, Atreyee, 357-59

septic tanks, 87-88, 89

service approvals, 78-80, 84-85, 123, 403

sewerage infrastructure, 87-88

sexuality, 246, 342-43, 389, 390

sex workers, 27, 45n103, 133, 271, 292,
295n6; Kamathipura, 23, 117-18, 145-51;
visits by ex-prisoners, 389, 390

shakhas, 238, 263, 268, 386

shame, arousing, 238, 270, 275-76

shareholders, 119, 158

Shetty, Prasad, 132, 363-64

Shivajinagar neighborhood, 51, 68-69,
72-75, 76nn1-3, 77n7

Shivaji Park: Mahaparinirvan Diwas at,
134-35, 135f, 136n8; temples, 111, 112, 130-
32; uses and transformations, 128-29

Shivkumar, Rohan, 298-99, 306n3

Shiv Sena, 113-15, 124, 129, 139, 303; BJP
alliance, 328n1; Bombay name change,
12, 36n1; ethno-religious riots and, 13;
hate-based politics, 359, 390; *hijras*
and, 237-38, 270-71; *karyakartas*, 141,
386; party publications, 326, 328n2;
prison surrogates, 386-89; Sena Bhavan, 367; Shiv Vada Pav initiative, 237,
241, 262-65, 267-68

Shree Udhyan Ganesh Mandir (temple),
111-12, 131

sign language. *See* gesture-based
communication

"silence zone," 129-30

Simmel, Georg, 30, 45n107

Simpson, Edward, 238-39, 241

Sindhis, 81, 192-94, 197n3

Singh, Bunty, 54-55, 59-60, 62-67

Singh, Simpreet, 17, 43n82

Singh, Tunku, 59, 65

sirdar, 101, 106-7

skills, 3, 4; bodily, 36n5; building, 181,
199-200; communication, 361-62;
deployment of, 33, 53; relational, 50, 52-53

Slum Rehabilitation Authority (SRA),
48, 49, 52, 79-80, 132, 408

slums: Dhaka, 207; evictions and resettlement, 19, 54, 60, 67n1, 79-80, 89, 143;
land transfer request, 16-17; Malabar
Hill, 324; monsoon season and, 358,
388; percentage of Mumbaikars living
in, 12; proof of tenure, 21, 49; redevelopment, 33, 48, 51-52, 408, 409, 411;
Shivajinagar, 68, 76n1; Sunderbaug
demolition, 408; surveys, 140, 405-6,
408-9; water infrastructure, 201, 203-6.
See also Bhim Nagar neighborhood

Slum Sanitation Program (SSP), 50, 87–93, 94n4
social impact assessment (SIA), 410
social infrastructure, 317, 319, 321, 351
sociality: of taxi space, 378, 382–83; urban, 351, 353
social mobility, 267, 305, 418; upward, 12, 67, 237, 264–65, 372
social norms, 54, 55, 103, 357, 372–73, 376. *See also* gender norms
social programs, 9
social relations, 31, 167, 178, 220, 304–5, 353; ethnographic practice and, 32, 213, 215; urban, 128
social workers. See *karyakartas*
Society for Promotion of Area Resource Centres (SPARC), 408
South Indian Udupi restaurants, 263, 264–65, 268
spiritual and religious practice, 105–6, 135, 230, 274; *bhakti*, 210, 214; *dua*, 254; help and healing, 228–29; Ismaili, 254–55, 258–59; leftover foods and, 209; *rangoli* rituals, 348; training, 226–28. *See also* gods/goddesses; tantrics
Srinivasachari, C. S., 417
state-society distinction, 18–19
Streeck, Wolfgang, 40n45, 40n48
street food, 263, 264–65, 268, 314; *puri*, 393. See also *vada pav*
Strohl, David J., 235–36, 240
subcontractors, 53, 74, 104, 363–64, 402, 409
Subramaniam, Radhika, 382
Summerscale, Kate, 372
Sunderbaug settlement, 406, 407–9, 411
Surgeon's Daughter, The (Scott), 416–17, 418, 423n21
surrogacy agents, 165, 167–68, 172, 175–81
surveys: community-led, 408; foreign researchers and, 409; Mithi River flooding, 363, 401–2; slips, 113, 140; slum, 140, 364–65, 405–6, 408, 409; truth of, 364
survival, 166, 181, 233, 264, 268, 300, 346; prison and, 358

sustainable development, 199–200, 206, 410
Swaminathan, R., 237–38, 241

Taloja Prison, 385
tamasha, 234, 241, 247, 249–51, 303
tantrics, 166, 167, 169; business improvement and politics, 229–31; forging *yantras*, 170, 172, 224–26, 229; help requests and healing, 228–29; preventing violence, 231–32; training and education, 226–28, 232n2
tapori, 34, 318, 351; *dhandha* distinction, 163–64, 171; language, 290, 293
Taskar, Aneri, 165, 167–72
Tata Institute of Social Sciences (TISS), 405, 407
taxi drivers, 359, 378–83
Team of Research Investigators and Process Services (TRIPS), 406, 409, 411
tea shops, 2, 20–23, 146
temples, 65–66, 111–12, 130–32, 155–56
temporality/time, 30–31, 168–69, 171, 209
textile industry, 167, 207, 417; Chinese-made fabrics, 191–92, 194–96; decline, 12, 41n53, 195, 230, 265; mill workers and strikes, 263–68; in Parel area, 275
Thackeray, Bal, 129, 368, 387
Thackeray, Udhav, 123, 263
Thane suburb, 81, 83
tiffins, 219, 266–67, 349; deliveries, 168, 208–14
Tilak Nagar neighborhood, 393–94
Tilly, Charles, 13
toilet blocks: operators and management, 50, 89–94, 330; overview of, 87–88
tours, 291–92; *dabbawala*, 212–14; "slum," 206; socio-architectural, 278, 284
trade: counterfeit commodity manufacture, 193; *dalals* and, 27; East India Company, 419–20; enterprise and, 13; exchange and, 164; fabric, 191–92, 194–96; from Kutch, 278; languages of, 288, 289f; leather, 351–52; networks, 167; suit, 193–94; value and, 26

train travel, 211–12, 273; Bandra station, 208, 211, 393; deaf people and, 361, 397; Elphinstone Road station, 270, 276n2; Victoria Terminus, 298

transferable development right (TDR), 48, 49

transgender community. See *hijras*

transgressions, 18, 317, 357, 373, 415

Transit Camp, 20–21

translators. See *dubashes*

traveling folk theater. See *tamasha*

Trawick, Margaret, 353

Truelove, Yaffa, 30, 110–11, 112, 116, 301

trust, 9, 10, 73, 220; building, 50, 63, 98, 222, 382; currency of food and, 172, 219; networks, 13, 150; sex work industry and, 117–18, 149–50

truth, 35, 355–65; detecting the, 370, 371, 373; smartphone technology and, 381, 383

Tsing, Anna, 15, 37n9

Tyabji, Badruddin, 293, 295n7

Udupa, Sahana, 359–60

Ulhasnagar city, 192–93, 195–97, 197n1

universal adult franchise (UAF), 159, 160

urban development, 12, 33, 47–49, 54, 68, 234; consultants, 402–4; illegality and, 111–12; of Kamathipura, 117–18, 151–52; primary data and, 410–12

urban India, 11–12

Urban Renewal Mission, 363, 402–3

Urdu: Bombay, 239, 287, 291, 293–94; education and literature, 287, 295n6; word translations, 288, 292

Uttar Pradesh (UP), 291, 315–16, 318

Vachani, Lalit, 111, 112

vada pav, 236–37, 262–68, 271, 276, 311

valorization, 4, 8, 53, 65, 166, 356

valuations, 27, 29, 164, 171, 184, 186, 188

value: of cash, 31, 171; creation, 166, 168, 171–72, 214; of doing business, 34; exchangeability, 45n106; labor theory of, 25–26; of land, 165; of local expertise,

28–29, 169–70; market, 167–68, 170; production, 164–65, 167; stored, 29–31, 167, 169–70; of time, 168; truth and, 35, 356, 362

Varkari Sampradaya sect, 210

Vasi Virar city, 54, 59, 63. *See also* Shivaji-nagar neighborhood

vegetable markets, 218

vegetarianism, 209

Venkatarama Ayyar, A. V., 415, 417

verification practices, 35, 356

Verkaaik, Oskar, 15, 43n74

Vevaina, Leilah, 112, 118–19

violence, 64, 93, 259, 421; circulation of images of, 359–60, 379, 381; gangster, 54, 65; Hindu nationalist, 254; police, 243; prison, 358–59

voluntary service, 119n4, 133, 136n5, 406; Ismaili, 253–56, 258–60

Walkers Ecology Movement Trust (WECOM), 129

waste management, 134, 136n5, 403. *See also* e-waste recycling

watchmen, building, 274–75, 277n12, 280

water infrastructure: access, 200–201, 202f; ATMs, 205; in Bhim Nagar, 138; lack of, 12, 87–88; pipe pressure, 89, 203; quality, 206; in rural Gujarat, 257; securing connections, 21, 32, 78–80, 84–86, 115; storage tanks, 89, 200, 203; sustainable solutions for, 200–201, 206–7

water tankers, 88, 206

wealth accumulation, 25–26, 96, 118

women, 64, 232n2, 283, 339, 342; Dalit, 246–47, 251–52; marriage expectations, 357, 368, 370–71; Parsi, 118, 155, 161n4; patriarchal norms and, 372–73; relational labor, 351; Tamil, 352, 353. See also *didi*; sex workers; surrogacy agents

yantra, 170, 172, 225–26, 229

Žižek, Slavoj, 41n62